Intercultural Communication with Arabs

Rana Raddawi
Editor

Intercultural Communication with Arabs

Studies in Educational, Professional
and Societal Contexts

 Springer

Editor
Rana Raddawi
American University of Sharjah
Sharjah
Utd.Arab.Emir.

There are instances where we have been unable to trace or contact the copyright holder. If notified, the publisher will be pleased to rectify any errors or omissions at the earliest opportunity.

ISBN 978-981-287-253-1   ISBN 978-981-287-254-8 (eBook)
DOI 10.1007/978-981-287-254-8
Springer Singapore Heidelberg New York Dordrecht London

Library of Congress Control Number: 2014955249

Printed on acid-free paper

Springer is part of Springer Science+Business Media (www.springer.com)

To my beloved parents, Majed and Maria,
who made me the person I am today
May their Soul Rest in Peace
To my dear brothers, Hareth, Muthanna,
and Muanna for being always there when
I needed them
To the treasure of my life and source of
inspiration,
Majdoline and Bader

Acknowledgements

I would like to extend my thanks to the contributors of this volume who responded enthusiastically to the invitation to contribute to this collection. I am also grateful to the reviewers whose suggestions helped the authors prepare the final draft of their papers. I would like to specially thank Susan Riley, Bill DeGenaro, and Nicole Smithson, without whom, this work would not have been completed. Many thanks also go to Sadaf Ahmad and Nour Arab for their precious assistance.

I would also like to thank esteemed Springer publishers, mainly Jayanthie Krishnan, for their insightful editorial guidance all along.

The editor, chapter authors, and publisher thank all individuals who gave their permission to use copyright material.

Last but not the least, I am so grateful to my family and friends who not only supported me in the completion of this book but also were patient and generous enough to sacrifice the time I was supposed to spend with them while I was working on this collection.

Preface

The present volume arose from the need for a book on intercultural communication (IC) with Arabs. IC has become a vital skill in the current time period. It has perhaps never been as rampant because globalization in the modern world has resulted in increased cross-cultural contact. The book provides readers with information that gives light to a new perspective of understanding Arabs from the Arabs themselves or from foreigners who have lived in Arab countries.

The book is divided into three main sections that include studies in educational, professional, and societal contexts. Contributors are Arab scholars or foreign scholars who live or have lived in the Arab world. In this volume, they provide an overview of their experience whether in the classroom or in professional settings or social settings drawing on current theory, research and practice.

The chapters include descriptive and narrative essays and case studies with some illustrations: tables or charts.

The reader would be aware of the ways Arabs communicate in different situations, contexts, and settings such as education, business, politics, media, healthcare, and society at large. The manuscript also describes how Arabs are portrayed by others in an attempt to project a more accurate and realistic image of them. I hope that this collection of original papers will be a valuable resource and reference for researchers and academics in the world. Undergraduate and graduate students who are studying about culture in the Gulf region and the Middle East or taking a course on IC can also benefit from this book.

Editor

Rana Raddawi

Contents

Contributors

Sarah Abdul–Hadi American University of Sharjah, Sharjah, United Arab Emirates

Khawlah Ahmed American University of Sharjah, Sharjah, United Arab Emirates

Rozz Albon Higher Colleges of Technology, Abu Dhabi, United Arab Emirates

LoriAnn Alnaizy American University of Sharjah, Sharjah, United Arab Emirates

Asma AlShamsi American University of Sharjah, Sharjah, United Arab Emirates

Bashaer Aref American University of Sharjah, Sharjah, United Arab Emirates

Omar Fayez Atari UAE University, Al-Ain, United Arab Emirates

Georgia Daleure Higher Colleges of Technology, Abu Dhabi, United Arab Emirates

Asiya Daud University of California, Irvine, CA, USA

William DeGenaro The University of Michigan–Dearborn, Dearborn, MI, USA

Melanie Gobert Higher Colleges of Technology, Abu Dhabi, United Arab Emirates

Hala Asmina Guta Prince Mohammad Bin Fahd University, Al Khobar, Saudi Arabia

Manssour Habbash University of Tabuk, Tabuk, Saudi Arabia

Geoff Harkness Grinnell College, Iowa, USA

Ayesha Heble Sultan Qaboos Univerity, Al Khod, Oman

Khaleel Hinkston Higher Colleges of Technology, Abu Dhabi, United Arab Emirates

Zenzele Isoke University of Minnesota, Minneapolis, USA

Magdalena Karolak Zayed University, Dubai, United Arab Emirates

Linzi J. Kemp American University of Sharjah, Sharjah, United Arab Emirates

Radia Kesseiri University of Leeds, Leeds, UK

John McKeown Higher Colleges of Technology, Abu Dhabi, United Arab Emirates

Michael J. Oghia American University of Beirut, Beirut, Lebanon

Rana Raddawi American University of Sharjah, Sharjah, United Arab Emirates

Sandhya Rao Mehta Sultan Qaboos Univerity, Al Khod, Oman

Irene Theodoropoulou Qatar University, Doha, Qatar

Hayfaa A. Tlaiss University of New Brunswick, New Brunswick, Canada

Salah Troudi University of Exeter, Devon, UK

Tarifa Ajaif Zaabi Higher Colleges of Technology, Abu Dhabi, United Arab Emirates

Chapter 1
Introduction

Rana Raddawi

Globalization is affecting every part of our life from what we eat to what we learn and do for a living to the people we interact with. Encountering people of different cultural backgrounds has become an everyday experience for many reasons including the development of an integrated global economy, sophisticated communication and technologies, migration, traveling, and education. Confirming the immense impact of globalization on intercultural communication (IC), Piller (2011) states that IC in practical life is "embedded in economic, social and cultural globalisation, transnational migration and overseas study" (p. 1). The more successful individuals become in their careers the more they deal with a variety of people from ethnically diverse backgrounds. People in various fields work beyond borders; they attend various discussions and conferences, outsource their businesses, or make branches of their offices in other countries. Therefore, one should not overlook the need to learn IC. IC helps communication between people from different national cultures. As an academic field of interest, IC aids engineers, business leaders, media authorities, law enforcers, teachers, and other professionals. We all need to be able to deal effectively and efficiently with diverse cultures.

In its simplest form, IC means the sharing or exchange of messages between people of different cultural and/or social backgrounds. This exchange can occur through verbal or nonverbal forms of communication. Jandt (2013) states that personal space, body movements, facial expressions, gestures, eye contact, the use of time, paralanguage, silence, the use of the sense of touch, clothing and physical appearance, and the use of the sense of smell are all forms of nonverbal communication. Because IC is concerned with people, Bardhan and Orbe (2011) maintain that it "involves the study of identities in communicative interaction in various contexts" (p. xiii). Another term that is frequently used in research with similar or overlapping meaning with the term intercultural communication is "cross-cultural communication." Piller (2011), however, draws a clear distinction between the meanings of these two terms. She explains that although studies in both "cross-cultural communication"

R. Raddawi (✉)
American University of Sharjah, Sharjah, United Arab Emirates
e-mail: rraddawi@aus.edu

© Springer Science+Business Media Singapore 2015   1
R. Raddawi (ed.), *Intercultural Communication with Arabs,*
DOI 10.1007/978-981-287-254-8_1

and "intercultural communication" begin with the assumption that there exist distinct cultural groups, the former compares communicative practices of these cultural groups in an analytical study while the latter investigates them "in interaction with each other" (p. 8).

Due to a globalizing world, IC is on the rise; new research keeps improving global citizen's view on diverse cultures and traditions. Borcoman (2011) states that as an academic field of study, IC is influenced by several other but related disciplines including sociology, anthropology, history, religious studies, ethnology, and geography, and it emerged toward the end of the twentieth century. The author continues that while IC was formally studied in the North American region in the 1960s, its European counterpart was reluctant to embrace this fledgling field of study. However, the rapid socioeconomic developments, the evolution of media, and the establishment of European structures such as the European Union warranted the advent of IC in Europe in the 1990s (Borcoman 2011). In essence, globalization has urged diversity and the mingling of cultures to the extent that practically there is no context in the world today where cultural exchange does not take place. Culture can be understood as a nation and/or ethnicity, or can be faith based or gender based or even discourse based (community speeches and styles) (see Paulston et al. 2012); or what Jandt (2013) calls "cocultures," i.e., a culture within a culture.

One part of the world that is constantly talked about and is always on the news is the Arab world. This culture is one that is distinctive in its own right. The Arab world consists of 22 countries; geographically it covers parts of North Africa: Algeria, Morocco, Tunisia, Libya, Sudan, Egypt, Djibouti, Somalia and Mauritania, and Western Asia: The Fertile Crescent or better known as the Middle East comprising Syria, Lebanon, Jordan, Palestine, and Iraq; The Arabian Peninsula also known as the Gulf States include Oman, Saudi Arabia, Bahrain, United Arab Emirates, Qatar, Kuwait, and Yemen; and last but not least the Comoros Islands situated in the Mozambique Channel.

Not all Arabs are Muslims and not all Muslims are Arabs. While approximately 85–90% of the Arab population is Muslim (Feghali 1997), Arab countries also embrace Christians and Jews who have lived together in the Arab region for hundreds of years. Conversely, there is the white Arab, the black Arab, and the brown-skinned Arab. There is also the brunette, the red head and the blond Arab, and the veiled and unveiled females just like there exist the tall, the mid-height, and the short Arab. Yet, despite their diversity, all Arabs are united by the Arabic language, by their origins and similar beliefs and traditions and most importantly, as this book shows it, by the need for support, love, and justice through a thorough understanding and tolerance of Arab cultural attitudes and patterns.

While IC studies have become widely offered in the West, scarcity is still persisting in the Arab world. Ivy League schools and other reputable universities in the USA and the West, in general, have programs directly related to cross-cultural and Intercultural Communication. Universities in the Middle East are at the initial starting point of tackling the topic of IC. The top-ranked universities in the Middle East such as the American University of Sharjah, the American University in Dubai,

Zayed University in UAE, King Saud University in Saudi Arabia, Qatar University, and American University of Beirut (AUB) in Lebanon are teaching courses in the area of IC. However, since the topic is fairly recent, literature for teaching IC among Arabs is practically nonexistent. Middle Eastern and Gulf States' universities use textbooks and teaching materials from the West. Since the two cultures are diverse, students from the collectivist culture end up learning more from the Western perspective than they do from the culture they are brought up in. Therefore, there is a need for textbooks and teaching materials in this field, which directly relate to the Arab world, and bring out their perspective on issues. Thus, the need is not just a textbook aimed for Arabs, but a book in which the authors are either from the same culture or have lived in the Arab world. Very little research is written on ways of interacting, accepting, and fully appreciating the richness of the Arab culture and the diversity of the people in Arab society. Published books on IC deal with various aspects of Western communication and focus on communicating with various ethnicities within the West. While some textbooks publish diverse and extensive chapters that deal with Japanese, Chinese, or African culture, they usually discuss the parts of traditional Arab culture and less of how to communicate with Arabs. Although some works of Arab intercultural communication scholars played an important role in understanding the connection between culture and communication and their manifestation in Arab societies and in settings that include education (Love and Powers 2004), communication patterns and intercultural competence (Zaharna 1995, 2009; Feghali 1997; Nelson et al. 2002), and discursive strategies (Umale 2011), the dearth of literature on IC in the diverse Arab world remains evident. Therefore, this book *Intercultural Communication with Arabs* fills in gaps of primarily dealing with Arabs.

The book is divided into three overarching themes: The first theme consists of the introduction and eight chapters while the second and the third themes comprise five chapters each.

The first theme, "Educational Contexts," explores how culture and language can shape the educational experiences of students and teachers and the impact and restrictions of IC in various educational settings.

In Chap. 2 titled "Intercultural Communicative Styles in Qatar: Greek and Qataris," Irene Theodoropoulou investigates the intercultural communicative styles used by Qatari female students and their Greek instructor in their academic interactions at Qatar University. The researcher concludes that although students and their instructor came from different cultural backgrounds, they could yet communicate in an effective manner.

In Chap. 3 titled "Perceptions of Indians in Oman: Exploring Aspects of Intercultural Communication," Sandhya Rao Mehta and Ayesha Heble examine the predominant perceptions that the Omani youths subscribe to in understanding the Indian community in Oman. The Omani youth could play a major role in breaking stereotypes between the two cultures and promoting cultural integration.

In Chap. 4 titled "Intercultural Communication in the Context of Saudi Arab Tertiary Education," Magdalena Karolak and Hala Guta used Hofstede's five-dimensional model to identify the patterns of communication that formed between students and their teachers in classrooms of educational institutions that adopted Western models and employed foreign educators in Saudi Arabia.

In Chap. 5 titled "The Discourse of Global English and its Representation in the Saudi Context: A Postmodernist Critical Perspective," Manssour Habbash and Salah Troudi use postmodern critical inquiry in their attempt to relate the aspects of English language education to broader sociopolitical and socioeconomic issues in Saudi Arabia. They examine the status of English as a lingua franca and its impact on shaping English educational policies in the country based on the views of a group of English language (ELT) teachers and students.

In Chap. 6 under this theme titled "Understanding Family Involvement in the Education of Emirati College Students in the United Arab Emirates (UAE)," Georgia Daleure, Rozz Albon, Khaleel Hinkston, John McKeown, and Tarifa Ajaif examine how understanding socio-demographic cultural influences on family involvement and parenting styles provide educators with significant insight that aids them in forging more effective communication with students and their families. The role of Saudi family involvement in terms of time and efforts in the academic success of their children is also highlighted.

In Chap. 7 titled "Taboo Topics in the English as a Second Language (ESL)/ English as a Foreign Language (EFL) Classroom in the Gulf Region," Melanie Gobert explores the topics considered taboo in ESL classrooms in the Gulf Cooperation Council (GCC) countries, the author sets out to define taboo topics and gives recommendations for teaching such topics alongside critical pedagogy.

In Chap. 8 titled "Intercultural Communication and Muslim American Youth in US School Contexts," Khawlah Ahmed looks at the consequences of ineffective IC of teachers and administrators in relation to Muslim American students in US school contexts. There are flaws in the academic system that need to be recognized and addressed to prevent an already existent cultural divide in the larger social context in the USA.

In Chap. 9 titled "Night School in Beirut and the Public Sphere: Student Civic Action Rooted in Liberal Secularism," William DeGenaro elaborates on the impact of nurturing a liberal-secular spirit among a group of undergraduate students in Beirut involved in a community literacy initiative. Using rhetorical-ethnographic methods, the researcher found out that this practice allowed the students to resist perceived institutional and dominant cultural values such as sectarianism.

The second theme "Professional Contexts" looks at the understanding and influence of culture with regard to business, health care, media, and politics as the backdrop.

In Chap. 10 titled "Culturally Different Perspectives of Time: Effect on Communication in Meetings," Lindsay Kemp uses an empirical study conducted in an Arab organization in the United Arab Emirates to investigate the cultural framework to time of 11 research participants of different nationalities. The objective is for those involved in intercultural business meetings to recognize a polychronic approach to time in the Arab world and adapt accordingly.

In Chap. 11 titled "Intercultural (Mis) Communication in Medical Settings: Cultural Difference or Cultural Incompetence?," I explore the linguistic and cultural challenges between non-Arabic-speaking healthcare practitioners and Arabic-speaking patients in the multicultural settings of the UAE and the USA. I underscore the significance of cultural competency in medical settings in the attempt to yield patient satisfaction, cost-efficiency, and improved health care and research outcomes.

In Chap. 12 titled "The Political TV Interview: Tim Sebastian's Interview with an Arab: A Venue for Reconciliation or Discord?," Omar Atari analyzes an interview to describe the interviewer and interviewee's communicative styles as influenced by their respective sociocultural backgrounds. The researcher demonstrates how the interview is not just a source of information and knowledge to viewers.

In Chap. 13 titled "The Role of 'Cyber Dissent' in Stimulating Democratization in the MENA Region and Empowering Youth Voices," Asiya Daud examines how social networking sites are used for political purposes to circumvent governmental constraints in the Middle East and North Africa (MENA) region. This practice is encouraged considering the widespread practice of press censorship and political restrictions in the region.

In Chap. 14 under this theme titled "The Political Discourse of the Arab Revolution: The Case of Egypt, Tunisia, Libya, and Syria," Radia Kesseiri closely analyzes the political discourse used by the leaders in Tunisia, Egypt, Libya, and Syria during the "Arab Spring." The author contends that the political leaders made deliberate language choices to justify their own policies during a period of intense turmoil.

The third theme "Societal Contexts" examines the impact of parenting styles, the perception of couple relationships, and the existence and interaction of cocultures in the Arab society.

In Chap. 15 titled "Impact of Parental Communication Patterns on Arab Women's Choice of Careers," Hayfaa Tlaiss examines parental communication patterns in the Arab world and draws attention to its impact on Arab women's education and career choices. The researcher calls for a change in Arab societies towards an egalitarian bias-free communication process between parents and children.

In Chap. 16 titled "Different Cultures, One Love: Exploring Romantic Love in the Arab World," Michael Oghia addresses the cultural and intercultural contentions related to the topic of romance and love in the Arab world. Conversely, he shows how love is defined and valued using a sample of students from AUB. The researcher findings reveal the need to rethink the definition of love relationships and marriage among the Arab youth in a globalized world.

In Chap. 17 titled "In the Zone: Female Athletes and Intercultural Contact in Iraq," Geoff Harkness views sports as an intercultural contact zone and considers its role in mitigating intergroup conflicts between Arabs and Kurds in Iraq within the Arab world. The researcher analyzes discursive practices used by Kurd and Arab female athletes to show differences and similarities and at the same time demonstrate how the basketball court and soccer pitch can lead to harmony between different ethnic groups.

In Chap. 18 titled "'Why Am I Black?' Gendering Hip-Hop and Translocal Solidarities in Dubai," Zenzele Isoke uses ethnographic fieldwork to find out about
multidimensional identities of "third" culture Afro-Arab women in Dubai, UAE.
She proposes that hip-hop provides a fertile platform for individuals to forge connections in ways that undermine national boundaries erected by states and reinforced through racializing practices.

In Chap. 19 titled "Integration of People with Disabilities in the United Arab
Emirates Society," Sarah AbdulHadi, LoriAnn, Bashaer Aref, and Asma AlShamsi
investigate the interplay between various sociocultural variables to identify the
multiple challenges that the disabled and their families face in the UAE. Recommendations are issued for a more effective communication process among theses
cocultures in Arab societies: individuals with and without disabilities.

The contents of the volume offer a rich and varied reflection of the communication of Arabs in different settings and countries in the Arab world. While there is a
concentration of studies from the Gulf Arab states, the collection spans perspectives
from Iraq, Syria, Lebanon, Egypt, Libya, Tunisia, and Sudan.

The studies also give an intimate, personal view of communication across a range
of subjects, from taboo topics in an ELT classroom in the Gulf, to hip-hop and Arab
"blackness," to ethnic tensions in post-conflict Iraq, to understanding the meaning
of "love" by Lebanese students, and to communicating disabilities and a mother's
concern for autistic child. The book reflects a view of IC from an Arab perspective.

As the first volume on IC in Arab societies, this book charts new territory and
seeks to lay the groundwork for future study of Arab communication from an Arab
perspective.

References

Bardhan, N., & Orbe, M. P. (2011). Identity research and communication: Intercultural reflections
    and future directions [MyiLibrary version]. http://lib.myilibrary.com.ezproxy.aus.edu/Product-
    Detail.aspx?id=498939. Accessed 4 Oct 2013.
Borcoman, M. (2011). Intercultural communication: Theoretical notions. *Review of the Air Force
    Academy, 9*(1), 131–135. http://ezproxy.aus.edu/login? url=http://search.proquest.com/docvie
    w/887908079?accountid=16946.
Feghali, E. (1997). Arab cultural communication patterns. *International Journal of Intercultural
    Relations, 21*(3), 345–378.
Jandt, F. E. (2013). *An introduction to intercultural communication: Identities in a global com-
    munity* (7th ed.). Los Angeles: Sage.
Love, D. E., & Powers, W. G. (2004). Differences in the persuasion strategies of Arab female
    students toward western instructors. *Journal of Intercultural Communication Research, 33*(1),
    1–13.
Nelson, G., Batal, M., & Bakary, W. (2002). Directness vs. indirectness: Egyptian Arabic and US
    English communication style. *International Journal of Intercultural Relations, 26*, 39–57.
Paulston, C. B., Kiesling, S., & Rangel, E. (Ed.). (2012). *The handbook of intercultural discourse
    and communication*. Malaysia: Wiley-Blackwell.

Piller, I. (2011). Intercultural communication: A critical introduction [Ebrary version]. http://site. ebrary.com.ezproxy.aus.edu/lib/aus/docDetail.action?docID=10477158 Accessed 6 Oct 2013.

Umale, J. (2011). Pragmatic failure in refusal strategies: British versus Omani interlocutors. *Arab World English Journal, 2,* 18–46.

Zaharna, R. S. (1995). Bridging cultural differences: American public relations and Arab communication patterns. *Public Relations Review, 21,* 241–255.

Zaharna, R. S. (2009). An associative approach to intercultural communication competence in the Arab world. In D. Deardorff (Ed.) *Sage the handbook of intercultural communication competence* (pp. 179–195). Thousand Oaks: Sage.

Part I
Educational Contexts

Chapter 2
Intercultural Communicative Styles in Qatar: Greek and Qataris

Irene Theodoropoulou

2.1 Introduction

I have been working in the Department of English Literature and Linguistics at Qatar University since September 2010. It was the first time that I ever stepped foot in any of the Gulf countries and it felt immediately like home, contrary to the UK where I spent five years having a rewarding academic life and fascinating social life but never felt at home. At first, I thought that the openness I was treated with by all Arabs, both inside and outside the university, was part of the traditional and widely known Arabic hospitality, and that every Westerner is treated like this. However, as I started learning Arabic and interacting with diverse speakers of Arabic dialects, I came to realize that between my native language and culture, Greek, and Arabic dialects and cultures there are many similarities, not only in terms of food and traditions but also and perhaps most importantly in terms of shared values, a factor that contributes to this communicative intimacy and easiness.

In exactly the same way that some of the most basic cultural values associated with the Arab world include collectivism, hospitality, honor, and modesty (Feghali 1997; Ayish 1998; Marsh 2010), Greeks also embrace these principles, albeit from a different perspective and through different forms. For example, modesty in the Greek world is realized through widows and nuns often wearing head scarves, as opposed to Gulf countries where many Muslim women veil their heads in public (though of course some women choose other semiotic means, e.g., through the wearing of elegant but not provocative clothing). Collectivism is common in the Greek world as well, especially nowadays with the financial crisis that the country is going through; a lot of young people return to their parents' home and they either support them financially or they are being supported by their parents. The family has always been seen as a core notion and a value in the context of Greek society, as in the Arab world, in the sense that one's immediate family members are seen

I would like to thank Rana Raddawi and the anonymous reviewer for useful feedback on an earlier version of this chapter.

I. Theodoropoulou (✉)
Qatar University, Doha, Qatar
e-mail: irene.theodoropoulou@qu.edu.qa

© Springer Science+Business Media Singapore 2015
R. Raddawi (ed.), *Intercultural Communication with Arabs,*
DOI 10.1007/978-981-287-254-8_2

as the omnipresent saviors of the person; they are expected to support each other economically, emotionally, psychologically, socially, and professionally. Along the same lines, the notion of community has been significantly enhanced during the past two years. This is evident in the number of socially oriented initiatives by various nongovernmental organizations (NGOs) and the Greek Orthodox Church, which aim at providing poor and homeless people with food.

Hospitality has been always dealt with as a core principle in the Greek society as well; from the Homeric era onward, the guest has been always treated as a sacred person who needs to enjoy one's home as if it were their own. The offering of drinks, coffee, food, and especially gifts (cf. http://greece.greekreporter.com/2012/12/20/a-greek-gift-guide-ideas-for-christmas/) is something which is still shared between the Greek and the Arab world; however, the basic difference is that in Greece gifts tend to be more modest than the ones offered in the Arab world not only nowadays but also throughout history, because one of the dominant ideas in the Greek-speaking world is that simplicity is always better than luxury. It goes without saying, of course, that luxurious gifts can also be offered to guests and hosts, but not as frequently as in the Arab world.

Finally, in terms of honor (Campbell 1964), the idea is pretty much the same in Greece as in all over the Arab world; people's behavior needs to be tailored according to the preservation of one's personal and their family's honor.

After having spent almost three years interacting with Arabs, I have come to realize that many of them share these values, although in different degrees depending on their religion, their families, their tribes, the country they are from, and their life experiences. In addition, through my learning Arabic I keep discovering many similarities in terms of the two languages as well: not only do we share much vocabulary in terms of food (e.g., fasulia [beans], which are *fa'solia* in Greek, and *faraoula* [strawberry], which is '*fraoula* in Greek) or clothing (e.g., *qamis* [shirt], which is *pu'kamiso* in Greek) but also in terms of wishes (e.g., birthday wishes in Arabic are expressed through "*kel 'am wnty/y bikhair*," which is the equivalent of "*na ta ekato'stisis*," meaning may you live 100 years). Discovering more and more of these similarities inspired me to investigate the relationship between Arabic and Greek communicative style and to delve into how these two styles express one's identity and culture. Given the diversity of the Arab world and the space restrictions, I focus my discussion only on a comparison between Qatar and Greece. After presenting the theoretical notions that I use in my analysis, I give a brief description of the methodology and data followed by the discussion of the results of my study. Finally, I conclude by suggesting that my findings can contribute toward the creation of a nascent research strand on the similarities and differences between Arabic and Greek, which can be further used for educational and business purposes.

2.2 Literature Review

By communicative style, I tentatively mean the choice of linguistic, paralinguistic, and discursive resources through which we manage our everyday life, translating into negotiating our and others' social identities, achieving our goals, sharing our ideas, problems, and thoughts, and eventually constructing social meaning. Social meaning is a pertinent notion in sociolinguistics and linguistic anthropology, two theoretical traditions in which this study is embedded, and it has to do with the ways we combine "people, practices, and linguistic varieties, in order to make sense of the society" (Coupland 2007, p. 104). Making sense of the society means that we are able to communicate with each other and, hence, to survive. In this process, language holds a dominant position, namely the specific code we are using, be it a dialect, a sociolect, a switching between different languages or dialects (code switching), the shifting in the level of formality in our speech (speech style) or even the sporadic uses of specific accents or words.

The dimensions of communicative style that can be seen as pertinent are the resources available to speakers, which can be (socio)linguistic, including specific features (lexico-grammatical and phonological systems) or whole dialects and speech varieties imbued with potential for social meaning, and communicative competence, namely linguistic awareness of social rules and norms for speaking (Coupland 2007). Speakers engage with social norms and practices based on their knowledge of what variables in their language index, a type of knowledge they have accumulated during their socialization process (Kiesling 2009) and their general exposure to social experience. This linguistic awareness manifests itself not only in speakers' ability to perceive the differences in what these linguistic features index (e.g., the greeting *assalamu alaykum* in the Gulf indexes formality, while *hala wallah* indexes informality and intimacy) but also through people's ability to comment on these differences metalinguistically (cf. perceptual dialectology studies (e.g., chapters in Preston 1999) that have tried to delve into both resources and competence).

This awareness could be seen as a type of reflexivity (Johnstone 2006), which allows speakers to design their own stylistic operations and attend creatively to the form of their linguistic products (Coupland 2007). It further suggests that awareness of the functional and indexical implications of people's utterances is a core quality of all communicative interaction, and as such, it can also lead people to question, resist, or even challenge social norms. This can be realized through the performativity of speaking or performance, which forms the third dimension of the resources in Coupland's framework. Performance, namely the "enacting of agency, its coming into being" (Duranti 2004, p. 454), can allow people to engage themselves in what Judith Butler has called "performativity of speaking" (1997), whereby they can challenge or even subvert the dominant ideologies and established social values. In this sense, people's styles can break with the social contexts in which they occur (Coupland 2007). Put differently, if performance is incorporated into a framework of how to deal with style, it can allow for realizing (and thus, capturing in the analysis) the possibility of speakers' undermining "the established, conventional meanings indexed by specific linguistic variables" (Coupland 2007, p. 101)

As a unifying thread, performance is the speech event where things are brought together and are synthesized, in order to produce the final product, namely the performed speech act, or to put it simply, the (contextualized) utterance. Through these three aspects of communicative style, namely sociolinguistic resources, communicative competence, and performativity of speaking, I argue that we not only manage our everyday life but also we at times consciously and subconsciously communicate our culture. In a course on language and culture, for instance, the metapragmatic awareness of cultural differences, namely the ability we have to reflect on them, comes at the forefront of every discussion in the same way that a discussion on the similarities and differences between various cultures makes it relevant.

Regarding the definition of "culture," I am aligning with Shaules' notion of "deep culture." He treats it as "the unconscious meanings, values, norms and hidden assumptions that allow us to interpret our experiences as we interact with other people" (2007, pp. 11–12). I consider this definitionpertinent to my data, inasmuch as it allows us to understand who we are according to how we position ourselves vis-a-vis ourselves, our interlocutors, and the society itself, something which is the gist of communication as well.

With respect to Arab communicative styles, a number of studies have focused on business communication between Arabs and Westerners (e.g., Haase 2011; Marsh 2010). These studies, however, do not delve into the nitty-gritty of the linguistics of these styles. On the other hand, Feghali (1997) has identified four features associated with communicative style in Arabic: (1) repetition, (2) indirectness, (3) elaborateness, and (4) affectiveness. All of these four are illustrated through examples from my own data in the analysis found below. These features are found in the use of the Arabic language, but it has been claimed that they also tend to be transferred to the use of Arabs' use of the English language as well. Nonetheless, the author's discussion does not include any actual data analysis, through which one could see the nuanced meanings of the aforementioned stylistic features.

Contrary to the increasing scholarly interest in Arabic communication styles, in terms of Greek communicative styles in professional contexts the literature is rather limited. Deborah Tannen (1984) has analyzed Greek speech style with a special focus on involvement, but her studies on Greek speech style focus on informal and casual interactions among friends and family members rather than people in a professional context. More specifically, Tannen has claimed that Greek speech style is characterized by high involvement, in the sense that Greek speakers participate in conversations in an enthusiastic and very talkative way (1984). From a cultural studies perspective, Broome (1996) shows that Greek communication style is a mosaic of different strategies and emotions, which are characterized by the interlocutors' tensions between saving and losing face. This study was not conducted in a professional/business context.

Aiming at filling this gap in the literature on professional Greek communicative style and drawing on this literature from the two languages, I have decided to focus on the aforementioned stylistic aspects, namely sociolinguistic resources, communicative competence, and performativity of speaking, and see how, on the basis of my ethnographic study, the communicative styles of Arabs and Greeks are similar and different from each other.

My motivation for conducting this type of research is that after working in an Arab country for 3 years, I have come to realize that doing business with Arabs in general, and Qataris in particular, entails the establishment of a solid relationship, which requires good and efficient communication targeted toward the maintenance of this relationship, contrary to the western world, where my experience in the UK has shown me that it is actions, practices, and choices associated with work rather than interpersonal relationships that need to be foregrounded and addressed via communicative styles. Using Hofstede's (1980) cultural values theory, one could argue that the communication with Arabs seems to be framed in a high-context culture, that is, it is interpersonal relationships oriented, contrary to the western communication, which despite its undeniable differences among different countries and continents seems to be overall embedded within a low-context culture, namely it is more transaction or goal oriented.

In light of this take on communicative style and culture, the two research questions which my study seeks to explore are the following: (1) What are the basic communicative styles used by the Greek instructor and her Qatari students, and how are they similar and different from each other? and (2) how do they contribute toward the construction of their perceptions of their own cultures?

2.3   Methodology and Data

In order to answer the guiding research questions, linguistic ethnography was used. As a method, linguistic ethnography is seen as "a method of social research, [which] seeks to capture and understand the meanings and dynamics in particular cultural settings" (Rampton et al. 2004, p. 2). Of the connected characteristics identified as relevant to ethnography in this definition, the most important, in my view, and the one that underlines my analysis is the "regard for local rationalities in an interplay between 'strangeness' and 'familiarity,' namely ethnography's effort to flesh out the meanings that participants take for granted in their everyday practices and render them construable to the audiences to which the research reports are addressed" (Rampton et al. 2004, p. 2). The reason why I foreground this feature of linguistic ethnography is because this interplay between strangeness and familiarity alludes to my personal initial strangeness toward the Arabic language, its dialects and the cultures attached to them, and my familiarity with the other, namely the Greek one.

Such a distinction resembles the distinction between what I would call hardcore ethnography, namely the type of research we engage ourselves in when we are not familiar with the culture we are about to research, and self-reflective ethnography, which we exercise when we belong to the culture under scrutiny. In the exploration of the relationship between Arab and Greek communicative styles and cultures, it is important to combine these two types of ethnography, without prioritizing the one at the expense of the other, in order to arrive at these nuanced meanings and dynamics within and across the language and the cultures.

Overall, the methodology of this study includes ethnographic participant observation (Emerson et al. 2001) and ethnographic interviews (Bucholtz 2007) . The
combination of these two methods aims at "informing the analysis of language
produced independently of the researcher's immediate involvement" (Tusting and
Maybin 2007, p. 579).

Regarding the data collection, I relied primarily on my field notes, the interview
data from my students and Arabic-speaking colleagues as well as e-mail exchanges
in my sociolinguistics, language and culture, and discourse analysis courses, which
I gave during the academic year 2011–2012. My data stem from 156 undergraduate female Qatari students' use of English and, in the cases of code switching, the
shifting between English and Arabic, which I have termed Arabizi, namely a written variety of Arabic which uses Latin characters to represent Arabic words. Due
to space restrictions, the stylistic patterns are illustrated through actual data from
online interactions I have had with five students from my sample. Upon their request, all names have been pseudonymized. I consider these data representative of
the patterns I analyze on the basis of their encapsulating the social meanings which
the vast majority of my students convey in their interactions with me.

Data Analysis

With a focus on four aspects of the communicative styles that my students and I
use the most, i.e., with a high frequency in our daily professional communication
regarding university-related issues, this section provides an analysis of e-mail exchange data sets between my students and me. The four aspects of communicative
styles that are of interest here and the ones that emerged as the themes of my analysis comprise the following: repetition patterns in university discourse (English),
indirectness patterns in university discourse (English), elaborateness patterns in
university discourse (English), and high-involvement style in university discourse
(English).

Repetition Patterns in University Discourse (English)

Regarding repetition, it has been observed that this stylistic feature forms an important part of Arabic communicative style(Feghali 1997), particularly when it is
realized through the use of pious formulae, mainly *insha'allah, alhamdullillah,
masha'allah, subhan allah, baraqalahu allah*. This is definitely the case with my
Qatari students' oral and written style inside and outside class, especially with the
use of *insha'allah* (cf. Sussex 2012), which I have noticed they use extensively
whenever they talk about the future and their future plans or whenever they make
promises. Another pattern I have noticed with my Qatari colleagues is that whenever I ask them to do something that I know they will not do (e.g., to come to a
party I am organizing, which does not correspond to their concept of a party given

the mixed gender invitees, the consumption of alcohol, etc.), they use *insha'allah*, which I interpret as the inability for them to come because Allah did not allow them to do it.

As a Greek, in my interactions with my Qatari colleagues and students, I tend to use not only the phrases like "hopefully" and "I hope" but also *insha'allah* with the meaning of "with the help of God." Greek language also has this, which expresses the idea that the future heavily depends on God and/or luck with the phrase *syn theo* or an *thelei o theos* (God willing); that is why the concept of *insha'allah* is familiar to me to use.

The following example illustrates the use of *insha'allah* in an online interaction between a Qatari student of mine and me[1]:

Example 1:

On Jan 4, 2012, at 2:28 PM, Sarah wrote:

> Dear Dr. Irene, assalam alaikum!
> Hope these words find you well.
> Kindly find the attachment (the extra work).
> I was waiting to set with my grandmother to ask her some questions about the family, but I won't be able to do that this weekend. I wrote what I know, I hope it is good.
> I will submit a hard copy on sunday, insha'Allah. Is that OK?
> Thank you and best regards
> Your student,
> Sarah Al Habibi
> Student id number

Example 2

> From: Eirini Theodoropoulou
> Sent: Friday, January 04, 2013 8:03 PM
> To: Student's email
> Subject: Re: Extra work
> Wa alaykum salam, ya Sarah!
> Thanks for this. No problem, you can submit the hard copy on Sunday—could you please drop it into my mailbox? Insha'allah, I'll be at QU in the afternoon to pick it up.
> Thanks,
> Dr. Irene

This e-mail exchange concerns my student Sarah's electronic submission of some extra credit work I asked her to do to make up for a missing quiz during the semester; I asked her to submit both a soft and a hard copy and, given that she knows how strict I can be unless students stick to deadlines, in her e-mail she makes a promise that she will submit her hard copy by the deadline, which is on that Sunday that she refers to in her e-mail. Her use of *insha'allah* indexes exactly the commitment she makes to the submission of her paper, which however she sees as depending on Allah. In my answer to her, I also use *insha'allah* but in my case it has the meaning that I hope to be able to go to Qatar University to pick it up on that day. The reason why in my data *insha'allah* has a slightly different meaning from Sarah's is because on that Sunday I had some professional obligations outside Qatar University and

---

[1] All of the examples are original ones; they have not been edited.

I was not sure when they would be over to allow me to go to my office in Qatar University.

Overall, all of these "religious" expressions used by Qataris have been secularized or dereligionized in the sense that many Westerners including myself, who are non-Muslims, also use them in their interactions with Qataris aiming to sound more polite and more likeable. This extended use of these expressions points toward them being a very good example of routine or fixed linguistic units, which form part of the repetitive style used by both my Qatari students and their Greek instructor. They are repeated but more often than not they carry different social meanings depending on the context and not on who is using them.

Indirectness Patterns in University Discourse (English)

By "indirectness" I align with the linguistic literature on viewing it as the conveying of unstated meaning (Tannen 2007). The basic idea behind indirectness is that you need to be able to read between the lines in order to decipher people's talk. Even though indirectness has been found as an important stylistic feature of Arabic communication style because of its association with being a high-context culture (see Feghali 1997; Nelson et al. 2002; Bassiouney 2009), from my experience I would claim that this is not always the case. While interacting in pleasant communication circumstances, such as giving compliments expressing admiration for something, my Qatari students tend to sound and seem indirect, but when it comes to requests for academic issues, such as deadline extensions, questions on which material to focus on for the purposes of final exams, and grade raising, they tend to be very direct. The following example from an e-mail exchange between a student and me illustrates this discrepancy:

Example 3

On Jan 7, 2012, at 1:42 PM, Noora wrote:

> Good afternoon Erine,
> As a student in this course, I am very keen to capitalize on my success. You have done a great deal and assisted me personally in many things, so thank you so much.
> To reach my goal of at least a B as a grade, I would like to know what are the specific things I should focus on for the final exam?
> Yours,
> Noora

Example 4

January 7, 2012 2:47:16 PM GMT+ 02:00

> Hi Noora,
> thanks for this and your kind words. I am afraid I cannot help you with this; as I said, you need to study everything that we have covered after the midterm exam. The questions I am going to ask will require your understanding of the phenomena that we have discussed in class.
> Best,
> Dr. Irene

Noora's e-mail contain indirect style in as much as it coincides with her camouflaged and concealed true intentions in terms of her wants, needs, and goals in the discourse situation (Gudykunst and Ting-Toomey 1988) she is trying to establish with me. To be more specific, through her e-mail she is trying to elicit information on what kinds of questions I am going to ask and which topics/notions I am going to focus on in the exam of the Introduction to Language course. Instead of asking this question directly, though, she decided to frame it as some sort of help I need to provide her with, in order for her to get a B. In other words, she positions me as someone who needs to offer her some sort of a *Sadaka*, namely some kind of a good deed. A practice like this is very common among students (at our university): they try to cultivate an atmosphere of flattery, and as soon as this has been established they ask for a favor in such a way that it is presented as if it were tied to the student's professional, academic, or even personal well-being.

Elaborateness Patterns in University Discourse (English)

Along the same lines of constructing flattery, elaborateness as a communicative style refers to creative, expressive, and almost poetic use of language. In the context of the Arabic language, this elaborateness is also seen as equivalent with the use of many words (Samovar and Porter 1991). In the literature on elaborateness in Arabic, two rhetorical strategies have been found to realize elaborated speech: exaggeration (*mubalagha*) and assertion (*tawkid*) (Badolato 1981; Rahim 2005).

Regarding exaggeration, in both our oral and written discussions with students I have found that both sides employ this stylistic feature but in different ways; while students in principle tend to construct whole discourses of exaggeration, I as the instructor tend to take on my students' exaggeration but through the use of "extreme" verbs as opposed to whole texts. The following examples from an e-mail exchange with one of my students illustrate these patterns:

Example of exaggeration (*mubalagha*)

Example 5

On Jan 9, 2012, at 1:47 PM, Mona wrote:

> From: XXXX
> To: irene.theodoropoulou@qu.edu.qa
> Subject: ...
> Date: Wed, 9 Jan 2012 13:39:50+0300
> Dear Doctor
> I promise to send my research paper in one houre
> am baging u to accept my final paper
> I cant find excuses to write for you, because I know that am not the only student who has pregnancy dificulties
> or academic pressure, even my husband said that to me in order to motivate me to finish my work
> I swear to God that I run through websits, reading some books and preparing a survey,
> I didnt even see my kids for more than two weeks!! I sent them to my mum house thinking that would help me to achieve somthing

But I miss that point, that my problem is within me. my problem that I was surrending to my negativity and like an old turtle I was racing against time
I was week and panic
Maybe am too old to be an acadamic student

Example 6

Hi Mona,
thanks for this. There is no reason for panicking! Just try to do the best you can with your final paper and you can submit it either today or tomorrow at the latest.
Thank you,
Dr. Irene
P.S. Could you please return the language attitudes book as well? I am doing a collaborative project with Dr. X on language attitudes and we need it! Thanks!

The poetic character in Mona's e-mail is already evident via the format of the e-mail; instead of writing one continuous text, which would be expected according to the e-mail writing conventions found in e-mails written in English (cf. Crystal 2012), she leaves a blank line between different sentences and phrases, maybe in order to emphasize the ideas that she wants to express. Similarly, the whole tone of the e-mail is quite poetic and expressive, indexed through the emotional strength of words and sentences such as "begging," "I swear to God," and "I haven't seen my kids." This poetic use is further enhanced via the use of psychology-related, in the sense of self-reflectional, expressions, like "my problem is within me," "I was surrendering to my negativity and like an old turtle I was racing against time," culminating in self-deprecating expressions, like "I was weak and panic," and "maybe am too old to be an academic student." My experience in Greece, Austria, and in the UK has shown me that such emotional expressions are rarely used in e-mail interactions between faculty members and students in the western world, even when emotions run high because of disagreements having to do with grades or general academic issues. Part of this emotionality in the case of my students in Qatar is also constructed through the mechanism of personalization and the sharing of personal information, which in the western context can be seen as more than necessary.

Example of assertion (*tawkid*)

Example 7

On Jan 7, 2012, at 4:59 PM, Alreem wrote:

>Hi dr
>How are you? I hope that you are fine
>I will graduate this semester and so afraid of my grades as you know my father died affected badly on my personality I always crying and can not focus on my exams. For seminar I did my best and if there is any method to increase my grade I will do it.
>
>Thank you for your helping
>
>Alreem

Example 8

------Original Message------

From: Eirini Theodoropoulou

To: Alreem
Subject: Re:
Sent: 8 Jan 2012 8:20 PM
Hi Reem,
thanks very much for your email. I do understand your situation and would like to help you out here; your overall grade so far is a D+, which can become a C, if you write a 250-word essay about the history and sociolinguistic features of your tribe. Please submit this essay no later than Sunday, the 13th of January.
Thanks,
Dr. Irene

Example 9

On Jan 8, 2012, at 8:33 PM, Alreem wrote:

Thank you for helping and I will submit it before sunday inshalla but please can you clarify the topic please
Alreem

In these three excerpts by student Reem and me, the mechanism of assertion is in full swing; in Reem's first e-mail, assertion takes two shapes—one referring to the past (I did my best) and one referring to the future (I will do whatever it takes to increase my grade). Even though the assertion regarding students' performance throughout the whole semester is not very frequent in my data, it can be seen as a powerful communicative stylistic practice whereby students, and in this particular example Reem, are trying to pave the way for asserting that they will do their best to get a good grade. In other words, by constructing the persona of a hardworking student, they hope to be able to persuade their instructors to give them extra credit work to do, in order to increase their grades. From my ethnographic participant observation, I have arrived at the conclusion that for my Qatari students getting a high grade is more a matter of prestige for themselves and their families than a matter of it securing them a good job or the ability to get a scholarship and carry on doing postgraduate studies in Qatar or abroad. From my part as an instructor, I am always trying to give students opportunities to improve their performance in general and their grades in particular. Nonetheless, in order not to create false impressions, namely that all students who are given extra credit work will automatically receive better grades, I am always trying to use modal verbs, such as can, could, and would, which are also to be found in example 8. In this way, I also employ the stylistic mechanism of assertion but not as directly and as straightforwardly as my students.

In a nutshell, both the strategies of exaggeration and assertion are claimed to establish and maintain credibility during interaction, in the sense that intimacy can be constructed via them, which in turn can secure honesty and trust in our interactions.

High-involvement Style in University Discourse (English)

Another stylistic feature which is relevant to intimacy and subsequent credibility between interlocutors is high-involvement speech. High-involvement speech style has been found to characterize Greek communication(Tannen 2005). It is realized through a range of different stylistic features, including few or no pauses, supportive tags (e.g., hm, mm, yes, ok), overlapping questions, fast-paced latching (elaborating on a topic), and undisrupted conversation. All of these features have been argued to show interest and rapport between interlocutors, and thus to establish intimacy and mutual trust between them (cf. Jandt 2012).

From my teaching experience both inside and outside of the classroom, I can say that both my Qatari students and I tend to use supportive tags in my interactions with students, primarily the English ones ok, and yeah but also the Arabic ones *aiuwa* (yes) and *sah*? (right?), especially when the discussion topic is pertinent to the Qatari dialect and culture. Regarding my students, they use the discourse marker *yani* (roughly translated as "namely") in their oral English discourse but never in their e-mails. In the latter, they tend to use tag questions at the end of their e-mails, and it is usually if they want to take the initiative for doing something, but they do not know whether I agree with it. In their e-mail, they would usually send their ideas/initiatives and at the end of the sentence(s) containing the initiatives they would put the tag question (see, for instance, Sarah's e-mail in example 1: I will submit a hard copy on sunday, *insha'allah*. Is that OK?

2.4   Implications

The data point toward one of the basic cultural features shared between Greek and Qatari deep cultures, is affect. As an example of subjective culture, namely as a cultural aspect that we cannot see or touch, as something that functions out of awareness (Triandis 1972), affect is identified with people's tendency to appeal to their interlocutors' emotional rather than rational aspects of their character. In light of this, I would say that the foregrounding and constant use of affect can be seen as equivalent to "doing drama," namely to deal with problems, challenges, and tensions in an emotional rather than rational way. This can be seen both inside and outside class and in both face-to-face and online interactions. Even though many times I have been tempted to accommodate this affect linguistically, i.e., to converge to it, I have decided to diverge instead, namely not to follow it, because of my role as an instructor and, hence, as a role model of rationality, which is, I think, the most impartial and thus fair way to deal with students in an academic and professional context such as a university.

Along the same lines of affect, both the students and I engage in the effort to construct intimacy rather than hierarchy, another subjective cultural pattern relevant to handling human relationships. The hierarchy dimension of course is there, indexed through the use of Dr. in my students' discourse, but my ethnographic participant observation has shown me that for many of my female students I act as a live (rather than popular culture related) bridge between them and the western world, hence they are trying to establish a friendly relationship with me, in order to learn as much information about the western world from me as possible. This is done through the use of the aforementioned stylistic devices (Coupland 2007), including repetition, indirectness, elaborateness (exaggeration and assertion), and high-involvement style (Tannen 2005), which can be argued to form wider communicative patterns of *filotimo*, a notion that has been claimed to characterize the Greek society only. Even though there is no exact translation in English or, for that matter, in Arabic, "*filotimo*" can be seen as the sense of obligation and responsibility to the in-group, including family, friends, and colleagues (Broome 1996, p. 66). This is the case because all these four stylistic mechanisms share the communicative pattern of being polite, tactful, respectful and, eventually, grateful (Triandis 1972) to one's interlocutors. It this way, *filotimo* can be seen as characterizing both my Qatari students and me, albeit from a different angle: my students' *filotimo* is constructed with a communicative emphasis on respectfulness and gratefulness, while I place an emphasis on the tactfulness aspect. At the end of the day, of course, all of us will convey *filotimo* in its multidimensionality either consciously or subconsciously in both our offline and online interaction, exactly because our communicative styles are trying to encode our respective sense of personal honor and self-esteem. Eventually, the safeguarding of *filotimo* secures equality, so no one of us interacting with each other feels inferior to the other. The latter requires courses on intercultural communication like the one I teach and also awareness with the aid of the media and the government to create not only knowledge but also tolerance. Yet, tolerance does not necessarily mean acceptance but just admitting that not everyone is like us or maybe that the so-called other is like us even if they speak a different language and come from a different country.

Conclusion

The current study attempted to investigate the communicative styles used by a number of young female Qatari students and their instructor, a Greek woman, and to understand how these styles contribute toward the construction of culture. The respective dimensions of communicative styles used in university-related communication included the following four: repetition patterns in university discourse (English), indirectness patterns in university discourse (English), elaborateness patterns in university discourse (English), and high-involvement style in university discourse (English). With respect to repetition, it has been found that it is primarily religious expressions, such as *insha'allah*, which are used extensively by both parties with the aim to render their communication more trustworthy and valid through its framing within a pious context. Indirectness is employed by my students as a mechanism to ask me to do favors for them, such as improving their grades. This strategy verifies the fact that the Qatari culture can be seen as a high-context culture (Hofstede 1980), where subtlety and indirectness are prized. Instead of getting down to business directly, my Qatari students tend to rely first on existing relationships outside the university so that shared understandings make explicitness unnecessary. Along the same lines, elaborateness realized through exaggeration and assertion on behalf of my students has a similar target, in as much as it aims at rendering the message more emotionally appealing and thus standing a good chance of accomplishing its mission. Finally, high-involvement style, evident through the use of few or no pauses, supportive tags (e.g., hm, mm, yes, ok), overlapping questions, fast-paced latching (elaborating on a topic), and undisrupted conversation at the level of classroom discussions and the use of supportive tags next to students' suggestions or initiatives can be seen as a prioritization of the cultivation of an interpersonal relationship with their instructor more than the accomplishment of a certain goal.

It goes without saying that the findings from this study are not generalizable, given that the analysis is qualitative and the data stem from a limited number of people and from a very specific context, which is that of an Arab university in Qatar. Nonetheless, the value of this study is that it introduces the idea of a correlation between communicative styles of people whose languages may be different, but who share a lot of cultural similarities. I hope the findings from this study will contribute toward the unlocking of the peculiarities associated with communicative styles, which sometimes prevent intercultural communication between an Arab and a non-Arab, hence they hinder the very process of learning. To this end, I would suggest the creation of an intercultural communication course attended by both students and non-Arab faculty members alike, which will focus on the understanding and interpretation of such empirical data and will seek to provide both types of target groups with the necessary tools that will help them gain cultural competence. Given the frequency and the nature of collaboration between them, cultural competence is a sine qua non for a successful student experience and faculty members' tenure at the university, respectively.

References

Ayish, M. I. (1998). Communication research in the Arab World. A new perspective. *The Public, 5*(1), 33–57.

Badolato, E. V. (1981). *The cultural impact of US-Arab military relations*. Newport: The Naval War College Center for Advanced Research. www.dtic.mil/cgi-bin/GetTRDoc?AD=ADA160865. Accessed 6 July 2012.

Bassiouney, R. (2009). *Arabic sociolinguistics. Topics in diglossia, gender, identity, and politics*. Washington, DC: Georgetown University Press.

Broome, B. J. (1996). *Exploring the Greek mosaic: A guide to intercultural communication in Greece*. Boston: Nicholas Brealey.

Bucholtz, M. (2007). *Interviews and interaction as sociolinguistic data*. Presentation at the 'Ethnographic Methods in Sociocultural Linguistics' workshop. Stanford University, July 14.

Campbell, J. K. (1964). *Honour, family and patronage*. Oxford: Clarendon Press.

Coupland, N. (2007). *Style. Language variation and identity*. Cambridge: Cambridge University Press.

Crystal, D. (2012). *Internet linguistics. A student guidebook*. London: Routledge.

Duranti, A. (2004). Agency in language. In A. Duranti (Ed.), *A companion to linguistic anthropology* (pp. 451–473). Malden: Blackwell.

Emerson, R. M., Fretz, R. I., & Shaw, L. L. (2001). Participant observation and fieldnotes. In P. Atkinson, A. Coffey, S. Delamont, J. Lofland, & L. Lofland (Eds.), *Handbook of ethnography* (pp. 352–368). London: Sage.

Feghali, E. (1997). Arab cultural communication patterns. *International Journal of Intercultural Relations, 21*(3), 345–378.

Gudykunst, W. B., & Ting-Toomey, S. (1988). *Culture and interpersonal communication.* Newbury Park: Sage.

Haase, F.-A. (2001). Contrastive studies in communication styles of Gulf Arab business culture and Western business communication cultures. http://ssrn.com/abstract=1937092 or http://dx.doi.org/10.2139/ssrn.1937092. Accessed 4 March 2013.

Hofstede, G. (1980). *Culture's consequences: International differences in work-related values.* Beverly Hills: Sage.

Jandt, F. E. (2012). *An introduction to intercultural communication. Identities in a global community* (7th ed.). London: Sage.

Johnstone, B. (2006). Reflexivity in sociolinguistics. In K. Brown (Ed.), *Encyclopedia of language and linguistics* (2nd ed., pp. 463–464). Oxford: Elsevier.

Kiesling, S. F. (2009). Style as stance: Stance as the explanation for patterns of sociolinguistic variation. In A. Jaffe (Ed.), *Stance. Sociolinguistic perspectives* (pp. 171–194). New York: Oxford University Press.

Marsh, D. (2010). *The Middle East unveiled. A cultural and practical guide for all western business professionals.* Oxford: Howtobooks.

Nelson, G. L., Al Batal, M., & El Bakary, W. (2002). Directness vs. indirectness: Egyptian Arabic and US English communication style. *International Journal of Intercultural Relations, 26,* 39–57.

Preston, D. (Ed.). (1999). *Handbook of perceptual dialectology* (Vol. 1). Amsterdam: Benjamins.

Rahim, Y. A. (2005). Imaging identity: A study of Aljazeera's online news and its representation of Arabness with particular attention to "Arabs in Diaspora". http://digitool.library.mcgill.ca:80/webclient/StreamGate?folder_id=0 & dvs=1380056777028~150. Accessed 12 Feb 2013.

Rampton, B., et al. (2004). UK Linguistic ethnography: A discussion paper. http:// www.ling-ethnog.org.uk/documents/discussion_paper_jan_05.pdf. Accessed 4 May 2011.

Samovar, L. A., & Porter, R. E. (1991). *Communication between cultures.* Belmont: Wadsworth.

Shaules, J. (2007). *Deep culture: The hidden challenges of global living.* Clevedon: Multilingual Matters.

Sussex, R. (2012). Switching in international English. In A. Kirkpatrick & R. Sussex (Eds.), *English as an international language in Asia: Implications for language education.* London: Springer.

Tannen, D. (1984). Spoken and written narrative in English and Greek. In D. Tannen (Ed.), *Coherence in spoken and written discourse* (pp. 21–41). Norwood: Ablex.

Tannen, D. (2005). *Conversational style: Analyzing talk among friends.* New York: Oxford University Press.

Tannen, D. (2007). *Talking voices. Repetition, dialogue, and imagery in conversational discourse.* Cambridge: Cambridge University Press.

Triandis, H. C. (1972). *The analysis of subjective culture.* New York: Wiley.

Tusting, K., & Maybin, J. (2007). Linguistic ethnography and interdisciplinarity: Opening the discussion. *Journal of Sociolinguistics, 11*(5), 575–583.

Irene Theodoropoulou is assistant professor in sociolinguistics at Qatar University and associate of King's College London. Her teaching and research interests include sociolinguistics, discourse analysis, rhetoric, and intercultural communication. She is currently working on two interdisciplinary projects funded by Qatar National Research Fund, one on the interface between sociocultural linguistics and traditional Qatari architecture and other on offline and online communication in Qatar. Her work has appeared in academic journals, including the Journal of Greek Linguistics, Articulo—Journal of Urban Research, and edited volumes.

Chapter 3
Perceptions of Indians in Oman: Exploring Aspects of Intercultural Communication

Sandhya Rao Mehta and Ayesha Heble

3.1 The Indian Presence in Oman: An Introduction

In 1781, a young Indian trader is said to have landed on the coast of the erstwhile Masqat kingdom in order to facilitate trade between Tipu Sultan of Mysore and the Al Said empire (Allen 1991). This gentleman was followed by numerous other traders who came to Oman in the following years, primarily from the Kutch area in the western coast of India, to be involved with the trade of dates and frankincense, bringing to Oman shipments of grains, cotton, and fresh produce (Allen 1991). As these traders gradually settled in the coastal town of Muscat, they brought their families with them and soon established themselves as a quiet but vibrant community. Since then, at times sporadically, the Indian presence in Omani society has been firmly entrenched, particularly after the first decade of the twentieth century and after the establishment of the modern Omani state in 1970. While the demographics of Indians in Oman shifted along with historical changes, they never completely left the region. According to Pradhan (2010), there are more than 600,000 Indians in Oman (a country of less than three million), making them the largest expatriate community in the country. While the first wave of Indians came to Oman in 1970 to aid the infrastructural development of the country, many more came as the economic prosperity of Oman demanded more technologically qualified manpower. Thus, as Pradhan (2010) states, the earlier workers in Oman were largely construction personnel and those in the oil rigs, but after the 1980s, more technocrats, doctors and nurses, and those in the education sector began to be part of the widening Indian community. Rahman (2009) states that more than 25% of Indians are in the unskilled category, 30% in semi-skilled, 35% in skilled, and 10% are in the upper level of corporate and government sectors.

S. Rao Mehta (✉) · A. Heble
Sultan Qaboos University, Muscat, Oman
e-mail: rao@squ.edu.com

A. Heble
e-mail: aheble@squ.edu.com

© Springer Science+Business Media Singapore 2015
R. Raddawi (ed.), *Intercultural Communication with Arabs,*
DOI 10.1007/978-981-287-254-8_3

This wide range of Indians in Oman has a direct effect on the way they are approached as a community by the host nation. Historically, the Indian diaspora has been active in many regions of the world, particularly as they went to the Caribbean and Fiji and Maldives as part of the first generation of indentured laborers. There was also the second wave of migration to Africa and then to the UK, following the violence of independence and the partition of India. The third wave, after the liberalization of immigration rules in the USA, consisted of well-qualified individuals who joined private industries and various medical and educational areas (Mishra 2007). As such, Indians have often been seen as being essentially multifaceted, good in technical and academic skills, and successful in their fields.

In the Arabian Gulf, however, and in particular in Oman, the high percentages of workers in lower-paying industries have led to the establishment of stereotypes of the community, which are at variance with the predominant communities across the world. While there are more than half a million Indians in Oman, the human face of this community of the diaspora is almost nonexistent. Viewed as statistics and a group that exists essentially to provide services to the local population, the Indian community is couched within stereotypes that are not only partially true but are also dangerous for the establishment of meaningful relationships between the two communities. While on one hand, Indians are primarily seen as being caregivers in the form of maids and nurses, as well as cleaners and construction workers, they are also the focus of much envy by the host community for the perceived usurpation of jobs that "belong" to them. In this way, the relationship between Indians and Omanis is couched in terms which defy interpretation or label, as they oscillate within a range of mixed emotions. The repercussions of this complete gap in communication could be tremendous, given that the relationship between these two countries is a historical given and not likely to change in the foreseeable future. It is imperative, therefore, to understand the intercultural communication which exists between Omani nationals and Indian expatriates to examine the ways in which they could be more usefully addressed. This chapter attempts to explore the attitudes that exist between the two communities of the Omanis and the Indians in Oman. Based on a series of questionnaires and interviews, it can be concluded that the Indian community is couched in terms of multiple stereotypes, owing largely to the lack of any real contact between the two social groups.

3.2 Establishing a Framework for Intercultural Communication: A Review of Literature

Intercultural communication, defined as "a symbolic process in which people from different cultures create shared meanings" (Lusting and Koester 1999, p. 52), has become one of the most significant areas of academic interest in the last few decades. Having got established with the increase in global trade and travel at the turn of the new millennium, research can be traced back to studies by Gudykunst and

Kim (2003), who focused on the notion that intercultural communication is primarily communication between different nationalities, and Martin and Nakayama, (2009) for whom the notion encompasses communication within the larger spectrum of race, gender, and region. The primary impulse for the academic study of this area, however, arises from the works of Kramer and Ikeda (1998) and their theories of dimensional accrual and disassociation, which underlines the distinction between assimilation, adaptation, and integration. Kramer and Ikeda's notion of cultural fusion focuses on the idea that the human mind can add to its learning with the increase of experiences. Thus, immigrants or host communities can learn new ways of approaching communities without having to "unlearn" their previous knowledge. In this way, the cultural fusion theory suggests that communities benefit from new arrivals as they add to the sum of human experiences already existent in the host and the new society. Kramer and Ikeda go on to add that this theory "assumes that all interaction involves interpretation, a process of making sense of one's surroundings, including Others' behavior" (Jackson 2010, p. 388). Further, Gudykunst and Lee (2003) developed the idea of cross-cultural adaptation as a more complex process of accepting and rejecting one's own and other cultures, ultimately leading to adaptation. The aim of this communication is to be able to establish a meaningful relationship between host and new groups of individuals: "Intercultural communication affects communication through its influence on cultural norms and rules related to group identities and the differentiation between members of in-group and out-groups" (p. 10). Further to this discussion dealing with various cultures, Edward Hall's distinction between high and low contexts adds to the notion that an understanding of these differences was an essential part of the intercultural communication, without which a modern society could not effectively involve its individuals. Samovar (2012) quotes an earlier study done by Hall to define this notion of contexts:

> A high context (HC) communication or message is one in which most of the information is already in the person while very little in the coded, explicit, transmitted part of the message. A low context (LC) one is just the opposite; i.e. the message is vested in explicit code (Samovar et al. 2012, p. 201).

3.3 Intercultural Communication in the Arab World

With this background of the way in which studies on inter- and cross-cultural communication have prioritized this area in academic fields, it can be seen that its focus in the Arab world remains relatively unexplored. The range of works which specifically focus on the Middle East is limited. Some of the most significant contributions remain those of Zaharna (1995) and Feghali (1997), whose "Arab cultural communication patterns" remains one of the most established academic studies in this field, focusing on defining the notion of "Arab" and continuing with an exploration of ways in which Arab verbal and non-verbal communication patterns differ fundamentally from those of the Western world. Feghali clearly states that "(t)he intent of this article is to critically review the existing limited and, in some cases, contradictory research on cultural communication patterns in the Arab world. Published investigations of communicative phenomena in this region have been largely absent in the field of intercultural communication..." (Feghali 1997, p. 7). Feghali goes on, in this study, to look at various features of Arab speech patterns, identifying such elements as indirectness, elaboration, and repetition as continuing patterns of Arab speech. This research was continued by Zaharna, who used emerging studies in intercultural communications and elaborated on the need for explaining Arab communication strategies to the Western world in order to be better understood. Zaharna (1995) divided language use into different dichotomous elements such as the high/low order, the direct/indirect forms, the doing/being dichotomy, the oral/literate differences, and the linear/nonlinear forms. Zaharna couched this need to understand differing cultures in terms of a wider context of avoiding conflict: "When ethnocentrisms occur, cultural differences are no longer neutral, but rather negative" (p. 242). Much before the world began to focus on the need to establish more effective relations with the Arab world, these studies pointed to the urgency of establishing effective modes of communication which would help to tide over stereotypes and quick judgments based on poor knowledge of "other" communities.

Other studies which focus on more specific areas as Arabic language use in Western contexts include those of Nelson et al. (2002), who worked on the idea of direct and indirect speech tendencies among Egyptians and Americans, particularly in using statements of refusals; Cohen (1987), who explored the implications of the use of indirectness by Arab negotiators in the Arab–Israeli conflicts, and Katriel (1986), who also explored the way in which American straightforwardness enabled a language in official documents which was diametrically different from those of the Arab speech communities, couched as they are in talk that is sweet as opposed to the direct speech of the Israelis.

In much of the research in intercultural communication, whether internationally or in the Arab world, it can be noted that the East–West divide is as clear and continuing as it has been historically. To a large extent, this is due to such influential academicians as Hall, E. and Hall, M. who connect as well as divide societies in a somewhat generalized fashion. Thus, Hall and Hall (1990) declares:

> Japanese, Arabs and Mediterranean peoples, who have extensive information networks among family, friends, colleagues, and clients...are high context.... Low context people include Americans, Germans, Swiss, Scandinavians, and other northern Europeans ... (p. 7)

Thus, intercultural communication assumes that the major divide in communicative theories remains that between the East and the West. While primarily true in the larger context, it is inevitable to accept that neither Western societies nor Eastern societies share a homogeneity of experience which could be contrasted to the "other" alone. This approach creates complications for just as Europeans do not necessarily share entire verbal and nonverbal patterns with Americans, Arabs do not necessarily share behavioral tendencies with Japanese and Indians in exactly the same manner, even if they were to be seen as a homogenous group of people, which they are not. This is a complication in intercultural communication theories which has failed to gain ascendency in current research concerned as it remains with addressing the singular issue of justifying eastern, in this case Arab culture, to the Western world. This is also, in part, what Jandt (2010) achieves in the book *An Introduction to Intercultural communication*. In a section on the Arab world, such clichés as terrorism and religion are frequently brought out in order to apparently clarify a variety of social issues of the Arab world to the Western readers. Beyond such generalities, very little work has been done within the Arab world on its own societies, exploring the increasingly divergent quality of its demographics and its resultant implications. While most literature in the Arab world, particularly in the Arab Gulf has contained itself to discussions on intercultural communication with the Western world, almost no effort has been made to explore the implications of not establishing effective intercultural communication within its geographical boundaries, given that so many inhabitants of these countries come from different parts of the world. It is imperative that the huge demographic shift in the countries in the Gulf region should lead to some changes in social perceptions and fears about usurpation of culture, language, and everyday life. It is precisely to address some of these concerns that it is important to understand the way in which other communities affect the host nation. As Indians comprise a large part of the expatriate community in the Gulf region, they could be a significant point of study in terms of the intercultural communication existing between them and the countries in which they reside.

3.4 Studies on Indians in the Gulf

Apart from official sources such as (Embassy of India in Oman 2012) records and other public documents such as those of the Gulf Research Center, studies on Indians in the Gulf have been minimal. Whatever records do exist point to economic factors such as annual remittances to and from the host nations, many generalized narratives of exploited workers, occasional suicides which make it to newspaper headlines as well as the success stories of the odd Indian businessperson as they receive a national or international award. Yet, Indians comprise a substantial part of the population of the entire region of the Gulf. According to Pradhan (2010), more than "5 million Indians live in the Gulf Co-operation Council (GCC) making them the largest expatriate community in the region" (p. 3). He goes on to show that in countries such as the United Arab Emirates, more than 30 % of the total population and more than 45 % of the total workforce is Indian and in other countries such as Bahrain and Kuwait they are the largest group of expatriates. His data also suggest that, while 90 % of the total number of Indians were in low-income jobs in the 1970s and 1980s, by 2008, more than 35 % of the Indians were in professional sectors such as medicine, education, and the software industry.

With such overwhelmingly large figures, the Indian community remains a standard presence in all the countries in the Gulf. Yet, research into the impact of this community on the host nation, as well as the reciprocal effect of the stay of these residents on themselves is an area which has been sparsely covered in the literature of intercultural communication, often leading to large areas of misunderstandings and potential conflict. Studies on the personal nature of Indians in the Gulf include Vohra's studies on the Indian community in the U. A. E., including her 2009 article entitled "The Precarious Existence of Dubai's Middle Class." Gardner's (2008) study "Strategic Transnationalism: The Indian Diasporic Elite in Contemporary Bahrain" examines the lives of a few successful Indians in that small nation while Beuthe's (2009) dissertation entitled "Social and Cultural Relations between Nationals and Expatriates in the Gulf Cooperation Council" deals with the way in which Indians are perceived in the Gulf region by the host countries. Thus, while a few studies exist on the Indian presence in the area, minimal information is available regarding any specific country within the GCC and Oman is no exception.

Historically and geographically, Oman is closest to India in terms of languages spoken, trade relations, educational access, and even proximity to the ruling classes. Rahman (2009), tracing the historical relations between the two modern-day countries back to almost 4500 years ago, describes the resurgence of the relationship following India's independence in 1947 when an embassy was established in Oman:

> As a result, centuries-old economic and commercial exchanges between India and Oman were further strengthened. The merchant community from India who has been living for several generations in Oman got the opportunity to interact with India. This interaction has helped in laying the foundation for a substantial multi-dimensional economic relationship between these two countries. This revitalized relationship has also added contemporary value to the historic ties which link India and Oman from ancient times (p. 101).

Rahman's study of Oman–India relations, while being one of the few pieces of sustained research into this area, remains primarily a macro-picture of the way in which the two nations have established economic and cultural ties. Such studies also include those of Allen (1987); Pradhan (2010); Peterson (2004) and Kechichian (1995). It would be, in fact, fair to say that there has been no sustained and specific study of the Indian community in Oman or the effect that this community has upon the host country. The only available general studies are those of Deffner and Pfaffenbach (2011) entitled "Zones of contact and spaces of negotiation: The Indian Diaspora in Muscat (Sultanate of Oman)" and Mehta and Sacheti's 2011 study of Indian diasporic artists in Oman entitled "Coastal Contacts: Oman in the Indian Imagination." Clearly, more sustained research is necessary in order to contextualize, analyze, and even understand this historical relationship.

3.5 Exploring Attitudes Towards Indians in Oman: Methodology

In order to better understand the way in which Omanis view Indians, it is important to recognize that they are an important part of their physical landscape in that they permeate almost every aspect of their working lives, from cleaners whom Omanis citizens encounter early in the morning cleaning the streets, professional doctors and teachers whom they meet officially, waiters and managers at big and small hotels and restaurants as well as other people they commonly see driving on the roads, in supermarkets, and other public spaces like parks. Even a cursory glance at everyday life in Oman suggests that it is impossible for an Omani, whether in the cities of Muscat, Sohar or Salalah or even in the interior towns and villages to remain unconnected with Indians in their daily lives. And yet, personal conversations as well as online forums often show Indians in a negative light. This prompted an investigation into the way in which Omanis actually viewed Indians and the role they seemed to play in Omani lives.

Based on the premise that the university community would have a deeper knowledge and awareness of the complexities of social life, a questionnaire was given to students and interviews conducted with three university professors of Sultan Qaboos University in order to gauge social perceptions as well as general awareness of young Omanis towards Indians. The students were selected as they were in the classes of the researchers and they were joined by some of their friends in other sections of the same course. All of them were informed of the objective of the questionnaire and that the information which would be collected would form part of a research project. Two interviews were conducted with Omani faculty members and one with an Indian faculty member to understand the situation from both points of view. Sultan Qaboos University is located in the center of the capital of Oman, Muscat and as such, has a diverse population within its campus, including Western expatriate teachers and Indians at various different levels. As they drive down the campus, students often encounter Indians in the form of gardeners, cleaners, and maintenance staff. They also tend to see them in classrooms as instructors, lab technicians as well as in official, secretarial roles. This diversity of roles would lead to the assumption that Omanis, particularly in their late teens and early twenties, would be able to assume a complex relationship with the Indian community which is always within the ambit of their mental vision. Omani university students, the hypothesis was, would be able to articulate the complexity of this relationship in their country, as they are being continually exposed to people from this particular ethnic group in various different ways. It was also assumed that, given the exposure to information and access to visual sources of various kinds, their knowledge of India would be somewhat correct.

As such, a series of questions were asked of 21–22-year-old university students who were English majors students of the Arts and Education program of the university. This major was selected as they were in the classes of the researchers and, therefore, readily accessible. They had been in the university for at least 3 years and came from different parts of Oman, its smaller towns and the capital city as well. While 52 questionnaires were handed out, 37 of them responded, with 15 of them saying that they did not have much to say about this topic.

The questions which were asked of these students included the following:

1. Do you know what the capital of India is?
2. Do you know the name of any Indian language?
3. Do you know approximately how many Indian languages are spoken?
4. Can you name any (around three to four) famous Indian personalities?
5. Do you encounter Indians in your daily life?
6. Do you personally know any Indian?

7. If you were to use a few adjectives to describe Indians, what would they be?
8. In your opinion, what are some of the positive effects of Indian presence in Oman?
9. In your opinion, what are some of the negative effects of Indian presence in Oman
10. What do you think can be done to make this relationship between Indians and Omanis better?

3.6   An Analysis of Student Perceptions

An interesting starting point towards analyzing the reasons for gaps in communication between the Indian community and Omanis is articulated by an Indian professor who views this in the context of power and identity:

> The attitudes to Indians in Oman, a country which is socio-politically more liberal seem conflicted and conflicting which is a part of narrative worth exploring. The relationship between the Indian Diaspora and Omani Community could be better articulated and explained in terms of sociolinguistic principles of power and solidarity and the construction and performance of identities, which is, to a large extent, influenced and regulated by the socio-cultural assumptions and practices of the two speech communities in question. (Personal communication, Jan. 12, 2013)

This interplay of identities is significantly brought out in the analysis of the questionnaires which were given to students of the English department at Sultan Qaboos University. The answers to these questions were interesting and surprising in some respects, although some of them were fairly predictable. As the questionnaire included short and long questions, percentages in this analysis have been given only where possible. Phrases used are those of the respondents and have not been corrected. Only 50% of the respondents said that Delhi was the capital of India while 15% said that it was Mumbai and the rest said they did not know. Asked about the number of languages spoken in India, students used words like "millions" while "hundreds" was more popular. Of course, the intention was not to get the correct number of languages but to see general awareness patterns. While only 55% of the respondents even said they knew the names of some of the languages spoken in India, most of them named Urdu, Bengali, Hindi, and "the language spoken by Kerala people" in that order. Although Keralites form the major group of the Indian expatriate labor force in Oman, Omani students themselves had never heard of their language, Malayalam.

Asked to name famous Indian personalities, the result was predictably unanimous. 100% of the students referred to the famous Bollywood actor Shah Rukh Khan, while 20% of them mentioned other actresses such as Katrina Kaif, Amitabh Bhachan, and other film personalities. Among the non-film personalities mentioned, Gandhi was the most prominent (15% of respondents) with one person mentioning writer Salman Rushdie and another, Indira Gandhi. To the question of whether they knew any Indians at a personal level, all of them mentioned teachers, doctors, and housemaids. One student mentioned knowing "my doctors and my family's farmer" while another said "yes, I know Indian teachers and our Indian maid and neighbor." When asked to describe Indians, 90% of the respondents used the word "hardworking" while others (1 each) used words like "active," "talkative," "patient." Negative adjectives used included "noisy," "angry," and "criminal." One student elaborated and said "some are criminals cuz nowadays they victimize ppl for their own benefits." When questioned about what they thought were the positive elements of Indian presence in Oman, the word "hardworkers" came up a few times (25%) again as did the notion that they built the country: "they provide us with facilities and have been good teachers of mathematics and English." "They work for many hours with low salary" and "they do some work which Omanis do not do like building." More than 90% of the students used words like "building," "infrastructure," and "development" to describe their view of the positive effects of Indians in Oman. While describing the negative effects, 40% of them said that there were none ("there are no negative points"; "no negatives") while others (20% of respondents) spoke about the criminal nature of some of the Indians: "Some Indian workers make crimes," said one student, while another mentioned "crimes, drugs, stealing." Yet others (30%) felt that the negative effect was the one that they were having on the culture and language in Oman: "Some Indians do not respect Omani culture, religion, and traditions"; "sometimes they don't respect our culture in the way of communicating with us" and, simply, "language and culture." One student remarked that a negative effect was that "The Omanis become dependent and lazy people."

Much of what was stated by the students was also corroborated by academicians in the area of intercultural communications and professors at the university. One such interview was with an Omani professor who, in response to a question posed on Omani students' perception of Indians in Oman, said that "(s)tudents can see Indians as being basically in the lower layer of society and therefore deserving pity or in the more influential layer of society and that generates envy. Most students oscillate between these two contradictory emotions" (personal communication, Dec. 29, 2012). Further elaborating on this complexity, another Omani professor of linguistics and intercultural communication more succinctly stated:

> I believe the relationship of Omanis to Indians could be best described as a love-hate relationship. Indian expatriates bring the best and the worst in Omanis. Like most interactions, it is, thus, a very complicated relationship fraught with contradictory feelings, attitudes and practices. On the one hand, Omanis view the Indian diaspora as a lower-status group, leading the former to treat them with disrespect. This disrespect manifests itself at different levels: abusing them at work, not paying them at times, and paying them less than what they deserve. They, both in lower-status and high-end jobs, thus, almost always find themselves at the receiving end of racism and discrimination (personal communication, Dec. 7, 2012).

When asked about what solutions they would offer to make the relationship between Indians and Omanis better, students were less vocal about their responses. 20% of respondents said that there was nothing to be done as it was already very good. Others (25%) suggested offering courses in Indian languages and culture ("I think it's already close. Furthermore, Indian courses in different fields such as Indian languages and Indian cooking"). Many of the students (20%) mentioned creating clubs where they could interact, having competitions ("arranging Indian-Omani gatherings and celebrations"), and even having more opportunities to work together. And 35 % of them mentioned that the media could also play a role in this ("Provide opportunities to identify with each other via the media"; "through the media which will help to bring us together"). One student suggested having public shows which would attract Omanis: "Plan for programs that can interest the Indians and Omanis—like what was done one when they brought an Indian magician."

3.7 Indians in Oman: An Academic Framework

These reactions are primarily substantiated by the very limited research which has been done on this area. Jain (2008) quotes Weiner's observation that "(m)igrants are incorporated into the economic structure, but are excluded from the social structure. Separation, not integration or assimilation, is the goal. Social contacts between Arabs and expatriates are minimized" (p. 193). Beuthe's 2009 study of expatriate relations led her to believe that "(p)articipants seemed to agree that interaction was not supported by the social system and hindered by stereotypes on both sides" (p. 36). She goes on to add that, while Indians in America have been traditionally seen as an ideal minority owing to their education and work ethics, it was exactly the opposite in the Gulf. This is largely corroborated by the research which was done in this study in Oman as well. In fact, Beuthe (2009) explains the primary purpose of her original research as being the exploration of the increasing relations between expatriates and nationals in the Gulf region but "(f)ar from finding anything of the sort, all sources have been essentially unanimous in one thing: there is no interaction" (p. 45). In fact, she ends on a more ominous note, stating that "the state of relations between the largest expatriate group and nationals is highly indicative of the problems in the region" (p. 45).

Vohra (2009) too arrives at a similar conclusion in her study of Indians in the U. A. E. when she says that "(w)hile the guest at the five star hotels and the guest workers of the labor camps have captured the global media's attention to date, they are not the entirety of the city, and they are not markers of a two-dimensional form of globalization" (p. 21). Gardner (2008) makes a similar observation in his study of the Indian business class in Bahrain, noting the way in which Indians and Bahrainis tend to lead separate lives: "(t)hese separate social worlds are characteristic of the Gulf, and the governance that produces this separation helps explain the function of exclusion and dominance in a plural society" (p. 64). More specific studies on Oman by Deffner and Pfaffenbach (2011) similarly conclude that "(a)s long as the lives of the Indians and the Omani remain separate they get on well together. This is the case as the expectations on both sides are clearly defined and the conditions and rights Indians are granted in the receiving and nonetheless hospitable and tolerant Omani society are obeyed by most of the immigrants" (p. 15).

3.8   Promoting Intercultural Communication: Some Recommendations

Al-Jenabi (2012), in her study on intercultural communication in the workplace in the U. A. E., suggests that private firms have a range of four different kinds of acculturation available including assimilation, separation, deculturation, and pluralism. Her conclusion that simple assimilation seems to be the most common method of dealing with the workforce is primarily indicative of the way in which relationships between various communities in the Gulf remain entrenched. The consequences of such a vacuum between communities sharing time and space together could only create needless concern and problems. As the students at the university concluded, it is of utmost importance that the dialogue between different communities, in this case, Indians and Omanis, should be encouraged in every possible way in order for a historical relationship to move ahead in a constructive manner. As it has been noted, "(t)he ultimate result of intercultural awareness is the creation of the atmosphere of mutual respect which is a prerequisite for real intercultural dialogue" (Mazi-Leskovar 2010, p. 10). Such an awareness could be promoted through increased and repeated exposure of young students to different cultures starting with Indians who form such a large part of Omani society, perhaps even through projects and field activities in school, long before their entry to the university and the workplace.

Taking a cue from the students and professors who responded to the set of questions posed to them, it seems that more cultural and educational forums are necessary to make a more effective communication between these two communities possible. It is also important to add some courses in intercultural communication at the school level in order to sensitize students early on to the complexities of living in a multicultural society. Given the historical links between India and Oman, activities such as road shows, promotion of tourist destinations, increased contact through schools and other public institutions as well as establishment of friendship associations may go a long way in creating a framework within which the two communities could mingle more creatively and usefully. AsHeble and Mehta (2013) note: "[i]n a context where the notions of multiculturality (with its associations of intercultural understanding and transcultural potential) are so pertinent, it seems to be very important that students be introduced and exposed in a sustainable manner to literatures across the globe in ways which reflect the complexity of both the reader as well as the text which they are confronting" (p. 9). Within the university, exposure to literature, history and language through interdisciplinary courses in cultural studies could also be more effectively used to expose students to the richness of intercultural experiences, thus bringing Omani students closer to their Indian neighbors. As university students are most equipped to be able to tackle emerging social situations, they remain a good point of contact for the introduction of ideas on intercultural communication which could then be applied in the world outside their immediate contexts.

Conclusion

It is thus interesting to note that, although most research on the area of intercultural communication between Indians and Omanis in Oman tends to point to the absence of constructive and meaningful relationships, most studies also note the potential consequences of not having a meaningful relationship. In a macrocosmic perspective, the void that exists between host nations in the Gulf, in this case, Oman, and the expatriate workers who are increasingly a significant part of the social landscape of the nation, could only be seen as worrying. While there is no doubt that continuing gaps between these two communities will need to be more usefully addressed, the precise way in which this would take place remains open to debate. As the analysis shows, students' attitudes are, at best, ambivalent towards a group of people who are an integral part of their public life. This ambivalence, in turn, opens the doors for further research into creating ways in which the communities could interact in ways which could benefit the host nation as well as those residing in it. Establishing a more effective relationship between these two communities is not impossible but it is most definitely imperative.

References

Al-Jenabi, B. (2012). The scope and impact of workplace diversity in the United Arab Emirates—Preliminary study. *Malaysia Journal of Society and Space, 8*(1), 1–14.

Allen, C., Jr. (1987). *The modernization of the Sultanate*. London: Westview Press.

Allen, C., Jr. (1991). The Indian merchant community of Muscat. *Bulletin of the School of Oriental and African Studies, 44*(1), 39–53.

Beuthe, S. (2009). Social and cultural relations between nationals and expatriates in the Gulf Cooperation Council. Spring. Retrieved 3 June 2013 from Washington research library consortium. http://hdl.handle.net/1961/4674.

Cohen, R. (1987). Problems of intercultural communication in Egyptian-American diplomatic relations. *International Journal of Intercultural Relations, 11*, 29–47.

Deffner, V., & Pfaffenbach, C. (2011). Zones of contact and spaces of negotiation: The Indian diaspora in Muscat. Proceedings of dealing with diversity in 21st century urban settings, Amsterdam.

Embassy of India in Oman. (2012). http://www.indemb-oman.org/. Accessed 12 Oct 2013.

Feghali, E. (1997). Arab cultural communication patterns. *International Journal of Intercultural Relations, 21*(3), 345–378.

Gardner, A. M. (2008). Strategic transnationalism: The Indian diasporic elite in contemporary Bahrain. *City & Society, 20*(1), 54–78.

Gudykunst, W. B., & Kim, Y. Y. (2003). *Communicating with strangers: An approach to intercultural communication*. Boston: McGraw Hill.

Gudykunst, W. B., & Lee, C. M. (2003). Cross cultural theories. In W. G. Gudykunst (Ed.), *Cross-cultural and intercultural communication* (pp. 7–34). Thousand Oaks: Sage.

Hall, E. T., & Hall, M. (1990). *Understanding cultural differences: Germans, French and Americans*. Maine: Intercultural Press.

Heble, A., & Mehta, S. R. (l2013). A tale of two cultures: The Omani-Indian encounter in the literature classroom. *Arts and Humanities in Higher Education, pre-print* ed., 1–9. doi:10.1177/1474022212467787.

Jackson, R. L. (2010). *In encyclopedia of identity*. California: Sage.

Jain, P. C. (2008). Globalisation and Indian diaspora in West Asia and North Africa: Some policy implications. In A. Alam (Ed.), *India and West Asia in the era of globalization* (pp. 161–187). New Delhi: New Century Publications.

Jandt, F. E. (2010). *An introduction to intercultural communication* (6th ed.). London: Sage.

Katriel, T. (1986). *Talking straight: Dugri speech in Israel Sabra culture*. Cambridge: Cambridge University Press.

Kechichian, J. A. (1995). *Oman and the world*. Santa Monica: RAND Corporation.

Kramer, E., & Ikeda, R. (1998). Understanding different worlds: The theory of dimensional accrual/disassociation. *Journal of Intercultural Communication, 2*, 37–51.

Lustig, M. W., & Koester, J. (1999). *Intercultural competence: Interpersonal communication across cultures*. New York: Harper Collins.

Martin, J. N., & Nakayama, T. K. (2009). *Intercultural communication in contexts*. London: McGraw Hill Ltd.

Mazi-Leskovar, D. (2010). Fiction for adults: Promoting intercultural and intracultural understanding. *Linguistics and Literature, 8*(1), 9–17.

Mehta, S. R., & Sacheti, P. (2011). Coastal contacts: Oman in the Indian imagination. Proceeding of Oman and India: Prospects and civilization, 337–345.

Mishra, V. (2007). *The literature of the Indian diaspora: Theorizing the diasporic imaginary*. New York: Routledge.

Peterson, J. E. (2004). Oman's diverse society: Northern Oman. *The Middle East Journal, 58*(1), 32–51.

Pradhan, N. S. (2010). India and the GCC: An economic and political perspective. *Strategic Analysis, 34*(1), 93–103.

Rahman, A. (2009). The socio-cultural dimensions of Indo-Omani relations. *International Politics, 2*(3), 99–113.

Samovar, L. A., Porter, R. E., McDaniel, E. R., & Roy, C. S. (2012). *Communication between cultures* (8th ed.). London: Wadworth Publishing.

Vohra, N. (2009). The precarious existence of Dubai's middle class. *Middle East Report, 252*, 18–21.

Zaharna, R. S. (1995). Understanding cultural preferences of Arab communication patterns. *Public Relations Review, 21*(3), 241–255.

Chapter 4
Intercultural Communication in the Context of Saudi Arab Tertiary Education

Magdalena Karolak and Hala Asmina Guta

4.1 Introduction

Saudi Arabia, along with other Gulf Council Cooperation member states, has been experiencing a rapid development of its tertiary sector of education stimulated by population growth, a planned transition from oil to a knowledge-based economy, as well as a growing role for women in the workforce. While in 2003 there were only eight universities in Saudi Arabia, "at least 100 additional universities and colleges have been created there since" (Romani 2009, p. 1).

New institutions in the Arabian Gulf often prefer to adopt an American model of education that is thought to provide adequate skills required in the workforce. These developments have led to a steady flow of foreign professors who, unlike in the past, come from outside the Middle East. The mutual impact on student–instructor relations is worth exploring. Various studies suggest that "in the classroom environment the interpersonal relationship between teacher and students is an important element contributing to the learning process of students" (Brekelmans et al. 2002), while in the multicultural context, "ethnicity is consistently associated with students' perceptions of their teachers [and] that the way teachers communicate varies according to the ethnicity of their students" (den Brok and Levy 2005, p. 75).

Intercultural communication, which "occurs whenever a person from one culture sends a message to be processed by a person from a different culture" (Samovar et al. 2009, p. 7), is especially interesting to assess in the case of Saudi Arab classrooms. Saudi Arab society follows a strict version of Islam. It is rigidly

M. Karolak (✉)
Zayed University, Dubai, United Arab Emirates
e-mail: Magdalena.karolak@zu.ac.ae

H. A. Guta
Prince Mohammad Bin Fahd University, Al Khobar, Saudi Arabia
e-mail: halaguta@gmail.com

© Springer Science+Business Media Singapore 2015
R. Raddawi (ed.), *Intercultural Communication with Arabs*,
DOI 10.1007/978-981-287-254-8_4

patriarchal and its educational system is based on segregation of genders (van Geel 2012); the latter is also enforced in public spaces (Yamani 2000). The contact between students and professors who embody values different from Saudi Arab is increasingly common. It is interesting to analyze how these sharp differences in cultural background between students and professors affect the educational process. The latter is also marked by the fact that intercultural communication occurs in English language and by a teacher through a student power relation.

This chapter is based on the case study of a university located in Al Khobar in the Eastern Province of Saudi Arabia. The institution is privately owned and has adopted a curriculum developed by Texas International Education Consortium (TIEC). It has two separate campuses, for males and females, respectively. This study has been undertaken at the female campus. Although most students are Saudi Arabs, the majority of professors are foreigners. In this context, the chapter assesses the cultural influences on communication between Saudi students and foreign professors from the students' point of view. Hofstede's five-dimensional model (Hofstede 2001) was applied for the analysis. The factors of analysis are uncertainty avoidance, individualism/collectivism, and power distance dimensions. The study also assesses the respect and identification with professors.

The study is comparative in nature, given the fact that students also have experience with local Saudi Arab professors. Through a series of in-depth interviews with 17 female students we investigate intercultural communication patterns. Given the fact that no studies in the past have undertaken intercultural communication research between students and professors in the context of Saudi Arabia, this chapter will provide an insight into the effects of culture on perception and it can serve to provide recommendations on how to improve culturally responsive education.

4.2   Literature Review and Theoretical Framework

As stated by Hall, (1994) cultural identities reflect "the common historical experiences and shared cultural codes which provide us, as 'one people', with stable, unchanging and continuous frames of reference and meaning, beneath the shifting divisions and vicissitudes of our actual history" (p. 223). As a result, the importance of cultural identities in the process of communication cannot be overstated. A brief overview of Saudi Arabia's cultural context is necessary to understand its impact on intercultural communication.

Saudi Arabia's society is largely conservative. Islam plays a central role in the Kingdom's culture, since it is the birth place of Islam and the host to Mecca, Muslim's holiest city where pilgrimage (Haj) is practiced. As argued by Alsaggaf and Williamson (2004), "religion and culture in Saudi Arabia not only shape people's attitudes, practices, and behaviors, but also shape the way they see and do things and perceive their lives" (para 5). In adherence with the Kingdom's traditions and Islamic teachings, Saudi society observes, for instance, a strict segregation between genders. Women are not allowed to mix with unrelated men in public. Most educational institutions, banks, restaurants, and work places have separate divisions for males and females. In addition, the importance of family and behavior that exemplifies the virtues of honor, manliness, and hospitality are other defining characteristics of the Saudi Arab society (Abdelman and Lustig 1981). Despite the existing scholarly interest in Saudi Arabia, studies of intercultural communication between Saudi and Western interlocutors are scarce. Abdelman and Lustig (1981) assessed the patterns of communication of American and Saudi Arab managers and concluded that, on the one hand, Saudi Arabs resented the Americans' inattention to social rituals as a prelude to task-oriented discussions. On the other hand, the American managers believed a lack of objectivity was the main problem of their Saudi Arab counterparts. Yet, differences in the organization of ideas were perceived as the major problem by both groups. Glowacki-Dudka and Treff (2011) pointed out the norms of high power distance and uncertainty avoidance that impacted the intercultural communication between professors of an all women college in Saudi Arabia. The authors observed, for instance, that due to these communication norms, faculty members were perceived as subordinates by the administrators. In addition, the patterns of communication were carried out in a manner to avoid any conflict or recourse from the faculty toward the administration. Lauring (2011) studied intercultural communication between Saudis, Danes, and other expatriates in a Saudi subsidiary of a Danish corporation. He concluded that intercultural communication was understood as slowing down the decision making process; as a result, some nationalities were excluded from the lines of communication. Interestingly, the Danish managers engaged in this behavior, which made their decisions impossible to question by the subordinates. However, Lauring noted that exclusion and mistrust between the managers and the subordinates led to counteractions by the latter. It may be inferred that Danish managers adopted the attitudes characteristic of the local Saudi organizational setting, thus switching the attitudes to the host culture.

Bruner states that "learning and thinking are always situated in a cultural setting and always dependent upon the utilization of cultural resources" (1996, p. 4). Consequently, understanding the cultural setting of the environment is essential when analyzing educational processes taking place within this setting. Hofstede's five-dimensional model (Hofstede 2001) provides a stepping stone for analysis of the Middle Eastern sociocultural context. The dimensions, namely, power distance, individualism versus collectivism, uncertainty avoidance, masculinity versus Femininity, and short-term versus long-term orientation were developed, based on a statistical method. Saudi Arabia was not assessed separately but together with other countries sharing similar cultures, hence in Hofstede's study the scores for each dimension are shared by the broader Middle Eastern region; the results provide us with preliminary considerations for the study. They also provide hints when it comes to the educational setting (Fig. 4.1).

The first dimension reflects the power distance, i.e., "the extent to which the less powerful members of organizations and institutions (like the family) accept and expect that power is distributed unequally" (Hofstede n.d., online document no page numbers). Saudi Arabia's high score indicates that people naturally accept a hierarchical order of society in which inequalities are inherent and subordinates

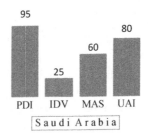

Fig. 4.1 Hofstede's 5-D model for Saudi Arabia. (Adopted from: Hofstede n.d.)

are expected to be told what to do. Within the context of large power distance, education is teacher-centered, unlike in societies with low power distance, where education focuses on the student. The second dimension indicates the low level of individualism, which means that Saudi Arab society is collectivistic. Consequently, people are born into extended families or clans which protect them in exchange for loyalty (Hijab 2002). Emphasis is put on belonging to a group and sharing their opinions and the group predetermines decisions. In the collectivist societies, the purpose of education is learning how to do; not learning how to learn (Hofstede and Hofstede 2005).

On the scale of masculinity versus femininity, with a score of 60, Saudi Arabia is a more masculine than feminine society. In this male-dominated society, the maximum emotional and social role differentiation between the genders is displayed through values such as strength, fight, and ambition that are expected from the men. Women should obey men and, unlike men, they are believed to embody emotions. The fourth dimension, uncertainty avoidance, indicates "the extent to which the members of a culture feel threatened by ambiguous or unknown situations and have created beliefs and institutions that try to avoid these" (Hofstede n.d., online document no page numbers). Saudi Arabia displays thus "firm strict behavioral codes, laws and rules, disapproval of deviant opinions, and a belief in absolute Truth" (Hofstede 2011, p. 10), which are supported by strict religious observance (Idris 2007). Despite the fact that not all rules may be respected on a daily basis, the members of society have an emotional need to have a proper structure to guide them. In the context of education, teachers are supposed to have all the answers. The last dimension has not been originally assessed by Hofstede, however more recent studies reported Saudi Arabia's score to be 36 (Hofstede et al. 2010) making it a short-term oriented society. Short-term oriented societies "foster virtues related to the past and present such as national pride, respect for tradition, preservation of 'face', and fulfilling social obligations" (Hofstede n.d., online document no page numbers).

Saudi Arabia's national culture is "fairly homogeneous"[1] (Idris 2007, p. 37), nonetheless, thanks to its location close to Bahrain, the Eastern Province is often considered one of the least conservative areas in the kingdom (Shifting Sands

---

[1] There is, however, a growing influx of foreign workers who currently constitute 31% of the total population of Saudi Arabia.

Documentary n.d.). The university in question was established in 2006 as a private institution with a curriculum fashioned after North American higher education. It offers BA degrees in business administration, information technology and computer engineering, and law for both men and women. The university also offers undergraduate degrees in electrical, mechanical, and civil engineering for men and interior design for women. Masters degrees are offered in business administration and education for both genders. Given the fact that it is the only US curriculum university where English is the language of instruction in this region of Saudi Arabia that accepts women, it also attracts students from distant locations in the province such as Qatif and Jubail. English is the medium of instruction and all students must demonstrate an advanced level of language proficiency to pursue their education. Due to the strict religious observance, female professors are not allowed to teach male students; however male professors are permitted to teach female students in specially designated zone of the female campus.

The faculty is very diverse, representing 27 different countries other than Saudi Arabia according to the Human Resources data as of December 2012. The four leading nationalities are American, British, Canadian, and Pakistani. Despite efforts to nationalize the workforce in Saudi Arabia, high numbers of foreign faculty were hired to compensate for shortage of skilled professionals among local population. Although statistics are not available for tertiary education, "expatriates made up 40 percent of the secondary teaching force" (Zafeirakou 2007, p. 28) and Prince Mohamed Bin Fahd University (PMU)'s faculty composition by nationality is revealing. For the purpose of the study, PMU has been selected because, given the ethnic mix, there is potential for in-depth exploration of intercultural communication between students and professors in the educational setting.

4.3   Methodology

Samovar et al. (2010) enumerate a number of factors that have to be taken into account when studying intercultural communication. These include (1) perception, (2) patterns of cognition, (3) verbal behaviors, (4) nonverbal behaviors, and (5) the influence of context. Perceptions, i.e., "ways of evaluating and assigning meaning to the stimuli" (p. 13) from the surroundings are strongly influenced by individual's beliefs, values, and attitudes shaped by the latter two. Overall, perceptions are reflected in the worldview, which is the understanding of abstract concepts such as nature, universe, etc. Those factors are reflected in Hofstede's five-dimensional model mentioned above. Our study focuses especially on power distance, uncertainty avoidance, and collectivism. Cognitive patterns include reasoning and approaches to problem solving, which are reflected in "different patterns of knowing and doing" (Samovar et al. 2010, p. 15). In the context of the university in question, education stresses the importance of critical thinking and problem solving as well as teamwork, leadership, and professional and technological communication competence. Verbal communication requires sharing of a common language, yet "lack of shared background knowledge leads initially to misunderstandings" (Gumperz 1995, p. 120). Nonverbal behavior, defined as "intentional uses as in using a non-spoken symbol to communicate a specific message" (Jandt 2010, p. 107), comprises eight nonverbal codes: "physical appearance, proxemics, chronemics, kinesics, haptics, oculesics, vocalics, and olfactics," (Andersen 2010, p. 293). The context of the intercultural communication is the university setting where student–instructor relations govern the interaction.

This study adopted a qualitative in-depth interviewing methodology. The purpose of the in-depth interviews "is to understand themes of the lived daily world from the subject's own perspective" (Kvale 1996, p. 27). Qualitative interviewing aids in gaining deeper understanding of the interviewee's thoughts, experience, and perspectives; "we interview people to find out from those things we cannot directly observe" (Patton 2002, p. 341). The study involved 17 undergraduate female students. Participation was voluntary and all participants received full disclosure of the purpose of the study and they have given their consent to publish interviews. The interviews were conducted in English and, in some cases, in Arabic and lasted between 30 min and 1 h. All interviews were conducted within the university premises.

4.4 Analysis and Findings

The findings of the study are organized thematically. We first focused on the importance of communication and then assessed Hofstede's dimensions of power distance, collectivism, and uncertainty avoidance.

Communication As mentioned earlier, interview questions concentrated on cultural variations in communication styles that are understood along the dimensions of power or influence and proximity (den Brok et al. 2002), power distance, uncertainty avoidance, and collectivism. Through a communication style, for instance, interlocutors can signal similarity and affiliation through "convergence on linguistic, paralinguistic and nonverbal features in such a way as to become more similar to their interlocutor's behaviour", while difference can be demonstrated through "divergence in communication style that accentuates differences between the speaker and the interlocutor". (Noels et al. 2012, p. 54)

Although most participants did not observe major differences in communication styles between Saudi and non-Saudi professors, most participants cited the easiness of communication with Arabic-speaking professors due to language familiarity. As one participant stated: "Actually, for me, I prefer the Arabs because I can communicate with them easily, we can talk in Arabic with them. Sometimes, I cannot explain what I actually want to say so they may misunderstand me when they are Westerners." Another participant felt that she could express herself better when speaking with Arabic speaking professors: "Of course, it is easier with Arabs, because sometimes if we cannot explain something, we can communicate more effectively with Arabs," She went on to explain that when using English she feels limited in expressing her views because: "Sometimes, maybe I cannot deliver the message like because of language ... I could not say something properly so I prefer not to say it sometimes." This limitation stemming from language barrier was highlighted also by other participants and in extreme cases may lead to a student withdrawing herself completely from class discussions: "Yeah ... it happens a lot, I don't say anything in class because of my English. Also, when I want to explain it happens they don't understand not because of my language because sometimes she is a native speaker and when I say 1 or 2 words she does not understand." This personal risk linked to being misunderstood when communicating with a "Westerner" was frequently stressed.

When it comes to the cultural background, students highlighted the learning process that allows foreigners to understand the cultural context: "From the point of view of the language it is easier [to communicate] with Arabs, but when it comes to culture not really. Westerners learn our culture and they respect it so over time they improve and there is no real difference."

Although most participants found it easier to communicate with Arabic speaking professors, they cited the importance of communicating in English with English speaking professors in their careers and future:

> Nowadays, life is not only the people around your home; there is more intercultural [connections], [and] globalization now. Even in my career life, in the future, I will for sure face many people from around the world so I have to be able to communicate. If I don't know any other language than mine, I won't be able to do so ...

Although another participant recognized the difficulties she faces with communicating in a language other than her native one, she emphasized the importance of communicating with non-Arabic speaking professors at PMU and the opportunities that come with such interaction:

> You see, sometimes I don't find the right words, so if my instructor is Saudi or Arab, I just say it in Arabic. But with Westerners it forces me to speak in English, which is very important to my career and future. I like it here at PMU that we have to speak English all the time.

Power Distance When it came to power distance, the findings of this study confirmed the findings of the literature about the high power distance score of the Saudi society. Students observed a hierarchical order of the society. That was apparent in the way students address their teachers. Almost all participants emphasized that they never address their professors by first name only. Most of them use the title "Miss" or "Doctor," but "Miss" is more common even if the instructor is a Ph.D. holder. One student indicated that "using Miss is less confusing because sometimes you do not know who is a Doctor and who is not." She went on to state that "the title Miss makes me feel more comfortable." It is likely that students carry on the traditions of high school where professors are addressed as Miss followed by their name.

Another area that illustrates the power distance is the participation in class. Most students interviewed indicated that they participated in class. However, when asked if Saudi or non-Saudi professors are easier to approach with their concerns, many participants stated that they found it easier to approach non-Saudi professors. One participant stated:

Sometimes, I think Westerner, I don't know…because Saudis they are used to and students come to them and they tell them lies. But sometimes, even when I have an excuse I would not tell the doctor because I don't want them to think I am lying although I am not…because I know girls are telling them the same excuse every day. But Western, even if they think you are lying, they would not say it even when it is obvious. Arabs they are used to these excuses as lies like not all students are sick…they already are suspicious they make it so obvious like really? That's your excuse? Westerners try to believe you.

Similar statements were reiterated by another student:

I feel comfortable approaching non-Saudis or even arguing with non-Saudis because they act very professional…Maybe I just have bad experiences so I don't want to be judgmental. I had a disagreement with a [Western] instructor, but she still gave me a full mark on my assignment…I feel they [Westerners] judge you fairly. I am not sure, but I think our culture is more subjective, may be our emotions interfere in our judgment. I am not sure.

Another student perceived that Westerners actually appreciate challenging them, but Arabs and Saudis prefer a more authoritative relationship:

Yeah [will say it if I disagree in class] because she [Westerner] will like my personality if I disagree [on] something. She will know I am with you in the class and Western will appreciate it more than Arabs. Arabs is like "you should listen". But Western is like "you are with me, you are following".

This participant felt that pleasing her Saudi professors will grant her a favorable evaluation, as their personal impressions about her will affect their assessment if she challenges their authority in class. The result was keeping the hierarchal societal structure with the teacher's superiority intact and his or her authority unchallenged. The authority of the instructor was especially visible in teamwork scenarios, where the majority of participants mentioned they would rather refer to the instructor if they encounter problems with their team members than looking for in-group solutions.

It is worth noting however, that although Saudi society and Arab culture at large has a high power distance, the issue of language made it easier for some participant to approach their Saudi and Arab professors than Western professors: "If I have an issue it is mainly if I want to talk more about it I prefer to have Arabic instructor cause my English is not [good]…so I prefer to communicate with Arabic one." With high power distance, it was expected that there would be differences in teaching styles. Within the context of large power distance, education is teacher-centered, unlike in societies with low power distance, where education focuses on the student. However, the findings of this study illustrated that this trend is changing. Students interviewed did not notice differences in teaching style between Saudis and non-Saudis or Westerners and Arabs[2] when it came to interactive class sessions, students' participation and students–instructor's interactions. Most participants stated that differences are more personal that cultural. In other words, different professors use different teaching styles based on their personality rather than where they come from. The one area where culture was observed as playing a role revealed to be the

---

[2] The study acknowledges the diversity among the group of Arab professors; the stress was put on Gulf Arabs (members of the Gulf Cooperation Council).

use of humor in classroom. As one student noticed "Arabs try to be more conservative so we do not get used to each other… like the instructor tries to have levels [of distance] and to [be] respect[ed]. But Westerners it's OK with them [to joke]." However, humor in many instances is culturally oriented, which is why using humor from a different culture might not resonate well or be understood by students. The differences in the use of humor were noted in previous studies that contrasted American and Arab approach to joking and types of jokes. For instance, Kalliny, Cruthirds, and Minor advised American managers to avoid self-defeating or self enhancing humor as "Arab followers are likely to misinterpret such overtures and form a negative impression which could be the basis of, or support, cross-cultural communication problems" (2006, p. 131). One of our participants stated the difficulty of understanding jokes:

> We had an instructor from New Zealand, sometimes she makes a joke and nobody understood but she realized that and she tried to explain so we don't feel like without understanding. Not the American professors though, because we are used to American series and TV shows and movies…

This confusion is sometimes masked:

> we just laughed [without understanding the joke] because [the instructor] laughed.

Individualism versus Collectivism The second dimension of Hofstede's five components of culture compares individualism to collectivism. In collective societies, ties between group members are stronger and individuals tend to act in the group's interest rather than the individual interest. Moreover, in collectivistic cultures, group members "are likely to seek to save face and to have a stronger commitment to their organization" (Whiteoak et al. 2006, p. 79–80). Schwartz and Bilsky (1990) identified three characteristics of collective cultures: the search for harmony of the in-group, the interdependence of group members, and the prioritizing of group goals over personal goals. The findings of this study illustrate that in the context of Saudi tertiary education, there are mixed elements of the national collectivistic culture as well as influence of individualistic Western culture. This may be linked most likely to globalization as well as the strong presence of Western professors and content in the university.

Most participants emphasized the importance of maintaining harmony within the group, which is visible in the high reluctance to be critical of the work of others: "*I will not say it [work of other students] is not good even if I know it is not.*" This reluctance was motivated by the possible negative consequences coming from the group: "*I don't know what they are going to do for me if I do.*" On the other hand, the collectivistic approach may also discourage students from standing out of the group in the context of positive appraisal. Most of the participants stated they would be reluctant to talk about their achievements in front of others as they could be misunderstood: "*they [other people] will say 'what she is trying to say' so it is better not to talk.*" It is thus rather common to downplay one's achievements as recalled by another interviewee:

I had a situation, for example, when Ms. X in administration asked me 'Are you a professional photographer?'; I said 'No'. Then, when she saw my picture, she said 'Why you said you are not a professional one?' I don't know, I don't like to show myself. Reaction of people may be bad if you do standout also.

However, preserving group harmony does not go to the extent of compromising one's ideas or grades for the sake of the group. One participant stated that she would let go of her ideas for the sake of the group harmony, but if that would influence her performance, she would try coming up with a third idea:

Maybe if it is about an idea, I will give them the space, OK I will ignore my idea, well I will try to convince them first. I don't want them to feel uncomfortable, I am not bossy. I will make them convince me first…I will try to come up with the third idea. I would not just give up. I have my personality too. My name will be on the paper too. I have to have an excuse, if the instructor asks me 'what is this?' I can explain but if I don't know anything like why I am I in this group, you can choose anyone else.

On the other hand, most participants showed a dimension of interdependence among members of the same group. Most participants cited the importance of having a network of friends contributing to their success. Helping each other with assignments and school tasks is another common trend among participants.PMU's academic culture emphasizes academic honesty and integrity, which was reflected in the participants' awareness of the consequences of plagiarism and copying from each other. Soliciting or offering help normally takes the form of explaining the main ideas of an assignment or offering examples of how to perform certain tasks rather than providing an assignment in place of one's friend:

Yes, I would give my work to a friend but I would tell them take it as an idea as an example an idea for you but not to use it of course. I don't give to anyone, I give only to my class friends. Sometimes like I cannot ask the instructor what's this, so I take my friends' assignments as a backup and read their part and understand. Like for the proposal I did not understand what is feasibility so I took my friends assignment and study from it. Even my subject was totally different so I cannot copy paste but just to have an idea.

Nonetheless, participants mentioned that the negative repercussions of plagiarism were the most important factor to limit sharing of their work only to an inner circle of friends, where relations are based on trust preventing practices that could put the members in trouble. Collectivism is also visible in the fact that students stick to groups of friends often coming from the same geographical areas, or Saudis as opposed to international students, as mentioned by a participant: "First semester I had one international friend, we did a presentation together. But it is easier to be friends with Saudis, because of our culture, our way of thinking." The group made up of Saudi members thus preserves consensus on cultural issues.

Uncertainty Avoidance Uncertainty avoidance is the fourth dimension this study assessed. In societies with high level of uncertainty avoidance, there exists high reliance on strict rules and instructions (Hofstede and Hofstede 2005). Members of these societies feel uncomfortable when they are in ambiguous or unknown situations. The academic culture of PMU relies heavily on providing students with detailed guidelines and assessment rubric for assignments. This combined with the national culture that emphasizes strict religious observance and respect for authorities, created a high level of uncertainty avoidance among participants. When asked if they feel uneasy in situations where there are no clear rules at the university, most participants answered positively. In collectivistic societies like Saudi Arabia, reliance on kin was a solution: *"My first year, I felt scared at PMU, writing essays was scary. My sister helped to find out what to do at PMU."*

It is worth noting though that some participants asserted the importance of thinking out of the box, yet they felt more at ease when they were given clear rules. Uncertainty avoidance was also reflected in participants' reluctance to accept changes in well established situations. Uncertainty avoidance was mentioned in the interviews as a factor limiting cooperation with friends: *"I think it is difficult to work with new people because I have to first get to know them."* However, some interviewees mentioned that the reason for avoidance could be pragmatic:

> With new colleagues, it can be an issue too. It takes a lot of time to assess who works hard or who just wants to get grades but not really works, so working with them can be a problem.

The participants did not observe differences between nonverbal codes of Saudi and Western professors as a group. Any differences perceived were attributed to personal traits rather than cultural and/or educational background of the professors. As striking as this result may be, other studies (Monthienvichienchai et al. cited in Mahon and Cushner 2012) clarify that such perceptions may be due to the inability of the students to grasp the specific aspects of culture in a consistent manner; hence, students would associate the differences they perceived between themselves and the professors to an individual professor in a classroom context rather than to a specific culture in general. The lack of sufficiently broad exposure to a foreign culture was noted as the factor influencing such perceptions students had.

4.5   Recommendations

Despite the differences in cultural background, Saudi students are keen to understand the foreign professor's culture and adjust to Western communication codes. In order to enhance their teaching, English-speaking educators should take into account certain factors.

First, professors should understand that students' participation might be challenged because of their limited ability to speak English. Therefore, those students' participation should be especially encouraged in order to decrease the apprehension of making mistakes in a foreign language. On the other hand, professors who are Arabic speakers should minimize allowing students to switch to their mother tongues.

Taking into account Saudi cultural values and nonverbal communication cues, especially the respect of authorities, it is vital to bear in mind that students may not say anything or nod, while in reality they do not agree or do not understand. This apprehension may become an obstacle during the learning process. Students may delay approaching the professor with their problems with understanding the course material and the assignments until they start failing the class. At that time, it may be too late to reverse the damage. In order to avoid such misunderstandings, it is important to observe the students' progress throughout the course and make sure they have internalized the guidelines of the assignments and are able to follow the course material.

The assessment or evaluation, especially critical, of other students' works will be muted if done in an open class forum. Encouraging constructive criticism practices, whether self-criticism or criticism of others' work, is advisable to overcome this initial apprehension by fostering a learning from mistakes approach. Furthermore, given the importance of face-saving, it is preferable if the professor addresses major problems concerning individual students in a private setting.

In order to decrease discomfort resulting from uncertainty, professors should provide clear and explicit directions in course objectives and for assignments because the students expect structure from authority; yet with the passage of time increasing the level of students' independence is advisable. Consequently, activities where students are required to take their own initiative should be encouraged to promote autonomy in the learning process.

Furthermore, given the collectivistic approach that compels students to remain within their close group of friends throughout their time spent at the university, activities involving changing group partners should be encouraged, and including team work skills in the curriculum is vital. Increased communication among different team members will have a beneficial effect on the students' intercultural competence defined as "empathy, openness, tolerance of ambiguity, readiness to decentre, willingness to engage with others and to try anything new" (Fleming cited in O'Dowd 2012, p. 367) as well as patience, flexibility, suspending judgment etc. Within the context of future career, intercultural competence will have a positive impact on the students' ability to collaborate in order to achieve a common goal as a team and their ability to deal with conflicts and to resolve them in a constructive manner (O'Dowd 2012). These skills are becoming increasingly important due to, for instance, virtual work arrangements promoting the formation of cross-organizational and cross-cultural innovative communities online (Heimburger et al. 2010). In a virtual world, such communities allow knowledge transfer between members and foster new knowledge creation.

In addition, engaging students in critical thinking activities and debates where individuals defend their views is necessary to make them overcome the collectivistic background. The ability to overcome such barriers will promote understanding of other cultures, and enhance intercultural communication skills and participation in collaborative international teams, which are a growing element of globalized economy.

Although the problem of plagiarism occurs worldwide, it has often been suggested that the phenomenon is particularly prevalent and acceptable in collectivist societies (McCabe et al. 2008). Indeed, learning in collectivistic societies such as China emphasizes the value of imitation of tradition and encourages memorization.

As a result, "how Chinese writers appropriate texts is deeply inherent in Chinese culture" (Bloch 2008, p. 222). The concept of plagiarism and that of originality may have a different meaning in collectivistic societies than in the individualistic ones (McCabe et al. 2008). Professors should be made aware of this approach to learning as repetition that students may carry as a habit from primary and secondary schools. This does not preclude introduction of the concept of plagiarism as it is understood by the Western academics into the university academic code of conduct; it is necessary however to put stress on explanation of the concept to students in detail and emphasize it throughout their studies. In addition, as some students may be focused on their scores only rather than learning specific skills, it is necessary to include topics and discussions that promote the awareness of course goals. Professors should also highlight the importance of course outcomes for students' future careers as some students may still perceive learning as mere memorization of course material.

Ultimately, the universities should offer intercultural communication courses and training sessions for both professors and students. Such sessions should be organized at the inception of professors' employment and students' enrollment but additional sessions should also follow up at later stages. Such initiatives will increase the students' intercultural competence fostering "tolerance and appropriate attitudes of curiosity and openness" (O'Dowd 2012, p. 350) in intercultural exchanges. In addition, they will facilitate the professors' role in educating students of different cultural backgrounds.

Conclusion

This chapter aimed at assessing the patterns of intercultural communication in the classrooms in tertiary education at one institution in the Eastern Province of Saudi Arabia. The data was drawn from in-depth interviews with 17 female students and used elements of Hofstede's five dimensional model as the basis for analysis. The study uncovered specific patterns of intercultural communication, peculiar to a Saudi Arab classroom setting. Understanding of these elements and their inclusion in development of holistic academic agendas will be beneficial to educators and educational institutions alike. The analysis provides guidelines on how to enhance the educational experience of Saudi students and instill new skills necessary in the modern, globalized economy.

The findings of this chapter confirm that although "cultural identities come from somewhere, [and] have histories. But like everything which is historical, they undergo constant transformation" (Hall 1994, p. 394). Although Saudi society can be classified as a collective society with high power distance and high degree of uncertainty avoidance according to Hofstede's theory, it is apparent that in today's globalized world cultures are more dynamic (Jandt 2012). Interactions between students and culturally diverse teachers, and the infusion of culturally responsible education could contribute to instilling critical thinking, individual creativity, and movement out of comfort zones, which will prepare students for the globalized job market's challenges. Given the fact that the majority of Gulf Cooperation Council citizens display "low societal capacities" (Hertog 2010, p. 5), which translate into low productivity and high expectation of redistribution of state resources, overcoming the barriers that hinder the advancement of the learning process in Saudi universities is an essential step to a greater economic sustainability in the future. The advancement of intercultural competence among the young generation of Saudis will foster collaboration, competition and innovation promoting Saudi Arabia's distinctiveness and contribution in a globalized world and will enable its citizens to become global citizens who understand and engage with other communities (Lu and Corbett 2012).

References

Abdelman, M., & Lustig, M. (1981). Intercultural communication problems as perceived by Saudi Arabian and American Managers. *International Journal of Intercultural Relations, 5,* 349–363.

Alsaggaf, Y., & Williamson, K. (2004). Online communities in Saudi Arabia: Evaluating the impact on culture through online semi-structured interviews. *Forum: Qualitative Social Research, 5*(3). http://www.qualitative-research.net/index.php/fqs/article/view/564/1225. Accessed 3 July 2013.

Andersen, P. A. (2010). Nonverbal communication. In L. A. Samovar, R. E. Porter, & E. R. McDaniel (Eds.), *Intercultural communication: A reader* (13th edn, pp. 293–312). Boston: Wadsworth.

Bloch, J. (2008). Plagiarism across cultures: Is there a difference? In C. Eisner & M. Vicinus (Eds.), *In originality, imitation and plagiarism: Teaching writing in the digital age* (pp. 219–230). The University of Michigan Press.

Brekelmans, M., Wubbels, T., & den Brok, P. (2002). Teacher experience and the teacher-student relationship in the classroom environment. In S. C. Goh & M. S. Khine (Eds.), *Studies in educational learning environments: An international perspective* (pp. 73–99). Singapore: World Scientific.

Bruner, J. (1996). *The culture of education.* London: Harvard University Press.

den Brok, P. J., & Levy, J. (2005). Teacher–student relationships in multicultural classes: Reviewing the past, preparing the future. *International Journal of Educational Research, 43,* 72–88.

den Brok, P. J., Levy, J., Rodriguez, R., & Wubbels, T. (2002). Perceptions of Asian-American and Hispanic-American teachers and their students on teacher interpersonal communication style. *Teaching and Teacher Education, 18,* 447–467.

Foppa, K. (Eds.) (1995). *Mutualities in dialogue* (pp. 101–123). Cambridge: Cambridge University Press.

Glowacki-Dudka, M., & Treff, M. (2011). Forming an institutional culture with multinational administrators and teachers at Effat College, Saudi Arabia. *Intercultural Education, 22*(2), 207–222.

Gumperz, J. J. (1995). Mutual inferencing in conversation. In I. Markova, K. Fopp & K. Graumann (Eds.), *in Mutualities in Dialogue.* Cambridge: Cambridge University Press.

Hall, S. (1994). Cultural identity and diaspora. In P. Williams & C. Laura (Eds.), *Colonial discourse & postcolonial theory: A reader.* New York: Columbia University Press.

Heimburger, A. et al. (2010). Context-based knowledge creation and sharing in cross-cultural collaborative communities. *Proceedings of the 2010 conference on Information Modelling and Knowledge Bases XXI* (pp. 76–88). Amsterdam: IOS Press.

Hertog, S. (2010). The sociology of the Gulf Rentier systems: Societies of intermediaries. *Comparative Studies in Society and History, 52*(2), 1–37.

Hijab, N. (2002). *Women are citizens too: The laws of the state, the lives of women.* New York: Regional Bureau for Arab States, UNDP.

Hofstede, G. (2001). *Culture's consequences: Comparing values, behaviors, institutions, and organizations across nations* (2nd ed.). Thousand Oaks: Sage Publications.

Hofstede, G. (2011). Dimensionalizing cultures: The Hofstede Model in context. *Online Readings in Psychology and Culture, 2*(1), 1–26.

Hofstede, G. (n.d.). *What about Saudi Arabia?* http://geert-hofstede.com/saudi-arabia.html. Accessed 14 Oct 2013.

Hofstede, H., & Hofstede, H. (2005). *Cultures and organizations.* Lund: Studentlitteratur.

Hofstede, G., Hofstede, G. J., & Minkov, M. (2010). *Cultures and organizations: Software of the mind* (Rev. 3rd ed.). New York: McGraw-Hill.

Idris, A. (2007). Cultural barriers to improved organizational performance in Saudi Arabia. *SAM Advanced Management Journal, 72*(2), 36–54.

Jandt, F. E. (2012). *An introduction to intercultural communication: Identities in a global community.* Thousand Oaks: Sage Publications.

Kalliny, M., Cruthirds, K. W., & Minor, M. S. (2006). Differences between American, Egyptian and Lebanese humor styles: Implications for international management. *International Journal of Cross Cultural Management, 6,* 121–134.

Kvale, S. (1996). *Interviews: An introduction to qualitative research interviewing.* Thousand Oaks: Sage Publications.

Lauring, J. (2011). Intercultural organizational communication: The social organizing of interaction in international encounters. *Journal of Business Communication, 48*(3), 231–255.

Lu, P., & Corbett, J. (2012). An intercultural approach to second language education and citizenship. In J. Jackson (Ed.), *The Routledge handbook of language and intercultural communication* (pp. 325–339). New York: Routledge.

Mahon, J., & Cushner, K. (2012). The multicultural classroom. In J. Jackson (Ed.), *The Routledge handbook of language and intercultural communication* (pp. 434–448). New York: Routledge.

McCabe, D. L., Fenghalli, T., & Abdallah, H. (2008). Academic dishonesty in the Middle East: Individual and contextual factors. *Research in Higher Education, 49,* 451–467.

Noels, K. A., Yashima, T., & Zhang, R. (2012). Language, identity and intercultural communication. In J. Jackson (Ed.), *The Routledge handbook of language and intercultural communication* (pp. 52–66). New York: Routledge.

O'Dowd, R. (2012). Intercultural communicative competence through telecollaboration. In J. Jackson (Ed.), *The Routledge handbook of language and intercultural communication* (pp. 340–356). New York: Routledge.

Patton, M. (2002). *Qualitative research and evaluation methods* (3rd ed.). Thousand Oaks: Sage Publications.

Romani, V. (2009). *The politics of higher education in the Middle East: Problems and prospects.* Crown Centre for Middle Eastern Studies, Middle East Brief.

Samovar, L. A., Porter, R. E., & McDaniel, E. R. (2010). *Intercultural communication: A reader.* Boston: Wadsworth.

Schwartz, S. H., & Bilsky, W. (1990). Toward a theory of the universal content and structure of values: Extensions and cross-cultural replications. *Journal of Personality and Social Psychology, 58*(5), 878–891.

Shifting Sands Documentary. (n.d.). http://insideout.wbur.org/documentaries/shiftingsands/part2.asp. Accessed 12 Oct 2013.

van Geel, A. (2012). Whither the Saudi woman? Gender mixing, empowerment and modernity. In R. Meijer & P. Aarts (Eds.), *Saudi Arabia between conservatism, accommodation and reform.* The Hague: Netherlands Institute of International Relations 'Clingendael'.

Whiteoak, J., Crawford, N., & Mapstone, R. (2006). Impact of gender and generational differences in work values and attitudes in an Arab culture. *Thunderbird International Business Review, 48*(1), 77–91.

Yamani, M. (2000). *Changed identities: The challenge of the new generation in Saudi Arabia.* London: Royal Institute of International Affairs.

Zafeirakou, A. (2007). Teacher policies for underserved populations: A synthesis of lessons learned and best practices. *Paper commissioned for The EFA Global Monitoring Report 2008, Education for All by 2015 Will We Make it?.* UNESCO retrieved from unesdoc.unesco.org/images/0015/001555/155594e.pdf. Accessed 8 July 2013.

Magdalena Karolak (Ph.D. in Linguistics, University of Silesia, Poland) is Assistant Professor of Intercultural Studies at Zayed University, UAE. Her research interests include transformations of societies in the Arabian Gulf and Slavic and Romance linguistics. For the past 5 years she has been conducting fieldwork in Bahrain. Dr. Karolak has published journal articles and book chapters on the shifting gender relations, social media, culture and identity, and political system transformations. She is the author of a monograph "The Past Tense in Polish and French: A Semantic Approach to Translation" (Peter Lang 2013).

Hala Asmina Guta (PhD of Mass Communication from Ohio University, United States) is Assistant Professor of Humanities and Social Sciences at Prince Mohammad bin Fahd University. Her research interests include communication for social change, and the intersection of communication, culture, and identity. Her publications and conference presentations include papers on the role of media in peace building in societies emerging from conflict, and the role media and other cultural institutions play in social change and the construction of identity.

Chapter 5
The Discourse of Global English and its Representation in the Saudi Context: A Postmodernist Critical Perspective

Manssour Habbash and Salah Troudi

5.1 Introduction

Today, English is recognized as a global language because most people believe that it has a special role globally (Crystal 1997). In fact, as Carli et al. (2003, p. 865) state, all discourses acknowledge the place of English as the "language of globalization" (as quoted in Findlow 2006, p. 20). In the Arab World, English has gained a higher status than ever before, particularly in the Gulf States where English, it is believed, unquestionably brings many advantages to the millions who learn it. In Saudi Arabia, command of English is seen now not only as prestigious but as an essential requirement for a better job and a window through which Saudis can integrate with the international community. English is in fact a crucial component in public and higher education, academia, international communications, the job market and all the domains related to science and technology

Since the discovery of oil in 1938, there has been a constant wave of American and British companies coming to Saudi Arabia with long-term strategic projects resulting in multibillion-dollar contracts. Many of these contracts involve the establishment of English language training centres with the aim of teaching the language to Saudis, a move which stemmed from the Saudi government's need for qualified citizens to manage and maintain contact with such companies (Al-Shaabi 1989). Parallel to this, the commitment of Saudi Arabia to the World Trade Organization (WTO) in 2005 and the need to cope with the rapid speed of development in technologies, economies and sciences have accelerated calls for more citizens who are proficient in the English language. Equally importantly, political developments

M. Habbash (✉)
University of Tabuk, Tabuk, Saudi Arabia
e-mail: M_HABBASH@ut.edu.sa

S. Troudi
University of Exeter, Devon, UK
e-mail: s.troudi@exeter.ac.uk

© Springer Science+Business Media Singapore 2015
R. Raddawi (ed.), *Intercultural Communication with Arabs,*
DOI 10.1007/978-981-287-254-8_5

(such as the events of 11 September 2001 and the War on Terror) have played a crucial role in changing the status of English.

Coupled with the general dissatisfaction with English language educational outcomes, these developments have led the government in Saudi Arabia to rethink its English language educational policy and to launch a large-scale curricular reform project, including changes to language curricula as well as considerable parts of the English language syllabuses (Al-Hazmi 2003). So far, the information available indicates that the reform process has resulted in the introduction of English, from the academic year 2004–2005, as a compulsory subject to be taught from the sixth grade of elementary school (at the age of 11) rather than from intermediate school (at the age of 12). Furthermore, although the basic educational system of the government mandates Arabic as the official language, the government passed a proposal at the beginning of 2007 that allowed private schools to teach core subjects, such as mathematics and history, through the medium of English (Al-Riyadh 2007, May 1). It should also be mentioned that English is taught as an independent subject from the kindergarten stage in these schools.

Furthermore, there has been recent controversy as to whether or not to teach scientific subjects through the medium of English at public schools so that students will become more capable of pursuing further studies at university level, where English is used extensively. From the above, one can conclude that there is a persistent conviction among government officials and stakeholders that English is necessary for access to success and modernity. Likewise, the assumptions of students, teachers and parents are not dissimilar to the official view. This is evident from the increasing number of parents who are willing to send their children to private schools, colleges, universities and other institutions where the utilization of English as a medium of instruction (EMI) is a key source of pride (Al-Shammary 2002). Among Saudi educationalists and applied linguists, however, official and public discontent with poor English language proficiency among students at the preuniversity level is coupled with concern that the government's curriculum reforms in public schools may be circumvented and will not best serve the future of the Saudi English language learners; neither will they safeguard their Islamic values and cultural heritage (cf. Al-Hazmi 2005; Al-Jarf 2004, 2005a, b, 2008; Al-Kahtani 2005).

Equally important is the fact that such decisions do not take into consideration the fact that English, as the language of globalization, is "unilateral in vision" (Zughoul 2003, p. 106) and could form a potential threat to Arabic if implemented in the absence of empirical research. According to Pennycook (1994, p. 8), such a widespread use of English "threatens other languages and resulted in English being the language of power and prestige in many countries, thus acting as a crucial gatekeeper to social and economic progress".

Moreover, such ad hoc, albeit vital, decisions could threaten the right of children to be taught in their own language, which constitutes a major violation of basic linguistic human rights (LHRs) (Skutnabb-Kangas 2000). Significantly, such policies may directly and/or indirectly contribute to deterioration in linguistic proficiency, resulting in more money and effort being poured into educational reform without obtaining the desired outcomes. Some research findings have shown that lowering the age of starting compulsory English language instruction negatively affects the child's native language and impedes the acquisition of both languages (Al-Shammari 2003; Aljamhoor 2000). This is also evident at the university level, where studies have found that education in a foreign language will not necessarily augment students' potential to acquire the subject knowledge; nor will it result in competent users in that language (Elley 1994; Al-Dhufairi 1999).

This study was stimulated by the concern outlined above that English in public education is unconditionally embraced in the Saudi context, and therefore, there is a pressing need in this context to examine alternative ways of approaching the phenomenon of global English. This research aims to critically examine and relate aspects of English language policies in public education to broader, current and/ or future social and political issues in the world's wealthiest oil-resource country, Saudi Arabia.

5.2   Relevant Literature

Global English has become a "buzz-word" in ELT and English language education circles. Sometimes the spread of English is attributed, especially by biased scholars (cf. Crystal 1997), to its inherent structure and capabilities, and at other times to what some call a fortuitous incident. Others reject this view, calling it a "nonsense" argument in favour of global English, and argue that the new status of English has not happened in a vacuum but that there are real political factors underpinning this global phenomenon.

Crystal (1997) posits that a language may have certain features that make it internationally appealing, such as its inherent structure and capabilities. He highlights a considerable number of features to enforce his argument in favour of English over other languages, as illustrated in the following extract:

> Learners sometimes comment on the *familiarity* of English vocabulary [...] English is in fact more a Romance than a Germanic language [and] the absence in English grammar of a system of coding social class differences, which can make the language appear more 'democratic' to those who speak a language [...] does not express an intrinsic system of class relationships. (Crystal 1997, p. 6) (Original emphasis)

Many years earlier Jespersen (1860–1943) also argued that the success of English is ascribed to its intrinsic superior qualities and described it as "vigorous, even manly" (cited in Melchers and Shaw 2003, p. 9). Although claiming to espouse an objective view, such a triumphalist tone is implicit in the ethnocentric views of some purist scholars such as those represented by Quirk (1990) and Honey (1997). The fact that English is a global language is often ascribed to its superiority as the language of modernity, success, science, democracy and other such positive features. As a major proponent of standard English, Honey (1997) states that "some languages are shown to be [...] more serviceable than others for certain functions" (p. 20).

Views expressed by the above scholars have been severely criticized both for their perceived triumphalism and their political naivety. In addition, English as a

world language is often cited in discussions of postcolonial relationships and domination, and therefore, a deeper analysis is needed. Lo Bianco (2004) remarks that
one cannot simply explain why it is instrumentally useful to learn English by opting
for its ease of learning or its inherent rationality. Phillipson and others take a more
critical stance and criticize views that try to "depoliticize" the issue of global English. For example, Phillipson and Skutnabb-Kangas (1999, pp. 22–23) contend that
"scholarship that purports to rise above politics when analyzing language policy
and global English (e.g. Crystal 1997) suffers from a high degree of self-deception,
particularly when a spurious 'neutrality' seems to reveal myopia about the way
power is approached in social or political science and in the humanities, and the
epistemological roots of scholarship in these areas". Several arguments have been
put forward by those who take a more critical stance on the spread of English; while
there was some common ground there was a tendency to take different approaches.

Phillipson's (1992) thesis of linguistic imperialism (1992) has proved to be a
major milestone in the literature for many reasons. His watershed publication has
been controversial and has stimulated much of the later scholarly work on the politics of English in the world, including Holliday (1994, 2005), Pennycook (1994,
1998, 2001), Phillipson and Skutnabb-Kangas (1995, 1996), Canagarajah (1999),
Jenkins (2000), Phillipson (2003, 2009a, b) and Ricento (2006), to name but a few.
Central to Phillipson's theory is the view that ELT is not a value-free activity and it
is inextricably linked to wider political issues. The phenomenon of global English
is thus seen as "linguistic imperialism", which Phillipson defines as:

> The dominance of English asserted and maintained by the establishment and continu-
> ous reconstitution of structural (material properties) and cultural (ideological properties)
> inequalities between English and other languages. (1992, p. 47)

The aforementioned example of the imposition of English in the Saudi context
helps to illustrate Phillipson's (1992) theory. Meanwhile, Phillipson's linguistic imperialism alone does not tell the complete picture. Canagarajah (1999, p. 41) offers
a different view stating that Phillipson's macrosocial theoretical perspective is "too
impersonal and global"; instead he inclines towards a form of resistance and appropriation of English. In a similar vein, Pennycook (2000) posits that although Phillipson's linguistic imperialism serves to map out "ways in which English has been
deliberately spread, and to show how such policies and practices are connected to
larger global forces", it is "too powerful" (ibid, p. 114). He adds that while Phillipson's view demonstrates discursive effects, "they are not so much about the effects
of the spread of English as about the effects of the ideological support for the spread
of English" (ibid, p. 114). Consequently this view "runs the danger of implying that
choices to use English are nothing but an ideological reflex of linguistic imperialism"; a position that can be rendered as lacking "a sense of agency, resistance, or appropriation" (ibid). This is why Pennycook (2001) goes beyond the idea of linguistic imperialism, or what he calls "English in the world", and takes up the concept of
discourse imperialism, or "the world in English". In doing so, Pennycook suggests
that the implications of the spread of English are "even greater than suggested in
structuralist analyses because of the connection between English and international
discourses" (2001, p. 84). Pennycook (2001) argues that language pedagogy has

been constrained by the dominant Western-based models of ELT, which are hegemonic in their impact on classroom practice. He suggests that applied linguists and ELT teachers should become political actors "engaged in a critical pedagogical project to use English to oppose the dominant discourses of the West and to help the articulation of counterdiscourses in English" (ibid, p. 87). Central to this view is that educational institutions are "cultural and political arenas" in which different values are in struggle (Pennycook 1994, p. 297). Indeed the growth of English as a global language has resulted in a complex relationship between language and culture in many ELT contexts. At the same time it has been increasingly recognized that classroom practices are a reflection of local cultural norms and values as well as language education policy within a particular country (Holliday 1994).

In Saudi Arabia there exist contradictory discourses about the role of English in education on one hand, and the preservation of Arabic and local culture on the other. The Saudi Government realizes that in an age of globalization interdependence between nations is unavoidable. In addition, because interdependence could lead to more mixing of cultures and languages, in this case English, the government has emphasized the importance of maintaining the local identity of Saudis as a Muslim Arab nation. That being said, as Adamo (2005) justifiably wonders "what kind of integration or interconnectedness the process of globalization entails when the net flow of information, knowledge, values and norms runs only one way, is one-sided, and is largely in one language" (p. 22).

In the Arab World and in the Gulf region in particular, there have been voices (Al-Askari 2001; Al-Dhubaib 2006) warning against the ideological implications of the spread of English on Arabic language speakers and their culture. It is equally important that the effects of this worldview of bilingualism and linguistic equality (Phillipson 2008), which have continued to reverberate throughout the Arab World, have perhaps been most evident in the legacy of a dual-language education (Al-Hazmi 2005). Troudi (2002), for example, describes the rationale behind English-medium instruction policy in the Arab World as fallacious. Al-Shammary (1998) contends that one of the major impetuses underpinning colonial support for English-medium education policy in the Arab World has been "to guarantee scientific, technological and economic backwardness in the Arab World and at the same time fights Arabic language and marginalizes its role among its people" (as cited in Al-Hazmi 2005, p. 496). In addition, research has highlighted the ideological implications of English-medium instruction policy on Arabic language speakers and their culture. Al-Jarf (2008) investigated 470 Saudi female university students' views of the status of English and Arabic as well as their attitudes towards using English and Arabic as media of instruction at the university level. Using survey questionnaires, her findings revealed that 96% of students consider English a superior language, being not only an international language but also the language of science and technology, research, electronic databases and technical terminology. Eighty-two percent believed that Arabic is more appropriate for teaching religion, history, Arab literature and education majors, whereas English is more appropriate for teaching medicine, pharmacy, engineering, science, nursing and computer science.

In the Arab World, a number of studies show that following an English-only policy can potentially lead to linguistic–cultural dualism in which English is seen as symbol for technology and modern life, travel and employment, while Arabic is educationally marginalized and is seen to represent tradition, religion and, even worse, backwardness (Findlow 2006; Al-Rubaie 2010; Troudi and Jendli 2011).

Troudi and Jendli (2011) investigated the views of 110 female university students in the UAE (18–22 years old) from a range of academic disciplines towards both Arabic as medium of instruction (AMI) and EMI at a university where more than 90% of instruction is delivered in English.

5.3 The Study

The current study takes what Crotty (1998, p. 14) refers to as a "postmodernist critical stance"—a preferable term being a postmodernist conceptualization of critical inquiry—in which an alternative truth as such is not sought. Rather, the whole issue of the English language in public education in this developing country, Saudi Arabia, is called into question, with the hope of offering new possibilities and ways in which the English language is perceived and utilized.

In this study a qualitative approach, informed by a postmodernist conceptualization of critical enquiry, is needed to explore in depth the complex relationships between the sociopolitical setting of public education in the Saudi context vis-à-vis the issue of global English, as the participants perceive them.

The study was guided by the following question:

How have dominant discourses of global English and their prevalent representations shaped the practices of, and views held by, Saudi ELT students and teachers about the language?

Little, if any, research has been conducted so far to empirically examine the significance of the spread of English and its dominant discourse in shaping the practices of, and views held by, Saudi ELT students and teachers about the language.

Although there are a number of research studies that are devoted to studying English language education in Saudi Arabia (Abdan 1991; Al-Banyan 2003), they have largely failed to place the sociopolitical and sociocultural repercussions of the spread of English under scrutiny.

Informed by a postmodernist conceptualization of critical theory, a central endeavour underpinning the present research has been to *reveal* the discourses that have contributed to shaping the participants' beliefs and practices as far as the English language is concerned. By doing this, it is hoped that the study will trigger some interest among TESOL researchers in the Saudi context and those in the wider region.

5.4 Data Collection and Analysis

For the purpose of the current study a qualitative approach has been adopted, in which two methods of data collection are used: documentary analysis and semistructured interviews. While data obtained from interviews revealed discourses of students and teachers on the phenomenon of global English, the documents and letters collected provided historical and contextual data.

Documentary analysis led to a better understanding of the government policy rhetoric and identified areas of potential conflict between language policy and practice.

Semistructured interviews were used as the main tool of data collection. This approach allows the participants to demonstrate in depth their unique views regarding the complex issue of the phenomenon of global English, more than they would in structured interviews. Moreover, because the complexity of the issue of global English and its related social and political aspects, semistructured interviews are deemed useful in this study because they keep the conversation focused while remaining open to the unexpected.

Data obtained from interviews and documentary analysis were analyzed qualitatively by adapting Radnor's (2002) qualitative data analysis technique.

5.5   Sampling

The data were drawn from a purposive and convenient range of participants. The sample comprised eight male secondary school students (aged 17–18) and ten male ELT teachers, all of whom held degrees, drawn from a large population that encompasses students and ELT teachers in public schools in Saudi Arabia. The majority of students and teachers belong to the middle socioeconomic class and come from rural and semirural regions of the Kingdom to work or study in these three urban areas. The main reason for deciding to include students and teachers in this research is that, while they are not normally involved in the decision-making processes, they are most affected by the consequences of the reform effort. Thus, allowing them to participate in the research is a way for them to contribute their views about an issue that is of major importance to them.

Throughout the present research, a number of procedures were taken to ensure full compliance with, and adherence to, the University of Exeter's regulations and guidelines on research ethics, which follow the British Educational Research Association (BERA) ethical guidelines.

5.6   Main Findings

English in the Saudi Context The findings suggest that the practices of, and views held by, ELT students and teachers about global English were, to a certain extent, directly or indirectly shaped by a complex juxtaposition of several internal and external processes. All respondents assigned a high priority to English as being "the strongest language in the world", "the language of the powerful", "the global language", "the language of sciences", "the language of medicine", "the language of technology", "the language of the economy", "the language of the military", "the language of politics" and "the language of international communication".

The findings suggest that English is seen as an invaluable asset, enabling Saudis to efficiently communicate with the wider community in the age of globalization. For Suleiman, a teacher interviewee, the Saudi people and their government had come to recognize the role of English as a global language as a reality, as he stated in the following extract:

> So what I believe now is that our government has realized that English is the global language now and it's the international language. Everybody is speaking English everywhere. It's a reality actually. Because everywhere you go, you have to speak English. Everywhere!

The analysis indicated that with English being the de facto language of the Internet, technology and popular media, the use of English was increasingly being entrenched in the Saudi context.

For example, Nadir, a teacher interviewee, illustrated this trend as follows:

> I think the media plays a good role here because you know in a media like for example the TV or the ads in the radio sometimes, they bring this broken Arabic or 'English' Arabic if you wanna say where they use English sometimes and insert Arabic and try to make it look like Arabized English. This is what drives students to speak even the English word without them realising that it's English. Let's have an example of this kind of words: 'inta' online? [Are you online?], 'fein al' mobile? [Where is the mobile?], 'Inta' 'be' 'te'mel' chat? [Are you chatting?], 'al' coffee shop [the coffee shop].

Similarly, another teacher interviewee, Samir, reported a case of Americanisation of the Saudi society to show how Saudis responded to the fusion of English which accompanied what has been hitherto popularized as a "global village", as follows:

> Even the advertisements in the streets are in English sometimes [for example] Radisson SAS. Even some of the […] let's take Starbuck's [as another example]. Yeah I do agree that some of these shops are of American brands, European brands, but why don't we translate them? The food. If you go to a restaurant, just pick up the menu. Most of the dishes are Arabic [of Arabic origin] but are written in English letters.

Student and teacher interviewees regarded English as a means of increasing the chance to gain better job opportunities. It was noted that English was important to Saudi students who intended to seek careers in the private sector after completing their education. At the same time, English as a job requirement in the government sectors was downplayed compared to the grades achieved in academic qualifications. For example, Salman, a student interviewee, outlined his view:

> Essentially, to get a job in the private sector you need to be competent in English along with knowledge of computer skills because you are more likely to deal with foreigners. This is different from the case in the public sector where your university GPA weighs more than English competence. (Translated from Arabic)

Arabic as the Language of the Qur'an and Islamic Tradition

The participants were asked about their personal views of Arabic as well as the importance they ascribed to it. The first set of findings shows that the importance assigned to Arabic was deeply entrenched in the student and teacher interviewees' worldview, which seemed to be ideologically constructed by their shared Arab–Islamic identity. The analysis suggests that this view of Arabic was highlighted to symbolize the participants' collective identity as members of the Muslim Arab nation. Just as importantly, Arabic was identified as the language of the Holy Qur'an: the religious text of Islam. For example, when asked what Arabic meant to him, Rafid, a student interviewee, said:

> It [Arabic] is my mother tongue and is the language of the Holy Qur'an. You can see, for instance, some non-Arabic speakers are interested to read the Qur'an and its interpretation. So they need to learn Arabic in order to be able to read it. (Translated from Arabic)

Rafid highlighted the importance of Arabic as the language of the Holy Qur'an for him as a Muslim and a native speaker of Arabic, but also for other Muslims from different linguistic backgrounds. Notably, the association of Arabic with the Qur'an and Islamic teaching and culture appeared consistently in the student interviewees' responses. The same applies to accounts by teacher interviewees. For example, Fahd, a teacher interviewee, reported that for him, Arabic and tradition are inextricably linked. He said: "Arabic is my mother tongue and my roots; it is the language of heritage" (Translated from Arabic).

The above findings suggest that the high value in which Arabic is held by the participants stems from its religious and cultural status in Saudi society. However, the esteem in which Arabic was held by the student and teacher interviewees did not extend to their views of Arabic as a language of education, modernization, and scientific and technological advancements. Thus, while for interviewees the meaning of Arabic was firmly tied to religion, culture and tradition, the link between Arabic and scientific advancement and modernization was considerably weaker, if not lacking. For example, Melfi, a student interviewee, said:

> First and foremost, Arabic is the language of the Holy Qur'an and it makes for all other languages. It's the mother tongue of all Arab nations. Nevertheless, I don't think it's a language of modernity. (Translated from Arabic)

Similarly, Faris, a teacher interviewee, emphasized that most scientific fields (such as medicine) are of a universal standard and only English, as a universal language, could be used to access them:

> No I disagree with you. Who said in France medicine is taught in French? No. It is taught in English. Medicine is very advanced and cannot be taught in Arabic. Medicine is universal and must be studied in English. (Translated from Arabic)

Thus, for Faris the assumption was that when it came to science, English is in some way more capable than Arabic. These views correspond to a large extent with the views held by policy makers in the country. Findings from the analysed documents suggest that the nationalist tendency, although reflected in the official policy documents, has to some degree been misinterpreted or contradicted by MoE as Ministry of Education confirmed officials, who seem to be convinced that English is the only hope for accessing the realm of scientific advancement and modernization. Assumptions underlying these views can be said to portray Arabic as lacking and

Arabs as inferior, leading to statements such as those reported by the participants above. In May 2007 the previous minister of education, declared that his ministry was in the course of implementing the European A B International Baccalaureate (EABIB) programme in public education, which entails the teaching of maths and science subjects through the medium of English or French at intermediate and secondary schools (MoE—Knowledge Journal, 2007 May 10). The minister justified this decision by stating that "they [English and French] are more linked to these two subjects [exact science and mathematics] than Arabic is" (ibid, p. 2).

These findings clearly show that these policy decisions are diametrically opposed, albeit tacitly, to the explicit rhetoric reflected in official government education policy documents. Moreover, they reflect an unquestioning acceptance of the hegemony of English and its underlying epistemology, which emphasizes its superiority and devalues any effort to cultivate Arabic.

The above findings suggest that although student and teacher interviewees value the fundamental role of Arabic and view it as integral to the local identity of Saudis as a Muslim Arab nation, they downplayed its use as a language of scientific advancement and modernization.

5.7   English Versus Arabic: Global-Local Tensions

While the student and teacher interviewees' responses tend to imply that Arabic cannot be a language of science because of its assumed inherent local features, a number of participants indicated that Arabic could not be a language of science because it lacks an equivalent scientific terminology and because of the limited efforts by Arab scientists to promote the use of Arabic in science. For example, Yaser, a teacher interviewee, speculated that:

> You don't have even some of the terminology. You don't have even equivalent in Arabic language. [This] may be because of our translators and scientists. Even our scientists, if you think about it, even our scientists don't use Arabic. So if our major scientists use English, how can we learn it as regular people in our life?

Nadir, a teacher interviewee, agreed with Yaser and reported that although Arabic had been the language of science in the past, a number of conditions needed to be met before it could resume its role in technological and scientific advancements in the world. When asked whether he viewed Arabic as a language of science, he explained:

> I think yes, but with one condition: if the Arabs are really good at updated translation. Here there are other demands. We need like a very good center for translation at least so the Arabs will keep updated like the French and Germans. They're keeping themselves updated with the other knowledge they've translated immediately.

Thus, making the effort to translate knowledge from other languages is an essential, albeit unattainable, condition for Arabic to be viewed as a language of scientific and technological advancement. Meanwhile, the findings suggest that even if such a condition were to be achieved, the dominant role of English in the scientific domain seems to have limited the use of Arabic by its speakers and led them to abandon it in favor of English. For example, when asked whether Arabic could be a language of science, Thamir, a student interviewee, said:

> Arabic is the language of the Holy Qur'an. For sure it can be a language of science but there is nothing to do about it now because most people use English. (Translated from Arabic)

Nevertheless, Hamdan was more pessimistic when asked if he viewed Arabic as a language of science:

> I wish it were, but you are talking about a global language. What is the percentage of Arabic language speakers in the world? It does not amount to even 10%. So you are talking about globalization. All sciences and technologies are in English now. So I don't think that computers will be in Arabic. I'm pessimistic in this regard. (Translated from Arabic)

Another teacher interviewee, Majid, argued that Arabic could potentially be a language of science, as it had been in the past. He posited that the current low status of Arabic as a language of science was not a consequence of assumed inability to lead in sciences. Rather, he speculated, the language itself had been weakened by its NSs:

> Arabic is a rich language and has the potential to override any hurdles. However, let me tell you something. It's the people of a language, be it Arabic or English, who elevate it and give a value to it. Unfortunately, because Arab nations are weak, passive and are lagging behind in many fields, Arabic is becoming weaker now. (Translated from Arabic)

Abdulaziz, a teacher interviewee, conceded that irrespective of whether he viewed Arabic as a language of science, he believed that Arabic was fighting a losing battle against English because of the status of its speakers, who were lagging behind first world nations:

> we [Arabic language speakers] are considered a third world country. In order to compete with the so-called British or European countries or America, we still have to introduce a lot of things. Therefore, it's very difficult just to translate all the basic science from English to Arabic. This will never ever happen because you're way behind.

According to the views outlined above, therefore, it is "global" English rather than "local" Arabic that Saudis need to use in order to become part of the international and advanced communities. The analysis suggests that the construction of participants' views on the role of English as a global language was significant in shaping the participants' views of the Arabic language. In fact, the participants described English as powerful, global and modern and associated it with knowledge and with technological and scientific advancement, whereas they seemed more inclined to describe Arabic as a weak, local and traditional language. Thus, in order to catch up and become a strong and advanced nation, Arabic language speakers would need to adopt the "powerful" English rather than the "weak" Arabic, as expressed by Nadir in the following interview excerpt:

> Nowadays, America is a very powerful empire. That's why we imitate whatever is taking place in the world. In the Middle East and in the Arab World people are really weak. We should submit to this fact first. We are inferior and they are the superior.

5.8   Discourses of Global English and its Representations
in the Saudi Context

The findings indicated that the construction of participants' views on the role of English as a global language was significant in shaping their views of Arabic. While the participants described English as powerful, global, and modern and associated it with knowledge, technological and scientific advancement, they seemed more inclined to describe Arabic as a local and traditional language. Student and teacher interviewees valued the fundamental role of Arabic as integral to the local identity of Saudis as a Muslim Arab nation. As a consequence, where English was considered appropriate to teach scientific subjects, Arabic was preferred to teach Social Sciences and Religion subjects at school. These results confirmed Findlow's (2006) research findings. The majority of interviewees in the present study justifiably indicated that currently sciences could not be taught in Arabic due to the lack of equivalent scientific terminology and the modest efforts by Arab scientists to promote the use of Arabic in sciences. However, their responses clearly reflected an unexamined affirmation of the hegemony of English and its underlying epistemology, which emphasizes its superiority and consequently devalues any efforts leading to the cultivation of Arabic.

Even those interviewees who did acknowledge the potential role that Arabic could play in scientific and technological advancement conceded that a number of conditions needed to be met before Arabic could take on this role. Nevertheless, they held a pessimistic view about the chances of meeting such conditions, hence adding another reason to abandon their mother tongue in favour of English. In fact, for some of the participants, Arabic is currently fighting a losing battle against English given the status quo of its speakers, who have been lagging behind first world nations; it was therefore enough for them to recall that their tongue had been the language of science and modernity in the past. While such discourses could be seen as short-sighted and based on views of power rather than on linguistic knowledge, they have nevertheless contributed to the expansion of English in the Saudi context. The discussion of these findings raises a number of questions that need to be addressed. These are: What makes a native speaker of Arabic, such as the interviewees in the current study, who have always studied scientific subjects in Arabic at school, think it is better to study them in English? Would a French or German person of the same age develop such an opinion? And what makes the Arab world in general vulnerable to such English expansionism?

A direct answer to important questions such as these is not an easy task. However, it has to be stated that the negative and self-defeatist stances among the majority of participants towards their home language are better described as symptoms of a serious epidemic that is sweeping into the minds of Saudis and the wider Arab communities, including the educated class. Against such a situation of feeling of loss and despair of progress, relentless support for English is being exerted by the government to elevate its status as a medium of education, despite the lip service paid to Arabisation processes. Supporting this view, Elkhafaifi (2002) makes the point that the Arabic-speaking countries, "while recalling with pride their historical dominance in the medieval scientific arena, are now struggling to prevent the language from an inundation of modern foreign terminology" (p. 253). Al-Dhubaib (2006) was among several Saudi and other Arab scholars and applied linguists who took this issue seriously and raised early concerns about the consequences of EMI on the future status of Arabic as a language of education (see also Al-Askari 2001; Zughoul 2003; Troudi 2009). These voices, however, are faint in the face of the pervasive, though inadequate, presumption of global English that continues to grant it a privileged position at the expense of Arabic. Al-Dhubaib (2006) contends that any threat to the collective identity of a nation implies a threat to its language, as language, along with religion, is central to the prominence of that nation. He states emphatically that in the current age of globalization, the Arabic language is facing the same kinds of challenges. These challenges, he continues, are a product of a sense of exaggerated importance of the English language, which is often a result of both a fascination with what is Western and a false belief that progress and prosperity come only through mastery of the language. This false belief in turn is the result of psychological defeats suffered by speakers of Arabic, and admiration for the makers of Western civilization, who are represented as the victors in our present age (ibid). Similarly, Al-Shammary in Al-Hazmi (2005) contends that one of the main malicious conspiracies of neocolonialism "has been the constant support of linguistic duality in education systems in the Arab World which has consequently led to distinct cultural and ideological divisions" (p. 496). He continues by stating that "the first division is social sciences in which Arabic is used; the second is applied and technological sciences in which English is used in the east Arab countries and French in west Arab countries" (ibid) (p. 496). His view is supported by the findings of the present research and gives evidence to counter the view that although externally imposed hegemonic forms of English were evident during the colonial age, those who choose to learn English today do so freely (Crystal 1997; Brutt-Griffler 2002). A case in point is Fishman's (1996) analysis, in which he describes the current status of English in most former British and American colonies and spheres of interest as:

> no longer as much a reflection of externally imposed hegemony [...] as it is part of the everyday discourse of various now substantially autonomous societies, all of whom are essentially following their own *common sense* needs and desires". (ibid) (p. 639) (emphasis added)

Such a stance is not supported by the findings of the present research. First, it has already been shown that the agency element behind the spread of English is evident in the Saudi context. As discussed previously in this top-to-bottom process the USA exercised its political power to impose changes in the Saudi school curriculum, which resulted in the "more English, less Islam" formula. Secondly, taking into account the above discussion of the participants' views, one can argue that English in the Saudi context is also expanding in a bottom-up process. While it has an element of realism, the interviewees' uncritical support for the enactment of an EMI policy at school was merely distorted common sense resulting from the international

discourse on global English (Pennycook 2001), rather than a response to what interviewees called "logic" or "reality". Such support is short-sighted and based on their
views of power rather than on linguistic knowledge. Similarly, Troudi and Jendli
(2011) assert that "neutral and pseudo empirical discourses in education, especially
in matters of language policy, can distort reality" (p. 42). Looking at the juxtaposition of English and discourses of power relations, both historically and currently,
it is evident that "those discourses have been facilitative of the spread of English
and that the spread of English has facilitated the spread of those discourses" (Pennycook 2001, p. 85). This kind of discourse and its associated typological ideology
is hidden and, therefore, dangerous (Phillipson 1992). Skutnabb-Kangas (2000)
succinctly describes the extent to which dominant discourses about global English
manifest themselves in today's ELT scene:

> through glorification, the non-material resources of the dominant groups, including the
> dominant languages and cultures, and maybe specifically English, are presented as better
> adapted to meet the needs of *modern*, technologically developed, democratic post-indus-
> trial information-driven societies – and this is what a substantial part of ESL ideology is
> about. The non-material resources of the dominated groups … including their languages
> and cultures are stigmatized as being traditional, backward, narrow, and inferior". (ibid)
> (p. xi) (original emphasis)

5.9   The Power of the Media and Social Prestige

The findings of this study suggest that the standpoints of the participants were also
a result of immense exposure to mass media and popular culture. Indeed a number
of teacher interviewees did acknowledge the role of media in reinforcing dominant discourses of linguistic and cultural superiority and inferiority. For example,
they reported instances where many words from English, including Internet terms,
were naturalized and have become indispensable media of expression among young
Saudis. Similar cases were reported in the research findings of Troudi and Jendli
(2011), in which reference is made to the use of English for communication at home
in the UAE, and in the work of Al-Rubaie (2010), where the home and peer contexts
in Kuwait created a wide array of chances for code switching with a domination of
Arabic. In this present study, the fusion of Western style dress and fast food habits among Saudi youth were reported as other signifying codes or, in Pennycook's
(2003) words, types of "mixing that comes about as a result of transcultural global
flows" (p. 151). However, in the present study, this blind mixing *per se* of English
with Arabic or the blending of modernization and localization is disproportionate to
"appropriation" (Canagarajah 1999). As such, it could be argued that English in the
Saudi context is practised as "a way of joining a community" (American speakers
of English in this case) rather than a way of "shuttling between communities" or
appropriating it to "serve local interests" (Canagarajah 2006, p. 210). It is a "stumbling block" which has wittingly or unwittingly kept modern standard Arabic in
general, and technical terms in particular, outside everyday use of the language and

has so far resulted in a lack of public interest in using both modern standard Arabic and systematically Arabised terminologies such as those set by respected translation centres (Ghazalah 2005). Findings from interviews with students complemented the observations reported by their teachers such as those above. It was revealed that while student interviewees tended to have a high regard for those who are proficient in English, the prestigious place that modern standard Arabic has long held in the Saudi society seemed to have lapsed, or as one student, Fahd, expressed it: "Its time is past and I'm not sure if it will come again". It is ironically interesting to observe how those students expressed their desire to retain their own culture and identity when they showed no hesitation about downgrading the role of their mother tongue, Arabic, in the society in their struggle to belong to English and in their pursuit of modernization and of becoming part of the global community. The same was true of the manner in which the nationalist tendency of the government rhetoric, explicit in the documents analysed, which emphasized integration in the world whilst maintaining sovereignty of the society, has been easily manipulated and contradicted as a consequence of receptive attitudes towards global English on the part of policy makers.

Considering the above discussion of the findings and supporting literature, it is the researchers' contention that the interviewees in this study were themselves strongly influenced by the dominant discourse of global English, not least of attitudes and practices of Saudi policy decision makers, who unconditionally embraced global English. Indeed, as two teacher interviewees reported in this study, by taking such vital language policy decisions as EMI, the MoE is "victimizing the Saudi English language learners". As Troudi (2002) asserts, "by studying all subjects in English, as is currently the case in some institutions, students would not be blamed for believing that Arabic is not a language of science" (p. 6). In fact, proceeding with a pro-Anglicization view of education and implementing a policy whereby English is introduced from the very early grades of elementary school and scientific subjects are taught in secondary school in English would have serious ramifications on students' lives and not least on their mother tongue.

Conclusion

It seems fair to conclude that the increasing reliance on English language in the Saudi context, particularly as a medium of education, is relegating Arabic to a second-class status. If this process is to be challenged, special efforts need to be made to strengthen the position of Arabic. However, this step will only become meaningful if the negative attitudes towards Arabic as a medium of instruction and as a language of science which are held by students, parents, teachers, policy makers and all individuals involved in the educational process are confronted and changed. This sociolinguistic issue needs to be a priority in the Saudi context, over and above any purely linguistic and/or economic aspects. This change will first require raising the importance of Arabic across Saudi society and stressing its potential in contributing to social and economic advancement. The use of the Internet, visual and written press and other types of media can in effect facilitate this. This development could be initiated by government bodies such as the Ministry of Culture and Information, the MoE, the Ministry of Youth and the Ministry of Higher Education as well as nongovernment agencies in the private sector such as privately owned media. For example, the Ministry of Culture and Information should encourage those working under its capacity, whether in radio broadcasting services, written or visual mass media, to seriously consider using modern standard Arabic and avoid all forms of superfluous code mixing between Arabic and English. This should not be seen as a discretionary role of their profession. Rather, local radio and TV presenters and newspaper writers should be aware that doing so is an ethical action and a legitimate part of their ethical and moral responsibility towards society.

In addition, the MoE should collaborate with the Ministry of Culture and Information to produce educationally oriented programs in Arabic with the aim of attracting the attention of school-age children and cultivating their interest in their mother tongue. This could also be achieved through use of the Internet. Indeed, as it has become part of the everyday life of Saudi youth, the Internet could be an invaluable asset in achieving this aim. Such a proposal is feasible in the sense that it is consistent with the new tendency by the MoE to bring the latest educational technologies into schools, such as smart classrooms and the student's electronic book box. Therefore, in addition to the above, school students should be introduced to the increasing number of websites with rich Arabic content which, in addition to educational materials, offer different types of culturally sensitive entertainment for children of different ages. One way this could be achieved is to compile these websites in collaboration with King Abdul-Aziz City for Science and Technology (KACST) as the government body which oversees the use of the Internet in the country. The MoE should then make these websites accessible to students by listing them on its main webpage. Because new similar websites often emerge and existing ones disappear or become outdated, the list should be updated by KACST at adequate intervals. That said, students' use of the Internet should not be limited to this list. They should be introduced to online search engines and given hands-on experience in using keywords in order to be able to create their own lists. This could be fostered by parental supervision at home.

The school has another major role to play in the preservation of Arabic. In addition to improving the quality of Arabic language teaching methodology, this role also entails consolidating the position of Arabic at school. One way to do this is to draw the students' attention to the importance of their mother tongue not only as a main component of their Arabic and Islamic identity also but as a language with universal character and the ability to assimilate emerging technological and scientific advancements. Students need to be encouraged to feel proud of Arabic and attend open days organized at schools specifically for this purpose. Indeed, the latter could also contribute to promoting a reading culture among Saudi students. Students' skills in Arabic should be nurtured through enriching their knowledge in the core skills such as reading, writing, speaking and critical thinking. According to

Al-Hazmi (2005), developing these skills "can be positively transferred to English language and other disciplines" (p. 501).

Similarly students need to be aware of the importance of English and be encouraged to learn it as a means to reach their goals rather than an end in itself. Teachers should equip their students with different ways in which they can appropriate it. One way to do this is by contrasting students' own culture with the English-speaking cultures. Zughoul (2003) argues that "in the face of the hegemonic character of English, there is the need to empower the learner to build more confidence in his culture through his exposure to another" (p. 133). In addition, this will not only enhance their understanding of the cultures of other speakers of English but will also contribute to bridging the gaps between these cultures and the local culture. Put differently, empowering students to talk about their local culture and other cultures will help them to better develop an attitude of tolerance and respect towards difference.

References

Abdan, A. (1991). An exploratory study of teaching English in the Saudi Elementary Public Schools. *System, 19*(3), 253–266.

Adamo, G. (2005). Globalization, terrorism, and the English language in Nigeria. *English Today 84,* 21(4), 21–24.

Al-Askari, S. (1 March 2001). Arabs and the Arabization of modern sciences? *Al-Arabi,* Issue 508. http://www.alarabimag.com/arabi/common/showhilight.asp. Accessed 15 July 2011.

Al-Banyan, A. (2003). The level of Saudi students at public and private intermediate and secondary schools: The problem and solutions: A comparative study. *King Faisal University Scientific Journal, 4*(1), 179–218.

Al-Dhufairi, M. (1999). *A study into the effect of English on Arabic language in elementary schools.* Al-Watan Kuwaiti News Daily. (26 January 1999).

Al-Dhubaib, A. (2006). *The Arabic language in the era of globalisation.* Riyadh: Obeikan.

Al-Hazmi, S. (2003). *EFL teacher preparation programs in Saudi Arabia: Trends and challenges.* TESOL Quarterly, vol. 37, No. 2, pp. 341–351.

Al-Hazmi, S. (2005). English and Arabization: Friends or foes? The Saudi experience. Proceedings of the language in the age of globalization conference (pp. 493–506). Saudi Arabia: King Khalid University Press.

Aljamhoor, A. (2000). The simultaneous teaching of Arabic and English of Saudi children in the US (in Arabic). *Educational Science Journal, 86,* 42–47.

Al-Jarf, R. (2004). Youth attitudes towards using Arabic and English in education. *The World Arabic* Translators Association Online Archives. http://www.arabicwata.org/Arabic/ our_library/researchers_and_thesis/2004/janu ary/research4.html. Accessed 7 June 2009.

Al-Jarf, R. (2005a). *The power of the English language in the past, present and future.* Proceedings of the language in the age of globalization conference, 20-22/2/2005. Saudi Arabia: King Khalid University Press, pp. 216–232.

Al-Jarf, R. (2008). The impact of English as an International Language (EIL) upon Arabic in Saudi Arabia. *Asian EFL Journal, 10*(4), 193–210.

Al-Kahtani, A. (2005). *Linguistic identity beyond ethnic boundaries.* Proceedings of the Language in the Age of Globalization Conference, 20-22/2/2005. Saudi Arabia: King Khalid University Press, pp. 400–420.

Al-Riyadh News Daily (1 May 2007). Not out of fear on the Arabic language, but for fear of loss of identity and cultural schizophrenia (in Arabic). Al-Riyadh, Issue 14190. http://www.alriyadh. com/2007/05/01/article246210.html. Accessed 1 May 2007.

Al-Rubaie, R. (2010). *Future teachers, future perspectives: The story of English in Kuwait*. Unpublished Doctoral Dissertation, University of Exeter: Exeter, UK.

Al-Shaabi, A. (1989). *An investigation study of the practical preparation in EFL teacher preparation programs in colleges of education in the Kingdom of Saudi Arabia*. Unpublished Doctoral Dissertation, University of Wales: Wales.

Al-Shammary, E. (1998). *The role of Arabizing scientific higher education in human resources development in Saudi Arabia*. Proceedings of the symposium on generalizing Arabization and developing translation in Saudi Arabia. Riyadh, Saudi Arabia: King Saud University Press, pp. 75–98.

Al-Shammary, E. (2002). Teaching english in elementary classes (in Arabic). *Al-Jundi Al-Muslim: A Quarterly Islamic Journal, 108*, 22–32.

Brutt-Griffler, J. (2002). *World English: A study of its development*. Clevedon: Multilingual Matters.

Canagarajah, S. (1999). *Resisting linguistic imperialism in English teaching*. Oxford: Oxford University Press.

Canagarajah, S. (2006). TESOL at forty: What are the issues? *TESOL Quarterly, 40*(1), 9–34.

Carli, A., Guardiano, C., Kaucic-Basa, M., Sussi, E., Tessarolo, M., & Ussai, M. (2003). Asserting ethnic identity and power through language. *Journal of Ethnic and Migration Studies, 29*(5), 865–883.

Crotty, M. (1998). *The foundations of social research*. London: Sage.

Crystal, D. (1997). *English as a global language*. Cambridge: Cambridge University Press.

Elkhafaifi, H. (2002). Arabic language planning in the age of globalization. *Language Problems and Language Planning, 26*(3), 253–269.

Elley, W. (1994). The IEA study of reading literacy: Achievement and instruction in thirty two school systems. Oxford: Pergamon Press.

Findlow, S. (2006). Higher education and linguistic dualism in the Arab Gulf. *British Journal of Sociology of Education, 27*(1), 19–36.

Fishman, J. (1996). Summary and interpretation: Post-imperial English 1940–1990. In J. Fishman, A. Conrad, & A. Rubal-Lopez (Eds.), *Post-imperial English: Status change in former British and American colonies, 1940–1990* (pp. 623–641). Berlin: Mouton de Gruyter.

Ghazalah, H. (2005). Arabization in the age of alienation. Proceedings of the language in the age of globalization conference, (pp. 93–101). Saudi Arabia: King Khalid University Press.

Holliday, A. (1994). *Appropriate methodology and social context*. Cambridge: Cambridge University Press.

Holliday, A. (2005). *The struggle to teach English as an international language*. Oxford: Oxford University Press.

Honey, J. (1997). *Language is power: The story of standard English and its enemies*. London: Faber & Faber.

Jenkins, J. (2000). *The phonology of English as an international language: New models, new norms, new goals*. Oxford: Oxford University Press.

Lo Bianco, J. (2004). Invented languages and new worlds. *English Today 78, 20*(2), 8–18.

Melchers, G., & Shaw, P. (2003). *World Englishes*. London: Arnold.

Pennycook, A. (1994). *The cultural politics of English as an international language*. London: Longman.

Pennycook, A. (1998). *English and the discourses of colonialism*. London: Routledge.

Pennycook, A. (2000). English, politics, ideology: From colonial celebration to postcolonial performativity. In T. Ricento (Ed.), *Ideology, politics and language policies: Focus on English* (pp. 107–119). Amsterdam: John Benjamins.

Pennycook, A. (2001). *Critical applied linguistics: A critical introduction*. Mahwah: Lawrence Erlbaum.

Pennycook, A. (2003). Global English, rip slyme, and performativity. *Journal of Sociolinguistics, 7*(4), 513–533.

Phillipson, R. (1992). *Linguistic imperialism.* Oxford: Oxford University Press.

Phillipson, R. (2003). *English-only Europe? Challenging language policy.* London: Routledge.

Phillipson, R. (2008). The linguistic imperialism of neoliberal empire. *Critical Inquiry in Language Studies, 5*(1), 1–43.

Phillipson, R. (2009a). *Linguistic imperialism continued.* New York: Routledge.

Phillipson, R. (2009b). English in globalisation, a lingua franca or a lingua Frankensteinia. *TESOL Quarterly, 43*(2), 335–339.

Phillipson, R., & Skutnabb-Kangas, T. (1995). Linguistic rights and wrongs. *Applied Linguistics Journal, 16*(4), 483–504.

Phillipson, R., & Skutnabb-Kangas, T. (1996). English only worldwide, or language ecology? *TESOL Quarterly, 30*(3), 429–452.

Phillipson, R., & Skutnabb-Kangas, T. (1999). Englishisation as one dimension of globalization. In D. Graddol & U. Meinhof (Eds.), *English in a changing world: IALA review* (pp. 19–36). Oxford: Catchline.

Quirk, R. (1990). Language varieties and standard language. *English Today, 21*(1), 3–10.

Radnor, H. (2002). *Researching your professional practice: Doing interpretive research.* Buckingham: Open University Press.

Ricento, T. (2006). Language policy: Theory and practice—An introduction. In T. Ricento (Ed.), *An introduction to language policy: Theory and method* (pp. 10–23). Oxford: Blackwell.

Skutnabb-Kangas, T. (2000). *Linguistic genocide in education or worldwide diversity and human rights?* London: Lawrence Erlbaum.

Troudi, S. (2002). English as a language of instruction in the UAE: What is the hidden message? *Perspectives: An English Language Teaching Periodical from TESOL Arabia, 9,* 5–10.

Troudi, S. (2009). The effects of English as a medium of instruction on Arabic as a language of science and academia. In P. Wachob (Ed.), *Power in the EFL classroom: Critical pedagogy in the Middle East* (pp. 199–216). Newcastle Upon Tyne: Cambridge Scholars Publishing.

Troudi, S., & Jendli, A. (2011). Emirati students' experiences of English as a medium of instruction. In A. Al-Issa & L. Dahan (Eds.), *Global English and Arabic: Issues of language, culture, and identity* (pp. 23–48). Oxford: Peter Lang.

Zughoul, M. (2003). Globalization and EFL/ESL pedagogy in the Arab world. *Journal of Language and Learning, 1*(2), 106–146.

Manssour Habbash is an assistant professor of education (teaching English to speakers of other languages, TESOL) at the University of Tabuk. Dr. Habbash holds a PhD in education (TESOL) from the University of Exeter. He is a member of many academic associations. His research interests include critical pedagogy, critical applied linguistics as well as curriculum design in TESOL and language program evaluation. Dr. Habbash can be contacted at M_HABBASH@ut.edu.sa

Salah Troudi is associate professor in TESOL and language education at the Graduate School of Education, the University of Exeter. He teaches and supervises master's and doctoral students in TESOL, critical applied linguistics, research methodologies and curriculum. His research interests include critical teacher education, language of instruction policies and critical issues in education

Chapter 6
Understanding Family Involvement in the Education of Emirati College Students in the United Arab Emirates (UAE)

Georgia Daleure, Rozz Albon, Khaleel Hinkston, John McKeown
and Tarifa Ajaif Zaabi

6.1 Introduction

The society, culture, and traditions of the United Arab Emirates (UAE) are in the midst of a transition. Rapid economic growth from the mid-1960s made possible by diversification of oil revenues, together with an influx of expatriate labor, enabled the country to progress from a traditional agriculture-based society to a techno-logically advanced knowledge-based society in about half a century (Alabed et al. 2008; Alsayegh 1998, 2001). Each consecutive generation adapted to technological advancement, economic development, and effects of globalization with differing degrees of comfort and assimilation causing social transitions that impacted inter-generational communication (Allagui and Breslow 2011).

According to numerous studies conducted in Western settings from the late 1970s to the publication of this study, understanding family involvement in educa-tion, one form of intergenerational communication, is crucial to enhancing student performance at all levels (Altschul 2011; Henderson and Berla 1994; Henderson and Mapp 2002; Klomgah 2007). From the mid-1990s increasing positive family involvement was considered a key factor for developing educational policies aimed at retention of students at the postsecondary level (Gifford et al. 2006; Gofen 2008; Graunke and Woosley 2005), especially, with student populations studying in a lan-guage not spoken in the home (Engstrom and Tinto 2008).

Widespread postsecondary education in the non-Western setting of the UAE is a recent development with the first university established in 1976, only 5 years after unification, when most of the population had little or no formal education (Alabed et al. 2008). The first federally funded technical colleges were estab-lished in 1988 to address the needs of the first generation of high school graduates

G. Daleure (✉) · R. Albon · K. Hinkston · J. McKeown · T. A. Zaabi
Higher Colleges of Technology, Abu Dhabi, United Arab Emirates
e-mail: gdaleure@hct.ac.ae

© Springer Science+Business Media Singapore 2015
R. Raddawi (ed.), *Intercultural Communication with Arabs*,
DOI 10.1007/978-981-287-254-8_6

preparing to obtain entry level jobs in the rapidly developing economy (Alabed et al. 2008). Federally funded postsecondary institutions were set up based on the North American model and allowed eligible Emirati students to attend free of charge. Since English was used as the medium of instruction for most courses in federally funded institutions, instructors, other than Emiratis, were employed from a wide variety of countries and regions including North America, Europe, Australia, the Indian subcontinent, and the Middle East (Alabed et al. 2008). When educators and students come from such diverse backgrounds and cultures, the possibility of misunderstanding arising in both verbal and nonverbal communication is high (Obeidat et al.; Klein and Kuperman 2008; Krieger 2007), especially when students study in a nonnative language (Engstrom and Tinto 2008).

This exploratory study examines types of family involvement in Emirati college student education in the non-Western context of the UAE in which little academic literature exists. Understanding family involvement in Emirati student education including cultural expectations and influences exerted on students, adds a dimension of insight critically needed for educators and policymakers to establish effective educational policies that promote retention and student success. Gaining more insight into family influences on students' behaviors may enable expatriate educators to develop more contextualized teaching and learning strategies aimed at increasing the effectiveness of communication between Emirati students and expatriate educators.

6.2   Literature Review

The effects of sociodemographic factors and culture on education are well documented in international literature (Henderson and Mapp 2002; Howland et al. 2006; Klomgah 2007). In contrast, academic literature on any aspect of society in the Arab world is limited with specific literature on education appearing in the early to mid-2000s. This study explores family involvement in college students' education in the little known context of the UAE.

The literature review is divided into two sections with appropriate subsections: social and cultural trends in Emirati society and family involvement in education in Western contexts.

Social and Cultural Trends in Emirati Society

This subsection introduces important characteristics of Arab societies, describes the Arab national culture, and presents transitions in Emirati society from unification to the present.

Introduction to Arab Societies

Klein and Kuperman (2008) contrasted Arab and Western societies pointing out areas that often lead to misunderstandings in verbal and nonverbal communication. According to Klein and Kuperman, Arab societies tend to be collectivist, promote interdependence, encourage discussion even in individual decision-making and value maintaining relations over efficiency and cost-effectiveness.

Western societies, according to Klein and Kuperman (2008) tend to be individualist, promote independence, encourage individual personal decision-making, and consider saving time and money more important than maintaining relationships. The concept of time is more relative and relaxed in Arab societies than in Western societies.

Members of Arab societies, according to Klien and Kuppeman (2008) often use the technique of *saving face*—diffusing, putting off, or ignoring an unfavorable idea or arrangement—rather than directly rejecting it. Arab decision-making may seem more emotional than logical to Westerners while Westerner's decision-making processes may seem coldhearted to Arabs perceiving it as devoid of the human elements such as illness or family problems. Westerners tend to speculate on hypothetical solutions to problems while Arabs tend to use concrete reasoning with the present or past as the frame of reference.

Arab National Culture

Obeidat et al. (2012) explored the differences between Arab cultures and Western cultures using Hofstede's cultural model. Obediat et al. found that seven Arab countries including the UAE have a specific *national culture* consisting of five dimensions: *power distance, uncertainty avoidance, collectivism, and masculine–feminine dimension. National culture* refers to "a collection of habits, traditions, and beliefs which differentiate one culture from another" (p. 514).

Power distance in the UAE tends to be large or near paternalistic in which "decisions are made on the basis of favors to subordinates and loyalty to supervisors, not on the basis of merit" (Obeidat et al. 2012, p. 512). Organizations tend to "emphasize dependency relationships between managers and subordinates" (p. 514).

Uncertainty avoidance tends to be low in the UAE. Islamic religious beliefs that people should remember God "even in material work" (Obeidat et al. 2012, p. 515) and that time is "controlled by God" (p. 515) contribute to low uncertainty avoidance.

Collectivism is high in the UAE. According to Obeidat et al. (2012) individuals tend to be more loyal to groups within organizations rather than the organizational goals.

Arab countries including the UAE have both *masculine*, preference for output and performance, and *feminine*, preference for processes and emphasis on aesthetics, and *cultural dimensions*. However, the UAE is closer to the *feminine* side of the continuum in establishing "friendly relationships with other people" (Obeidat et al. 2012, p. 515). The authors describe the masculine dimension as *living to work* and the feminine dimension as *working to live.* Expanding the authors' description, Emiratis work more to cover the costs of life and less for self-fulfillment.

Arab countries including the UAE have a *long-term orientation.* The focus is on future results preferring "a stable progression toward long-term goals" (Obeidat et al. 2012, p. 516).

"Culture and its implications play an important role in how people behave, act, and respond to things in their communities" (Obeidat et al. 2012, p. 513). According to Obeidat et al., this raises questions about the appropriateness of applying policies and procedures developed in one country on populations of other countries with different cultures.

Emirati Society in Transition

Prior to being a British protectorate, isolated and deprived of contact with the rest of the world, the area now known as the UAE was composed of thriving commercial communities engaging in trading, pearling, cultivating dates, fishing, and herding (Alabed et al. 2008; Alsayegh 2001). After independence in 1971, the leadership of the UAE used the new found oil wealth to establish a basic physical and social infrastructure including transport and communication systems, hospitals, and schools (Alsayegh 2001).

By the early 1990s, the primary and secondary education systems were in place, landline phones and televisions were common, and transportation systems allowed people to move freely inside and outside the country (Alsayegh 2001). By the early 2000s, technology, including computers, internet, and mobile phones, had become an important part of the growing economy (Alabed et al. 2008).

Rapid development in the UAE necessitated importing labor needed to perform jobs from domestic service to medical doctors and university professors. At the time of this study the expatriate labor force comprised 80% of the population and about 90% of the labor force (United Arab Emirates National Bureau of Statistics 2012). English, rather than Arabic, was most commonly used in most business communication and in postsecondary education. In the lifespan of a single generation, the grandparents of the present day college students, the country progressed from an isolated monocultural agriculture-based society to a technologically advanced multicultural society-based on the knowledge economy.

Changing communication styles contributed to a shift in interfamilial interaction and social concerns. Allagui and Breslow (2011), reported that the majority (67%) of young Emiratis (aged 18 years old) surveyed indicated they spent more time on the internet chatting with friends than visiting family members. Deterioration of Arabic language proficiency among youth was attributed to widespread use of English language, social media, and popular websites in the same study.

The top social issues concerning Emirati university students, according to Hassane and Abdullah (2011), were road accidents (86%), smoking (85%), high divorce rates (84%), and high school dropout rates (80%). The results of the study highlighted the concerns of young Emiratis including smoking related health problems occurring at a higher rate among Emirati males, high number of traffic fatalities occurring with Emirati males, increasing divorce rates occurring within newly married Emirati couples, and Emirati male education attrition rates, especially at the postsecondary level where males persist less than half as frequently as females (Ridge 2010).

Simidi and Kamali (2004), reported that religion, followed by family expectations, were the most important factors influencing behaviors of Emirati males and females. According to Schvaneveldt et al. 2008), supported by Crabtree (2005) families (extended, nuclear, and male with multiple wives) are considered the basis of Emirati society. Marriage is an expectation for Emirati males and females because being married and having children help improve familial status. However, Emirati people, especially women, are getting married later in life, hence the family size is decreasing. In Crabtree's study, students who were unmarried at an age of 22–24 had mothers who had married at an age of 13–15 and students who had eight or nine siblings anticipated having five or less when they eventually marry. The qualitative findings of Crabtree and Schevaneveldt et al. are supported by Tabutin and Shoumaker's (2005) empirical study entitled *The demography of the Arab World and the Middle East from the 1950s to the 2000s: A survey of change and a statistical assessment.*

Age is respected, with older men and postmenopausal women often consulted for their opinions. Younger unmarried women generally stay at home unless suitably accompanied. Married women have begun chaperoning younger unmarried sisters on outings, in contrast to the experience of women in past generations (Crabtree 2007; Schvaneveldt et al. 2005).

According to Crabtree (2007) and Schevanevldt et al. (2005) education is seen by Emirati families as a necessity in the modern life for both males and females. However, as reported by Ridge (2009) and supported by Zuraik (2005), family educational expectations for males tended to be lower than females, particularly in families in which parents have low education. Females, on the other hand, were encouraged to study at least up to the point of marriage offers. Crabtree (2007), and Schvaneveldt et al. (2005) found that Emirati families expected their sons to work after completion of studies but did not have the same expectation for their daughters. Mothers in both studies expressed approval for their daughters to study and but not all expected their daughters to work.

Alsayegh (2001), Crabtree (2007), Simidi and Kamali (2004) and Schvaneveldt et al. (2005) reported concerns that the relatively relaxed standards of personal freedom experienced by some Emirati males did not enable them to develop the discipline and strength in character to meet the cultural expectations of becoming heads of households and community leaders. Ridge (2010) recommended that parents demand "higher standards from their [male] children" (p. 29) so that they perform better in school, continue on to postsecondary education, and become better prepared to enter the workforce.

Summary

In a collectivist society such as the UAE, "people belong to groups or collectivities which are supposed to look after them in exchange for loyalty" (Hofstede and Bond 1984, p. 419 quoted in Bright and Mahdi 2012). The social norms of dominant groups, i.e., families, highly influence the behavior of the individuals (Bright and Mahdi 2012). Cultural differences between home environment and learning environment can contribute to the differing views held by students, parents, and educators (Cutright 2008); therefore, understanding family involvement in the case of the UAE is especially important.

Family Involvement in the West

Literature from the mid-1990s began using the term *family* involvement instead of *parental* involvement, acknowledging the shift from nuclear two-original parent households to single-parent, blended, extended, and alternate family structures (Henderson and Berla 2002). The current study uses the terms *family involvement* and *parenting styles* assuming that *parenting* is increasingly done by individuals who are neither biological parents nor family members. This section presents literature on family involvement in education in the existing literature on Western contexts to establish the framework for building survey items and developing an analysis model. The first subsection describes parenting styles, followed by a discussion of home environment characteristics that affect family involvement.

Parenting Styles

Henderson and Mapp (2002) discussed three distinct parenting style groupings:

- *Authoritarian*: characterized by punishing for earning poor grades, and responding to good marks by insisting on better performance.
- *Authoritative*: characterized by frequent discussions, encouraging all family members to contribute to decision making, responding to good grades with praise and poor grades with restrictions, and providing academic assistance when needed.
- *Permissive*: characterized by being indifferent to grades, and not establishing household rules or routines concerning TV watching, bedtimes, household chores, time spent outside the house, time with friends, or time on the phone.

Dornbush et al. (1987) (cited in Henderson and Berla (1994)) found that students from authoritative parenting environments tended to have the highest academic performance, while students from permissive parenting environments tended to have the lowest. Clark (1983) (cited in Henderson and Berla (1994)) found that a warm and nurturing home environment with well-defined limits and abundant encouragement from family members was found to stimulate independence and high achievement.

Bechler (1984) (cited in Henderson and Berla (1994)) reported that a home environment with little or no encouragement from family, less than daily family interaction, poor monitoring of activities, and poorly defined limits on behavior was associated with poorer performance. Rumberger, Ghatak, Poulas, Ritter, and Dornbush (1990) found that school dropouts tended to come from permissive parenting environments. In addition, students reporting authoritarian family interactions were less confident and more often frustrating leading to lower performance.

Sociodemographic Factors Associated with Family Involvement in Education

Kells (1993) found that low achieving students often have behavioral issues associated with family structure breakdown and lack of parental involvement as evidenced by: lack of parental support; lack of parental concern for academic progress; little or no parental contact with school representatives even when requested by the school; little or no monitoring or encouragement for students to complete homework assignments; lack of support for school rules and disciplinary procedures. Clark (1993), quoted in Henderson and Berla (1994, p. 104) added that uninvolved parents often lacked "knowledge of how to help" the students.

Eagle (1989) developed a Home Environment Scale (HES) incorporating key attributes of home life and background finding five key attributes of home life associated with student academic performance: mother's education; father's education; family income; father's occupation; and number of key possessions. Eagle hypothesized that students with higher academic performance tended to have highly educated parents with greater financial stability allowing them to have a rich and stimulating home environment. Henderson and Berla (1994) concurred and added that students with low to very low socioeconomic status (regardless of academic performance) tended to have the following challenges:

- Ethnically diverse backgrounds but living in low income areas with high concentrations of the same ethnic, racial, or social minorities.
- Larger families with more extended family members living in the same households.
- Parents who did not complete high school.
- First language other than English used in the home (supported by Engstrom and Tinto 2008).
- Financial constraints and lack of parental support for education.
- Pressure for young people, particularly males, to work during school years, not pursue higher education, or even drop out of high school before completing.
- Household headed by mother with an absent father, grandparent raising one or more grandchildren, or foster parents.
- Low emphasis or indifference toward education for females assuming that females would be married to males who would provide for them.

Yeung et al. (2001) and Thompson and Pong (2005) concluded that the blurring of traditional family structures and roles of mothers and fathers in modern society can create more complex and intense social pressures which can be stressful for children leading to lower academic performance.

Muller (1995) supported by Eagle (1989) and Milne (1995) found that children across all socioeconomic levels whose mothers are part-timers achieved higher levels of academic performance than students with nonworking mothers or students with full-time working mothers. In some racial subgroups students from low socioeconomic status households headed by full-time working mothers outperformed all other groupings (Battle 1997). Henry et al. (2008) reported that males performed better when they perceived that their mothers believed in their ability to succeed.

Summary of Literature Review

The literature review shows the transition that is occurring in Emirati society. The effects of rapid economic development after nationalization have affected each consecutive generation and led to social trends including: increasing need for higher levels of education to enter the workforce, tendency for developing nuclear families, decreasing definition of gender roles, increasing marriage ages especially for females, decreasing family sizes, younger parents with higher levels of education than their own parents, more working mothers, and rise in divorce rates.

Combining concepts from both sections of the literature review, several areas for exploration arise from the literature presented on Western contexts to be explored in this study. Which parenting styles do Emirati families tend to use with college students in the transitioning society? Do parenting styles differ depending on the gender of the student? Is parenting style linked to academic achievement? Are home environment behaviors linked to parenting styles in the Emirati context? Are specific home environment factors associated with high or low academic achievement?

6.3   Methodology

The quantitative methodology of this exploratory study was designed based on six original research questions derived from the literature; however, this chapter reports on the two questions specifically related to the theme of this book.

1. How are Emirati families involved in their college students' education?
2. How does family involvement vary when controlling for sociodemographic variables?

Survey Instrument and Question Development

After carefully teasing out the specific family involvement behaviors present in each of the parenting styles (authoritative, authoritarian, and permissive) and presented in the literature on Western contexts, three interrelated constructs were isolated: *engagements, influences,* and *enablers.* Presence or absence of these specific family involvement behaviors, according to the literature, determine the parenting style and are associated with students' academic performance.

Engagement is defined in this study as the direct and demonstrable interaction between students, families, and educators. Examples in this study are interaction between family members, discussion, encouragement, and restrictions.

Influence is defined as interaction intended to leads to change in student attitude, opinions, or behavior. Examples are stressing importance, supporting participation, planning for the future, and expressing approval and disapproval.

Enablers are defined as financial, logistical, physical supports required for students to persist in their studies. Enablers do not indicate the affluence of the family, but rather the priority of using resources for education.

Reporting questions were developed to glean information about specific family involvement behaviors. When developing items for the survey instruments, statements were phrased so that responses of *strongly agree/agree or always/most of the time* indicated highest levels of involvement and authoritative parenting style and conversely responses of *disagree/strongly disagree and sometimes/never* indicated lowest levels of involvement and/or the presence of authoritarian or permissive parenting styles.

Research Design

The study utilized a bilingual online survey to target 800 male and female students, and a telephone survey administered in Arabic for 30 randomly selected guardians. Both surveys were piloted prior to implementation and contained items designed to gather data on family involvement constructs, and sociodemographic information. Student and guardian survey data was first analyzed using descriptive statistics, correlations (Pearson's r), and linear regression with Statistical Package for the Social Sciences (SPSS) and StatPlus software packages.

In the second phase, index tables, or composite indicators, were created corresponding to engagement, influence, and enablers by assigning weightings to student responses and calculating the weighted averages in each category. The table was extended by controlling for sociodemographic variables discussed in the literature. Advantages to using indexes include: the ability to summarize complex, multidimensional data; ease of interpreting data with multiple related items; ability to identify trends over time; and ability to capture and incorporate large data sets into a manageable information base (Organization for Economic Co-operation and Development (OECD) 2008). Guardian data were not directly combined with student data, nor were they in the Index tables. Rather, guardian data were used to supplement, support, and affirm interpretations of the student data.

Instruments

The bilingual student survey containing 66 items was reviewed for cultural sensitivity, translated into Arabic, and verified before piloting with 37 students. After incorporating feedback, the student survey was made accessible through the college portal and at the end of first week, 1173 completed surveys were obtained surpassing the target of 800 usable surveys. The total population was slightly over 2800 students.

The parent telephone survey containing 29 questions was vetted for cultural sensitivity, translated into Arabic, verified, and piloted. The Arabic speaking interviewer was trained by a research team member and a pilot study was conducted using the first five potential guardian numbers out of a pool of 100 guardians of randomly selected students. Each survey was estimated to take between 15 and 20 min to complete, but most took substantially longer and required multiple contacts. The target of 30 completed surveys, kept intentionally low due to the novelty of obtaining personal information by telephone at the time of the study, was reached after 59 attempts.

Special care was taken to maintain cultural sensitivity in the telephone survey since conducting phone surveys was not common at the time of the study. According to the Emirati member of the research team, some questions perceived as common and acceptable in the international literature may cause discomfort in the Emirati context and result in the respondent discontinuing the phone survey. Those contacted may feel uncomfortable giving personal information to an unknown person who has contacted them by telephone. To make potentially sensitive questions more palatable, for example, asking about salary ranges was reframed into a question asking about type of income, *limited, moderate,* and *extended,* understood in the cultural context of the UAE respectively as *living off retirement income or government assistance, at least one parent working with a perceived middle income salary,* and *above working class income.* Another question considered too sensitive for a phone interview was marital status. Female guardians may perceive the question as too invasive while male guardians, potentially having more than one marriage, may fit into multiple categories resulting in an uncomfortable discussion resulting in discontinuance of the phone interview.

6.4   Findings

This section presents and discusses results of the student and guardian surveys.

Student Survey

This subsection gives general student information and presents results for engagements, influence, and enablers from the student survey (See Appendix 1 for complete list of student survey questions).

General Student Information

The sample group consisted of 1173 male and female Emirati students from a postsecondary institution in the UAE. About 90% (1059) of the students were female and 10% (114) were male from all programs, year levels, and credential levels including diploma, higher diploma, and bachelor degrees. Most of the students (81%) were between the age of 19 and 22. About half (54%) of the students were from the main catchment area with around 46% from outlying areas. Most were single (88%) and nearly all (95%) were not working.

Engagements

Engagements are present in Chart 1 in descending order. (See Appendix 1 for Survey Questions.)

Chart 1: Engagements

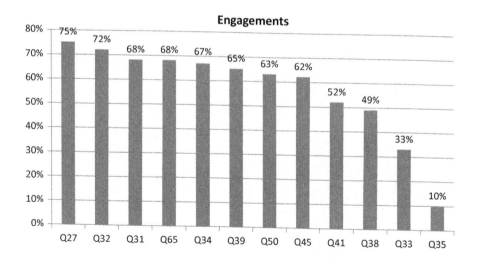

The results of the engagement questions indicated that family involvement is stronger in the areas of general encouragement and weaker in monitoring activities. The most frequently indicated activity is *spending leisure time with family at least once*

per week (75%) and the least frequently indicated activity is *having someone quiz the student* (10%). More than half (64%) the students responded that their *families try to limit the amount of TV, video game playing, or talking on the phone* while about half (52%) of the students responded that their families try to *limit the amount of time students visit their friends.* The pattern indicates a mix of authoritative and permissive parenting styles.

When reporting which family members encouraged students to do well in college, the most frequent choices were parents (83%), siblings (sister 45% and brother 31%), aunt (16%), and uncle (15%). Most married students (99 out of 138 or 72%) indicated that they felt encouraged and supported to do well in college by spouses. Students could choose multiple family members.

When asked to indicate with whom students discuss their problems of college at home, students responded most frequently with parents (49%), followed closely by sisters (47%), then cousins (28%), uncles (20%), and brothers (18%). From the 138 married students, 79 reported spouse (57%). Students were allowed to choose multiple family members.

Students considered their families to be generally supportive and seek the assistance of different family members for different purposes.

Influences

Influences are presented in Chart 2 in descending order. (See Appendix 1 for a list of survey question by number.)

Chart 2: Influences

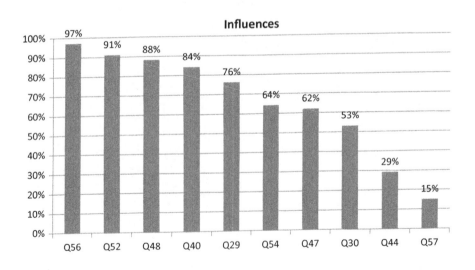

The results support the literature indicating that families are very influential in students' lives with 97% responding that their families encouraged them to go to college and 91% responding that their families were interested in their progress.

Enablers

Enablers are present in Chart 3 in descending order. (See Appendix 1 for complete question list.)

Chart 3: Enablers

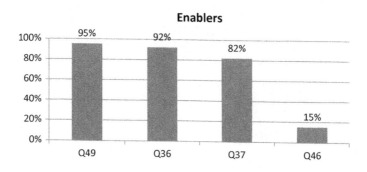

The results show the most frequently provided enabling family involvement is financial support, i.e., providing money for food every day (95%) and computer, printer, paper, and other materials needed to study (92%). Only working males indicated *not* receiving financial support from their families.

Correlational analysis confirmed that family involvement tended to be higher for enablers, followed by influences, then engagements. Nearly all of the general engagement behaviors were moderately correlated to each other ($r = 0.315 - 0.475$, $p < 0.01$). The most specific engagement, *family checks to see that homework and other college tasks are done,* correlated with four other specific engagement behaviors ($r = 0.402 - 0.475$, $p < 0.01$) indicating that all five behaviors were not widespread but rather carried out mostly in the same families. A few students (6%) responded *no one gives support or encouragement* and had negative correlations ($r = -0.326$ to -0.212, < 0.01) with most other engagements.

Guardian Survey

The guardian survey data is reported in the following subsection.

Sociodemographic Data

The summarized results are given in Appendix 5. Chart 4 shows the guardian relationship to student.

Chart 4: Guardian Relationship to Student

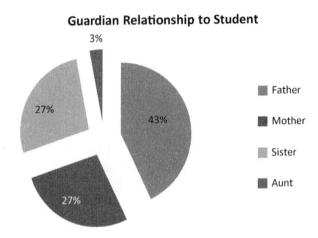

Chart 5 shows the occupations of the guardians with most of the mothers being housewives and all of the fathers identified themselves as retired, officers, office workers, or professionals. All sisters and the aunt were working and/or studying.

Chart 5: Guardian Occupation

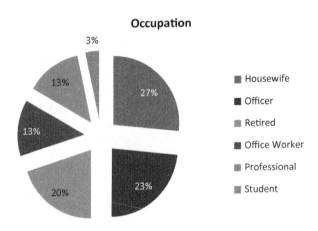

Charts 6 shows the educational level of the guardians. All eight sisters and eight of the fathers had postsecondary education.

Chart 6: Guardian Education Level

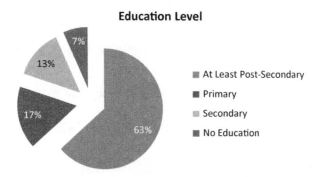

Chart 7 shows that more than half of the guardians indicated medium family income, understood as at least one person in the family is working with moderate income.

Chart 7: Guardian Income Level

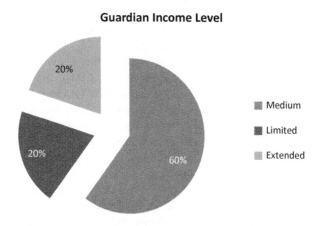

In summary, most guardians were fathers followed by mothers and sisters, mostly educated to at least the high school level, mostly working and/or studying, and most indicated medium income.

Family Involvement

The guardians were asked a series of engagement questions with the following shown in Chart 8.

Chart 8: Guardian Engagements

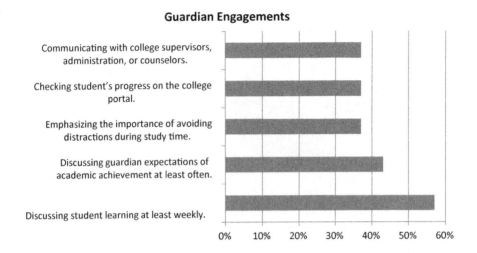

The guardians' engagement results show the same pattern as the student survey with least specific engagement reported more frequently and more specific engagement reported less frequently. Students reported much higher levels of family involvement than guardians reported giving to the students.

Evidence from the guardian survey indicates that family involvement varies depending mainly on the education level of the guardian, which member of the family is the guardian, and income level. Education level was moderately correlated with the following family involvements: *belief that family should be involved in students' education* ($r=0.4$, $p<0.01$); *belief that the guardian has the skills to help the student* ($r=0.56$, $p<0.01$); *willingness to learn more about helping the student succeed* ($r=0.42$ $p<0.01$); *frequency of discussing academic expectations* ($r=0.44$, $0<0.01$); *level of involvement in college experience* ($r=0.35$); *frequency of communicating with college representatives* ($r=0.37$, $p<0.01$); and *frequency of accepting invitations to college* ($r=0.33$, $p<0.01$). Occupation was moderately correlated with belief that guardian has the skills to help the students ($r=0.30$, $p<0.01$). Income level was moderately correlated with *belief that guardian should be involved in students' education* ($r=0.30$, $p<0.01$); frequency *of discussing expectations with student* ($r=0.41$); and *engaging in discussions with student about college* ($r=0.31$, $p<0.01$).

Guardians were asked which enablers (types of supports) they provided with the results given in Chart 9.

Chart 9: Guardian Enablers

Guardian Enablers

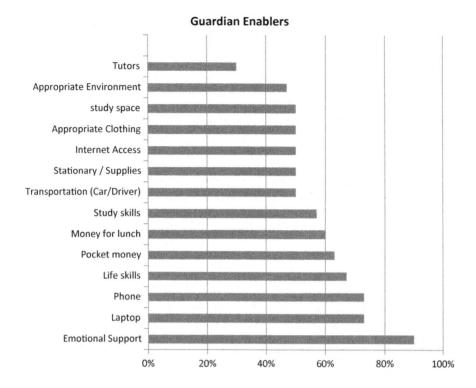

The results show that guardians most commonly provided emotional support, followed by the essentials to study at college, laptop, and mobile phone. Most of the other supports listed in Chart 9 are provided by only half of the guardians. Students rated the provision of lunch money, supplies, and many types of supports much higher than the guardians. In the Emirati extended family model, multiple family members, not only guardians, provide support as appropriate and available. Older working sisters tended to be more active in the specific family involvement behaviors than other guardians in the study, while fathers tended to more frequently provide financial and material support.

Most guardians (63 %) believed that college students needed family involvement and 70 % believed they had the skills and knowledge to be involved with 90 % of the guardians giving tips or advice on college work at least sometimes. Most of the guardians (77 %) responded that they believed that their student was doing well enough at college and did not have to ask for help. Most of the guardians (67 %) responded that they were involved in their student's college education at a medium level or high level.

6.5   Results and Discussion

Results of the student survey supported by the guardian survey are discussed in this section and grouped by research question.

Q1 How are Emirati Families Involved in Their Students' Education?

The study found three categories of family involvement discussed in order of frequency of reporting: enablers, influences, and engagements.

Enablers

Nearly all students, with the exception of working males, reported physical and material support in the financial and logistical areas including daily lunch money (95%), computer, paper, and supplies (92%), and daily transport to college (82%). The most frequently reported physical and material supports by guardians were laptops (73%), phones (73%), pocket money (63%), and money for lunch (60%) with academic support in the form of providing students with study space (50%); an appropriate environment for studying (47%); or hiring a tutor (15%) was least frequently provided.

According to Wagie and Fox (2005), eligible Emiratis attend federally funded postsecondary institutions without paying for tuition or books. However, students must provide their own supplies and equipments required for specific programs such as laptop computers, iPads, drawing kits, or other specialized items as well as transport. The data suggest that the presence of enabling family involvement is crucial for college student persistence as related by Eagle (1989) and Henderson and Berla (1994). Further investigation with nonpersisting students is recommended.

Influences

Authoritative parenting style behaviors, reported in the literature to be the most conducive to high performance, varied greatly in frequency suggesting that the nature of the involvement was more significant than the style of parenting. For example, the two influences that were the most frequently reported, *family encouraged me to go to college* (97%) and *family is very concerned about my academic progress* (91%) represented the most general involvement. More specific involvement, families *being complementary of good grades* (76%); families *showing disapproval for bad grades* (53%); and families *supporting participation in college clubs, activities, or sports* (29%) were reported less frequently. The data suggests that nearly all families were concerned with students' persistence and success but most did not try to influence students to develop behaviors that ultimately lead up to it, a sign, according to the literature, of permissive parenting.

Engagements

Engagement survey items were the least frequently reported involvement items, yet were the most specific in terms of participation in the educational process. Engagements including *spending leisure time with family at least once per week* (75%), *discussing college work with family* (69%), *informing family of grades* (68%), *telling family when preparing a project, paper, or test* (67%), *encouraging students to speak to a teacher, counselor, or supervisor when they have a problem at college* (63%), *asking about friends at college* (63%), *discussing college activities or events* (31%), and *allowing family to view student information on college portal* (28%) suggest only moderate involvement in the educational process. The results are in line with Hoover-Dempsey and Sandler (1995) who stated that parents choose not to be involved in specific academic tasks when they believe that they do not have the skills needed to assist, their assistance does not make a difference, or that their children or their children's teachers do not want them to be involved.

In summary, family involvement was concentrated in the areas of financial and logistical support and general support for educational persistence and success. Families tended to be less involved in influence and engagement behaviors that lead students to be successful.

Q2 How Does Family Involvement Vary when Controlling for Sociodemographic Variables?

General family involvement patterns were discussed in the preceding section indicating a mix of authoritarian and permissive parenting styles. This section discusses significant sociodemographic factors, defined as the highest or lowest index score on a given survey item. (See Appendices 2 to 4 for Index tables for Engagements, Influences, and Enablers).

Family Size

As shown in Chart 10, 23% of the students came from families with one to six members while about half (51%) come from households with nine or more members. Most students (78%) reported having at least one sibling studying at the post-secondary level.

Chart 10: Family Size

Family Size

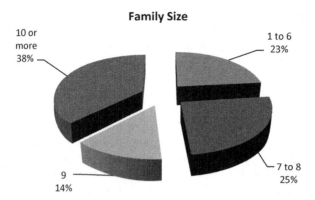

Crabtree (2007) and Alsayegh (2001) indicated that young adults generally live with their parents and/or extended family members until married and often with their parents or in-laws even after marriage.

Students from families of one to six members had the lowest index score for Q27 and the highest index score for Q31 and Q50. Most students in the sample with six or less members were married students living with their spouses and children. Of the 138 married or previously married students, more than half (52%) indicated that they had at least one child, with 41% indicating up to three children, and 11% indicating between four and ten children. Most students were not working (95%). Students who are themselves parents have little leisure time and discussion with family would likely be confined to the student communication with his or her spouse.

Students from families with nine or more family members had the lowest score for Q35 and Q44 and the highest scores for Q48 and Q56. With most of the students (86%) reporting four or more siblings and about half (51%) reporting seven or more siblings, parental attention is spread over a large number of children with little time for individual quizzing, discussing, and transporting students to and from extracurricular activities. Students from large families could have older parents with a traditional perception of respecting education and authority.

Gender

Males had the highest index scores in eight engagement and three influence items (Q32, Q33, Q34, Q35, Q38, Q39, Q43, Q45, Q44, Q48, Q56) and the lowest score in Q54. Males more frequently reported encouragement, discussion, restrictions, and support to participate in extracurricular activities and less frequently reported families influencing their chosen field of study. According to Crabtree (2007) and Alsayegh (2001), Emirati females typically have more restrictions on their personal freedom than Emirati males. Perhaps the males perceived any type of restriction on personal freedom as significant, while females, having less personal freedom, considered family involvement concerning education supporting rather than restrictive.

Table 6.1 Parent's education level

Responses	Father's education		Mother's education	
	Frequency	Percentage	Frequency	Percentage
No education	161	14	202	17
Primary school	287	25	317	27
Secondary school	343	29	355	30
College/University graduate	212	18	196	17
Master's qualification or higher	41	4	14	1
I don't know	129	11	89	8
	1173	100	1173	100

With females outnumbering males nearly 65–35 % in postsecondary education, families may feel that young males warrant more involvement to ensure completion of their degree. Males tended to have the most engagement and influencing behaviors and were performing higher academically.

Parents' Education

Students with either mother or father with no education had the lowest index scores for ten engagement items and four influence items (Q27, Q32, Q33, Q34, 45, Q50, Q31, Q30,Q40, Q44, Q47), while students with either mothers or fathers having at least postsecondary education had the highest score in two engagement items, two influence items, and three enabler items (Q27, Q38, Q29, Q47,Q36, Q37,Q46), with Q27 and Q47 in both groupings exhibiting the same trend as seen in the literature that students with parents who have low education, less frequently report family involvement and students with highly educated parents more frequently report family involvement. Mothers and fathers within families tended to have similar education levels especially at the higher education levels as indicated by the moderate correlation ($r = 0.566$, $p < 0.001$) and Table 6.1.

Mother's Working Status

Students with working or retired mothers had the highest index scores for two engagement items, six influence items, and five enabler items (Q27, Q38, Q30, Q40, Q44, Q47, Q52, Q54, Q35, Q37, Q46). Students with working or retired mothers reported most influence and enabler family involvement. Parents' employment is shown in Table 6.2.

Half the students (50 %) indicated that their fathers were working. The other half indicated that their fathers were either not working or retired (47 %), or they did not

Table 6.2 Parents' employment

Responses	Father's employment		Mother's employment	
	Frequency	Percentage	Frequency	Percentage
Don't know	37	3	12	1
Not working or retired	549	47	972	83
Working	587	50	189	16
	1173	100	1173	100

know (3 %). Less than one-fourth of the students (16 %) indicated that their mothers were working. No significant correlation was observed between divorced parents and working mothers or between nonworking fathers and working mothers. The literature states that older women are respected and often consulted for their opinions. Perhaps older working or retired women contribute financially as well.

Student's Marital Status

Students who were married, divorced, or widowed had the lowest scores on four engagement, and four enabler items (Q39, Q41, Q43, Q50, Q37, Q46, Q49). Most of the students (1035 or 88 %) indicated that they were single. Of the 138 married or previously married students, more than half (52 %) indicated that they had at least one child, with 41 % indicating up to three children, and 11 % indicating between four and ten children. Most students were not working (95 %).

Parent's Marital Status

About 8 %, (99 students) indicated that their parents were divorced. Students with divorced parents have the lowest scores in one engagement, four influence, and one enabler item (Q38, Q29, Q48, Q52, Q52, Q56) and highest in one engagement and one influence item (Q41, Q57). The results coincide with the literature which states that students with divorced parents have less family engagement, less concern for academic success, less respect for teachers and institutional rules, and more pressure to pursue a major they do not want.

Implications for Educators

Educators can develop policies and introduce initiatives that support struggling students who may not have enough family, emotional, or academic support. Initiatives aimed at students could include remedial sessions, peer tutoring, academic advising, and increasing opportunities for participation in extracurricular activities.

Educators should try to initiate programs aimed at raising family and guardian awareness of the realities of the modern UAE work environment, the importance of making appropriate career choices based on the individual's skills and aptitudes not family perceptions about lucrative jobs, and the importance of soft skill development gained by participating in extracurricular activities.

Conclusion

Findings indicated that the students with the most engagement behaviors were males. Almost all students, except working males, received financial support from their families and most students report strong encouragement to study and emotional support from their guardians. However, academic support including providing an atmosphere conducive to studying at home and assisting with college work is often lacking.

Elements of Emirati family structure and social life may affect student academic achievement negatively or positively. Extended family living situations put pressure on the family financial resources and increase the need to assist the higher number of children in the household with academic support. Students with divorced parents tended to have less financial support. Extended families with older siblings or similar age relatives who have attended college or university can provide an increased emotional and academic support for Emirati college students. Working sisters, as indicated by the student survey and guardian survey, are increasingly advising, guiding, and serving as guardians for their younger siblings. The availability of older siblings and other extended family members may help to fill the gap left in support when parents have little educational experience.

Results from both the student and parent surveys indicate that families are generally supportive in their students' education and provide the financial support for students to persist. Families and guardians are becoming more educated, sophisticated, informed, and capable of providing support needed for students to succeed, especially in cases of students who are at risk of failing. In families with low education, however, parents may not know how best to support students who are exhibiting low academic achievement although there is evidence that they are trying to support their children.

As the Emirati society continues to evolve, relationships between college students and their families will continue to be in transition. As more Emiratis with higher formal education become parents, some of the issues raised in this chapter will subside. However, issues related to national culture in the midst of rapid economic development and increasing globalization will take more concerted and structured efforts to resolve.

Appendix 1: Survey Questions Used in Indexes Listed by Number

Q29	My family is complimentary when I get good grades
Q30	My family shows disapproval if I get bad grades
Q31	I inform my family about my grades
Q32	I allow my family to use the College portal to check my student information
Q33	My family checks to see that I've done my homework and other academic tasks
Q34	I tell my family when I have a project, paper or test to prepare for
Q36	Someone in my family will quiz me to help me study before a test
Q36	My family provides the computer, printer, paper and other tools I need to study
Q37	My family ensures I am at College in time for my classes
Q38	My family encourages me to get enough rest to be alert in college each day
Q39	My family tries to limit the amount of time I watch TV, play video games, talk on the phone because it may interfere with my studies
Q40	My family stresses the importance of getting good grades
Q41	My family tries to limit the amount of time that I can visit with friends when I have College the next day
Q42	My family ensures I have breakfast before college each day
Q43	My family discusses College activities or events with me
Q44	My family supports my participation in College clubs, activities or sports
Q45	My family encourages me to speak to my teacher, counselor, or supervisor when I have a problem in College
Q51	My family is willing to speak to someone from the College when I have a problem in College
Q52	My family is very interested in my academic progress
Q53	I am passionate about my chosen field of study
Q54	My family influenced my chosen field of study
Q55	I work hard in College to satisfy my family
Q56	My family encouraged me to go to College
Q57	I am considering or pursuing a major I don't like in order to please my family
Q58	I work hard in College to satisfy myself
Q59	College level students do not require family involvement
Q60	I think students with high family involvement in their learning process are more successful
Q61	My family will find me a job when I graduate College
Q62	My family will not allow me to work when I graduate from College
Q63	The level of my family's involvement in my studies was greater before I came to College
Q64	There are enough opportunities to involve my family at the College
Q65	I would do better in College if I had more support from my family

Appendix 2: Engagements

Sociodemographic variables	Number	Q27	Q31	Q32	Q33	Q34	Q35	Q38	Q39	Q41	Q43	Q45	Q50	All
All	1173	0.696	0.743	0.489	0.520	0.749	0.361	0.819	0.576	0.607	0.518	0.720	0.706	0.619
SMC	114	0.695	0.776	0.550	0.581	0.781	0.417	0.857	0.618	0.588	0.559	0.776	0.702	0.655
SWC	1059	0.696	0.739	0.483	0.514	0.746	0.355	0.814	0.572	0.609	0.514	0.714	0.706	0.615
Family size 1–6	273	0.625	0.779	0.531	0.547	0.745	0.389	0.843	0.572	0.590	0.530	0.734	0.736	0.636
Family size 7–8	299	0.691	0.727	0.482	0.509	0.750	0.360	0.822	0.579	0.589	0.518	0.735	0.691	0.615
Family size 9	160	0.700	0.719	0.472	0.503	0.761	0.347	0.825	0.583	0.631	0.522	0.695	0.702	0.614
Family size 10 or more	441	0.694	0.739	0.474	0.518	0.747	0.349	0.799	0.574	0.621	0.510	0.710	0.699	0.613
Father no education/do not know	290	0.625	0.717	0.457	0.484	0.716	0.352	0.775	0.558	0.591	0.509	0.674	0.674	0.592
Father primary/secondary school	630	0.697	0.745	0.502	0.539	0.757	0.363	0.826	0.585	0.618	0.518	0.735	0.718	0.628
Father postsecondary education	253	0.727	0.766	0.493	0.516	0.768	0.366	0.850	0.576	0.599	0.529	0.736	0.712	0.628
Mother no education/do not know	291	0.625	0.706	0.467	0.497	0.714	0.356	0.813	0.570	0.605	0.516	0.700	0.680	0.619
Mother primary/secondary school	672	0.698	0.753	0.507	0.533	0.765	0.368	0.817	0.580	0.613	0.517	0.724	0.718	0.627
Mother postsecondary education	210	0.696	0.760	0.461	0.511	0.746	0.344	0.833	0.571	0.593	0.525	0.736	0.702	0.617
Father not working/do not know	275	0.696	0.743	0.489	0.520	0.749	0.361	0.819	0.576	0.607	0.518	0.720	0.706	0.606
Father retired	489	0.684	0.734	0.482	0.517	0.753	0.353	0.811	0.576	0.622	0.516	0.725	0.712	0.618
Father working	409	0.702	0.770	0.505	0.523	0.756	0.380	0.836	0.580	0.611	0.525	0.722	0.702	0.628
Mother not working/do not know	887	0.693	0.736	0.494	0.523	0.747	0.360	0.814	0.580	0.607	0.516	0.718	0.705	0.618
Mother retired	97	0.727	0.745	0.472	0.510	0.773	0.363	0.858	0.562	0.580	0.513	0.714	0.722	0.619
Mother working	189	0.625	0.772	0.474	0.513	0.747	0.364	0.821	0.566	0.620	0.532	0.730	0.700	0.622
Student marital status single	1035	0.695	0.742	0.489	0.523	0.749	0.360	0.819	0.584	0.612	0.523	0.721	0.709	0.621
Student marital status married/divorced/widow(er)	138	0.703	0.750	0.487	0.496	0.754	0.366	0.819	0.516	0.569	0.484	0.714	0.679	0.603
Parents are divorced	99	0.674	0.745	0.530	0.548	0.770	0.366	0.768	0.614	0.649	0.523	0.707	0.692	0.628
Parents are not divorced	1074	0.698	0.743	0.485	0.518	0.747	0.360	0.823	0.573	0.603	0.518	0.721	0.707	0.618

SMC: Sharjah Men's College

SWC: Sharjah Women's College

Appendix 3: Influences

Sociodemographic variables	Number	Q29	Q30	Q40	Q44	Q47	Q48	Q52	Q56	Q57	Q54	All
All	1173	0.827	0.665	0.850	0.499	0.702	0.903	0.863	0.895	0.440	0.583	0.723
SMC	114	0.825	0.680	0.873	0.522	0.695	0.923	0.855	0.917	0.428	0.542	0.726
SWC	1059	0.827	0.663	0.848	0.497	0.703	0.901	0.864	0.892	0.441	0.587	0.722
Family size 1–6	273	0.832	0.666	0.856	0.518	0.708	0.912	0.875	0.902	0.434	0.645	0.735
Family size 7–8	299	0.839	0.661	0.855	0.498	0.697	0.886	0.866	0.890	0.447	0.628	0.727
Family size 9	160	0.838	0.652	0.861	0.497	0.711	0.920	0.875	0.913	0.425	0.603	0.729
Family size 10 or more	441	0.811	0.672	0.840	0.489	0.700	0.902	0.849	0.887	0.443	0.621	0.721
Father no education/do not know	290	0.796	0.620	0.813	0.483	0.677	0.880	0.840	0.899	0.469	0.644	0.712
Father primary/secondary school	630	0.831	0.669	0.858	0.502	0.706	0.915	0.860	0.889	0.427	0.607	0.726
Father postsecondary education	253	0.851	0.706	0.875	0.513	0.722	0.899	0.897	0.904	0.437	0.652	0.746
Mother no education/do not know	291	0.804	0.621	0.834	0.483	0.670	0.901	0.845	0.899	0.453	0.620	0.727
Mother primary/secondary school	672	0.833	0.675	0.854	0.503	0.707	0.901	0.860	0.896	0.438	0.618	0.728
Mother postsecondary education	210	0.837	0.692	0.860	0.512	0.733	0.912	0.899	0.885	0.427	0.661	0.742
Father not working/do not know	275	0.827	0.665	0.850	0.499	0.702	0.903	0.863	0.895	0.440	0.626	0.726
Father retired	489	0.827	0.654	0.851	0.491	0.709	0.904	0.870	0.894	0.443	0.613	0.726
Father working	409	0.833	0.674	0.851	0.510	0.700	0.898	0.852	0.898	0.441	0.639	0.730
Mother not working/do not know	887	0.824	0.652	0.847	0.493	0.694	0.901	0.856	0.894	0.438	0.614	0.721
Mother retired	97	0.838	0.714	0.884	0.513	0.722	0.907	0.918	0.892	0.448	0.680	0.752
Mother working	189	0.836	0.697	0.847	0.521	0.734	0.910	0.868	0.898	0.442	0.652	0.740
Student marital status single	1035	0.824	0.664	0.849	0.500	0.703	0.904	0.862	0.895	0.439	0.629	0.727
Student marital status married/divorced/widow(er)	138	0.844	0.670	0.859	0.491	0.701	0.899	0.875	0.889	0.447	0.605	0.728
Parents are divorced	99	0.773	0.667	0.823	0.500	0.710	0.866	0.831	0.876	0.467	0.611	0.712
Parents are not divorced	1074	0.832	0.665	0.853	0.499	0.702	0.906	0.866	0.896	0.437	0.580	0.724

Appendix 4: Enablers

Sociodemographic variables	#	Q36	Q37	Q46	Q49	All
All	1173	0.929	0.853	0.382	0.962	0.750
SMC	114	0.923	0.866	0.375	0.963	0.754
SWC	1059	0.930	0.851	0.383	0.962	0.750
Family size 1–6	273	0.945	0.847	0.388	0.956	0.760
Family size 7–8	299	0.926	0.855	0.405	0.958	0.758
Family size 9	160	0.952	0.869	0.381	0.964	0.759
Family size 10 or more	441	0.914	0.849	0.364	0.967	0.737
Father no education/ do not know	290	0.916	0.840	0.361	0.952	0.741
Father primary/secondary school	630	0.929	0.860	0.382	0.963	0.752
Father postsecondary education	253	0.945	0.850	0.408	0.971	0.758
Mother no education/ do not know	291	0.921	0.855	0.377	0.958	0.750
Mother primary/secondary school	672	0.924	0.856	0.378	0.959	0.747
Mother postsecondary education	210	0.957	0.837	0.405	0.975	0.755
Father not working/ do not know	275	0.929	0.853	0.382	0.962	0.753
Father retired	489	0.919	0.846	0.371	0.957	0.750
Father working	409	0.943	0.853	0.388	0.964	0.750
Mother not working/ do not know	887	0.923	0.855	0.373	0.959	0.750
Mother retired	97	0.956	0.871	0.428	0.966	0.769
Mother working	189	0.943	0.829	0.401	0.971	0.744
Student marital status single	1035	0.931	0.860	0.387	0.964	0.754
Student Marital Status married/divorced/ widowed	138	0.918	0.797	0.348	0.949	0.725
Parents are divorced	99	0.874	0.838	0.379	0.955	0.728
Parents are not divorced	1074	0.934	0.854	0.383	0.963	0.752

Appendix 5

Guardian survey demographics	Frequency	Percentage
Relationship to student		
Father	13	43
Mother	8	27
Sister	8	27
Aunt	1	3
	30	100
Occupation		
Housewife	8	27
Officer	7	23
Retired	6	20
Office worker	4	13
Professional	4	13
Student	1	3
	30	100
Education level		
At least postsecondary	19	63
Primary	5	17
Secondary	4	13
No education	2	7
	30	100
At least postsecondary education		
Sister[a]	8	42
Father	8	42
Mother	2	11
Aunt	1	5
	19	100
Income level		
Medium	18	60
Limited	6	20
Extended	6	20
	30	100

[a] Sisters' ages 22–33 and all working and/or studying

References

Alabed, I., Vine, P., Hellyer, P., & Vine, P. (2008). *The United Arab Emirates: Yearbook 2008*. London: Trident.

Allagui, I., & Breslow, H. (2011). The internet, fixity, and flow: Challenges to the articulation of an imagined community. In R. Fisher & D. Riha (Eds.), *New media and the politics of online communities*. Oxford: Inter-Disciplinary.

Alsayegh, F. (1998) Merchants' role in changing society: The case of Dubai, 1900–1990. *Middle Eastern Studies, 34*(1), 87–102.

Alsayegh, F. (2001). Women and economic changes in the Arab Gulf: The case study of the United Arab Emirates. *DOMES, 10*(2), 17–28.

Altschul, I. (2011). Parental involvement and the academic achievement of Mexican American youths: What kinds of involvement in youths' education matter most? *Social Work Research, 35*(3), 159–168.

Bright, L. K., & Mahdi, G. S. (2012). U.S./Arab reflections on our tolerance for ambiguity. *Adult Learning, 23*(2), 86–92.

Carter, S. (2002). *The impact of parent/family involvement on student outcomes: An annotated bibliography of research from the past decade*. Washington, DC: CADRE.

Catsambis, S. (1998). Expanding knowledge of parental involvement in secondary education. Effects on high school academic success. *Center for Research in Education of Students Placed At Risk (CRESPAR) Report 27*, John Hopkins University, ED 426174.

Catsambis, S., & Garland, J. E. (1997). Parental involvement in students' education during middle school and high school. *Center for Research in Education of Students Placed At Risk (CRESPAR) Report 18*. John Hopkins University, ED 423328. http://www.csos.jhu.edu/crespar/techReports/Report18.pdf. Accessed 11 June 2012.

Charlton, J., Barrow, C., & Hornby-Atkinson, P. (2006). Attempting to predict withdrawal from higher education using demographic, psychological, and educational measures. *Research in Post-compulsory Education, 11*(1), 31–47.

Chee, K. H., Pino, N. W., & Smith, W. L. (2005). Gender differences in the academic ethic and academic achievement. *College Student Journal, 39*(3), 604–622.

Coburn, K. L. (2006). Organizing a ground crew for today's helicopter parents. *About Campus, 11*(3), 9–16.

Crabtree, S. (2007). Culture, gender, and the influence of social change amongst Emirati families in the United Arab Emirates. *Journal of Comparative Family Studies, 4*(38), 575–587.

Cripps, K., & Zyromski, B. (2009). Adolescents' psychological well-being and perceived parental involvement: Implications for parental involvement in middle schools. *RMLE Online, 33*(4), 1–13. http://www.amle.org/portals/0/pdf/rmle/rmle_vol33_no4.pdf. Accessed 14 June 2012.

Cutright, M. (2008). From helicopter parents to valued partner: Shaping the parental relationship for student success. Understanding current trends in family involvement. In B. Barefoot (Ed.), *New Directions for Student Services, 144*, 39–48.

Daehlen, M., & Odd, B. U. (2009). Low skilled adults in formal continuing education: Does their motivation differ from other learners? *International Journal of Lifelong Education, 28*(5), 661–674.

DeBerard, S. M., Julka, D. L., & Spielmans, G. I. (2004). Predictors of academic achievement and retention among college freshmen: A longitudinal study. *College Student Journal, 38*(1), 66–74.

Desforges, C., & Abouchaar, A. (2003). *The impact for parental involvement, parental support and family education on pupil achievement and adjustment: A literature review*. Research Report No. 433. London: UK Department of Education and Skills.

Donohue, T. L., & Wong, E. H. (2005). Achievement motivation and college satisfaction in traditional and non-traditional students. *Education, 118*, 237–243.

Donovan, J. A., & McKelfresh, D. A. (2008). In community with students' parents and families. *NASPA Journal, 45*(3), 384–405.

Eagle, E. (1989). Socioeconomic status, family structure, and parental involvement: The correlates, of achievement. In A. T. Henderson & N. Berla (Eds.), *A new generation of evidence:
The family is critical to student achievement* (pp. 59–60). Washington, DC: Center for Law
and Education.

Engstrom, C., & Tinto, V. (2008). Access without support is not opportunity. *Change, 40*(1), 46–51.

Gifford, D. D., Briceno-Perriot, J., & Mizano, F. (2006). Locus of control: Academic achievement
and retention in a sample of university first year students. *Journal of College Admission, 191*,
18–25.

Gofen, A. (2008). Family capital: How first-generation higher education students break the inter-
generational cycle. *Family Relations, 51*(1), 104–120.

Graunke, S. S., & Woosley, S. A. (2005). An exploration of the factors that affect the academic
success of college sophomores. *College Student Journal, 38*(2), 367–376.

Hassane, S., & Abdullah, A. (2011). Exploring the most prevalent social problems in the UAE.
International Journal of Academic Research, 3(2), 572–577.

Henderson, A. T., & Berla, N. (Eds.). (1994). *A new generation of evidence: The family is critical to student achievement* (A report from the National Committee for Citizens in Education).
Washington, D.C.: Center for Law and Education.

Henderson, A. T., & Mapp, K. (2002). *Annual Synthesis 2002: A new wave of evidence: The impact
of school, family, and community connections on student achievement*. SEDL Texas: National
Center for Family and Community Connections with Schools.

Henry, C. S., Plunkett, S. W., & Sands, T. (2008). Neighborhood, parenting, and adolescent factors
and academic achievement in Latino adolescents from immigrant families. *Family Relations,
57*(5), 579–590.

Hoover-Dempsey, K. V., & Sandler, H. M. (1995). Parental involvement in children's education:
Why does it make a difference? *Teachers College Record, 97*(2), 310–331.

Hoover-Dempsey, K. V., Battiato, A. C., Walker, J. M. T., Reed, R. P., Dejong, J., & Jones, K. P.
(2001). Parental involvement in homework. *Educational Psychologist, 36*(3), 195–209.

Howland, A., Anderson, J. A., & Smiley, A. D. (2006). School liaisons: Bridging the gap between
home and school. *School Community Journal, 16*(2), 47–68.

Jeynes, W. H. (2011). Parental Involvement research: Moving to the next level. *School Community
Journal, 21*(1), 9–15.

Kells, R. (1993). Principals' perceptions of factors affecting student achievement. *Education,
113*(4), 617–623.

Klein, H. A., & Kuperman, G. (2008). Through an Arab cultural lens. *Military Review, 88*(3),
100–105.

Klomgah, R. Y. (2007). Predictors of academic performance of university students: An application
of the goal efficacy model. *College Student Journal, 41*(2), 407–415.

Krieger, Z. (2007). Saudi Arabia puts its billions behind western-style higher education. *Chronicle
of Higher Education, 54*(3), A1–A20.

Obeidat, B., Shannak, R., Masa'deh, R., Al-Jarrah, I. (2012). Toward better understanding for
Arabian culture: Implications based on Hofstede's cultural model. *European Journal of Social
Sciences, 28*(4), 512–522.

Organization for Economic Co-operation and Development (OECD). (2008). Handbook
on constructing composite indicators: Methodology and user guide. www.oecd.org/
publishing;corrigenda. Accessed 11 May 2012.

Ridge, N. (2009). The hidden gender gap in education in the UAE. *Policy Brief No. 12*, Dubai:
Dubai School of Government.

Ridge, N. (2010). Teacher quality, gender, and nationality in the United Arab Emirates: A crisis for
boys. *Working Paper Series 10–06*. Dubai: Dubai School of Government (May).

Schvaneveldt, P. L., Kerpelman, J. L., & Schvaneveldt, J. D. (2005). Generational changes in
family life in the United Arab Emirates: A comparison of mothers and daughters. *Journal of
Comparative Family Studies, 36*(1), 77–91.

Simidi, F. A., & Kamali, M. A. (2004). Assessing the values structure among UAEU students.
Social Behavior and Personality, 32(1), 19–26.

Tabutin, D., & Schoumaker, B. (2005). The demography of the Arab World and the Middle East from the 1950s to the 2000s: A survey of change and a statistical assessment. *Population, 60*(5/6), 505–616.
Taub, D. (2008). Exploring the impact of parental involvement on student development (15–28). In C. Carney-Hall (Ed.), *New Directions for student Services*. No. 122.
Thompson, G., & Pong, S. L. (2005). Does family policy environment moderate the effect of single-parenthood on children's academic achievement? A study of 14 European countries. *Journal of Comparative Family Studies, 36*(2), 227–248.
United Arab Emirates National Bureau of Statistics. (2012). Demographic and social statistics. http://www.uaestatistics.gov.ae/EnglishHome/ReportsByDepartmentEnglish/tabid/104/Default.aspx?MenuId=1&NDId=16. Accessed 12 April 2012.
Wagie, D., & Fox, W. (2005/2006). Transforming education in the UAE: Contributing to social progress and the new economy. *International Journal of Learning, 12*(7), 277–268.
Yeung, J. W., Sandberg, J. F., Davis-Kean, P. E., & Hofferth, S. (2001). Children's time with fathers in intact families. *Journal of Marriage and Family, 63*, 136–154.
Zuraik, E. (2005). A study of success and failure patterns in the public high schools of the Emirate of Sharjah in the UAE. *UNESCO Report.* (Arabic and English).

Georgia Daleure PhD currently holds the position of Faculty at Sharjah Higher Colleges of Technology after serving as the applied business technology program chair for 4 years. Dr. Georgia completed her Bachelor of Science specializing in entrepreneurship and small business management at Ball State University, Muncie, Indiana, USA, and then switched over to the Education Department to pursue Master of Arts and doctorate in educational leadership specializing in adult education and curriculum/assessment development. Prior to coming to the UAE, she was employed in private not-for-profit training and placement serving as training and placement subcontractors for the State of Indiana. Dr. Georgia seeks by her research to contribute to the knowledge of best practices in education leading to successful placement, maintenance, and advancement in employment of Emiratis in the UAE.

Rozz Albon PhD her extensive career in education has ranged from lecturing in educational psychology to Director of teaching and learning. She is currently the academic coordinator in education at SWC and teaches in the Bachelor of Education early years and primary education programs at SWHCT specializing in research, and administration and management. Her PhD emanated from her passion and interest in the most able and gifted of children which then resulted in a book on young gifted children. She has researched and written across a wide field in education including giftedness, motivation, teaching and learning models, teaching in English, the development of a team learning model, and most recently, family involvement and Emirati college students' achievement.

Khaleel Hinkston PhD received his doctorate in counseling psychology from the University of Nebraska-Lincoln in 1991. Prior to this, he served as an educational opportunity program counselor/college recruiter and later held the position of assistant director of Outreach Services for California State University, Bakersfield (his alma mater). He worked in various mental health related settings while serving in the US Army in the 1970's. His post doctorate work experience includes 12 years employed by the Veterans Affairs of Western New York Healthcare System. For five of those years, he served as the post traumatic stress disorder treatment program coordinator and 7 years as a clinician in the Mental Health Clinic. During his stay in the Middle East he has taught psychology at Abu Dhabi University (United Arab Emirates) and currently serves as a college counselor/occasional teacher for the Higher Colleges of Technology, Sharjah.

John McKeown has a bachelor's degree in IT and a master's degree in business administration, both from the University of Kent in the UK. Since 1984, he has taught in Japan, Turkey, Egypt, and the UK before coming to work nearly 10 years ago at the Sharjah Higher Colleges of Technology in the UAE. John teaches a wide variety of business related subjects including operation management, business math, statistics and management information systems reflecting his keen interest in statistics and devising innovative methods of statistical analysis and design incorporating spreadsheet design and presentation of statistics.

Tarifa Ajaif Zaabi currently occupies the position of the acting dean of student affairs and college advancement at Sharjah Higher Colleges of Technology in the UAE. She has 12 years of experience in skills development for youth in higher education organizations in UAE (Zayed University and Higher Colleges of Technology). Tarifa's qualifications include: near completion of doctoral degree in education from the British University in Dubai—researching social responsibility education in higher education; Executive Master of Business Administration from the University of Sharjah; and a Bachelor of Business Administration from the Dubai Higher Colleges of Technology. Tarifa has represented the UAE in several conferences and international events including: "Women as Political Leaders," an exchange program with US government; presenter at the Women's as Global Leader Conference; presenter at the event "United in Responsibility: Exploratory workshop on social responsibility concept of Emirati students using LEGO Serious Play"; and other national and international events and conferences.

Chapter 7
Taboo Topics in the ESL/EFL Classroom in the Gulf Region

Melanie Gobert

7.1   Introduction

The word "taboo" came into English from the Tongan word "tabu" at the end of the eighteenth century that simply means "to forbid" or "forbidden," and is applied to any prohibition (Radcliff-Brown 1939, cited in Allan and Burridge 2006, p. 2). In 1777, Captain James Cook referred to the concept of taboos before actually using the word in his ship's log saying it generally means forbidden but has a comprehensive meaning that includes actions which cannot be done, objects which cannot be touched, or words that cannot be said (Allan and Burridge 2006). Taboos may be religious, dietary, or cultural (Keturi and Lehmonen 2011). Crystal (2003) defines taboo language as language that people avoid using because they view it as harmful, embarrassing, or offensive, and that it is commonly characterized by a tacit understanding between people of what is acceptable to do or say, which can change over time. MacAndrew and Martinez (2001) identify three broad categories of taboos: (1) swearing, talking about death, and prostitution; (2) serious issues such as racism and genetic engineering; and (3) personal matters such as appearance, hygiene, and nudity.

Taboos are usually culturally specific. That which may be discussed or done in one culture (abortion, sex change, legalizing drugs, same-sex marriage, etc.) may be highly taboo in another culture. This chapter looks at taboo topics in Gulf Cooperation Council (GCC) country classrooms. The GCC countries are Saudi Arabia, the United Arab Emirates (UAE), Oman, Kuwait, Bahrain, and Qatar. In the GCC countries, Islam is the official religion and 95–100 % of the national population is Muslim. In addition, many follow a strict interpretation of Islam influenced by the Wahabism movement, which is a conservative branch of Sunni Islam that originated in Saudi Arabia in the eighteenth century (Allen 2006). There are over 40 million people living and working in the GCC countries, and over 13.6 million (34 %) are nonnationals comprising Asians, Europeans, and other Arab nationalities (see Table 7.1).

M. Gobert (✉)
Higher Colleges of Technology, Abu Dhabi, United Arab Emirates
e-mail: mgobert@hct.ac.ae

© Springer Science+Business Media Singapore 2015   109
R. Raddawi (ed.), *Intercultural Communication with Arabs*,
DOI 10.1007/978-981-287-254-8_7

Table 7.1 The population and percentage of Muslims, nationals, and nonnationals in the GCC. (Compiled from the World Factbook 2013)

Country	Muslim percentage (%)	Population	Number of nonnationals	National percentage (%)	Nonnational percentage (%)
Saudi Arabia	100	26,534,504	5,576,076	79.0	21.0
UAE	96	5,314,317	4,304,596	18.6	81.4
Oman	75 (Ibahdi Muslim)	3,090,150	577,293	81.3	18.7
Qatar	77.5	1,951,591	1,701,591	12.8	87.2
Kuwait	85	2,646,314	1,291,354	48.7	51.3
Bahrain	81.2	1,248,348	235,348	81.2	18.8

The GCC is made up of oil and gas-rich countries that import educators, administrators, and curriculum, in order to improve the knowledge capacity of their citizens and raise their standard of English for global communication. Many educators arrive to teach in the GCC without a firm understanding of what topics are considered taboo (Moore 2011), which has caused some to lose their jobs (e.g., Rashid 2006). Topics that seem innocuous in Western societies such as dating before marriage or drinking alcohol may be offensive to Gulf Muslim Arabs because they are either forbidden by their cultural norms or expressly forbidden by their religion. Other topics that have been suggested as appropriate topics in critical pedagogy, such as the spread of AIDS and honor killings (Akbari 2008) may not be considered appropriate for the classroom in the Gulf region (Khuwaileh 2000; Zaid 1999).

Teachers should be aware that there may be differences even between different countries in the GCC, such as Saudi Arabia and the UAE, and Muslims or Muslim families, about what it is acceptable as a classroom topic. Factors that may play a role in these differences are exposure to other cultures, studying abroad, globalization, and family background.

The Brazilian educator Paulo Freire introduced the idea of critical pedagogy in the 1960s in *Pedagogy of the Oppressed* (Izadinia 2009). Critical pedagogy holds the position that the role of education has been taken over by the economic status quo to maintain its position, thereby propagating beliefs about the rights of the ruling class and the place of the underprivileged. Freire specifically advocated a transformation of the role of teachers and students to critical examiners of the ritualized hidden syllabus. Freire's work was a precursor to the work of French sociologist Pierre Bourdieu, whose work *Distinction: A Social Critique of the Judgment of Taste* published in 1971 empirically proved that social status was inherited (McLaren 2009). According to Akbari (2008), in English language teaching, critical pedagogy "is an attitude which relates the classroom context to the wider social context and aims at social transformation through education" (Akbari 2008, p. 276). On one level, critical pedagogy works as a vehicle for transformation by which the oppressed members of a society may come to critically examine and reject the status quo of that society. For example, students may be asked to critically examine why some are favored in society over others (e.g., Why is the teachers' parking lot closer to the building than the students' parking lot?) On another level, critical pedagogy may usurp one society's values for that of another. For example, setting Gulf Arab Muslim students the task of debating same-sex marriage is advocating a position that may be held by certain Western societies, but again, is expressly forbidden by their religion which is Islam.

In today's world, according to Kachru and Smith (2008), 25 % of the most educated and influential people speak English, and the spread, status, and functions of English have never been matched historically by any other language. English is used as a medium of communication between many speakers of other languages from different cultures and it is used in the Gulf Arab states as a lingua franca (Randall and Samimi 2010). It has replaced Arabic as the language of the workplace because of the many linguistically diverse groups working in the region from Arab to European to Asian (Randall and Samimi 2010). However, as a result of that demographic melting pot, there are indications that the government is worried about the continuation of the local culture with its values and the degree to which it is being assaulted by the other cultures of the large expatriate population living and working in the country (Findlow 2006).

Previously in the nineteenth century, culture was a synonym for "Western culture," but today the concept of culture is the totality of thought, experiences, behavior, concepts, values, and assumptions made by a group that is self-sustaining (Jandt 2012). Some scholars believe that "we can have no direct knowledge of a culture other than our own" (Jandt 2012, p. 16). Intercultural communication is the act of sociality between cultures: a way to create and preserve social relationships (Huang et al. 2012). People with shared backgrounds share the same perceptions of the world. Some English as a second language (ESL) teachers believe that students will have an easier transition and better grasp of English if they are specifically taught American, English, or Australian values (Huang et al. 2012). However, this teaching philosophy ignores ESL students' cultures (Huang et al. 2012). Not valuing the students' cultures as much as the target language's culture can "jeopardize the psychological well being of the students" (Anderson 1992, p. 5).

There may be a large distance between the students' culture and the culture of the language they are learning. This distance may alienate the student so much that learning the target language may be severely impeded. Thus, it is not simply a matter of teaching students that red wine is eaten with meat and white wine with chicken or fish, for example, in teaching them about "English culture" (i.e., language), but the teacher is teaching them about the consumption of alcohol. The path is one of delicate balance, teaching students about the target culture for effective intercultural communication, without inadvertently encouraging them to adopt the cultural norms of the target culture (in this case English), forsaking their own culture which may specifically prohibit such things as abortion, homosexuality, dating, and alcohol. So, for example, while the target language culture (in this case English) is currently debating the legalities of same-sex marriage, a discussion of same-sex marriage as a topic may not be appropriate in the language classroom in the GCC countries because Islam specifically condemns homosexuality.

7.2   Teaching Taboo Topics

There are several levels of factors at work when bringing taboo topics into the classroom including what is considered taboo in the society, how both teachers and students feel about discussing the topics in class, and what may happen if the topics are brought into class. For example, Khuwaileh's (2000) study found that female students in Jordan refused to write about AIDS, sexual diseases, contraception, condoms, kissing, homosexuality, and heterosexuality, asking why they should use words like these that do not pertain to the degree they are getting, their personalities, their religion, or their idea of what it is appropriate for women to talk about in their society. Khuwaileh concluded that teachers need to create their own culturally specific teaching materials to lessen the gap between Western English language teaching/English as a foreign language (ELT/EFL) theory and overseas practice.

On the other hand, Tekin (2011) examined Turkish students' attitudes toward including the topics of homosexuality and adultery/premarital sex in a study aimed at gauging the students' reactions to using the taboo topics as a means of English language learning. Tekin used extensive postlesson questionnaires to find out that while most students agreed that these topics are seen as taboo by the majority of Turkish people, they did not find the subjects unspeakable in the classroom and did not have a negative attitude about them being included as discussion topics. Eighty-five percent of the students who participated in the study felt that objective materials used by an objective teacher were very important in the discussions of these two taboo topics. No point of view, pro or con, was offered in the materials; they were factual and unbiased. In addition, the teacher did not interject any opinion in the discussion.

In an Asian context, Timina and Butler (2011) surveyed 70 Taiwanese students to find out which topics they would feel uncomfortable discussing in the classroom and found that students would not like to discuss their private life (weaknesses, mistakes, illnesses, boyfriend/girlfriend relationships), sex, politics, personal family income, personal appearance, single-parent families, death, homosexuality, personal religious beliefs, and superstitions. The number one reason given by the students for not wanting to discuss the topics was because they are taboo in the students' culture and not often discussed in their native language.

Furthermore, Haynes's (2000) study on the taboo topic of AIDS and teacher reluctance found that many Japanese EFL teachers were reluctant to address any sort of controversial issues in class citing concerns about presenting issues fairly and objectively or the possibility of offending someone in the class. The teachers also expressed fears of objection to the material by students or administration.

7.3   Taboo Topics in ESL/EFL

What may be considered taboo topics depends on the context and culture of the learners. For ESL learners in general, according to Bell and Gower (1998), the main taboo topics of EFL course books are sex, drugs, religion, and death. Thornbury

(2010) writes that mainstream ELT publishers have an acronym for topics that are universally understood to be prohibited in textbooks, PARSNIP, which stands for politics, alcohol, religion, sex, narcotics, -isms, and pork. Gray (2002) adds anarchy, AIDS, and Israel to the list of taboo topics in the ESL classroom. In a different Western context, Keturi and Lehmonen (2011) added suicide, violence, abortion, cursing, and smoking in an analysis of four series of EFL course books published in Finland by Finnish publishers that targeted junior to senior high school English language learners. All of these topics would also be considered taboo in Gulf Arab Muslim classrooms in the GCC, but perhaps not in other Muslim or Arab contexts such as Pakistan or Lebanon.

7.4   Taboo Topics in the Gulf Region

Other topics that may offend Muslim Gulf Arab students are the consumption of pork, Christian holidays, the zodiac, and ghosts (Gobert 2003). The consumption of pork is prohibited in Islam and belief in the zodiac and fortune telling is also prohibited. Ghosts (a spirit of the dead which lingers in this world after death) also do not exist in Islamic epistemology. In addition, in Saudi Arabia, the public celebration of Christian holidays such as Christmas and St. Valentine's Day is prohibited (see Religious 2012). Two more topics that may be considered taboo in Muslim Gulf Arab student classrooms, especially in the post-9/11 and emerging Arab Spring world, are war and politics. For example, students themselves were reluctant to talk about the crisis in Syria in the author's classroom. They felt that the topic was not appropriate for the classroom because Middle Eastern politics were involved. Thornbury (2002) writes that he was admonished not to mention the war when he first started his teaching career in Egypt at the time of the October 6th War in 1973, so the taboo against talking about politics in Middle Eastern classrooms goes back quite a long way.

In a discussion of the cultural confrontation and resulting cognitive dissonance that may occur among Gulf Arab Muslim students when teachers are called upon to teach from culturally conflicting material, Zaid (1999), lists 16 cultural values of non-Islamic societies said to be particularly offensive to Muslims. The topics are:

Boyfriend/girlfriend.
Dating.
Beach/bikini wear.
The consumption of wine and alcohol.
Dancing.
Hugging.
A picture of an uncovered breast.
Fortune tellers and predicting the future.
A cross worn by a man subliminally conveys an advocacy of a Christian perspective.
The Christian church
Sexism

Superstitions
Guns
Teen suicide
Life after death
Birth control

The next section will discuss each of these topics in turn. The author will draw upon relevant literature and the author's personal narrative experiences teaching in Saudi Arabia and the UAE to discuss whether the topic can be handled appropriately in the classroom or whether the topic is better left out of the classroom altogether.

7.5 Boyfriends/Girlfriends and Dating

Moore (2011) recounted an anecdote when first teaching females in the UAE. When asked by students what he had done on the weekend, he referred to spending time with his girlfriend to the sound of titters in the classroom. He was disconcerted; no one had told him that girlfriends/boyfriends and dating are taboo topics in the GCC classroom. Many course books from mainstream ESL publishers also feature girlfriend/boyfriend relationships and dating in innocuous grammar and speaking practice examples (i.e., "Do you have a girl/boyfriend?" see Gobert 2003). Course books that target the Middle Eastern market have more recently issued specific editions of their books, such as *New Headway Plus Elementary*, Middle Eastern version (Soars and Soars 2011), that remove all references to pork, alcohol, and dating. Dating before marriage is not permitted in Islam (Liaise n.d.), and for many Gulf Arab Muslim students,

> The reality of God in the world, the truths God revealed to man in the revelation of the Koran, and man's accountability to God for his response to the truths, are all as plain and beneficial as the air he breathes to stay alive. So, in the Arab world, God remains socialized in a way we have not seen in Europe since perhaps before the Enlightenment. God is omnipresent in the community and not, as for those in the West, simply reckoned to be as a matter of personal belief. The implications are vast. (Allen 2006, p. 26)

Much of what other nationalities or religions consider appropriate in class and part of normal daily life (i.e., dating, girlfriend/boyfriend relationships, male/female hugging and kissing) is taboo in the Gulf Muslim Arab classroom because of their interpretation of what their religion permits. This is not to say that no Gulf Muslim Arabs have girlfriend/boyfriend relationships; many do in today's modern world. As Allen (2006, p. 44) comments, "…a culture that stresses so much the autonomy of the individual has a layered and deep awareness of individual needs and rights and these are a matter of stringent respect…the sense of the personal, and many of its associations which we would call 'private,' is very strong." However, bringing girlfriend/boyfriend relationships and dating into the public sphere of the classroom may not be appropriate.

Most families in the Gulf region have arranged marriages and often a period of engagement occurs before the wedding. A couple is considered affianced once the marriage contract is signed, which usually occurs before the wedding party, and thus it is perfectly permissible to substitute fiancé for boyfriend/girlfriend. How much the couples are able to see of each other and under what circumstances is also a family matter. In my experience, some couples are allowed to talk on the phone, some are allowed to go out unescorted, and some are not allowed to have any contact with each other prior to the wedding.

Marriage is not a taboo topic in the classroom in the UAE. However, it is not appropriate to ask publically in the classroom what a male student's mother's/wife's/ or sister's name is in front of other students, and it is never appropriate for a male instructor to do so. This is because of the private realm of the man's haram, coming from the Arabic root HRM because it is reserved or sacred, as in *al-haram*, the Holy Ka'abah built by Ibrahim in Mecca, and that which he must defend, the idea of which runs across centuries, fashion, culture and social mores (Allen 2006, pp. 60–61). However, male students are happy to discuss their daughters and even show photos on their phones, computers, or iPads, as long as their daughters are still considered children. I have had many successful lessons when I have brought "problem pages" into the classroom from the local press or Internet that feature married couples. In one such letter, a man cheating on his wife was hotly debated throughout the lesson. In addition, I have taught classes where the discussion topic was how different societies espouse men and women, comparing arranged marriages with nonarranged marriages, and my students were interested to compare the two means of finding a lifetime partner. I have even brought in Muslim matrimonial ads in English from local newspapers or the Internet to introduce the topic. Students are interested in discussing or writing about the pros and cons of arranged marriages versus "love matches" (Allen 2006, p. 68).

7.6   Hugging and Kissing, Music, and Dancing

Hugging, kissing, and dancing between a male and a female in public are taboo although hugging, kissing, and dancing are permissible between those of the same gender. Most mainstream ELT course books now avoid these areas, at least in their Middle Eastern editions, but why are these topics taboo? Hugging and kissing between a man and a woman is for private, not public, consumption and it is prohibited between an unmarried couple. This can make it difficult to find inoffensive films to broadcast in the classroom. I suggest a careful checking of content before showing, a quick hand on the remote control, or allowing the students to take control of the device while screening. However, if a teacher is not quick with these, Gulf Arab students will feel very uncomfortable during kissing, sex, or sexy scenes in a film. Many will look away or ask to go pray. Also, if there are students in class that are particularly religious, especially male students, some may refuse to watch films at all, although some may not refuse to watch digital content on the Internet. This is best handled by having an alternative activity they can work on outside of class or not using video technology while you are teaching that particular class.

Some students do not listen to music for religious reasons while some may know all about the latest pop or rap artist and even pick up some urban slang used in those forms of communication. Teachers can give students projects to do on their favorite singer, band, or poet, Arabic or English, which is something many young persons are enthusiastic about and motivated by. Giving a poet as an option solves the problem of having students in the class who do not listen to music for religious reasons. An additional benefit is that students can share Arabic singers and poets with the teacher. Arabic poetry, locally known as Nabati poetry, is a long-held folk-loric tradition in the Gulf, and one that many are proud to have prowess in. There is even a reality TV show known as the Million's Poet where the prize is between 1–5 million AED (US\$ 272,294–1,361,470).

Music and dancing are seen as such innocent crosscultural topics that they have been featured as speaking topics on International English Language Testing System (IELTS) and other international exams. However, many Gulf Arab students freeze on these questions. They need to be taught that music and dancing include traditional music and dancing so that they can relate to these topics. Every country has traditional music and dancing, and even though some very strict Muslims may not listen to or participate in traditional music and dancing, most do. The problem is due to the idealized middle-class world presented in ESL textbooks (Akbari 2008; Rinvolucri 1999; Thornbury 2002) where the poor have to be non-American and Londoners John and Mary are the only ones who plan holidays in the Caribbean (Banegas 2011). The result is when Muslim Arab students are asked, "Do you like dancing?", all they can picture is discos and nightclubs whereas their traditional dances are just as much dancing as the gyrations of the club scene.

7.7 Beach/Bikini Wear/Nudity

In Muslim cultures as well as other conservative cultures in Asia, the propriety of dress is one of modesty for teachers and students alike. Mainstream ESL course book publishers have become more attuned to this need, and recent editions of course books destined for the Middle East, particularly the Saudi market, have removed any pictures that might be considered immoral or immodest. While teaching in Saudi Arabia, I saw many textbooks with the bodies blacked out in photos of beach-wearing holiday makers. I have also seen the arms and necklines of women blacked out as well as nude images of classical Roman or Greek statues. In the UAE, I have not witnessed this kind of visual censorship in any way and in fact, the UAE minister of higher education and research has stated publicly that "No book should be banned and no information should be withheld from the public in this day and age" (Al Nowais 2005, para. 4). However, nudity, sex, or sexy scenes, make most Gulf Arab students feel very uncomfortable because of the conservatism which exists in their society which is based on both their cultural tradition and Islam.

7.8 Fortune Tellers, Predicting the Future, Superstitions, and the Zodiac

Some English grammatical concepts seem offensive to some GCC Muslim students depending on how those concepts are explained by the teacher or in textbooks. For example, in Islam, fortune telling, soothsayers, and magic are all evil practices (History n.d.). Bringing them into the classroom as examples or text contravenes Islam. Many mainstream ESL course books teach one of the uses of "will" for future predictions. Arab students tend to overgeneralize the use of the word "will" in their interlanguage as a future tense marker as in Arabic. Students should be taught that will is not a future tense marker in English and that which tense form speakers choose to use depends on how the speaker sees the future (i.e, *My flight leaves at 10:00, My flight's leaving at 10:00, My flight is going to leave at 10:00, My flight will leave at 10:00*, etc.).

Muslims always preface or postscript their statements about the future with "insha'allah" which translates as "god willing." For example, if a teacher asks a student "Do you think you'll get married one day and have children?" for future prediction, the answer will be "Yes, I think I'll get married one day and have children, insha'allah." This means, when the teacher says "See you tomorrow at 3," and they answer "insha'allah" that they will do their best to come at that time, but that something unforeseen may intervene because only Allah (God) knows the future. Many teachers become discomfited by this difference between the English and Muslim Arab languages and culture. Acceptance of this difference on the teacher's part leads to a greater understanding of the students' culture. Even teachers may do their best to get something done or be somewhere at a certain time in the future and be unable to accomplish it because of unforeseen circumstances. In reality, the future is unknown and English is not the only language or world view.

The idea of superstitions is also not familiar to Gulf Muslim Arab students. From the Islamic Centre's (Leicester, UK) website: "Islam does not acknowledge the concept of superstition" (What is the view in Islam on superstitions n.d., para. 2). Course book writers have long relied on superstitions to teach conditionals. Lessons built around superstitions, (e.g., black cat walking across your path, walking under a ladder, breaking a mirror, etc.), are never successful. Gulf Muslim Arabs cannot relate to them. Asking students if they have a lucky object to activate their schemata of superstitions bears no success. At this point, it is worth asking if it is necessary for students using English as a world language for global communication to be familiar with English superstitions or if course book writers and publishers are tailoring language to suit a grammar syllabus without examining a corpus.

Regarding the zodiac, "There is absolutely no evidence in the Quran and Sunnah that one carries particular traits, habits, or drawbacks which are peculiar to his zodiac signs or stars…" (Astrology n.d., para. 2). However, several years ago a colleague reported a very successful student's presentation on the zodiac in which the student categorized other classmates according to their zodiac. Zodiac horoscopes are also a regular feature of a national newspaper in the UAE. This may be because

of ideas regarding what is individualistic and personal versus what is public and socially acceptable in Muslim society. Some teachers may feel comfortable teaching
the zodiac or Chinese zodiac for language learning purposes. Furthermore, students
may be interested in the topic while scoffing at its validity.

7.9   Religion

In a study by Gobert (2003) on four mainstream English language intermediate textbooks, there were 33 references to Christianity, including four full-length reading
texts while there were only two references to Islam (an imam [preacher] who lived
to be 136 years old and an article comparing weddings in different countries). There
were two references to Hinduism, one to ancient Greek gods, and two mentions of
Buddhism. There were also 21 references to Christmas and one to Valentine's Day,
while there was no reference to Ramadan (the month of fasting in Islam), Eid Al Fitr
(celebrating the end of Ramadan), or Eid Al Adha (the celebration at the end of the
Haj [pilgrimage to Mecca] for Muslims). This may be because of the inseparability
of language and culture, i.e., the English language and the influence of Christianity.
On the other hand, it fails to show the reality of current English-speaking societies,
which are multicultural and practice multiple religions.

The Quran (the Islamic holy book seen by Muslims as a revelation from Allah
[God] to the founder of Islam, Mohamed, the Prophet) calls for respect and toler-
ance to be shown to Christians and Jews because they worship the same God of
Ibrahim (Abraham), Isma'il (Ishmael), Musa (Moses), and the other prophets (Al-
len 2006), including the Christian prophet, Esau (Jesus), the founder of Christianity.
Christmas can be referred to as "Prophet 'Issa's birthday" in class and Gregorian
dates (b.c. and a.d.) in teaching materials, can be referred to as "before the time of
Prophet 'Issa's birth" or "after the birth of Prophet 'Issa."

A number of Muslim Arabs in the UAE and Saudi Arabia celebrate Valentine's
Day while in Saudi Arabia, the Organisation for Promoting Virtue and Discouraging
Evil confiscates red roses and Valentine's Day cards from shops ("Religious police
swoop," 2012). Texts on the origins of Valentine's Day using articles recounting
Shiv Sena's objections to its celebration in India in the UAE can be successful in
class. Students can debate and write about whether Muslims should celebrate Valentine's Day.

Once a colleague used a text to teach about Veteran's Day in the USA (similar to
Armistice Day in Europe) from materials compiled by the US Department of State's
(Foreign Secretary) English Language Office. The class was in a primary school in
the UAE, and the summer program was funded by the US State Department in the
aftermath of 9/11 and the Second Gulf War in an effort to redress anti-American
sentiment in the region. There were images of crosses across the graveyard of the
unknown soldiers. The parents came to the school and complained to the principal.
Muslims are buried in unmarked graves wrapped in shrouds within 3 days of death.

Once in Saudi Arabia in my early teaching days, I asked students about the split in Islam between Shi'a and Sunni. Saudi students were quite prepared to discuss this topic, but one student from Jordan whose grandfather had been given Saudi nationality after World War II said something to the students in Arabic and they all became silent and told me that there was no split in Islam. From that experience I learned from the students that it was not my place to probe them about their religion to see what they would say.

One of the goals of education in modern society is to indoctrinate young individuals into the social and religious mores of the society in which they are born (Tozer et al. 2008). Students from Gulf countries, therefore, do not learn a lot about Christianity or the history of the European world, and the founding of America. Students have asked me for brief explanations about Protestantism and Catholicism in class. The Pope is called El Baba (Father) in Arabic.

There was a great deal of outrage in the Muslim world following the publication of the Danish cartoons that depicted Prophet Mohamed in images in 2006. Muslims are not allowed to represent human images (thus the geometric patterns in Islamic art), and for them it is sacrilegious to depict Prophet Mohamed. One professor at a university in the UAE brought copies of the cartoons into the classroom for discussion and was fired on the orders of the highest authority of higher education in the country (Rashid 2006). On the other hand, a university in Sharjah held a public debate after the publication of the cartoons where one of the main themes of the discussion was the issue of freedom of speech versus respect for religions (Za'za 2006). It is vital for teachers to know that while some topics may be appropriate for discussion, such as freedom of the press versus publishing cartoons that are sacrilegious to Muslims, the act of showing the cartoons to students was unacceptable. New teachers coming into the Gulf need to be made very aware of the consequences that can occur for doing something that is considered blasphemous in Islam by Gulf Arab Muslims when working in the Gulf.

7.10   Alcohol, Pork, and Drugs

Muslims are prohibited from consuming alcohol and pork, and from using drugs. In fact, the penalty for drug trafficking in the Gulf states is death. In the USA, people are not expected to do something that is against their religion. For example, Quakers (who are pacifists) were exempted from the draft, and when I was growing up in the USA, female Pentecostal students were exempt from gym class because they were not allowed to wear shorts or pants. Previously, publishers were oblivious to the inclusion of consuming alcohol and pork in course books (Gobert 2003); however, most course books, at least Middle Eastern editions, avoid these topics nowadays. Such examples as "Wine is made in France" are relatively unobjectionable.

7.11   Guns

Guns are strictly controlled in the GCC member states, but are available and part of their cultural heritage. There is a large annual hunting and equestrian exhibition in Abu Dhabi with a large display of rifles and handguns. However, my students have told me that if you buy a gun in the UAE, the insides are removed by the police so that the weapon does not fire. I have heard of a female relative getting hit in the leg with a stray bullet at a wedding party when shots were fired in the air while she was sleeping on the balcony in a more remote region of Saudi Arabia and occasionally there are stories of guns being used as weapons ("One wounded," 2001). Guns and gun control are not controversial topics in the Gulf countries because guns are already controlled.

7.12   Teen Suicide and Abortion

Suicide is against Islam as it is against all major religions, and it is also against the law in Gulf countries. However, it does occur ("Unemployed youth," 2001). Suicide and assisted suicide are not permitted in Islam and are not suitable for discussion. Abortion is also not permitted in Islam; however, under some circumstances such as rape or incest, or when the mother's health is in danger, it may be acceptable according to a religion scholar's interpretation of the Quran. Some teachers may feel comfortable using the acceptability of abortion in certain cases in Islam as a discussion topic. This is not to say, however, that suicide or abortions do not occur in Muslim Arab society, but they are not suitable for discussion in scenarios in the Gulf region. In conversation or writing prompts such as "Are you for or against abortion?" or "Are you for or against assisted suicide?" Muslim Arab's religion dictates what their answer will be.

7.13   Life after Death and Ghosts

Muslims believe in heaven (paradise) and hell. If a teacher's personal beliefs contravene Islam (e.g., atheism), this does not belong in the classroom. The idea of a human spirit lingering on earth after death, (i.e, a ghost), does not exist in Islam. Course book writers often use ghosts to teach the third conditional, (i.e., What would you do if you saw a ghost?) but this prompt is not effective for Muslim Arab students. However, *jins* (e.g., the genie in Aladdin, evil spirits) exist and were created by Allah (God) in the Muslim world view. Substituting jins for ghosts in classroom activities is an effective way of teaching the third conditional. Many Gulf Muslim students' favorite movie genre is horror, but for them ghosts are as make believe as the whole cinematic world. Students are often interested in why people like scary movies and like to be scared.

7.14   Birth Control

Although some schools of Islamic thought state that birth control is not allowed in Islam, many Arab Gulf Muslims practice family planning which connotes the spacing of children and having a smaller family. Birth control pills are readily available in pharmacies in Saudi Arabia and the UAE, and condoms are readily available in large supermarkets and pharmacies. The ideal family size makes for an interesting class discussion as we begin to see the effects of economic growth influence (usually diminishing) the size of the family.

7.15   Sexism and Sexuality

Women being paid less than men for doing the same job, or how few women are in leadership positions in US politics, or the differences between genders regarding sports and video games are effective topics in the classroom and not taboo. Male and female students are open to discussing these issues, along with "Should women work outside the home?", "Should women be allowed to drive?" However, wearing a scarf or veil is a matter of personal or family choice and cultural traditions and it is not a suitable topic to discuss in the classroom (i.e., "Should women wear a veil?"). However, in my experience at one college in the UAE, the first-year research topic was changed from the AIDS epidemic to third world debt by the head of instruction at the last minute because AIDS can be a sexually transmitted disease. Sex education is lacking from the syllabus of many schools in the Muslim Gulf Arab countries although the Quran has verses that give ample explanation on sexual intercourse and sexuality (e.g., Surat al Baqara). Reading the Quran is open to all regardless of age group. It would seem that sometimes the lack of knowledge from the side of students boosts these unjustified taboos, yet taboos are both cultural as well as linguistic.

7.16   Swearing and Racism

Most students in the Gulf are aware of taboo words in English and do not use them in the classroom, though sometimes a minor s*** will be heard and quickly suppressed. If students are shown an action film, there may be a great deal of swearing, and often students simply ignore it. Informants say that swear words are removed from the Arabic subtitles for movies shown in the cinema or on television, so if these are used in class and the students are not very proficient, they might not understand what is being said. Students should be taught "profanity" or "swearing" if it comes up in a context (e.g., discussing the positives and negatives of Hollywood films) or they will simply use "bad words" in all contexts no matter what their level of English.

Incidences of racist remarks have occurred in Gulf Arab classrooms when mainstream course book writers have used photos of Africans or African Americans as role models. Students also complain sometimes because of other students' racist remarks. Teachers need to be aware of this and intervene by having a private word with the student who is making racist remarks or teaching a text on racism. Bringing to class English texts whether prose or poetry that are written by non-American and non-British writers such as African, Indian, Pakistani, or Malaysian writers could also help in spreading awareness on diversity and intercultural communication (which is part of critical pedagogy) and denouncing racism.

7.17   War and Politics

My career in the Gulf spans two Gulf Wars, 9/11, and their aftermath. I was advised early in my career that if students wanted to talk about politics, I should say that I would be happy to talk about American (national) politics. I have taken this advice to heart throughout my teaching career in the Middle East. As Americans, my children were made to feel uncomfortable by comments made by their Spanish teacher at the French school during the Second Gulf War. I have had a student comment to me at the time of Saddam Hussein's death, that it was not right to execute him, and a student comment to me that it was not right to kill Osama Bin Laden without a trial.

The Arab Spring is another more recent major political event in the Arab world. One after another, rulers were forced from power in Tunisia, Egypt, Libya, and Yemen, and major protests broke out in Algeria, Iraq, Jordan, and Morocco. Syria is in a state of civil unrest. Some Gulf states stopped issuing visas to countries that were experiencing the Arab Spring to prevent dissidents from entering the country (Thomas 2012) due to the fear that they may propagate the Arab Spring in the region.

7.18   Palestinian Conflict

I once had students ask me if they could watch a documentary in Arabic about the Palestinian refugee camps in Israel and Lebanon with English subtitles. We did not discuss or write about the film because in this case a picture was worth a thousand words. I use the term Palestine to refer to the region in class and have learned the Arabic word for Jewish if needed to briefly gloss for students. Some teachers are disturbed at the way that the situation between Palestinians and Israelis is handled in the Gulf, but the lack of acknowledgement of Israel on maps and in textbooks is a result of the GCC countries' nonrecognition of Israel as a state. Yet, most students are interested in Palestine, occupied territories, and Palestinians' rights.

7.19 Implications

As stated earlier, among the calls for critical pedagogy in the language learning classroom (Akbari 2008), there is an equal need to balance critical pedagogy topics with students' religious and cultural beliefs and values. Teachers in GCC countries need to be careful about which topics they bring into the classroom from both mainstream ESL/EFL course books and for the sake of critical pedagogy. There are certain topics such as boyfriends/girlfriends and dating, abortion, homosexuality, euthanasia, drinking alcohol, and taking drugs, which are specifically prohibited by Islam and there are certain topics that are politically sensitive such as 9/11, the Iraq War, Israel, and the Arab Spring. There is no legal protection for teachers who embark on teaching social issues in the guise of critical pedagogy as there is in the USA (Evans et al. 2000) if students or parents complain to the authorities about the teaching of a topic that they consider taboo. On the other hand, if students and teachers negotiate a syllabus of topics together, perhaps they can settle upon topics that are both relevant to the students' lives and uncontroversial. In the studies of both Kulchytska (2000) and Banegas (2011), the students' offerings of topics that interested them were not as "taboo" as the topics proposed by the teachers. Teachers offered the topics of child abuse, drug abuse, discrimination, and immigration and students offered the topics of:

Psychological disorders
Divorce
Politics
Eating disorders
The Catholic Church
Single parenting
The individual and society
Alcoholism
Smoking and drug abuse
AIDS
People's values
Human rights
The world after World War II
Careers
Man and nature
Youth culture
Women and society
The art of love

A negotiated syllabus of topics which may include critical pedagogy topics such as single-parent families and divorce is perhaps the best route for teachers to take in the GCC when teaching Arab Muslim students so that students are interested in the topics and will not feel cognitive dissonance in the classroom because the topics are so remote from their culture and religious beliefs, topics such as abortion and homosexuality. Also, because the topics are negotiated and found acceptable to both parties, the risk of job endangerment or students feeling uncomfortable with the topics will greatly diminish. We can bring more socially relevant English language teaching into our students' lives without negatively affecting their desire to learn English for studies and job prospects or offending them thus empowering both our learners and our classrooms. Promoting courses and training on intercultural communication (IC) in the ELT preservice and in-service teacher education can help in understanding IC, diversity, racism, ethnocentrism, stereotyping, and know how to deal with these concepts in the ESL classroom. Teachers should know about their own and other cultures especially the cultures of their students.

Conclusion

This chapter was written for teachers new to the Gulf Muslim Arab classroom or ESL/EFL teachers who are thinking of coming to teach in the Gulf. There are many topics considered taboo in the classroom such as drugs, alcohol, sex, religion, and death. In Muslim Gulf Arab classrooms other topics such as boyfriends/girlfriends, nudity, dating, and superstitions may also be considered taboo because of both their religion and culture, which tend to be conservative and traditional. Bringing such topics into the classroom may cause the students to feel uncomfortable and this may affect their learning of English. Teachers should be aware of their students' cultures and the topics that are considered taboo in their culture so that they can bring critical pedagogy topics into their classrooms without offending the sensibilities of their learners. This will result in positive IC both on the side of the teachers who will learn about their students' culture and on the side of the students who will not feel that their culture is being overwhelmed by the onslaught of Western values and culture.

References

Akbari, R. (2008). Transforming lives: Introducing critical pedagogy into ELT classrooms. *ELT Journal, 62*(3), 276–283.
Allen, M. (2006). *Arabs*. London: Continuum.
Allan, K., & Burridge, K. (2006). *Forbidden words: Taboo and the censoring of language*. Cambridge: Cambridge University Press.
Al Nowais, S. (1 April 2005). No book should be banned in this age of information. *Gulf News*. http://gulfnews.com/news/gulf/uae/general/no-book-should-be-banned-in-this-age-of-information-1.282872. Accessed 12 June 2012.
Anderson, G. (1992). Multicultural sensitivity: An essential skill for the ESL/EFL teacher. (Master's thesis) School for International Training, Brattleboro, Vermont.
Astrology star zodiac signs. (n.d.). http://www.islamhelpline.net/node/570. Accessed 11 May 2012.
Banegas, D. (2011). Teaching more than English in secondary education. *ELT Journal, 65*(1), 80–82.

Bell, J., & Gower, R. (1998). Writing course materials for the world: A great compromise. In B. Tomlinson (Ed.), *Materials development in language teaching* (pp. 116–129). Cambridge: Cambridge University Press.

Crystal, D. (2003). *The Cambridge encyclopedia of the English language* (2nd ed.). New York: Cambridge University Press.

Evans, R., Avery, P., & Pederson, P. (2000). Taboo topics: Cultural restraint on teaching social issues. *The Clearing House, 73*(5), 295–301.

Findlow, S. (2006). Higher education and linguistic dualism in the Arab Gulf. *British Journal of the Sociology of Education, 27*(1), 19–36.

Gobert, M. (2003). Avoiding cultural confrontation in the classroom: An analysis of four mainstream intergrated ESL textbooks. In S. Zafar (Ed.), *Culture, context, and communication in English language teaching, Proceedings of the 3rd Annual Teacher-to-Teacher Conference* (pp. 220–233). Abu Dhabi: Military Language Institute.

Gray, J. (2002). The global coursebook in English language teaching. In D. Block & D. Cameron (Eds.), *Globalization and language teaching* (pp. 151–167). London: Routledge.

Haynes, L. (2000). The taboo topic and teacher reluctance: An investigation into attitudes among university EFL teachers in Japan (Unpublished Master's thesis). Newport Asia Pacific University, Anaheim, CA.

History of fortune telling. (n.d.). http://www.islamiccentre.org/index.php?option=com_content&view=article&id=505. Accessed 23 June 2012.

Huang, J., Dotterweich, E., & Bowers, A. (2012). Intercultural miscommunication: Impact on ESOL students and implications for ESOL teachers. *Journal of Instructional Psychology, 39*(1), 36–40.

Izadinia, M. (2009). Critical pedagogy: An introduction. In P. Wachob (Ed.), *Power in the EFL classroom: Critical pedagogy in the Middle East* (pp. 7–16). Newcastle: Cambridge Scholars.

Jandt, F. (2012). *An introduction to intercultural communication: Identities in a global community*. New York: Sage.

Kachru, Y., & Smith, L. (2008). *Cultures, contexts, and world Englishes*. New York: Routledge.

Keturi, S., & Lehmonen, T. (2011). *Taboo or not taboo: A study taboo content in Finnish EFL learning materials* (Unpublished Master's thesis). University of Jyväskylä, Finland.

Khuwaileh, A. (2000). Cultural barriers of language teaching: A case study of classroom cultural obstacles. *Computer Assisted Language Learning, 13*(3), 281–290.

Kulchytska, O. (2000). The alternative textbook and teaching English in the Ukraine. *Journal of the Imagination and Language Learning and Teaching*, 5. http://www.njcu.edu/cill/journal-index.html. Accessed 3 Feb 2012.

Liaise with a boy/girl prior to marriage? (n.d.). http://www.islamiccentre.org/index.php?option=com_content&view=article&id=257. Accessed 1 June 2012.

MacAndrew, R., & Martinez, R. (2001). *Taboos and issues*. London: Language Teaching Publications.

McLaren, P. (2009). Critical pedagogy: A look at the major concepts. In A. Darder, M. Baltodano, & R. Torres (Eds.), *The critical pedagogy reader* (pp. 61–83). New York: Routledge.

Moore, P. J. (November 2011). *Teaching approaches and practices in varying cultures*. Paper presented at the 15th Annual Current Trends in English Language Testing Conference, Dubai, United Arab Emirates.

One wounded as youth opens fire on worshippers. (6 January 2001). *Arab News*. http://arabnews.com/node/212575.

Randall, M., & Samimi, M. (2010). The status of English in Dubai. *English Today, 1*(1), 43–50.

Rashid, M. (8 February 2006). Professor sacked for displaying blasphemous drawings in class. *Khaleej Times*. http://www.khaleejtimes.com/DisplayArticle.asp?xfile=data/theuae/2006/February/theuae_February225.xml&section=theuae. Accessed 11 July 2012.

Religious police swoop on Valentine's Day lovers. (15 February 2012). *ABC News*. http://www.abc.net.au/news/2012-02-15/saudi-heart-breakers/3830624.

Rinvolucri, M. (1999). The UK, EFLese sub-culture and dialect. *Folio, 5*(2), 12–14.

Soars, L., & Soars, J. (2011). *New Headway plus elementary*. Oxford: Oxford University Press. (Middle Eastern ed.).

Tekin, M. (2011). Discussing the unspeakable: A study of the use of taboo topics in EFL speaking classes. *Journal of Theory and Practice in Education, 7*(1), 79–110.

The World Factbook. (2013). https://www.cia.gov/library/publications/the-world-factbook/. Accessed 14 June 2012.

Thomas, J. (25 August 2012). Firms see obstacles in hiring from Arab Spring nations. *The National*. http://www.thenational.ae/news/uae-news/firms-see-obstacles-in-hiring-from-arab-spring-nations. Accessed 11 Mar 2012.

Thornbury, S. (2002). Don't mention the war! Taboo topics and the alternative textbook. *It's for Teachers, 3*, 35–37.

Thornbury, S. (27 June 2010). T is for taboo. [Web log]. http://scottthornbury.wordpress.com/2010/06/27/t-is-for-taboo/. Accessed 11 June 2012.

Timina, S., & Butler, N. (2011). *Uncomfortable topics and their appropriateness in Asian EFL classes*. Retrieved from ERIC database. (ED515120).

Tozer, S., Violas, P., & Senese, G. (2008). *School and society: Historical and contemporary perspectives* (6th ed.). Boston: McGraw-Hill.

Unemployed youth in critical condition after suicide attempt. (7 January 2001). *Arab News*. http://www.arabnews.com/node/212394. Accessed 11 July 2012.

Zaid, M. (1999). Cultural confrontation and cultural acquisition in the EFL classroom. *International Review of Applied Linguistics, 37*(2), 111–126.

Za'za, B. (5 February 2006). Muslims 'should stand united.' *Gulf News*. http://gulfnews.com/news/gulf/uae/general/muslims-should-stand-united-1.224100. Accessed 1 Nov 2012.

Melanie Gobert is on the faculty of Abu Dhabi Men's College at the Higher Colleges of Technology in the United Arab Emirates where she has served as a course team leader and academic coordinator. She has presented and published extensively in the region on reading, writing, speaking, vocabulary teaching and learning, assessment, independent learning, and online learning. She was the recipient of an Emirates Foundation Grant in 2009 for studying the effects of reading Emirati literature on national identity. She was a featured speaker at the Second World Congress on Extensive Reading in Seoul, Korea in September, 2013. She has a BA in English composition, an MA in applied linguistics/Teachers of English to Speakers of Other Languages (TESOL), and an EdD in educational leadership. She is currently the editor of Perspectives, the TESOL Arabia peer-reviewed journal and vice-president/president elect of TESOL Arabia. She is also the cochair of the Middle East and North Africa Extensive Reading Foundation.

Chapter 8
Intercultural Communication and Muslim American Youth in US School Contexts

Khawlah Ahmed

8.1 Introduction

"If you can't listen, why don't you take off your scarf so you can hear better" said a teacher to her female Muslim student. It is no wonder that at the beginning of the twenty-first century, issues of culture, ethnic identity, and recognition are still conundrums that spur some of the most heated debates at the highest levels of the social, political, and academic fronts in many parts of the world. In the USA, for example, major concerns still "abound concerning the origins, the present state, and the future of ethnic identity and ethnic communities" (Kivisto 1989, p. 11). One minority community that has been at the forefront of heated debates and controversies, especially after 9/11, is the Muslim American community. Issues ranging from their origins, present state, to their faith resurfaced with a vengeance, in the media and in politics, with repercussions that rippled through society and into the classrooms bringing toxic effects on the Muslim American youth and their school experiences.

A remark such as that above, coming from a teacher in a US high school context, raises a great deal of concern, cultural as well as pedagogic and psychological. It reflects the fact that US schools are still validating and reinforcing the cultural capital of dominant groups in society and devaluing and marginalizing others. This represents symbolic violence against the devalued groups (Nieto 1996), and positions their members to either discard their indigenous cultures or be excluded (Miller and McCaskill 1993). It raises questions about the educator's awareness and understanding of the pedagogic and psychological ramifications of such a remark and their understanding, or lack of it, of the theories that link culture to education and school outcomes. It suggests that there is a gap in the education system—one that requires culturally competent teachers with intercultural awareness, understanding, and communication skills that sensitize them to the importance and ramifications such remarks can have on all students.

K. Ahmed (✉)
American University of Sharjah, Sharjah, United Arab Emirates
e-mail: Khawlah@aus.edu

© Springer Science+Business Media Singapore 2015
R. Raddawi (ed.), *Intercultural Communication with Arabs*,
DOI 10.1007/978-981-287-254-8_8

In a country where it is estimated that the minorities will represent the collective majority by 2050 (U. S. Census Bureau 2008), we see that schools fail to realize this reality. Research shows that there is little, if any, consideration paid to the needs of children from different cultures and backgrounds as in how the students' psychic or internal development is impacted by the school (Alexander et al. 2005) to how their identities can be supported or rejected by the curricula and the school environments (Liese 2004). Today, according to Johnson (2010) "urban school leaders… face a plethora of cultural challenges—political, economic, and pedagogical" with "education leadership" that has "failed to evolve at the same pace as the[ir] cultural changes" and that there is "a need to hire, support, develop and promote culturally competent leaders in school districts and college campuses throughout the nation" (Johnson 2010, p. 2). For many Muslim American students, research shows that the symbolic violence Nieto (1996) refers to has developed into physical, verbal, and psychological abuse, some of which has been contributed to by educators in the school context whose actions and treatment of these students reflect a lack of cultural sensitivity, understanding, and awareness that may be promoting some of the prejudices and ethnocentric ideas about Muslim Americans drummed up by the media and the political rhetoric.

8.2   Making Connections: Intercultural Communication, Cultural Competence and Multicultural Education

We see a burgeoning amount of empirical studies and theoretical literature on second generation Muslim youth (e.g., Maira 2004; Sarroub 2005; Siren and Fine 2007; Sensoy and Stonebanks 2009; Surez-Orozco and Suarez-Orazco 2001) and there are many lenses through which the Muslim American students' lived experiences in US school contexts can be examined. In Tindongan (2011), we see that as a minority with roots in colonial countries, theories and approaches that can be utilized to examine these experiences may range from postcolonial to transnational. Sensoy and Stonebanks (2009) use student narratives and experiences, referred to by Nelson (2001, cited in Sensoy and Stonebanks 2009, p. x), as the transnational which is used to "empower and repair damaged group and individual identifies that emerge from dominant-group constructs of Muslim people" (p. x). In Sensoy and Stonebanks (2009), there are calls for the "interaction of th[e] knowledge disciplines of education of cultural studies and education," which can offer, " a rejuvenating, optimistic and positive perspective on education and educational institutions… rigorous analysis of the interrelationship between pedagogy, popular culture, meaning making, and youth subjectivity" and a need for "understanding of cultural pedagogy's (education that takes place outside of formal schooling) role in the shaping of individual identity—youth identity in particular—[and] the role educators play in the lives of their students" (p. piii).

The role that intercultural communication can play in academic contexts may also be an important component that needs to be examined. Intercultural communication, simply put, deals with communication between cultures. Yet, as Jandt (2007) explains, there was and continues to be a disagreement about defining the term culture. He shows that differing definitions have come about throughout the past centuries, beginning with a definition in the nineteenth century that was "synonymous with Western civilization" and moving to a definition today that "is no longer synonymous with countries" (Jandt 2007, p. 16). He also asserts that whether we analyze it through an ethnographic or a culture studies approach, both analyses are to a large extent "complementary and together can help our understanding of breakdowns in intercultural communication" (Jandt 2007, p. 16).

An intercultural communication (IC) approach recognizes that "Culture and communication are influenced by societal changes, and these changes need to be acknowledged, both in theory development and in classroom instructional methods" (Samovar et al. 2012, p. 45). Intercultural understanding, that is "the ability to understand the perceptions concerning one's own culture and the perceptions of the people who belong to another culture, and the capacity to negotiate between the two" is a basis for "multicultural or intercultural communication" (Samovar et al. 2012, p. 52) and a valuable asset, especially in today's US multicultural schools.

Culture, according to Samovar et al. (2012), "is first of all perceptions concerning our system of values, our ways of thinking, our beliefs, our psychological orientations" (p. 52). It is "the totality of [a] group's thought, experiences, and patterns of behavior and its concepts, values and assumptions about life that guide behavior and how those evolve with contact with other cultures" (Jandt 2007, p. 16). Studies have shown that inclusion, and/or exclusion of students' cultures, whether on the social, psychological, or academic level, can have major effects on students who are members of these groups (Seller 1992; Nieto 1996, 2002; Banks and Banks 1997). Identity and pride in cultures gives individuals a sense of belonging and group membership (Ferdman 1990; Berry 1986). They also answer the important question "Who am I?" (Gordon and Browne 1996), and legitimize the existence of the members in the eyes of others (Takaki 1993). The role that culture plays in school outcomes has been debated in both the literatures of multiculturalism and the anthropology of education literature (Ogbu 1991; Abu-Lughod 2006). Some argue that culture is connected with literacy in a substantive manner (Nieto 2002; Ferdman 1990; Apple 1996; Applebee 1974). They believe that students are socialized by the culture of their home and community (Vygotsky 1978, 1986) and problems can arise if what the student has learned at home clashes with the school culture.

Samovar et al. (2012) explain that "Something as simple as an awareness of cultural variations in eye contact can help teachers achieve great communication effectiveness in the multicultural classroom" (p. 3). They believe that "many cross-cultural problems can be resolved or avoided through an awareness and understanding of the components of intercultural communication" (p. 3). Being culturally competent, according to Johnson (2010), "means frequently discussing at length and with consistency how to engage, educate, understand and lead multicultural populations" (p. 3) and "culturally competent educational leaders, can model and shape the way others perceive human diversity in a positive way" (Henze et al. 2002, p. 11).

Multicultural education, defined by the National Association for Multicultural Education (2003) as "a philosophical concept built on the ideals of freedom, justice, equality, equity, and human dignity" is a "process that means to ensure the highest levels of academic achievement for all students while developing a positive self-concept from knowledge about the histories, cultures, and contributions of diverse groups for their responsibilities in an interdependent world" (para. 2). For many decades in the past, the philosophical concept of multicultural education was believed "to have the capacity to address the educational needs of a society that continues to struggle with the realization it is not monocultural in any aspect" (Hanley 1999, para. 1), and "to promote educational equality and justice for all groups" (Banks and Banks 1997, p. xiii). But this does not seem to be the case as research and literature show. Some believe that the inclusions made by multicultural education have been superficial, represented by a few posters on walls and holiday celebrations once a year, and that minority groups are still "ghettoized" (Diaz 2001). The goals of multicultural education have not yet been realized, because to do so, the curriculum needs to not just incorporate minority cultures, but to respect and tolerate their differences, and provide them with equal opportunities for education and include their narrative, stories, and contributions (Banks 2006). Multicultural education and culturally relevant pedagogy have actually failed to support teachers in applying that cultural knowledge in teaching and learning environments in an effective manner (Murrell 2007).

What seems to be the problem, as we see from Johnson's (2010) explanation is that

> Since multiculturalism means different things to different people, there must be a basis from which to speak. Ironically, diversity educators, those professionals trained to teach diversity, face similar challenges creating consensus in defining what multicultural education means in the traditional school setting. Therefore, it should come as no surprise that culturally competent research implies these shortcomings are due in part to "cultural incompetence." (p. 3).

According to Leef (2009, cited in Johnson 2010), "The opposite of 'cultural competence' is not 'cultural incompetence,' but rather the belief that schools should be places where all students are just taught the academic basics; the belief that students shouldn't be hectored about the supposed evils of society" (p. 3). But since the classroom is a microcosm of society, it should come to no surprise that the evils in it will be reflected in the classroom, as is the case with the Muslim American students.

8.3   Muslim Americans and the US Society

There are over 8 million Muslim Americans in the USA today (Ghazali 2008) and about 3 million speakers of Arabic as a mother tongue (Gordon 2005). Both the terms Arab and Muslim have become confused and conflated in the West, especially at the beginning of the twenty-first century. Each is an umbrella term for a multitude of cultures, ethnicities, and differences, and many are unaware that only about 10% of the Muslim population are Arab. The confusion has largely been due to the political rhetoric and the media portrayal and stereotyping that lumps all Arabs as Muslims, all Muslims as Arabs, and refers to all militant parties that are shown, as "Muslims," "as if all followers of Islam share one ethnic or political identity" (Wright 1995, p. 7). Despite all the events that have occurred and coverage these two terms have received, Americans today are, as Moore (2009) explains, still "profoundly ignorant regarding Islam and often conflate [it]…with terrorism and political regimes that unjustly conscript Islam to justify their oppressive policies and practices" (p. 142).

As a result of 9/11's social and political reaction to this group of individuals, factors such as ethnicity that differentiated the members of this group have, in a sense melted, unifying them under one new identity label, that of Muslim American (Sirin and Fine 2008). This "all-encompassing category… could be problematic" because it has become "ascribed to people originating from the Middle East or who have Middle Eastern features or who appear to identify with the Islamic faith" (Zaal et al. 2007, p. 165). The perpetuations of stereotypes had serious effects after 9/11. Whether you are Arab, Muslim, or you just "looked" Muslim, you become a target, intimidated, and discriminated against (Maira 2004; Levin and McDevitt 2002; Bennett 2007). You become a member of a "community… deemed suspect" (Nguyen 2005, p. 140). All Muslims became victims of guilt by association through the linking of Islam to extremist political violence portrayed in the media and by political leaders and other groups, which has caused unimaginable harm to the image of Islam in the USA (Ghazali 2008). These images have become "so much a part of the political and cultural discourse…in American society today that most do not even recognize it as racism" (El-Amine 2005, cited in Zaal et al. 2007, p. 165). They became members of a group who has been cast as the other. They have become targets of the wrath of many powerful governments that have constantly attacked their faiths and limited their civil rights and liberties.

According to Sirin and Fine (2008), since 9/11 and the subsequent "war on terror," it has become a far more challenging task growing up as a Muslim in the USA. They are continuously contending with stereotypical and popular cultural representations of Muslims being terrorists among other things, and the suspicion of not only the US government, but of the police, strangers, teachers, administrators, and peers. Sirin and Fine (2008) explain that this youth, in the USA, are "both culturally grounded and nationally uprooted, transnational and homeless, and swirling psychologically in a contentious diaspora" (p. 2). It is not only about "alienation and struggle, but also about their engagement with mainstream U.S. culture" (Sirin and Fine 2008, p. 2) that needs to be considered.

8.4   Muslim American Students' School Experiences

Schools, according to Tindongan (2011), are "microcosms of society" and have come to "reflect the narrow and negative representations of Muslims in the wider world" (p. 73). Today Muslim American students have become "situated on the intimate fault lines of global conflict" and are now "carry[ing] international crisis in their backpacks and in their souls" (NYU Press website commenting on Sirin and Fine's 2008 book, para. 2). They have, as Sirin and Fine (2008) explain, become morally excluded as the other and an enemy in a place they call home (Sirin and Fine 2008). They face, as Abo-Zena et al. (2009) point out,

> qualitatively different identity tasks than do their peers. Feelings of defensiveness and of being under attack or scrutiny because of their religion are widely considered to be part of the fabric of a Muslim youth's life experiences, and thus this psychological dimension and fear of being an outcast is an aspect of their lives within the school context. (Kahf 2006; Beshir 2004; Zine 2001, p. 5)

In 2006, for example the Council on American Islamic Relations (CAIR) shows that 7% of all reported discrimination cases towards Muslims occurred in schools (2006). This do not represent the unreported events of bullying or hostile behavior Muslim American students continuously endure. Reports of bullying (Eslea and Mukhtar 2000) and abuse range from locking students in closets (Marzulli et al. 2007), chasing them and pulling off their hijabs (Vaishanav 2001) to having teachers asking female students to take their hijabs off in the cafeteria in front of other students (Council on American Islamic Relations, CAIR 2007). Faith bullying has even been incorporated by the state and federal governments into general anti-bullying initiatives (Milne 2006). Though many schools have taken precautionary steps to protect students from discrimination after 9/11, Muslim American youth are still victims of violence and discrimination (Haynes 2004 cited in Moore 2009).

The current political, social, and unfortunately the academic contexts, have positioned the students to be seen as a problem. This is not surprising since "The politics and education about Islam, Muslims, Arabs, Turks, Iranians and all that is associated with the West's popular imagination of the monolithic "Middle-East" has long been framed within problematics" (Sensoy and Stonebanks 2009, p. ix). In many cases, it has become inescapable to be considered a problem if you are a member of this culture

> From the Crusades to Gulf War 2, we, as that diverse group of people that represents the West's *Islamic World*, whether "over there" or "right here" and "home grown" are a problem, and perhaps nowhere does this problem discourse play out more intricately than in schools and other non-formal locations of education. (Sensoy and Stonebanks 2009, p. x)

Furthermore, for the students, and Muslim American youth in general, "there have been systemic efforts to locate the crux of their crisis in the "clash of culture" which is perceived to be inherent in their backgrounds as practicing members of the Islamic faith and residents of a democratic and secular United States" (Sensoy and Stonebanks 2009, p. xi). They further show that mainstream schools are still "ignorant… about the lives … experiences… coping strategies" and the "volume of dominant societal messages that Muslim youth must navigate" (Sensoy and Stonebanks 2009, p. xii). And unfortunately, some educators have actively participated, intentionally or unintentionally, in fostering prejudice and racism toward these students. Whether it is by simply asking these students "if they knew anything about the terrorist attacks…made fun of their ….names or looked the other way when other students harassed them" (Wingfield and Karaman 2001, p. 133), according to Jandt (2007), "Communication can play a role in either spreading prejudice and racism or stopping their spread" and that "Just overhearing racist comments has been shown to nega-tively affect the listener's evaluation of the person being spoken about" (pp. 39–41). So when teachers use racial slurs such as, "camel, go back home" and tell Muslim girls in class to take their hijabs off if they can't hear in class (Ahmed 1998), or tell them to take their hijabs off in the cafeteria in front of their classmates (see CAIR 2007) and wave a piece of pork meat in a second grade student's face arguing that it is not going to bite him (Mossalli 2009), teachers are contributing to what is known as "othering." As Jandt (2007) explains, "othering" refers to the "labeling and de-grading of cultures and groups outside of one's own (Riggins 1997)" and are creating two categories that of "us," and "not us" or "them" (p. 42). Such cultural insensitiv-ity and cultural incompetency, as in examples seen above, may not just perpetuate and contribute to creating prejudice and racist hostile learning environment, but have been seen to have other toxic effects on the Muslim American students.

Studies show that students are struggling to find spaces and construct identi-ties. Muslim-American youth "wherever they are on the continuum of secular to orthodox, continue to struggle in negotiating intersecting, and sometimes dissecting, meanings of self-their religion, race, ethnicity, culture, way of life, community and knowledge" (Sensoy and Stonebanks 2009, p. x). To some students "everything is becoming a big blur" (Ahmed 1998, p. 136). Feelings of confusion and disrespect for their culture seem to be affecting their overall sense of themselves and their identity. For example in Ahmed's (1998) study, Rami knows that he is an Arab and a Muslim, has pride in his culture and respects its values and principles, yet he seems to be more inclined to want to identify with the group he hangs around with, mostly white students who are part of the school band, because they get, according to him, "more respect" (Ahmed 1998, p. 151). For Layla, in Sarroub's (2005) study "it was not al-ways clear to her whether she was an American or a Yemeni, and her attitude toward her home and school lives reflected her consternation with both identities" (p. 30).

Whether these youth are, to use Zaal et al. (2007) words, "negotiat[ing] their sense of self," or "fusing their identities," they are "struggling to find balance" which is becoming an even greater challenge "in a highly politicized context marred by intolerance" not only "from outside their communities" but sometimes "from within" (p. 168). The variety of reactions and emotions may result in a state of flux that can have effects not only at the academic and social levels but the psychologi-cal as well, creating individuals who feel as if, as Sarroub (2005) explains, they are living lives as sojourners. Sarroub explains that the struggle they are going through to construct, negotiate, or sustain some kind of identity remains a struggle because they "remain geopolitically, linguistically, religiously, and culturally isolated from American life" (p. 22).

They feel confused and alienated, such as the female Muslim student who is not allowed her elected position because she cannot participate in the school dance (Bayoumi 2009) and the one not able to participate in gym class because she wears a gym suit instead of shorts (Ahmed 1998). This is portrayed in Aisha's question, in Zaal et al. (2007) study, when she asks: "Why is [this country] treating me like an outsider? I'm not…I don't feel [like] an outsider and I shouldn't be treated like one, and neither should any other Muslim who resides here…we, as Americans here, haven't done anything directly to hurt any other Americans, so why are we being treated like this?" (p. 170). Some, like Abbid who are yelled at by their parents and told to ignore insults and not react until physically abused, pretend that he does not care about what others say about his culture, yet he exerts a conscious effort at reading about it so he "can correct any misinformation" his teachers or classmates may make (Ahmed 1998, p. 108). Some are defiant, like Manal, who is holding on to her culture's dress code despite the insults, ridicule, and accusations she has encountered and has a hard time in relating stories which have offended and made her angry to the point that she feels that there is "no reason" to complain because "no one will do anything" (Ahmed 1998, p. 118). Others feel that with the events of 9/11, their identity as Muslim kids has "fossilized" because they, like other youth, have become scapegoats and have become associated with everything that America was angry about (Mourchid 2009). As Mourchid shows, students like those in his study end up distancing themselves from their religious identity and asking their parents to move somewhere else where no one knew they were Muslim. Some begin to bear the burden on their own and take on the responsibility of correcting the distorted image of their culture, as those in Zaal et al. (2007) and feel that "they had to "step up" and dispel myths" (p. 173) and "just show them you are a good person" (p. 175) instead of "worry[ing] their families" they "choose to carry the silence and the burden alone, feeling that they have few trusting supporters to whom they can turn" (p. 173). And though many of these students may be successful at school, as Sensoy and Stonebanks (2009) explain, one needs to ask "at what costs was this success achieved" (p. xii).

The constant struggle, whether of "negotiating," "fusing," "balancing layered identities", and "living within and between identities" or simply developing coping strategies, constantly worrying and living in fear, trigger "social and psychological stresses" that are, as Zaal et al. (2007) conclude, "of concern in a neoliberal society in which the state has relinquished responsibility for the social welfare of its people," where these students have been forced to "pick up the responsibility" (p. 175).

8.5   Finding Solutions

Today both Muslim students and schools seem to have been placed in a predicament. Students have been placed in negative and even hostile learning environments that the education system seems to be contributing to. The school officials who sympathize and may want to accommodate the different needs of these students, especially when it comes to the issues of faith, will face problems because they are violating "First Amendment Violation...Under the establishment clause, administrators may not organize, sponsor, or otherwise entangle themselves in religious activities during the school day," (Accommodating Muslims in Public School: Where to Draw the Line? 2004, para.9). Imam (2009) explains that many of the policies that school administration tends to fall back on to explain to Muslim parents a great deal of what cannot be done, fall under religion and that they observe separation of church and state. Yet, these minorities, as Iman says, are quite involved in the religious activities of other faiths despite the schools' discourse about the separation of church and state.

A great deal of the initiatives that aim at bringing cultures together in education, such as multicultural education, have concentrated on materialistic changes in the school curricula, but not on the teachers and administrators. With the shortcomings of the education system in the USA, it is worth taking the suggestions of those who believe that culturally competent research has a point in saying that these shortcomings in today's education system "are due to cultural incompetence" and that there is "a need to hire, support, develop and promote culturally competent leaders" in school districts and college campuses throughout the nation" (Johnson 2010, p. 2). It may be as Hofstede (2001, cited in Samovar et al. 2012) explains that "intolerance of ambiguity and dogmatism is primarily a function of the uncertainty-avoidance dimension rather than the power-distance dimension" (pp. 288–313) and that learning, understanding, and being able to communicate with other cultures are crucial components in today's multicultural classroom.

Cultural competence is now seriously being considered in many institutions in the USA, such as in the fields of psychology, business administration, nursing, medical education, and the military. In the US military, for instance, the "U.S. Army has instituted the Human Terrain System, which co-locates civilian socio-cultural experts with commanders and staff to prove a source of knowledge on local peoples and their cultures ("Human," 2010)" (Samovar et al. 2012, p. 5). The importance of cultural competence and intercultural communication are bound to grow due to the increased economic and social integration of national populations and ethnicities. The need to understand cultural differences and communicate across cultures has become very important in today's world of global societies, world communities, and homogenized cultures (McDaniel et al. 2012, in Samovar et al. p. 4).

Jandt (2007) says that approaching intercultural communication from the perspective of attempting to learn all of the norms of all cultures would be impossible. He explains that a better approach is to examine the barriers to intercultural communication such as those developed by Barna (1997) which he cites: "anxiety, assuming similarity instead of difference, ethnocentrism, stereotypes and prejudice, nonverbal misinterpretations, and language" (p. 72). These barriers, according to Jandt, result in "a rejection of the richness and knowledge of other cultures… impedes communication and blocks the exchange of ideas and skill among peoples" (2007, p. 72). Chen and Starosta's (1996 cited in Jandt 2007) model of intercultural communication competence includes three perspectives that may produce the required outcomes: the "affective or intercultural sensitivity to acknowledge and respect cultural differences," the "cognitive or intercultural awareness-self-awareness of one's own personal cultural identity and understanding how cultures vary," and the "behavioral or intercultural adroitness—message skill, knowledge of appropriate self-disclosure, behavioral flexibility, interaction management, and social skills" (p. 45).

Introducing such a model of intercultural communication in the educational system, whether in the curriculum or in the teacher preparation programs, for example, may bring about the culturally competent leaders, as suggested by Johnson (2010). Such educators will be able to view students' experiences as "part of an interlocking web of power relations," especially in cases like the ones discussed above, where "some groups of students are often privileged over others" (Giroux 1994, p. 17). As Giroux explains, becoming effective intercultural communicators will lead teachers to critically examine the cultural backgrounds and social formations out of which students produce the categories they use to give meaning to the world. It will lead to teachers being aware that what is presented in the social and cultural levels can become internalized mentally (Vygotsky 1987), and that it is through these messages that individuals begin to internalize ideas about themselves and others (Gudykunst 1994). They will become aware that this knowledge and the social identities produced are formed in a variety of sites "including schools" (Giroux 1994, p. 132). As teachers and administrators, they will learn that, as research shows (Giroux 1994; Cortes 1991; Triandis 1990; Brislin 1990), new identities might be formed while others might be destroyed because of the messages received whether they are about one's sense of worth or where one fits (or does not fit) in the grand scheme of things, especially in the formative stages of the school years. In essence, there is a need for educators who "understand the potentially detrimental and cumulative effects government policies and social practices can have on the lives of young Muslims in the U.S. and in Europe" (Zaal et al. 2007, p. 175).

In the case of Muslim Americans, Moore (2009) suggests that "It is in America's best interests—given the global expansion of Islam, the high birth rates in Muslim countries, the fusion of Islam with political and nationalist causes, and the rapid increase of Muslims in the United States—to educate citizens about this diverse and dynamic religion" (p. 144). Everyone in society, from students to teachers, as Murrell (2007) explains, are all valuable members of this community and we are all responsible for educating ourselves and those that we are sharing with society about our culture. It is only then that we will appreciate not only our cultures but those around us and it is then that our differences will be tolerated. He further explains that the challenge for educators is developing a more reflective and responsive approach to the educational environment created, and to the students whom we share learning spaces with. If we were to consider the messages that these students are getting about their culture, their religion and their sense of self and importance in the school and social settings and the relations that are legitimated and disseminated in these messages, we would need to ask that profound question that Giroux (1987) asks, which he believes that education should enable the student to answer, *What is it this society has made of me that I no longer want to be?*

Conclusion

The cases discussed here are not isolated cases within the US school contexts. There are bound to be innumerable cases that have not been studied. As Moore (2009) explains, "For most of American history, public schools—via school board policies, segregation, community pressures, textbooks, curriculum, and instructional activities—have ignored, distorted, downplayed, or lied about the treatment of many minority and immigrant populations " (p. 144) in the USA.

Muslim American youth have had to add to their baggage the "moral exclusion," of becoming "the other" who had to be watched, detained, and sometimes deported, in order to save "us" (Sirin and Fine 2008, p. 1). The challenges, difficulties, and struggle of finding safe spaces to foster identities, feeling value and worth, and finding a sense of belonging and stability have intensified. They are currently made to inhabit spaces that may be shaping their identities in harmful ways (Giroux 1994). They are no longer just being positioned within forms of knowledge, representations, and images that have a creeping or quiet kind of hegemony about them, as Giroux explains (1994), but are getting loud and clear messages embodied in the wrath of a government and a society that now deems them as the enemy.

There are gaps and shortcomings in the academic system that need to be recognized and examined to prevent a cultural divide that already exists in the larger social context created by politics and the media. What is not needed is a further divide in the classrooms. Teachers are the most important factors that governments and agencies should be focusing on when it comes to building cultural understanding and effective communication between cultures. Teachers not only mold minds, in terms of instilling knowledge into these minds, they play crucial roles in maintaining stereotypes or fostering positive cultural attitudes and perspectives that become part of the students' experiences. These experiences will most likely be internalized and may reflect on how they treat, accept, or reject people of other cultures.

There is a need to acknowledge, as Carter (2005) explains, that "Multiple cultural repertoires do and should exist, and the common cultural repertoire that we share should be continually checked and balanced, revisited, revamped, and revitalized to insure that it is representative of the whole society" (p. 1). This acknowledgement comes in the form of not only curriculum inclusion, but effective culturally competent teachers and academic leaders who matter most. As Carter (2005) rightfully explains, students "require guidance in how to maintain several cultural competencies" and that can only be achieved if we have culturally competent individuals who "simply listen carefully to students as they describe their school experiences" and "figure[e] out how to mend the cracks in our elementary and secondary school systems" (p. 1). "It is these students, as Carter says, who reveal that they experience schools as organized ineffectually and blind to their social, cultural and material realities" and it is these voices that should "direct educators, social scientists, and society's attention to areas that must be addressed in order for them to have academic success" (2005, p. 1).

References

Abo-Zena, M., Sahli, B., & Tobias-Nahi, C. S. (2009). Testing the courage of their convictions. In O. Sensoy & C. D. Stonebanks (Eds.), *Muslim voices in school: Narratives of identity and pluralism* (pp. 3–23). Rotterdam: Sense Publishers.

Abu-Lughod, L. (2006). Writing against culture. In E. Lewin (Ed.), *Feminist anthropology: A reader* (pp. 153–166). MA: Blackwell Publishing Ltd.

Accommodating Muslims in Public School: Where to Draw the Line? (2004). http://www.firstamendmentcenter.org/accommodating-muslims-in-public. Accessed 10 June 2013.

Ahmed, K. (1998). Voices from within the invisible minority: A phenomenological study of school and social experiences of Arab American students. New York: State University of New York University Press. (Doctoral dissertation, see *Dissertation Abstracts International, 59/05,* 1433.).

Alexander, B. K., Anderson, G. L., & Gallegos, B. P. (2005). *Power, pedagogy and the politics of identity.* Mahwah: Lawrence Erlbaum Associates, Inc., Publishers.

Apple, M. W. (1996). *Cultural politics and education.* NY: Teachers College Press.

Applebee, A. (1974). *Tradition and reforming the teaching of English: A history.* Urbana: National Council of Teachers of English.

Banks, J., & Banks, C. (Eds.) (1997). *Multicultural education: Issues and perspectives* (3rd ed.). Boston: Allyn and Bacon.

Banks, J. A. (2006). Cultural diversity and education. *Foundation, curriculum and teaching* (5th ed.). Boston: Allyn & Bacon.

Barna, L. M. (1997). Stumbling blocks in intercultural communication. In L. A. Samovar, & R. E. Porter (Eds.), *Intercultural communication:* A reader (8th ed., pp. 337–346). Belmont, CA: Wadsworth.

Bayoumi, M. (2009). *How does it feel to be a problem: Being young and Arab in America.* New York: Penguin Press.

Bennett, C. I. (2007). *Comprehensive multicultural education: Theory and practice.* Boston: Allyn & Bacon.

Berry, J. W. (1986). Multiculturalism and psychology in plural societies. In L. H. Ekstrand (Ed.), *Ethnic minorities and immigrants in a cross-cultural perspective* (pp. 35–51). Berwyn: Swets North America.

Beshir, S. (2004). Everyday struggles: *The stories of Muslim teens.* Beltsville, MD: Amana Publishing.

Brislin, R. (1990). Applied cross-cultural psychology: An introduction. In R. Brislin (Ed.), *Applied cross- cultural psychology.* Newbury Park: Sage.

Carter, P. L. (2005). *Keepin it real: School success beyond black and white.* Cary: Oxford University Press.

Chen, G. M., & Starosta, W. J. (1996). Intercultural communication competence: A synthesis. In B. R. Burleson (Ed.), *Communcation yearbook 10* (pp. 353–383). Thousand Oaks: Sage.

Cortes, C. (1991). Empowerment through media literacy: A multicultural approach. In C. Sleeter (Ed.), *Empowerment through multicultural education.* Albany: State University of New York Press.

Council on American-Islamic Relations. (2006). *Results that speak for themselves: 2006 annual report.* www.cair.com/Portals/0/pdf/2006_Annual_Report.pdf. Accessed 5 Sept 2013.

Council on American-Islamic Relations CA. (2007, November 21). Rising harassment of minority students in school. http://www.cair.com/ArticleDetails.aspx?ArticleID=23813&&name=&&currPage=1&&Active=1. Accessed 11 June 2013.

Diaz, C. F. (2001). *Multicultural education in the 21st century.* New York: Addison-Wesley Educational Publishers Inc.

El-Amine, R. (2005). The making of the Arab menace. Left turn magazine, 16. Retrieved from http://www.leftturn.org/Articles/Viewer.aspx?id=615&type=M.

Eslea, M., & Mukhtar, K. (2000). Bullying and racism among Asian schoolchildren in Britain. *Educational Research, 42*(2), 207–217.

Ferdman, B. (1990). Literacy and cultural identity. *Harvard Educational Review, 60*(2), 181–204.

Ghazali, A. S. (2008). *Islam & Muslims in the Post 9/11 America. A source book.* Modesto: Eagle Enterprises.

Giroux, H. A. (1987). Critical literacy and student experience: Donald Graves' approach to literacy. *Language Arts, 64,* 175–181.

Giroux, H. A. (1994). *Disturbing pleasures*. Great Britain: Rutledge.

Gordon, R. (Ed.). (2005). *Ethnologue: Languages of the world* (15th edn.). Dallas: SIL International.

Gordon, A., & Browne, K. (1996). *Guiding young children in a diverse society*. Needham Heights: Allyn and Bacon.

Gudykunst, W. (1994). *Bridging differences: Effective intergroup communication*. Thousand Oaks: Sage.

Hanley, M. S. (1999). The scope of multicultural education. http://education.jhu.edu/PD/newhorizons/strategies/topics/multicultural-education/the-scope-of-multicultural-education/.

Haynes, C. (2004). Accommodating Muslims in public schools: Where to draw the line. http://www.firstamendmentcenter.org/accommodating-muslims-in-public-school-where-to-draw-the-line. Accessed 16 June 2013.

Henze, R., Katz, A. Norte, E., Sather, S. E., & Walker, E. (2002). *Leading for diversity*. Thousand Oaks, CA: Corwin Press.

Hofstede, G. (2001). *Culture's consequences: Comparing values, behaviors, institutions and organizations across nations*. Thousand Oaks, CA: Sage.

Imam, S. A. (2009). Separation of what and state: The life experiences of Muslim with Public schools in the Midwest. In O. Sensoy & C. D. Stonebanks (Eds.), *Muslim voices in school: Narratives of identity and pluralism* (pp. 41–54). Rotterdam: Sense Publishers.

Jandt, F. E. (2007). *An introduction to intercultural communication: Identities in a global community* (5th ed.). California: Sage Publications.

Johnson, L. M. (2010). Cultural competence: Laying the foundation for education and leadership. http://www.wtamu.edu/webres/File/Journals/MCJ/Volume5-2/johnson.pdf. Accessed 11 May 2013.

Kahf, M. (2006). *The girl in the tangerine scarf*. New York: Carroll & Graf Publishers.

Kivisto, P. (1989). Overview: Thinking about ethnicity. In P. Kivisto (Ed.), *The ethnic enigma* (pp. 11–25). Cranbury: Associated University Press, Inc.

Leef, G. (2009). *Only leftists can be good teachers*. Retrieved from http://www.popecenter.org/clarion_call/article.html?id=2273.

Levin, J., & McDevitt, J. (2002). *Hate crimes revisited: America's war against those who are different*. Boulder: Westview Press.

Liese, J. (2004). The subtleties of prejudice: How schools unwittingly facilitate Islamophobia and how to remedy this. In B. Van Driel (Ed.), *Confronting Islamophobia in educational practice* (pp. 63–76). UK: Stoke on Trent.

Maira, S. (2004). Youth culture, citizenship and globalization: South Asian Muslim youth in the United States after September 11th. *Comparative Studies of south Asia, Africa and the Middle East, 24*(1), 219–231.

Marzulli, J., Einhorn, E., & Divito, N. (2007 31 July). NY: Arab boy bound & beaten in class, suit Says. *New York Daily News*. http://www.nydailynews.com/news/crime_file/2007/07/31/2007-07-31_arab_boy_bound__beaten_in_class_suit_say.html. Accessed 4 June 2013.

McDaniel, E., Samovar, L., Porter, R. (2012). Using intercultural communication: The building blocks. In Samovar, L., Porter, R., & McDaniel, E. (Eds.), *Intercultural communication: A reader* (13th ed. pp. 4–19). US: Wadsworth Cengage Learning.

Miller, S., & McCaskill, B. (Eds.). (1993). *Multicultural literature and literacies: Making space for differences*. Albany: State University of New York Press.

Milne, J. (2006). Plan to beat faith bullies. *Times Educational Supplement, 1*, 5.

Moore, J. R. (2009). Why religious education matters: The role of Islam in multicultural education. *Multicultural Perspectives, 11*(3), 139–145.

Mossalli, N. N. (2009). The voice of a covered Muslim-American Teen in a southern public school. In O. Sensoy & C. D. Stonebanks (Eds.), *Muslim voices in school: Narratives of identity and pluralism* (pp. 55–70). Rotterdam: Sense Publishers.

Mourchid, Y. (2009). Left to my own devices: Hybrid identity development of religion and sexual orientation among Muslim students in the United States. In O. Sensoy & C. D. Stonebanks (Eds.), *Muslim voices in school: Narratives of identity and pluralism* (pp. 99–116). Rotterdam: Sense Publishers.

Murrell, P. C. Jr. (2007). *Race, culture, and schooling: Identities of achievement in multicultural urban schools*. New York: Routledge.

National Association for Multicultural Education (NAME). (2003). http://www.nameorg.org/resolutions/definition.html. Accessed 16 June 2013.

Nelson, H. L. (2001). *Damaged identities, narrative repair*. New York: Cornell University.

Nguyen, T. (2005). *We are all suspects now: Untold stories from immigrant communities after 9/11*. Boston: Beacon Press.

Nieto, S. (1996). *Affirming diversity: The sociopolitical context of multicultural education*. NY: Longman Publishers USA.

Nieto, S. (2002). *Language, culture, and teaching: Critical perspectives for a new century*. NJ: Lawrence Erlbbaum Associates, Publishers.

Ogbu, J. (1991). Cultural diversity and school experiences. In C. Walsh (Ed.), *Literacy as praxis: Culture, language and pedagogy*. Norwood: Ablex Publishing Corporation.

Riggins, S. H. (Ed.). (1997). *The language and politics of exclusion*. Thousand Oaks, CA: Sage.

Samovar, L. A., Porter, R. E., & McDaniel, E. R. (2012). *Intercultural communication: A reader*. USA: Wadsworth, Cengage Learning.

Sarroub, L. K. (2005). *All American Yemeni girls: Being Muslim in a public school*. Philadelphia: University of Pennsylvania Press.

Seller, M. S. (1992). Historical perspectives on multicultural education: What kind? By whom? For whom? And why? *Social Science Records, 30*, 11–30.

Sensoy, O., & Stonebanks, C. D. (Eds.). (2009). *Muslim voices in school: Narratives of identity and pluralism*. Rotterdam: Sense Publishers.

Sirin, S. R., & Fine, M. (2007). Hyphenated selves: Muslim American youth negotiating identities on the fault lines of global conflict. *Applied Developmental Science, 11*(3), 151–163.

Sirin, S., & Fine, M. (2008). *Muslim American Youth: Understanding Hyphenated Identities through multiple methods*. NY: NYU Press.

Suárez-Orozco, C., & Suárez-Orozco, M. M. (2001). *Children of immigration*. Cambridge, MA: Harvard University Press.

Takaki, R. (1993). *A different mirror: A history of multicultural America*. Canada: Little, Brown and Company Ltd.

Tindongan, C. W. (2011). Negotiating Muslim youth identity in post –9/11 world. *The High School Journal, 95*(1), 72–87.

Triandis, H. C. (1990). Theoretical concepts that are applicable to the analysis of ethnocentricisrn. In R. Brislin (Ed.), *Applied cross-cultural psychology*. Newbury Park: Publishers, Inc.

U.S. Census Bureau. (2008). *An older and more diverse nation by midcentury. U.S. Census Bureau News*. Washington, DC: Author. http://www.census.gov/Press-Release/www/releases/archives/population/012496.html. Accessed 2 April 2010.

Vaishanav, A. (2001, November 12). Somali parents aim to end school violence. Boston Globe.

Vygotsky, L. S. (1978). *Mind in society: The development of higher psychological processes*. Cambridge: Harvard University Press.

Vygotsky, L. S. (1986). *Thought and language*. Cambridge: MIT Press.

Vygotsky, L. S. (1987). Thinking and speech (N. Minick, Trans.). In R. W. Rieber, & A. S. Carton (Eds.), *The collected works of L. S. Vygotsky*. Problems of general Psychology (1), (pp. 39–285). New York: Plenum Press. (Original work published 1934).

Wingfield, M., & Karaman, B. (2001). Arab sterotypes and American Educators. http://www.adc.org/index.php?id=283. Accessed 11 May 2013.

Wright, J. W. (1995). Social distance, discrimination, and political conflict: Arab-ethnics in America. *The Journal of Intergroup Relations 21*(4), 3–11.

Zaal, M., Salah, T., & Fine, M. (2007). The weight of the hyphen: Freedom, fusion and responsibility embodied by young Muslim-American women during a time of surveillance. *Applied Development Science, 11*(3), 164–177.

Zine, J. (2001). Muslim youth in Canadian schools: Education and the politics of religious identity. *Anthropology & Education Quarterly, 32*(4), 399–423.

Chapter 9
Night School in Beirut and the Public Sphere: Student Civic Action Rooted in Liberal Secularism

William DeGenaro

9.1 Introduction

"Night School" (NS) is a literacy initiative organized by undergraduates at a private university in Beirut, Lebanon. Undergraduate volunteers teach basic English to university and university hospital staff members who wish to pass English language exams the university requires of its staff members before they receive promotions. NS language learners consist of janitorial and kitchen staff who devote two evenings per week to 90 min of English as a second language (ESL) instruction. A student organization, Civic Welfare League (CWL), started NS in 1930 (the program has gone through periods of activity and inactivity) and continues to lead the program, recruit undergraduate instructors, provide textbooks and rudimentary training and support, liaise with human resources, and assess the language learners using the Elementary English Test (EET). The number of volunteers and language learners fluctuates each year, but the EET places learners into one of four levels of instruction, Level 1 being the most basic and Level 4 the most advanced, and the CWL prefers to have two teachers present each evening to serve as coteachers.

I studied the program throughout the 2010–2011 academic year, interviewing volunteers and observing instruction. I wanted to arrive at a deep, ethnographic understanding of the classroom dynamics at play. I hoped to find out what motivated this group of undergraduates to lend time to this initiative. I wished to rhetorically analyze their descriptions of the service work and reflect on how their words imagined and represented the civic engagement work they were doing. What ideological, cultural, and/or individual assumptions motivated and informed the work of volunteers and how do those assumptions fit into theoretical models of participation in the public sphere?

W. DeGenaro (✉)
The University of Michigan–Dearborn, Dearborn, MI, USA
e-mail: billdeg@umd.umich.edu

© Springer Science+Business Media Singapore 2015
R. Raddawi (ed.), *Intercultural Communication with Arabs,*
DOI 10.1007/978-981-287-254-8_9

9.2   Background

By getting involved with the NS initiative, volunteers engaged the public sphere. Primarily interested in Western democracies, Habermas (1962) described the public sphere as individuals coming together to deliberate on social matters and involve themselves in public life. Habermas suggested the public sphere mediates between the state (where policy is set) and the private sphere (where we live our work and family lives), fosters intervention into the workings of society, and checks state authority. The public sphere is "the sphere of private people come together as a public" (Habermas 1991, p. 27). When we perform service or debate a social issue with others, we are engaging the public sphere. Giroux (2004) has suggested public spheres—with their opportunities to critique the state and its apparatuses, express dissent, and perform work that promotes social change—shrink as globalization and its forces commercialize "public" spaces, spread capitalism, and ask individuals to focus on private pursuits instead of the common good.

The growth of the Habermasian public sphere was made possible by liberal and technological revolutions and the growth of a middle class with access to information, literacy, and policy makers. Critics of neoliberalism like Giroux worry that the eras of expanding power and prerogative for middle classes have come to an end. By taking time from their private lives preparing for careers, NS volunteers expressed concern for the common good. Many in the West as well as the Arab world believe that higher education has as one of its primary goals educating students for public participation. In cultural contexts where deliberative participation is valued, society looks to universities to foster literacies, values, and skills that promote civil society.

In the Arab world, a vibrant public sphere (defined more broadly, of course, than Habermas's conception of the bourgeois after Western liberal revolutions) flourished earlier, some scholars argue, than in the West. Early Islamic dynasties, for instance, granted "a high degree of autonomy to civil society" (Ismael and Ismael 1997, p. 79); souqs served as marketplaces of ideas as well as goods. Most scholars, though, posit the birth of the Arab public sphere with the introduction of print media at the turn of the nineteenth century, after which an ethos of civic engagement evolved despite colonialism (Ayish 2008). Authoritarian regimes have limited the autonomy and agency of the "public," but an estimated 70,000 civil society organizations (for example, nongovernmental organizations working on human rights) exist in the Arab world (Ismael and Ismael 1997, p. 85). Somewhat pessimistically and monolithically, some critics in the years prior to the Arab Spring suggested the Middle Eastern public sphere was weak due to "state authoritarianism, global imperialism, and narrow-minded fundamentalism" (Ayish 2008, p. 29). Others, though, see a great deal of potential for vibrant deliberative action, for instance, in a context like Lebanon where religious and political diversity signifies potential for pluralistic dialogue and collective action (Khalaf 2006).

To understand the role that universities play in fostering civic engagement, scholars have developed taxonomies for public-sphere engagement among college students who may be doing volunteer work through student life offices, advocacy work through student organizations, and service learning in their classes. Morton (1995) proposes three overlapping paradigms—charity, project, and social change—and suggests each can be effective if "grounded in deeply held, internally coherent values; match means and ends; describe a primary way of interpreting and relating to the world; offer a way of defining problems and solutions; and suggest a vision of what a transformed world might look like" (p. 28). Charity involves face-to-face service; project models develop plans for solving community problems; social change paradigms critique problems and fights for radical policy change.

Others have suggested "charity" leaves undergraduates feeling rewarded but rarely benefits the common good. An activist or advocacy orientation, some scholars argue, is more effective for challenging assumptions and making structural changes in society (Bickford and Reynolds 2002; Coogan 2006; Herzberg 1997; Weisser 2002). According to these scholars, service learning—wherein undergraduates do public-sphere work as part of an academic course—in particular have an obligation to address root causes of community problems (Herzberg 1997), attend to material conditions and the materiality of place (Coogan 2005; Coogan 2006; Marback 2003; Mutnick 2007; Weisser 2002), pay attention to the politics of difference (Green 2003; Himley 2004; Reynolds 2004; Welch 2002), and contextualize critically any direct service that students perform (Bickford and Reynolds 2002; Hesford 2005; Herzberg 1997). This movement toward activism has sometimes resulted in a gulf between student ideologies (which often favor the ethic of charity, according to much of the literature) and advocacy-inclined faculty ideologies (Bickford and Reynolds 2002; DeGenaro 2010; Reynolds 2004).

A group of undergraduates in the USA composed a fascinating statement on civic engagement, "The New Student Politics," arguing that even the volunteer model often critiqued by scholars represents a political orientation and provides opportunities for contextual understanding of the public sphere (Long 2002, p. 18). The statement suggested the scholarship sometimes overlooks student motives such as religious convictions (rarely written about among scholars in the West). Looking at what motivates students in 13 nations to volunteer, Gronlund et al. (2011) found that structural factors and culturally specific values play an important role; for example, cultures that place the highest value on individualism (particularly liberal democracies) are more likely to volunteer as a resumé filler.

A healthy public sphere differs depending on cultural context. Most Western critics value secularism, situating activism in a realm separate from religious beliefs, which are framed as personal and private (cf. the mythic quality of the US Constitutional principle of "the separation of church and state"). In much of the Arab world, this distinction does not exist, certainly in states where Islam is the official religion, but also in Lebanon where ethno-religious affiliation is a fundamental identity marker. From an intercultural communication perspective, an anecdote may be instructive. A colleague from the USA was visiting me in Lebanon. A Lebanese friend privately asked me the religion of my US colleague and was shocked that I did not know. "I thought you knew her well," my Lebanese friend commented. "The subject rarely comes up," I responded. "How could it not come up?"

Still, the distinction is not that simple and we should avoid rushing to contrast. Habermas (2006) has emphasized "the political awakening of an ongoing strong religious consciousness in the United States" (p. 2), citing the growing power of the religious right as evidence that US conceptions of civic virtue are in flux when it comes to God. Indeed, Costrange (2012) sees religion's role in the public sphere increasing *globally,* singling out the USA and Lebanon as prominent venues where political discourse and civic action are *both* informed by religion and religious rhetoric. The fear is that neoliberalism decreases civic participation and that in the Arab world, sectarianism represents an acute threat to open deliberation. Ofeish (1999) argues that sectarianism remains the status quo in a context like Lebanon by allowing elite policy makers to "control" the masses, keeping them competing for resources, professing loyalty to partisan leaders, and taking for granted that those same leaders of the same sect must be working in their interests. Costrange (2012) is more optimistic, laying out a theoretical framework for an ecumenical, religiously pluralistic public sphere, echoing Khalaf (2006) but with an emphasis on the potential of religion as a civic virtue. Similarly, Kandil (2004) surveys a range of service projects in the Arab world and finds a promising diversity of university-sponsored, community-based programs.

This optimism about a vibrant Arab public sphere where plural and tolerant conceptions of faith—and the creative vision of the crafters of the "New Student Politics" statement in the USA with its inclusive conception of civic engagement— suggest that higher education in both the West and the Middle East might ultimately contribute to virtuous civic spheres by providing opportunities for engagement where diverse beliefs and ideologies mingle. NS represents such an opportunity.

9.3 Methodology

In order to gain a deep, descriptive understanding of how one group of undergraduates in Lebanon understands the public sphere and articulates cultural, ideological, and personal motivations for engagement therein, I obtained Institutional Review Board permission to study NS for 1 year. I relied on ethnographic, participant-observer methodology as well as interviews with volunteers. During NS sessions, I sat in the back of the classroom and took notes using a double-voiced system, wherein one column was objective observations and the other column included commentary, critical thoughts, and even the beginnings of connections among disparate ideas. Most weeks I attended four evenings per week; each session was 90 min long, resulting in about 6 weekly hours of observation during the year. I interviewed all 17 volunteers at the beginning and end of the year, and had less structured discussions in between, maintaining open-ended field notes of both formal interviews and informal conversation.

I consider my methodology "rhetorical" for several reasons. Cushman (1996) defines the role of a rhetorical researcher as "an agent of social change" (p. 7), a scholar using disciplinary knowledge for ethical ends. We study the circulation of language and take on action-oriented projects in order to intervene. Studying NS, I wanted to understand, of course, but I also wanted to serve. For example, as the academic year moved forward, I became more and more of a participant. My participation at first was minimal but the teachers began to ask me to participate with the language learners as conversation partners. Sometimes, they would ask me a question asking for clarification on a matter of language (often a punctuation rule or a spelling). Later, the teachers' (and sometimes the language learners') questions became more involved, encompassing questions about US culture and trivia and even dialectical differences. Like any ethnographer, I was a participant observer, but I considered moments of participation to be *interventions,* sharing what I knew (about English, the USA, teaching methods) for a positive end (more effective instruction, language acquisition, and, ultimately, social mobility for the language learners). Likewise, in my interviews and conversations with the undergraduate volunteers, I saw myself rhetorically intervening, listening to their stories and histories but also interjecting with thoughts, advice, and perspective, when requested and/or appropriate. I say this not to suggest I am somehow inherently wiser. On the contrary, echoing Cushman's methodological framework, I saw my relationship with my informants to be "reciprocal" (Cushman 1996, pp. 16–17); they provided me a deeper understanding (not to mention data that lead to published scholarship and my own material advancement), and I provided them with support to be more effective in the classroom and more reflective as they thought about their own work. We had a two-way relationship.

Further, the project was an ethnography of literacy, in at least two senses of "literacy." The first is literacy as proficiency in understanding and manipulating symbol systems, most notably language. Since the early 1980s, ethnography has dominated empirical studies of literacy due to the ethnographic gaze's unique ability to facilitate descriptions of language use in real social contexts. Influential studies by Heath (1983), Scribner and Cole (1981), Szwed (1981), and Street (1984) influenced methodological trends within burgeoning disciplines like new literacy studies in the UK (Baynham 2004) and composition studies in the USA (Cushman et al. 2001). These foundational studies taught us that reading, writing, and language acquisition are social practices, and foregrounded the ethnographic method as uniquely capable of a higher level of detail and a focus on "the local, situated nature of literacy" (Baynham 2004, p. 289), what Street calls "the contextualizing features" (2004, p. 329). The other sense of the word literacy is the notion of civic literacy, as defined by Lazere (2005), echoing Habermas, as the proficiencies in reading, writing, and critical thinking most useful for participation in *public*. Methodologically, I wanted to engage with the language learners and, most especially, the undergraduate language teachers in order to observe, participate, and intervene in a venue where basic and civic literacy intersected.

9.4   Participant Testimonials

Of the 17 volunteers, 15 were Arabs, and 2 were Westerners. Some Muslim and some Christian, they represented a wide variety of majors including engineering, agriculture, biology, education, and political science. Many were involved with the sponsoring student organization. All informants professed an abiding, optimistic belief in the potential of community service to transform the public sphere. They possessed distinct ideas about Lebanese society and the on-campus climate and frequently saw their own involvement with NS as a corrective to disturbing trends. Their own experiences with civic engagement were diverse and ambitious. This section outlines four themes that emerged during interviews, conversations, and NS sessions: past experience in public-sphere work, critical attitude toward university culture, nostalgia for nationalism, and antisectarianism.

Past Civic Engagement Work

The undergraduates brought extensive past experience in the public sphere. The sheer amount of such experience underscores the imperative for universities to respect and honor undergraduates and not paternalistically assume they are "introducing" students to activism or community service. One informant had spent a year doing environmental organizing and education and teaching environmental science to children. One had done sustained volunteer work building homes with Habitat for Humanity in Costa Rica. One worked at a home for the disabled in Kuwait. One had assisted at a library, one at a children's cancer center, and another at a camp for the children of divorced or widowed expatriate domestic workers. Many had spent several weeks living in refugee camps within Lebanon performing services including caring for recently orphaned children, providing day care, and tutoring school children. These experiences often occurred during high school breaks via trips organized by the schools themselves; many reported that their high schools mandated a certain number of hours of volunteer services and that such trips were ways to fulfill the service requirement.

Many were doing other projects concurrently with NS. These included tree planting, organizing a local literary and arts organization, clothing drives, women in engineering mentoring program, and tutoring programs both in public schools and on refugee camps. When speaking about these experiences (especially refugee relief work), the informants were often animated and lively. Hands-on contact seems to have had a profound impact, affectively speaking, and that affective dimension was palpable based on their enthusiasm. Also, their word choices revealed this level of enthusiasm and even hyperbole (one used the word "exhilarating") when speaking about these experiences. One called service "A way for me to … justify my existence." Another, speaking of community engagement, said, "I feel like a human." In addition to enthusiasm, they also were interested in engaging about the esoteric, abstract *idea* of community-based work; they were comfortable getting "meta."

One informant brought me coffee when we met in my office and said she liked talking about these matters. Another used analytic, nearly jargon-heavy discourse when describing community-based work; she referred specifically to the benefits of service work that foreground the "assets" not the "deficits" of those served. Still another abstracted the notion of identity during her discussion of service work: "[The] process of building identity is not an individual process. It's a community, collective process." Frequently, our discussions began with passionate discourse about volunteerism, but evolved into abstract insights about identity and justice, suggestive of hands-on work's potential to lead to something more—even if that something more is discursive discovery.

Critiques of University Culture

Participants were critical toward campus culture and the institution itself. One informant commented, "Boys driving Ferraris aren't doing service work, that's for sure," suggesting impatience with materialism among the student body. Though her comments may contain a problematic assumption, they show an awareness of privilege and class. "You're not really a part of the community until you get to know more people here…[including] those who make the University work." The undergraduates saw a problem with the sharp division between students and workers. Another recounted a conversation with a friend in the dorms who, upon hearing about NS, asked her, "Why would you want to work with workers?" Several informants complained that university administration focuses too much on the promotion of social activities like dances and parties; one informant, familiar with the functioning of student programming on campus, said such activities received approval and funding with greater expedience than activities rooted in advocacy, service, or social change.

Almost invariably, the informants voiced support for the university instituting a mandatory service program, which they suggested would serve as a corrective to privilege, apathy, Westernization, and even sectarianism. One informant was especially vocal about the university needing to play more of a role in critiquing and working to change social structures in Lebanon. He argued that pushing students toward club culture instead of the public sphere replicates the social structure. "Students are making the effort, not the University," he commented. Lebanon, he continued, "has humanitarian needs" that we should assess and try to meet. His critique of campus life brings to mind Ofeish's argument (1999) that maintaining the status quo in the Arab world benefits the elites and harms the health of the civic sphere. Even civic activities on campus, this same informant argued, are designed for a like-minded audience of students; in rhetorical terms, his critique suggests that his perception of public sphere activities on campus is that they are *ceremonial,* not *deliberative,* meaning there is little dialogue across difference, little mingling of perspectives. Not coincidentally, he went on to say that although there should be "tension" and "debate," the goal could be dialogue, not just multiple sides retreating into their own entrenched positions. This informant essentially recites the tenets of a healthy public sphere: robust and civil debate, forums for airing multiple perspectives, engagement across difference. Rhetorically, his view is Burkean, suggesting that purposeful discourse establishes humane connection and identification among language users (Burke 1969).

The discourse students used suggested they reject individualism and exclusive focus on one's studies—especially the notion that one's studies are only meant to benefit the individual: "I didn't join anything in my first year. I just wanted to study. But second year I changed my mind. I needed to feel like I had an impression on others." Another: "Before NS, I was much of a confined individual. My life could be summarized in one work 'academy.' All I did was … study. NS made me realize how wrong that was." Another: "At the end of NS days I feel like I did something important. On other days, not so much." Yet another: "I have a problem with school. It's self-centered."

Nationalism and Nostalgia

A third theme was a nostalgic longing for the Beirut of the 1960s. One volunteer summed up this sentiment by saying, "Priority has shifted from activism to getting high grades." Beirut universities in the 1960s were hotbeds of student organization against sectarianism (Ofeish 1999, p. 102). Several voiced a consciousness of this history of higher education in the Lebanese capital being a site for youth movements. They expressed a desire to create an alternative university culture more like the past, whether mythic and imagined, real, or somewhere in between. They wished the university could advance an *Arab* nationalism and promote *Arab* identity. When talking about the kind of society they wished for, many alluded to the prominence and visibility of Western logos and fast food chains. One informant even contrasted the image of Western restaurants near campus with the image of bookstores, which he learned from his father (a shopkeeper) were more common during the elder's tenure at the university. He complained that the neighborhood had fewer cinemas and bookstores than restaurants and nightclubs, unlike the mythic old days.

Another informant also invoked *her* father, explaining that she was majoring in art history because she had been influenced by her dad to care about Arab nationalism and wanted someday to work in cultural preservation of Middle Eastern artifacts. She said she convinced her father to give his blessing for her art history major (he had encouraged her to go into medicine) by appealing to his sense of regret that so many artistic treasures in the region had been lost or looted. Her professional objectives are rooted in civic commitment. The informants sometimes expressed nostalgic discourse regarding the curriculum as well, one calling for "less rote education," like it was before, "more choice, more history, more humanities."

Was the 1960s a critical time for Arab nationalism, youth culture, and social movements in the Arab world including at universities? Yes, just as the same can be said about US universities in the 1960s being sites for organizing peace and civil rights movements. Still, disgust with apathy is likely a part of each generation's experience of higher education. Interculturally, the rhetoric my informants used to talk about the past—the tendency to invoke "the good old days"—is remarkably similar to rhetoric among Western university students. It is a rhetoric of nostalgia, a representation of a perceived, not always factual, past.

Antisectarianism

A fourth theme was a belief that NS signified a small way of supporting national unity, a resistance to sectarianism (a fundamental part of Lebanese society by virtue of its confessional, or sect-sharing, system of government, wherein parliamentary representation is based on one's confession—the major three being Maronite Christianity, Sunni Islam, and Shi'a Islam), and an alternative to what they perceived to be the dominance of sect-specific political organizations on campus. Political parties are nearly always affiliated with a specific ethnoreligious group and those parties have significant power on college campuses. One woman who volunteered with NS even ran for student government as an independent during the academic year; doing so is somewhat rare at this university, where most student organizations and most students running for office have the backing of a party. My informants criticized the dominance of sectarianism in the Lebanese public sphere; it became clear to me that NS was providing a particular group of undergraduates a refuge from what they saw as Lebanese dominant culture. Their language (despite a sense of optimism) belied a resigned sense that eventually they would take their places as members of mainstream society but for a brief period they could resist by affiliating with an organization that is "independent" and "alternative." In this way, membership in the CWL fit into many informants' professed ideological leanings; many, for example, mentioned to me their support of secular reforms like instituting civil marriage in Lebanon. One identified herself as a feminist and atheist.

NS provided a space for rejecting norms and values. The same student running for office without partisan affiliation commented, "I [usually] don't get into student clubs because I know how things work in this country." Her campaign for office was viable and, she said, as the election approached she began to feel pressure from a political party to affiliate. She maintained her independent status and, for now anyway, her strong sense of antisectarianism. Others echoed this view, albeit in less explicit terms, calling for the university to be more inclusive and for clubs within the university to do more cosponsoring of events, events that might foster "skepticism" and critical thinking across difference. There is a "strong culture" of helping and giving one's time, one informant commented, "but students are often only involved if it's helping their own. You don't just want [the University] to be a microcosm of Lebanese society … People need to be more comfortable with each other."

The campus boasts approximately 50 student organizations, well over half of which have some type of civic engagement focus, meaning the emphasis is on the public sphere. Examples include the Red Cross, Freedom Club, Palestinian Cultural Club (a group that also organized ambitious community-based literacy work with high school students from a nearby refugee camp), and the Cultural Club of the South. A few of these organizations have explicitly secular identities or missions but most have partisan affiliation. Even many of the clubs without overtly *political* sponsorship have a connection to a particular sect, a connection sometimes implicit in the name of the organization ("the South," for example, often implies a particular affiliation, so including that phrase in the name of the organization signals who the organization represents). One volunteer told me that due to this climate, "There's no identity, no nationalist identity." Organizations should be working toward "Lebanese goals" instead of bringing in "their own" speakers, he said, placing stress on the words "their own."

One undergraduate reported that when she began tutoring Palestinians she felt more effectual: "Finally something other than protesting at the Israeli border, which I feel is not going to accomplish anything." Her rhetoric suggested that she desires to work outside the world of political agitation. This could stem from volunteerism's affective resonance, but she also was skeptical of sectarianism and her statement about protest suggests a desire to move beyond the status quo. One informant admitted that rallies are "kind of fun" but ultimately ineffective. He desired a new civic politics rooted in hand-on work and cooperation across difference.

9.5   Classroom Observations

In addition to interviews with NS volunteers, ethnographic observation of instruction was also used to understand informants' civic literacy. Seventeen undergraduates volunteered during the 2010–2011 academic year, allowing the CWL to have two or three coteachers present at each session. Each level met two evenings per week, but each undergraduate only needed to teach one night per week (aside from the first night when all teachers show up for introductions and aside from Level 4 which decided that they would all attend all classes).

Level 1	Monday/Wednesday 5:00–6:30	Two volunteer coteachers on Monday	The other two on Wednesday
Level 2	Tuesday/Thursday 5:00–6:30	Two volunteer coteachers on Tuesday	The other two on Thursday
Level 3	Monday/Wednesday 5:00–6:30	Two volunteer coteachers on Monday	The other two on Wednesday
Level 4	Tuesday/Thursday 5:00–6:30	Three volunteer coteachers on Tuesday	The other two on Thursday

During ethnographic observations, four particularly noteworthy themes emerged: the advantages of the impromptu ethos of the program, the frustrations that volunteers sometimes experienced, the formation of a socially bonded community of teachers, and the complex relationships between the undergraduates and the language learners.

An Impromptu, "Do-It-Yourself" Ethos

The lack of formal training and the impromptu ethos of the program was a source of ambivalence. One informant told me he regrets that there is "no structure to the curriculum—we made it up as we went along." Another articulated to me the obvious reality that the volunteers have "little training in ESL instruction." This inexperience often made the undergraduates stick very close to the textbook. They were slow to incorporate technology and audiovisual materials, though I often encouraged them to take advantage of the screens, projectors, and instructor computer station in the classrooms. They felt the most legitimate classes were the classes where they were delivering information from the front of the room, perhaps a reflection of the dominance of rote learning in the Lebanese education system.

The language learners agreed; for example, the learners were especially resistant to writing on each other's papers during group work or even filling in each other's scavenger hunt sheets during a creative language game. During the scavenger hunt, they were supposed to find someone in the room who had seen a particular movie or who had eaten a particular type of food for lunch and have those individuals fill in blank squares on their pages. Some refused to take part; others wrote in Arabic instead of English. I thought this game was going to be a success. A Level 1 instructor, an education major, made the comment, "The Mideast system encourages passive learning—tests, copying off the board, memorizing." Especially early in the academic year, the methods the volunteers used were often consistent with passive learning. And of course a closely related challenge was the lack of resources they had. Still, it was the do-it-yourself, *make-it-up-as-we-go* ethos that served to bond the volunteers together.

That bond eventually facilitated greater experimentation. The most enthusiastic, dynamic sessions were often those in which the undergraduates made use of innovative pedagogies. The only education major among the volunteers was adept at coming up with unique ideas like a Picture of the Day freewriting session and other holistic methods. She was comfortable teaching without following the flawed textbook and got the learners writing and talking with relative ease. Another creative volunteer, working in Level 4, brought in several English-language pop songs (e.g., "Ironic," by Alanis Morissette) and asked the class to listen to the lyrics, write down familiar vocabulary words, and even write in response to the lyrics. The volunteer teachers grew enthusiastic and more dynamic when the language learners were talking, laughing, and engaged with activities. After an animated class, one informant commented, "multiple languages expose you to other points of view—magazines, books, news…." Getting the classes writing and bringing in materials like pop music immersed the learners in language, but also culture, and the undergraduates were aware of both.

Learning language and learning culture (including intercultural communication skills, language/culture misunderstandings, and the dynamics of cultural differences) overlap, especially in a multilingual setting like the NS classroom. On one occasion, one instructor started class with an informal question, "Anybody have any dreams over the weekend?" The language learners thought he meant any aspirations. Another evening, a sample Test of English as a Foreign Language (TOEFL) test sample from evolutionary biology made a statement that people are animals, which prompted condemnations from many language learners in the class. On the evening of Halloween, the Hangman word was "costume," leading to a discussion about the word's meaning in which language learners and volunteers talked about whether the word can mean "uniform" depending on context (there was much disagreement about this matter).

Despite the inexperience and lack of formal training, the volunteers showed a great deal of ingenuity. Level 2 established an especially nice interplay among coteachers in which one was always at the board and one was always circulating, helping language learners with whatever exercise they were working on. Level 4 frequently started class with a spirited game of Hangman (the first night's words were "Fairuz," the iconic singer, and "rainbow"). Level 1 created a word wall containing new words the learners could use during exercises and writings; the word wall facilitated freewriting, for instance, during one session when learners were asked to write "I am..." sentences using an adjective-only word wall for help. On another occasion, the word wall was all nouns and learners wrote "I wish for..." sentences. Several levels had language learners correct homework in small groups and circulated among groups to help with the process. Several had language learners practice giving visitors to the hospital directions ("Where is the cafeteria?", etc.), which was practical and rooted in the learners' authentic contexts.

Level 4 had more opportunities for creativity and sometimes had especially interesting freewriting prompts (e.g., If you could go anywhere in the world during any period of history, where and when would you go?). This led to one of the most interactive, dynamic classes of my year of observation, as the language learners/writers became engaged with their thinking and with their language use. Several wrote compellingly about going back to visit deceased parents, for instance.

A Community of Volunteers

In these evening sessions, NS volunteers formed a strong community. They thrived and found the most success when they took advantage of the collaborative design of NS instruction (the fact that multiple instructors were present at sessions). They had expressed in some cases a critical attitude toward the outward signs of Westernization in Beirut and even on campus and, pedagogically, they rejected a kind of Western atomized individualism. They frequently seemed to be "teaching together," or "teaching communally." I think this communal attitude translated into classroom success in multiple ways; for instance, volunteers used humor with one another as they gave their lessons. They never got flustered when power would go out (somewhat regularly in Beirut). And they frequently mentioned these things to me in our discussions before and after class: satisfaction and relief that their coteachers were also present, the creativity encouraged by drawing on different strengths (e.g., having one native speaker of English and one native speaker of Arabic both in front of the room). There was a kind of collectivist pedagogy that emerged, one rooted in the social and collaborative nature of the volunteer work (some informants even praised NS as a way to help them get involved in social life on campus). Teaching was a "social" event.

Already there was a communal vibe on the first evening of instruction. In Level 1, the four instructors, all women, illustrate the diversity of NS staff: one in full abaya, one in high Western fashion, and two (one of whom is a Westerner) in casual wear including jeans and summery blouses. Four language learners—this number fluctuated throughout the year, often on a night-to-night basis—are present, dressed in work uniforms. All eight individuals introduce themselves. Whenever a language learner needs help with a word, one of the instructors, an education major, writes the word on the board in both English and Arabic and pronounces it several times. The instructors have created a makeshift alphabet on taped-together sheets of computer papers. The tape fails several times during the session, but the sign shows ingenuity and is the basis for the night's activity: recitation of the alphabet, first together, then individually. This takes up the bulk of class time as teachers interject with corrections of pronunciation. Electricity goes out several times but everyone keeps doing what they were doing. Some struggle with recognizing lower-case letters, but all do fairly well. The atmosphere is familial and light, the instructors appearing perfectly comfortable asking each other questions and asking each other to perform particular tasks. This is only one interaction among the students but it is suggestive of the potential for civic activities to bring together diverse constituents. Lebanese society can be segmented and the diversity of Level 1, comprised of both Muslims and Christians, creates a setting for members of multiple ethno-religious sects to work together for a common cause.

I also visit Level 4 on the first evening of instruction. Five Level 1 instructors are present: three young women in casual but fashionable attire, another woman in what might be described as "English major chic," and a young man from the West in a hipster, thrift shop getup. Twenty-three language learners show up (that number would fluctuate wildly, though Level 4 was consistently the largest class), some in hospital uniforms and others in jeans and, at least two, in leather jackets. Most are men. The language learners group together by department: kitchen, physical plant, housekeeping, etc. The teachers introduce themselves and talk a little about NS, emphasizing sentiments such as "it's your time," and reiterating that they can direct class in whatever ways the learners will find most useful. They are greeted with a cacophony of suggestions; it seems that half the class wants to meet for 3 h one night a week instead of 90 min twice per week. The teachers table this conversation and ask the language learners to write one or two paragraphs about their expectations for the course. I give paper and pen to four different individuals. Most finish this assignment in about 10 min. The teachers explain they will read the essays and start in earnest on Thursday night. I watch the stragglers finish their essays. Through the classroom window, I see one of the first to finish waiting for his friends; he is not much older than the undergraduates who are teaching the class and is enjoying a cigarette, tapping one of his workboots impatiently on the ground. Once all are finished, the teachers quickly read the writing samples and use them as diagnostic tools. As they are reading, the electricity goes out and they all get out cell phones to use as flashlights, not missing a beat. They decide they will all come to class on both Tuesday and Thursday and each will be in charge of a small group (about 4–5) of learners. They use the diagnostic writings to make sure that each small group has a range of skill levels.

Even on the first night, the instructors draw on each other's strengths, communicating with one another, and cooperating to accomplish a task—essential skills and activities of any civic activity. As they communicate, organize, and plan, they rely on intercultural communication skills in that they are communicating with individuals of different backgrounds, governed—quite visibly—by different norms (for example, the co-teachers wearing varieties of clothing, Islamic and otherwise). The volunteers would likely go home in the evening and be with a more homogeneous collective (i.e., their families), but during hours in the "public sphere," they are interacting with a more diverse, heterogeneous community—a community of volunteers who come from multiple backgrounds.

Complex Relationship with Language Learners

If they formed a community with their fellow undergraduate volunteers, their connection to the language learners was more complicated. They sometimes used overly familiar tropes when characterizing language learners: "The students taught me more than I taught them," for instance, and "Wonderful and devoted students made me love teaching and even consider applying for a PhD program." They expressed positive regard toward their "students," but sometimes characterized them in overly idealized (e.g., *wonderful*) ways. Their representation of the language learners was at times sentimental in its tone. What often emerged in the NS sessions was the coming together of individuals from different classes, the undergraduates being from more elite socioeconomic backgrounds and the language learners from the working class; perhaps the social class disparity explains the undergraduates falling back on clichés—the only vocabulary they had, perhaps, for describing experiences divorced from their own. Some made comments like "they study a lot given that they work long hours" *and* "they work really hard because they've been deprived," suggesting a burgeoning awareness of this social class divide. Another informant finds the learners receptive to lessons "despite their social standing." Another expressed her desire to move faster and assign more homework "but we don't know what their home life is like." The volunteers sometimes seemed to desire greater understanding of the material realities of the language learners; one stated, "I give the lesson and that's it. Not much of an emotional bond." In his influential critique of undergraduate service learning programs, Herzberg (1997) suggested that hands-on work and volunteerism too often neglect root causes and yet NS, though a "volunteer" initiative, at the very least prompted reflection about complex matters like social class in Beirut society. Perhaps the students are not engaged in activist modes of civic engagement, but the experiences seem to be building a consciousness.

Many informants had talked to me about the role that English plays in material success and in the establishment of cultural capital in Lebanese society. The interaction in the classroom *with the language learners themselves* proved to be valuable social interaction as well. Students had the opportunity to interact with diverse people—specifically, individuals from very different social classes than their own. The language learners, in contrast with the undergraduate volunteers, were largely working class, of which their lack of English language fluency was a marker. Of course Beirut is multilingual, the ubiquity of Arabic, English, and French reflecting Lebanon's cosmopolitan and colonial history. After the fall of the Ottoman Empire in the early twentieth century, French was the dominant "second language," particularly during the decades of French mandate. More recently, English has achieved cultural hegemony (as a lingua franca of science, business, and popular culture) and surpassed French as the nation's "second language." The language learners in the NS program had largely attended public schools—as opposed to private European or international academies— in the decades before English became such a dominant second language and hence lacked fluency.

One thing that provoked more than a little discomfort for the NS instructors was how to negotiate authority. Invariably, they saw the role of the "teacher" as being an authority, so they felt regretful about having to tell the language learners (their elders) what to do. They would regularly ask me questions about how to assign homework and correct the pronunciation of their elders. This made issues of discourse and power explicit as they taught their classes, felt these feelings, and discussed the issue with me. They were gaining a more conscious, deliberate understanding of difference, language, and why/how we talk to each other. "Unlike the kids at the refugee camp, you can't yell at them or offer simple rewards. It's an adult relationship, with respect, mutual respect," one of the informants expressed to me. Another said it was "kind of awkward" to be called Miss since "I could be their granddaughter." Still another: "It feels weird to call them by name because they are older. Sometimes, yanni, they interrupt each other and you want to yell but you can't." She later told me, "In the Arab world, usually you call older men by titles, so it takes getting used to calling them by name." Levels 1 and 2 both had standoffs of sorts between "teachers" and "students" in which the volunteers had become frustrated due to learners not completing homework assignments. In Level 2, the volunteer maintained a smile and kept the tone more collegial and friendly. In Level 1, the volunteer did not and the atmosphere was more awkward. In both cases, the stalemate involved the volunteer making the point that homework must be completed and the learner making the point that sometimes there simply is not enough time before or after work to complete the work. These exchanges further reinforced the conscious level of awareness of materiality of difference and culture

Much like their discourse about volunteer work writ large, which would begin at the affective-emotional level and evolve into abstract, meta-awareness of deeper insights, their discourse about their relationship to language learners also moved along a similar trajectory. One informant commented, "Just because someone is working a blue-collar job doesn't mean they should be under-privileged." Another: "Everyone has the right to good education [though] they come from lower socio-economic status." Many of the critiques of volunteerism situate hands-on work in a different realm than activist work, but the discourse of my informants suggested that volunteer service can be motivated by justice and can *lead to* insights regarding social justice. Here, too, I see the undergraduates implicitly challenging the Western critics who too readily dismiss the potential of hands-on work to promote social change. Significantly, it is students themselves who are embodying the link between "mere volunteer work" (allegedly a feel-good activity) and a deeper understanding of issues and a commitment to advocacy and activism. The Western service-learning students who created the Wingspread Statement wrote, "Those who develop connections to larger systemic issues building on their roots in community service adopt a framework through which service politics leads to greater social change" (Long 2002, p. 18).

Conclusion

NS, though no panacea, offers a strong corrective to the problematic scenario described by critics like Ayish (2008) who suggest a weakness in the Arab public sphere. The NS effort embodies a "do-it-yourself" ethos, without official sanction. The problem, of course, is that this also means a lack of resources. The NS program created a kind of "public space" on the university's campus, a public space where individuals of different religions and social classes interacted. The undergraduates built this space with little material support from the university and, indeed, operated under an ideological position that in some ways went against the dominant (i.e., sectarian) model. Khalaf (2006) has crafted an especially compelling historical and cultural study of the Bourj, Beirut's central public square (the area of Beirut's city center that houses both Martyr's Square and the memorial to assassinated Prime Minister Hariri). Khalaf sees the site as multivalent but ultimately finds much cause for optimism in the square's use as a public place of organizing, particularly in the weeks following Hariri's assassination in 2005. For Khalaf, the Bourj represents Lebanon's diversity, its potential for "collective mobilization" (p. 15), its "emergent composite identity" (p. 244). The NS program, a small, little discussed (even on campus) operation, obviously lacks the visibility of the Bourj but, similarly, the program illustrates the cosmopolitan potential of civic action. If NS was a "public space," it was also a *playful* public space. Informants were able to play and imagine something different for themselves and for their society.

The CWL embraced—at least during the 2010–2011 academic year—the secularist ideology that many young, liberal Lebanese espouse. The ideology is somewhat countercultural in that Lebanese society is heavily invested in sectarianism by virtue of its confessional system and the influence of sectarian politics is even felt at the level of higher education, where student organizations enjoy sponsorship from political parties. The CWL's mission statement articulates this support of secularism explicitly: "[T]hrough certain activities ranging from lectures to fun events, we look forward to promoting our idea of a civil society by endorsing secularist concepts such as civil marriage and non-sectarian interaction within society." The rhetoric is assertive, explicit, and proactive, sounding almost as if the mission is addressing the society write large. In short, it sounds like a manifesto. If the club's mission statement is its manifesto, then its NS operation puts the manifesto into action.

This theory-informed action does indeed reject particular institutional and dominant cultural ideas. As stated previously, the sectarian identity of student organization on campus can be quite intense, which further illustrates the CWL's proverbial *against-the-grain* ethos. For example, on student government election day, the university increases security and restricts visitors due to large campus rallies sponsored by national (and beyond) political parties who are endorsing particular candidates. Rarely do independent candidates (those lacking the support and affiliation from a national political party) win student elections there. This is the type of tendency against which the CWL pushes.

A healthy public sphere depends upon the active engagement of community members working together to support the common good. Higher education institutions in both Western and Middle Eastern contexts can promote a robust and engaged society by making a variety of public-sphere activities available to students. The present study suggests those activities can fruitfully include volunteer activities, especially those that allow students to organize, take on leadership roles, contextualize the volunteer work within broader societal contexts, and make sense of the world through independent critical thinking instead of partisan political ideology. Further, the data support the notion that interaction among diverse members of society (e.g., those from different socioeconomic strata and different ethnoreligious affiliations) fosters a critical, metacognitive understanding of how a society functions. When the various agents who interact in public-sphere activities come from diverse backgrounds, there is the added potential for intercultural understanding and reduced sectarianism and divisiveness as well—a desirable outcome in both Western and Arab contexts, to be sure.

References

Ayish, M. (2008). *The new Arab public sphere*. Berlin: Frank & Timme.
Baynham, M. (2004). Ethnographies of literacy: Introduction. *Language & Education: An International Journal, 18*(4), 285–290.
Bickford, D. M., & Reynolds, N. (2002). Activism and service learning: Reframing volunteerism as acts of dissent. *Pedagogy, 2*(2), 229–252.
Burke, K. (1969). *A rhetoric of motives*. Berkeley: University of California Press.
Coogan, D. (2005). Counterpublics in public housing: Reframing the politics of service learning. *College English, 67*(5), 461–482.

Coogan, D. (2006). Service learning and social change: The case for materialist rhetoric. *College Composition and Communication, 57*(4), 667–693.

Corstange, D. (2012). Religion, pluralism, and iconography in the public sphere: Theory and evidence from Lebanon. *World Politics, 64*(1), 116–160. http://ezproxy.aus.edu/login?url=http://search.proquest.com/docview/917954457?accountid=16946. Accessed 10 June 2010.

Cushman, E. (1996). The rhetorician as an agent of social change. *College Composition and Communication, 47*(1), 7–28.

Cushman, E., et al. (Eds). (2001). *Literacy: A critical sourcebook*. Boston: Bedford (St. Martin's).

DeGenaro, W. (2010). The affective dimensions of service learning. *Reflections: A Journal of Community Literacy and Service Learning, 9*(3), 192–220.

Giroux, H. (2004). *The terror of neoliberalism*. Boulder: Paradigm.

Green, A. (2003). Difficult stories: Service-learning, race, class, and whiteness. *College Composition and Communication, 55*(2), 276–301.

Grönlund, H., et al. (2011). Cultural values and volunteering: A cross-cultural comparison of students' motivation to volunteer in 13 countries. *Journal of Academic Ethics, 9*(2), 87–106. doi:http://dx.doi.org/10.1007/s10805-011-9131-6. Accessed 10 June 2013.

Habermas, J. (1991). *The structural transformation of the public sphere: An inquiry into a category of bourgeois society*. (trans. T. Burger). Institute of Technology. (Original work published in 1962).

Habermas, J. (2006). Religion in the public sphere. *European Journal of Philosophy, 14*(1), 1–25.

Heath, S. B. (1983). *Ways with words*. Cambridge: Cambridge University Press.

Hesford, W. S. (2005). Global/local labor politics and the promise of service learning. In L. Gray-Rosendale & S. Rosendale (Eds.), *Radical relevance: Toward a scholarship of the whole left* (pp. 183–202). Albany: State University of New York Press.

Herzberg, B. (1997). Community service and critical teaching. In L. Adler-Kassner (Ed.), *Writing the community: concepts and models for service learning in composition* (pp. 57–69). Washington, DC: American Association for Higher Education.

Himley, M. (2004). Facing (up to) "the stranger" in community service learning. *College Composition and Communication, 55*(3), 416–438.

Ismael, T. Y., & Ismael, J. S. (1997). Civil society in the Arab world: Historical traces, contemporary vestiges. *Arab Studies Quarterly, 19*(1), 77–87. http://ezproxy.aus.edu/login?url=http://search.proquest.com/docview/220600343?accountid=16946. Accessed 4 May 2013.

Kandil, A. (2004). Civic service in the Arab region. *Nonprofit and Voluntary Sector Quarterly, 33*(4), 39S–50S.

Khalaf, S. (2006). *Heart of Beirut: Reclaiming the Bourj*. London: Saqi.

Lazere, D. (2005). *Reading and writing for civic literacy*. Boulder: Paradigm.

Long, S. E. (2002). *The new student politics: The wingspread statement on civic engagement* (2nd ed.). Providence: Campus Compact.

Marback, R. (2003). Speaking of the city and literacies of place in composition studies. In B. McComiskey & C. Ryan (Eds.), *City comp: Identities, spaces, practices* (pp. 141–155). Albany: State University of New York Press.

Morton, K. (1995). The irony of service: Charity, project, and social change in service learning. *Michigan Journal of Community Service Learning, 2*(1), 19–32.

Mutnick, D. (2007). Inscribing the world: Lessons from an oral history project in Brooklyn. *College Composition and Communication, 58*(4), 626–647.

Ofeish, S. A. (1999). Lebanon's second republic: Secular talk, sectarian application. *Arab Studies Quarterly, 21*(1), 97–116. http://ezproxy.aus.edu/login?url=http://search.proquest.com/docvie w/220604218?accountid=16946. Accessed 11 Nov 2013.

Reynolds, N. (2004). *Geographies of writing: Inhabiting places and encountering difference*. Carbondale: Southern Illinois University Press.

Scribner, S., & Cole, M. (1981). *The psychology of literacy*. Cambridge: Harvard University Press.

Street, B. (1984). *Literacy in theory & practice*. Cambridge: Cambridge University Press.

Street, B. (2004). Futures of the ethnography of literacy? *Language & Education: An International Journal, 18*(4), 326–330.

Szwed, J. (1981). The ethnography of literacy. In M. F. Whiteman (Ed.), *Writing: The nature and development of written communication: Vol. 4. Variation in writing: Functional and linguistic cultural differences*. Baltimore: Lawrence Erlbaum.

Weisser, C. R. (2002). *Moving beyond academic discourse: Composition studies and the public sphere*. Carbondale: Southern Illinois University Press.

Welch, N. (2002). "And now that I know them": Composing mutuality in a service learning course. *College Composition and Communication, 54*(2), 243–263.

Part II
Professional Contexts

Chapter 10
Culturally Different Perspectives of Time: Effect on Communication in Meetings

Linzi J. Kemp

10.1 Introduction

Meetings are organizational phenomena during which employees describe, explain, and decide on actions that in turn affect the organization. But, as a subject for research, meetings have been greatly overlooked (Leach et al. 2009; Schwartzman 1986). Furthermore, Jarzabkowski and Seidl (2008) claim that "despite their pervasiveness, we know little about the effects of meetings upon the organizations in which they take place" (p. 1392). Meetings are pervasive in organizational life, and therefore a study of time in meetings is worthy of investigation (Hatch 1997). However, to date, there have been no academic studies focused on meeting time in the United Arab Emirates (UAE).

Findings from Hall's (1981) theory of time suggest that monochronicity is related to a Western context, and polychronicity to the Arab culture. It is, therefore, pertinent to test this theory in an empirical study of intercultural meetings conducted in an organization in the Arab world (CIA 2010). To that end, qualitative data were collected through nonparticipant observation of two meetings within an organization in the UAE. Other authors recommend qualitative methodology for the study of culture and organizational behavior, and so it is appropriate to rely on that research approach in this study (Denzin and Lincoln 1998; Sonnentag and Volmer 2009). The data are collected from an organization employing a multicultural workforce and located in a country within the Arab world. As such, this study on meeting time fits within the publication theme about communication with Arabs.

Vignettes are constructed from the meeting observations to illustrate how time was treated by the participants, and the effect on meeting communication. Analysis of the meeting time reveals delayed starts, extensions to meeting duration, and interruptions. Findings show that intercultural meeting communication in the Arab world fits within a polychronic dimension of time. Those involved in intercultural

L. J. Kemp (✉)
American University of Sharjah, Sharjah, United Arab Emirates
e-mail: lkemp@Aus.edu

© Springer Science+Business Media Singapore 2015
R. Raddawi (ed.), *Intercultural Communication with Arabs,*
DOI 10.1007/978-981-287-254-8_10

communication with Arabs need to adapt meeting time accordingly to achieve effective meeting practice. The scholarly contribution of this study adds to the body of knowledge on intercultural communication in meetings. The study is limited by findings within one organization in the UAE, leading towards a research direction to replicate such studies in other Arab organizations.

10.2   Literature Review

Meetings

Meetings are defined in this research as "purposeful work-related interactions occurring between at least two individuals" (Rogelberg et al. 2010, p. 2). We regard meetings as an element of the social construction of organizations, because meetings bring together certain people "during a particular space and time, while bracketing out others" (Jarzabkowski and Seidl 2008, p. 1394). Meetings occur regularly in both the public and private sectors (Adams 2004; Hallett et al. 2009), and are attended by all organizational peoples, from top management (Bang et al. 2010; Carrington and Johed 2007) to middle management (Schwartzman 1987), and other employees (Schwartzman 1986). Employees are brought together in an organizational meeting as it is the "principle vehicle for communicating and disseminating information" (Rogelberg et al. 2010, p. 155).

Although meetings are a common aspect of international business life, studies on them have been conducted for the most part in a Western setting (Gersick 1989; Millhous 1999). It is therefore, important to study meetings held in an intercultural setting, otherwise, in an absence of such studies, knowledge will reflect only the Western perspective of meeting behavior (Leach et al. 2009). For example, we would expect individuals from different cultures to hold dissimilar understanding about social constructs, and time is such a social construct (Hong 1999; Rutkowski et al. 2007). Meanings associated with time may be established and taken for granted in a dominant culture but the latter may also overlook the fact that there could be alternative meanings about time held by those from other cultures (Bluedorn 2000; Schein 1992). A domination of Western studies leads to academic concern that "people from Western countries have shown a certain kind of arrogance in assuming that concepts/results obtained in one culture apply anywhere" (Van Emmerik et al. 2010, p. 359). Therefore, it is anticipated that rich data can be drawn from a study of intercultural meeting behavior, and this will add to understanding of communication with Arabs.

Meetings and Time

An understanding about a particular organization and its people can be gained through the study of meetings as organizational phenomena (Hong 1999; Kay

1995). It is important to extract meanings about meetings because of their frequency and duration which affects employees (Hatch 1997). In illustration, Peters (cited in Deal and Kennedy 2000) quantitatively analyzed meetings in one organization, and found that 97% of the working hours were spent in meetings. The analysis initially led to a conclusion that employees were spending too much time at too many meetings and business results were poor as a consequence. However, the more important meaning to emerge from this study arose from a qualitative analysis, when the meetings were revealed to be too large for effective communication, and therefore lacked results.

The complexity of meeting activity, which includes the communication that takes place, has been diagnosed as a "waste" of time (Elsayed-Elkhouly et al. 1997). Through describing meetings within such a metaphor, it then comes to represent meetings as not only a problem but also the organizational culture itself (Cornelissen et al. 2005; Tourish and Hargie 2012). Schwartzman (1986) follows this idea of meetings as indicative of organizational culture, through the metaphor of "meetings as symptoms" (p. 237). Another theme of the literature that considers meetings as symptomatic of organizational culture is through the focus on meeting inefficiency (Johann 1994; Mintzberg 1973, cited in Rogelberg et al. 2006). We hear, for example, that employees spend "inordinate amounts of time" in meetings for no tangible reason (Schwartzman 1986, p. 253). Lakoff and Johnson (1999, p. 150–151) captured the "crime" of inefficient use of organizational time in their metaphor "time theft."

As Tipton (2008, p. 18) points out, the previous metaphors are based on the concept of "time as money" which reflects Western values that are "commonly held to cause problems for American executives in other countries." Tourish and Hargie (2012) refer to the "principle of exclusion" whereby categories of meaning are excluded because of a reliance on research within a particular social framework (p. 1048). Thus, when research takes place about meetings it needs to recognize that indigenous meanings about time need to be included. Time is a social construct, and an understanding of its value across cultures is therefore worthy of investigation (Rutkowski et al. 2007). An understanding of the value of time in multicultural organizations can be gained through interpretation of meeting behavior. We aim, therefore, to extract meaning from meetings held in the UAE, based on research that uses a cultural framework of time.

A Theory of Time

Time has been almost totally ignored as a research topic in the organization sciences. (Bluedorn 2000, p. 117)

Hall's (1981) cultural framework of time is defined as "the set of values and beliefs people hold about organizing and sequencing activities" (Bluedorn 2000, p. 119). The definition supports this study to investigate the set of values and beliefs held about organizing and sequencing meeting activity. Different dimensions to the organization of time have previously been found between Western and non-Western settings, and these are classified as "monochronic" (M) and "polychronic" (P) (Hall 1981).

Monochronicity is related to a culture where people's preference is for attention on one thing at a time. There is concentration on the particular task, promptness is emphasized, and time commitments (deadlines, schedules) are taken seriously. People need information (facts) to complete tasks, and they are committed to the job, and adhere to plans to achieve tasks (Hall 1981). Polychronicity relates to treating time as less defined, and is negatively correlated with values of punctuality, schedules, and deadlines (Bluedorn 2000). Hall (cited in Bluedorn 2000) states the existence of a polychronic culture, where peoples' preference is to be engaged in many things at one time. Distractions of people and events may interrupt the achievement of an objective, plans are changed to support the relationships between people, and information is dependent on relationship building. A cultural analysis of time has previously concluded that Arabs are more polychronic, and Westerners more monochronic (Hall 1981). It is, therefore, appropriate to test this framework to time through a study on intercultural meetings.

10.3 Methodology

To understand meetings in their organizational context, requires time spent in the organization getting to know people, places, customs, and rituals (Islam and Zyphur 2009; Van Maanen 1988). The fieldwork conducted in this study consists of a short immersion, via nonparticipant observation, at two formal meetings in the naturalistic setting of one organization (Olesen 1990; Sutter 2000). Qualitative research methodology that makes extensive use of nonparticipant observation is justified because it is anticipated to expose organizational dynamics (Burnett 1991; Crabtree et al. 1994).

The organization, henceforth, is given the pseudonym NWC for reasons of confidentiality (Lofland 1989). NWC has been in existence for 20 years, with offices located in the UAE and the Kingdom of Saudi Arabia. It is an industrial company that manufactures cables mainly for the domestic market, and for export to other Arab Gulf countries. NWC is a private, family-owned company, as is usual in the Middle East and common for firms worldwide (Constantinidis and Nelson 2009). NWC was chosen as an organization as it employs more than 200 people from 18 nations, 15% of whom are Arabs (Kemp and Williams 2013).

The criterion for selection of the participants was that they should be department managers, i.e., employees who were more likely to attend or hold regular meetings with others. The study participants were from various nationalities/ethnicities, and this information was ascertained from company documentation or from individual interviews. The official language of the company is English. As the observed meetings took place in an organization composed of mixed nationalities and the participants were from various nations, we consider the study is representative of "intercultural communication."

Data Collection

The study began with an introduction by the researcher, who stated that the theme of the research was about meetings. Each of the managers involved was asked to sign a consent form, was thanked for that consent, and was promised confidentiality. To preserve that confidentiality, employees were assured that anything they said would be treated with anonymity, and would not be repeated to others within the organization. A first name pseudonym is used here to preserve that confidential agreement. The formal address, Mr./Mrs., is also given because in the meeting documentation that was the reference. Furthermore, it was noted in the fieldwork that managers verbally referred to each other as Mr. or Mrs. first name.

Participants

In this study, we focus on two meetings led by two department managers (sales and quality). Mrs. Rania is Iraqi; she is the quality assurance manager at NWC and is leader of the quality meeting. Other participants at the quality meeting were Mr. Asif, Indian, quality control manager, and Mr. Hassan, Syrian, plant and production manager.

Mr. Bassan is Lebanese, and as NWC's sales manager, he leads the sales meeting. There were seven attendees at the sales meeting; six male sales engineers (SE) and a female secretary. It was not possible to establish the nationalities nor ethnicities of these particular employees at the time; however, company records helped with this. Besides the manager, there are 11 employees in the sales and marketing department; the majority are Indian (6), 4 Filipinos, and a Syrian. It is likely that the secretary is Filipina as it is common to see female nationals of that country in such roles in the UAE (Kemp 2012).

Analysis

Analysis was based on field notes from each of the observed meetings, supported by material extracted from organizational documentation (Yin 2009). The analysis is divided into four sections and presented as Table 10.1. The four sections of the observation compare poignant observation cues about meeting time during each of the two meetings (quality and sales).

The Quality Meeting

Place The quality meeting takes place weekly. It did not have a preset duration; the meeting lasts for as long as necessary to finish the business of the meeting. Occasionally, as happened at the observed meeting, a follow-up meeting is needed

Table 10.1 Meeting time analysis

Section	Quality	Sales
Place—where and when the meetings took place	Weekly. No set duration. Office of quality controller	Weekly. No set duration. Conference room in the sales office
Purpose—the rationale for the meeting is given	Checking of the noncompliant records	To share project details between members of the sales team. A different purpose was then stated at meeting commencement
Pre-meeting—the events prior to the meeting are reconstructed	Scheduled to begin at noon, phone call received that delayed start	Scheduled to begin at 1 pm. The sales manager calls people together for the meeting
Communication—the meeting behavior is interpreted	Phone calls responded to. Other personnel enter into the meeting space. Nonmeeting work carried out as meeting progresses	Phone calls received and made. Nonmeeting personnel enter the meeting space. Participants leave and reenter

to finish up any business left outstanding. The observed meeting took place as usual in the quality controller's office, where the attendees sat around a circular table. Both doors of the office remained open during the meeting, a secretary was in a room off the office, and the testing area was through the other door.

Purpose The meeting is referred to as "the NCR meeting" by Mr. Asif, who also stated its purpose to be for "continual improvement." Improvement is achieved through the checking of the noncompliant records (NCRs); an NCR is "opened" when an incident in the factory contravenes the quality standards. The meeting participants discuss the noncompliance, reach agreement on the cause, and agree ways to resolve the incident. The NCR is then signed off by each manager, and copies are filed.

Pre-meeting The telephone call to Mrs. Rania had been to inform her that there were external visitors, and she had been asked to meet with them. Mrs. Rania then continued her phone call with the administration manager, presumably in an attempt to rearrange her other meeting. Mr. Asif, whose office it was, left the meeting table and returned to sit behind his desk to make a telephone call. Mr. Hassan also left the meeting room, and returned a few minutes later. Whereupon, despite the call for postponement, the meeting continued and all meeting participants sat down to start the meeting at 12:13 pm

Communication Mr. Asif and Mr. Hassan sat next to each other, with Mrs. Rania opposite. As the manager of the quality department, Mrs. Rania is equal to the other managers in the organizational hierarchy as they all report to the general manager. However, she was referred to by Mr. Hassan during the meeting as the "NCR meeting leader." To add to our consideration of Mrs. Rania as meeting leader, she took control at the beginning: "one second Mr. Hassan before we start."

At the start of the meeting, each participant laid their cell phone beside them on the meeting table. During the meeting, cell phones were occasionally picked up and glanced at when text messages came in. Mr. Asif's cell phone rang during the meeting, and later it rang again—each time with a different tune. This raised a laugh from the others, and Mr. Asif was teased by Mr. Hassan with the comment, "nice tune!" During the meeting, the office telephone rang a few times, and was answered by the secretary, and Mr. Asif called over to the secretary to ask, "who was on the phone?" Mr. Asif also left his chair to receive and make telephone calls on his office telephone, and arose at one point to refer to something on his office computer. During those intervals, Mrs. Rania and Mr. Hassan conversed in Arabic to each other. At one point, Mr. Asif handed over a document to an employee who walked in through the secretary's office.

The meeting ended with a telephone call calling Mr. Asif elsewhere, and the others urged him to go. They all decided to finish this meeting at 2.04 p.m., and then meet again the next day to complete the remaining NCRs.

The Sales Meeting

Place It is a weekly meeting. The sales meeting took place in a meeting room at the sales office in Dubai where the sales team is located. The meeting room adjoins the sales manager's office through a glass wall, and it houses an oblong meeting table. The door remained open throughout the meeting; next to the open door was a whiteboard which designated the front of the room.

Purpose Mr. Bassan (sales manager) had previously informed me of the meeting purpose, "I want everyone to know what his colleague is doing, it is to share ideas in front of everyone." He had previously drawn up a checklist of project details to be reported on by each Sales Engineer (SE), "have that instead of an agenda...this will be discussed at such a meeting."

Pre-meeting The meeting was due to begin at 1 p.m. At 1 p.m., Mr. Bassan could see through the glass that, as yet, none of the SEs were in the room. He requested his secretary to "call everybody to the meeting," and the secretary went to each office. Mr. Bassan then stood in the office corridor and shouted "Yallah" (Arabic for "come"). About 10 min after the planned start time for the meeting, the meeting commenced when the other participants were seated, and Mr. Bassan walked in.

Communication Mr. Bassan took his place at the meeting table, at the end nearest the whiteboard. He brought his coffee with him, and set the mug on the table, sipping from it occasionally. Mr. Bassan also smoked during the meeting, an accepted company practice as during the fieldwork it was noted that other managers smoked in their offices. The secretary sat next to the sales manager and took notes. During the meeting, Mr. Bassan stood for the majority of the time, and wrote on the whiteboard. In front of each participant was a photocopied list, the checklist that Mr. Bassan had previously mentioned. SE5 had an open diary in front of him, two others placed their cell phones on the table, another his wallet, and another had an open laptop in front of him. Mr. Bassan opened the meeting by standing and stating to the SEs the meeting is to "assess your plans and talk about the difficulty you have to reach your objective." Each SE in turn gave a verbal report, where they read aloud from a document in front of them. Some, during their report, maintained no eye contact, others had some eye contact with Mr. Bassan, but not with their colleagues. As each in turn gave his report, questions were asked of them by Mr. Bassan in the form of repeatedly asking, "what else?" The other SEs sat quietly as each team member reported.

When SE1 had finished his report, the whiteboard was full of notes as written up by Mr. Bassan. He then attempted to wipe the board clean, but unfortunately could not. One of the SEs left the room to call in the office boy, and he came in to clean the board with soapy water. It is common for a UAE organization to employ someone in this role of "office boy." During this period, there was "off meeting" conversation and laughter between some. This issue of wiping the board and calling in the office boy was repeated after each report. The passing of meeting time to sort out the whiteboard problem rather hinted that its use was an unusual event; use of the whiteboard was perhaps just inaugurated for the observation.

During the report by SE2, Mr. Bassan and he conversed in Arabic, although the majority of the meeting was conducted in English. SE3 gave his report with his cell phone in his hand, and answered a question put to him by Mr. Bassan by replying rather formally, "No Sir." As SE3 was reporting, SE4 looked at photographs on his laptop, and also opened his email account showing something to SE2. SE4 read his report from his laptop. SE1 received a call on his cell phone and answered it while sitting at the meeting table. Another participant also left the room at one point to go to his office, and the secretary was asked to call him back. They all eventually returned, and in the meantime SE5, who was giving his report at the time, had continued. SE6, the final reporter, said that there was no need to write on the board as "I only have a few things," whereupon, Mr. Bassan sat down.

Having finished the reports, there was a short general discussion about issues, and how to overcome problems. Mr. Bassan asked "anybody have any conclusions?" One of the SEs spoke up and there was a short conversation at this point. Towards the end of the meeting, an SE left the room while speaking on his cell phone, and stood in the corridor talking into his phone. The conversation was loud enough to be overheard in the meeting room as the door was open. Mr. Bassan shouted out to him, "Yallah, we want to close the meeting!" By this time, other participants were respectively doodling, SE4 was typing on his laptop, and there was conversation between two SEs in another language. Mr. Bassan looked at his cell phone and began scrolling through it, at the same time asking, "anything else? OK thank you very much." The meeting finished at 2.17 p.m.

In the findings below, deeper insight is offered into the effect of time on meeting communication.

10.4   Findings

Table 10.1 is now extended to incorporate the observation cues from the meetings to enable a comparison between the M and P dimensions of time (Bluedorn 2000; Hall 1981). Table 10.2 illustrates the communication expectations of a meeting

Table 10.2 M and P time—the expected and observed meeting communication. (Based on Bluedorn 2000; Hall 1981)

Monochronicity (M)	Meeting communication expectations	Polychronicity (P)	Observation	
			Quality	Sales
Adhere religiously to plans	There is an agenda for the meeting which is followed	Change plans often and easily	Phone call from manager to change scheduled meeting	Participants prepared to wait until all called together
Emphasize promptness	The meeting begins and ends on time	Base promptness on the relationship	Delayed start	Delayed start
Are committed to the job	The meeting is prescheduled. All participants know about the meeting	Are committed to people and human relationships	Meet as needed, and if participants available	The sales manager called meeting attendees together
Concentrate on the job	The participants concentrate on the meeting progress	Are highly distractible and subject to interruptions	Open door. Secretary comes in and out	Open door. Office boy enters and leaves
Do one thing at a time	Participants focus on each agenda item in turn avoiding interruptions	Do many things at once	Cell phones that rang were switched off or responded to	Calls were made or texts sent
Need information	Meeting documentation is shared beforehand. Each participant has prepared from that documentation	Already have information	Written information in the NCRs, added to by manager's tacit knowledge about noncompliance	Checklist followed by manager as SE communicated from a pre-compiled report
Take time commitments (deadlines, schedules) seriously	The agenda items are timed, the chair keeps participants to time. The meeting ends at the scheduled time	Consider an objective to be achieved, if possible	Business of meeting ends abruptly without completing all NCRs	Weekly meeting to share information. The sharing continues depending on the participant input

according to monochronic time. Then the dimension P is given, and the findings from the observations of the quality and sales meetings are exhibited. The observation findings show that the meetings followed the polychronic dimension to time.

10.5   Discussion

The discussion follows the literature review, analysis (Table 10.1), and findings (Table 10.2). The communication at the two meetings is discussed in relation to the dimensions in the cultural framework to time (Hall 1981). In qualitative research, the reader can gain an impression of an observed scenario through a vignette that illuminates particular data (Stake 2010). The impression of each observed meeting is given in a vignette to illuminate the interpretation of time from each of the observed meetings.

Vignette 1—The quality meeting

> The meeting was scheduled to begin at Noon, but Mrs. Rania, accompanied by the researcher, only left her office at that time. During the walk across the factory to the meeting room, Mrs. Rania received a call on her cell phone from the Administration Manager. On arrival to the meeting room, Mrs. Rania immediately requested of the other participants that the meeting be postponed.

Vignette 2—The sales meeting

> When SE1 had finished his report, the whiteboard was full of notes as written up by Mr. Bassan. He then attempted to wipe the board clean, but unfortunately could not. One of the SEs left the room to call in the Office Boy, and he came in to clean the board with soapy water. During this period there was "off meeting" conversation and laughter between some.

Meeting *plans were changed often and easily.* In a meeting where participants have a monochronic perspective, a rating of the effectiveness of a meeting is whether it begins on time, despite who is present (Arrow et al. 2004). In the quality meeting, a request for postponement at the time of the meeting considerably delayed the start. The stated time for the start of the sales meeting was likewise delayed as participants were "rounded up" by the sales manager. In the multicultural meetings observed, there was a theme of polychronicity as meetings began when all participants were present. The latter incidents also suggest that *promptness is based on the relationship* between people, because meeting attendees were prepared to wait for others to begin the meeting or were "late" themselves.

Within this diverse environment, employees accommodate to each other, rather than to a scheduled meeting time, through *their commitment to people and human relationships.* In a monochronic context, these delayed starts to meetings, and requested changes of time are perceived as ineffective (Luong and Rogelberg 2005). In the polychronic understanding of time, the value of effectiveness is rated differently as flexibility towards planned time.

We noted that participants were *highly distractible and subject to interruptions* in the movement of people around the meeting room, and other nonmeeting members came in and left the meeting space. Evidence of the attendees doing *many things at once* was shown in the actions of writing, listening, holding conversations on cell phones, and conducting off-meeting chat with each other. Multitasking in meetings is considered as possibly contributing to ineffectiveness in meetings in monochronic cultures (Benbunan-Fich and Truman 2009; Hopper 1991). Multitasking was the norm and integrated as common practice in the observed meetings through a general acceptance to ignore or absorb the practice (Stephens and Davis 2009). It has been stated by Schwartzman (1986) that managers complain about the number of meetings as interference with their daily work: "complaints about meetings are so prevalent in American organizational life" (p. 249). In these intercultural meetings, there may not have been voiced complaints, but the multitasking suggests similar issues to those in American organizations where other work is "juggled" around meetings.

There were findings that showed employees were following the polychronic element of *already having information*. The verbal discussions at the quality meeting shared the tacit knowledge held by each participant, in addition to the data contained within written documentation (Myers 1986). Similar to the meetings described by Peters (cited in Deal and Kennedy 2000), the sales meeting was a time for sharing information rather than meetings only being a forum for making decisions (Farmer and Roth 1998; Kemp and Williams 2013). The sales manager did say to the observer that the meeting was an opportunity to "share" information, but that purpose was restated to the participants as being for assessment of their work. It was also left rather unstated by the sales manager as to how any shared knowledge was to be managed after the meeting (Cummings 2004; LaForce 2009).

Monge et al. (1989) reported that two thirds of meetings have a written agenda, the purpose of which is to control how time is spent at meetings so that objectives are achieved. There was documentary evidence to support the meeting objectives: NCRs; note-taking; checklist; and reports (Boden 1995; Niederman and Volkema 1999). Thus, participants had *an objective to be achieved, if possible*; in the form of agreement on noncompliance (quality meeting), and in the delivery of reports (sales meeting). In Gersick's (1989) fieldwork and laboratory experiments, "the sharper a group's time constraints, the more frequently participants will pay explicit attention to time and pacing" (p. 305). The "time message" in the quality meeting was prompted by the number of NCRs that formed the meeting. Time was an uncontrollable resource for the participants as they continued discussion in attempts to reach agreement over each NCR. A duration for each participant's report was unstated in the sales meeting, but everyone had to report in the time available, an underlying "time message" that controlled the pace of the meeting. The time for each SE report differed, dependent on how much time the sales manager spent in extracting the information from each person.

Each of the meetings came to an abrupt end, the quality meeting with a participant having to leave, and some of the SEs drifting off to other business. Similarly to Perlow's field study (1999), there was evidence of "time famine," of having too much to do and not enough time to do it (p. 57). The meetings were held in an organization situated in the UAE, and that organization also has its roots in another

Arab country, i.e., the Kingdom of Saudi Arabia. Meeting participants therefore constructed a local, social view of time, less controlled by time set by the clock or a preset agenda.

Evidence was found in this study that meeting time is treated differently in the Arab culture, defined as polychronic, to meeting time in a monochronic context (Hall 1981). Time in these observed meetings integrated elements that fit more within the dimension of polychronicity: flexibility towards planning; multitasking; absorption of interruptions; adaption to participant behavior; and information known and shared based on relationships (Benbunan-Fich and Truman 2009; Carlozzin 1999). As meetings are considered representative of the organizational culture, we concur with Schwartzman (1986); the interpretation of time from the observed meetings represents the NWC organization "writ small" (p. 250).

10.6   Limitations and Future Research

A critique is made of the approach to the research, and how this could have been improved upon. By just being there in the field, the researcher intervened and disturbed the normal routine of events, as it is not the norm to have a researcher present in day-to-day work. It must be taken into account that the researcher did make a difference to the meeting setting, although apparently she was accepted and her presence ignored.

The interpretation in this study of one organization in the Arab region is that a polychronic approach to meeting time is a norm. Qualitative research can be undertaken of other intercultural meetings within the UAE, and outwards to further investigate intercultural communication with Arabs. The purpose of that geographical widening will be to gather data about meetings from an as yet under-researched part of the world. Comparisons can then be made as to how time in meetings is understood differently or similarly in intercultural situations. Understanding that emerges will add to the body of academic knowledge, and will be of practical benefit for the management of intercultural meetings internationally.

Conclusion

Western meeting behavior has been the predominant research context (Rogelberg et al. 2007). In this research, it was noted that there were some similarities to Western meeting behavior but also dissimilarities. In particular, it was discovered that meeting time in an Arab context, with intercultural participants, fits more within a polychronic than monochronic dimension to time. The findings expand current knowledge of meeting time which, "in an era of globalization" is "very important" in terms of organizational understanding (Soin and Scheytt 2006, p. 2).

The findings raise awareness for those conducting and attending intercultural meetings. Time is a social construct, and the meaning attached to the construct cannot be overlooked as values ascribed to time do, and will, affect meeting communication (Giddens 1996). The study emphasizes the importance of intercultural studies for their impact on training for meetings in a multicultural context. The call for similar studies to be conducted in the Arab region is particularly pertinent as the region lacks such research. A recommendation is for individuals engaged in multinational businesses to recognize there are differing perspectives to time. In order to achieve effective meetings, participants, and those who lead meetings, require flexibility in their approach to meeting time. It is recognized that this is one story of meetings, and is not necessarily the same story for other intercultural meetings (Boje 1999). By interpretation through a cultural framework to time, some sense-making about intercultural meetings has emerged (Soin and Scheytt 2006; Weick 1995).

References

Adams, B. (2004). Public meetings and the democratic process. *Public Administration Review, 64*(1), 43–54. doi:10.1111/j.1540-6210.2004).00345.x.

Arrow, H., Poole, M. S., Henry, K. B., Wheelan, S., & Moreland, R. (2004). Time, change, and development: The temporal perspective on groups. *Small Group Research, 35*(1), 73–105. doi:10.1177/1046496403259757.

Bang, H., Fuglesang, S., Ovesen, M., & Eilertsen, D. (2010). Effectiveness in top management group meetings: The role of goal clarity, focused communication, and learning behavior. *Scandinavian Journal of Psychology, 51*(3), 253–261. doi:10.1111/j.1467-9450.2009.00769.x.

Benbunan-Fich, R., & Truman, G. (2009). Multitasking with laptops during meetings. *Communications of the ACM, 52*(2), 139–141. doi:10.1145/1461928.1461963.

Bluedorn, A. C. (2000). Time and organizational culture. In N. M. Ashkanasy, C. P. M. Wilderom, & M. F. Peterson (Eds.), *Handbook of organizational culture & climate*. Thousand Oaks: Sage.

Boden, D. (1995). Agenda and arrangement: Everyday negotiations in meetings. In A. Firth (Ed.), *The discourse of negotiation: Studies of language in the workplace* (pp. 83–100). Oxford: Pergamon.

Boje, D. M. (1999). Qualitative methods for management and communication research. http://cbae.nmsu.edu/. Accessed 2002.

Burnett, R. (1991). Accounts and narratives. In B. M. Montgomery & S. Duck (Eds.), *Studying interpersonal interaction*. New York: Guildford Press.

Carlozzin, C. L. (1999). Make your meetings count. *Journal of Accountancy, 187,* 53–55.

Carrington, T., & Johed, G. (2007). The construction of top management as a good steward: A study of Swedish annual general meetings. *Accounting, Auditing & Accountability Journal, 20*(5), 702–728. doi:10.1108/09513570710779018.

CIA. (2010). Geography, people. Middle East: United Arab Emirates. The world fact book. https://www.cia.gov/library/publications/the-world-factbook/geos/ae.html. Accessed Oct 2011.

Constantinidis, C., & Nelson, T. (2009). Integrating succession and gender issues from the perspective of the daughter of family enterprise: A cross-national investigation. *Management International, 14*(1), 43.

Cornelissen, J. P., Kafouros, M., & Lock, A. R. (2005). Metaphorical images of organization: How organizational researchers develop and select organizations. *Human Relations, 58*(12), 1545.

Crabtree, B. F., Miller, W. L., Addison, R. B., Gilchrist, V. J., & Kuzel, A. (Eds.). (1994). *Exploring collaborative research in primary care*. London: Sage.

Cummings, J. C. (2004). Work groups, structural diversity, and knowledge sharing in a global organization. *Management Science, 50*(3), 352–364. doi:10.1287/mnsc.1030.0134.

Deal, T. E., & Kennedy, A. A. (2000). *Corporate cultures, the rites and rituals of corporate life* (2nd ed.). Cambridge: Perseus.

Denzin, N. K., & Lincoln, Y. S. (Eds.). (1998). *The landscape of qualitative research, theories and issues*. California: Sage.

Elsayed-Elkhouly, S. M., Lazarus, H., & Forsythe, V. (1997). Why is a third of your time wasted in meetings? *Journal of Management Development, 16*(9), 672–676. doi:10.1108/02621719710190185.

Farmer, S. M., & Roth, J. (1998). Conflict-handling behavior in work groups: Effects of group structure, decision processes, and time. *Small Group Research, 29*(6), 669–713. doi:10.1177/1046496498296002.

Gersick, C. J. G. (1989). Making time: Predictable transitions in task groups. *Academy of Management Journal, 32*(2), 274–309. doi:10.2307/256363.

Giddens, A. (1996). *In defence of sociology, essays, interpretations and rejoinders*. Cambridge: Polity Press.

Hall, E. T. (1981). *Beyond culture*. Garden City: Anchor Books.

Hallett, T., Harg, B., & Eder, D. (2009). Gossip at work: Unsanctioned evaluative talk in formal school meetings. *Journal of Contemporary Ethnography, 38*(5), 584–618.

Hatch, M. (1997). *Organization theory, modern symbolic and postmodern perspectives*. Oxford: Oxford University Press.

Hong, I. B. (1999). Information technology to support any-time, any-place team meetings in Korean organizations. *Industrial Management & Data Systems, 99*(1), 18–24. doi:10.1108/02635579910247145.

Hopper, R. (1991). Hold the phone. In D. Boden & H. Zimmerman (Eds.), *Talk and social structure studies in Ethnomethodology and conversation analysis*. Cambridge: Polity Press.

Islam, G., & Zyphur, M. (2009). Rituals in organizations: A review and expansion of current theory. *Group & Organization Management, 34*(1), 114. doi:10.1177/1059601108329717.

Jarzabkowski, P., & Seidl, D. (2008). The role of meetings in the social practice of strategy. *Organization Studies, 29*(11), 1391–1426. doi:10.1177/0170840608096388.

Johann, B. (1994). The meeting as a lever for organizational improvement. *National Productivity Review, 13*(3), 369.

Kay, G. (1995). Effective meetings through electronic brainstorming. *The Journal of Management Development, 14*(6), 4. doi:10.1108/02621719510086147.

Kemp, L. J. (2012). Implications for recruitment in a multinational organization: A case study of human resource management in the United Arab Emirates. *Emerging Market Case Studies*. doi:10.1108/20450621111192780.

Kemp, L. J., & Williams, P. A. (2013). In their own time and space: Meetings behavior in the Gulf Arab workplace. *International Journal of Cross Cultural Management, 13*(2), 215–235.

LaForce, T. (2009). Action-oriented meetings. Transforming workplace teams. http://tomlaforce.com/action-oriented-meetings-2/. Accessed 11 June 2011

Lakoff, G., & Johnson, M. (1999). *Philosophy in the flesh: The embodied mind and its challenge to western thought*. New York: Basic Books.

Leach, D., Rogelberg, S., Warr, P., & Burnfield, J. (2009). Perceived meeting effectiveness: The role of design characteristics. *Journal of Business and Psychology, 24*(1), 65–76. doi:10.1007/s10869-009-9092-6.

Lofland, L. L. (Trans., & Ed.). (1989). On fieldwork, Goffman E. (1974). *Journal of Contemporary Ethnography, 18*(2), 123–132. doi:10.1177/089124189018002001.

Luong, A., & Rogelberg, S. G. (2005). Meetings and more meetings: The relationship between meeting load and the daily well-being of employees. *Group Dynamics: Theory, Research and Practice, 9*(1), 58–67. doi:10.1037/1089-2699.9.1.58.

Millhous, L. M. (1999). The experience of culture in multicultural groups: Case studies of Russian-American collaboration in business. *Small Group Research, 30*(3), 280–308. doi:10.1177/104649649903000302.

Mintzberg, H. (1973). The Nature of Managerial Work. New York:Harper & Row

Monge, R., McSween, C., & Wyer, J. (1989). *A profile of meetings in corporate America: Results of the 3M meeting effectiveness study*. Los Angeles: University of Southern California Press.

Myers, F. R. (1986). Reflections on a meeting: Structure, language and the polity in a small scale society. *American Ethnologist, 13*(3), 430–447. doi:10.1525ae198613.3.02a00020.

Niederman, F., & Volkema, R. J. (1999). The effects of facilitator characteristics on meeting preparation, set up, and implementation. *Small Group Research, 30*(3), 330–360. doi:10.1177/104649649903000304.

Olesen, V. (1990). Immersed, amorphous, and episodic fieldwork: Theory and policy in three contrasting contexts. *Studies in Qualitative Methodology, 2*, 205–232.

Perlow, L. A. (1999). The time famine: Toward a sociology of work time. *Administrative Science Quarterly, 44*(1), 57–81.

Rogelberg, S. G., Allen, J. A., Shanock, L., Scott, C., & Shuffler, M. (2010). Employee satisfaction with meetings: A contemporary facet of job satisfaction. *Human Resource Management, 49*(2), 149–172. doi:10.1002/hrm.20339.

Rogelberg, S. G., Leach, D., Warr, P., & Burnfield, J. (2006). Not another meeting! Are meeting time demands related to employee well-being? *Journal of Applied Psychology, 91*(1), 83–96. doi:10.1037/0021-9010.91.1.83.

Rogelberg, S. G., Scott, C., & Kello, J. (2007). The science and fiction of meetings. *MIT Sloan Management Review, 48*(2), 18–21.

Rutkowski, A.-F., Saunders, C., Vogel, D., & Van Genuchten, M. (2007). Is it already 4 a.m. in Your time zone?: Focus immersion and temporal dissociation in virtual teams. *Small Group Research, 38*(1), 98–129. doi:10.1177/1046496406297042.

Schein, E. H. (1992). *Organizational culture and leadership* (2nd ed.). San Francisco: Jossey Bass.

Schwartzman, H. B. (1986). The meeting as a neglected social form in organizational studies. *Research in Organizational Behavior, 8*, 233–258.

Schwartzman, H. B. (1987). *The meeting: Gatherings in organizations and communities*. New York: Plenum Press.

Soin, K., & Scheytt, T. (2006). Making the case for narrative methods in cross-cultural organizational research. *Organizational Research Methods, 9*(1), 55–77. doi:10.1177/1094428105283297.

Sonnentag, S., & Volmer, J. (2009). Individual-level predictors of task-related teamwork processes: The role of expertise and self-efficacy in team meetings. *Group & Organization Management, 34*(1), 37. doi:10.1177/1059601108329377.

Stake, R. E. (2010). *Qualitative research: Studying how things work*. Guilford Publications. http://lib.myilibrary.com.ezproxy.aus.edu?ID=249017. Accessed 8 May 2013.

Stephens, K., & Davis, J. (2009). The social influences on electronic multitasking in organizational meetings. *Management Communication Quarterly, 23*(1), 63–83. doi:10.1177/089331890335417.

Sutter, E. A. (2000). Focus groups in ethnography of communication: expanding topics of inquiry beyond participant observation. *The Qualitative Report, 5*(1, 2). Retrieved from http://www.nova.edu/ssss/QR/QR5-1/suter.html). Accessed 3 Oct 2012

Tipton, F. B. (2008). Thumbs-up is a rude gesture in Australia: The presentation of culture in international business textbooks. *Critical Perspectives on International Business, 4*(1), 7–24.

Tourish, D., & Hargie, O. (2012). Metaphors of failure and the failures of metaphor: A critical study of root metaphors used by bankers in explaining the banking crisis. *Organization Studies, 33*(8), 1045–1069. doi:10.1177/0170840612453528.

Van Emmerik, H., Gardner, W. L., Wendt, H., & Fischer, D. (2010). Associations of culture and personality with McClelland's motives: A cross-cultural study of managers in 24 countries. *Group & Organization Management, 35*(3), 329–367. doi:10.1177/1059601110370782.

Van Maanen, J. (1988). *Tales of the field on writing ethnography*. Chicago: University of Chicago Press.

Weick, K. (1995). *Sensemaking in organizations*. London: Sage.

Yin, R. K. (2009). *Case study design, research & methods* (4th ed.). Thousand Oaks: Sage.

Linzi J. Kemp (Ph.D., Manchester Metropolitan University; MBA, Brunel University; B.Ed. (Business), University of Huddersfield; Diploma in Marketing, Chartered Institute of Marketing) is assistant professor with the American University of Sharjah, teaching *organizational behavior and leadership* to undergraduate and graduate students. Her research focuses on organizational communication with a particular interest on meeting behavior. Further research is on women in employment and leadership in the Middle East.

She has worked internationally; in the USA with distant learning and international programs; in the UAE, as a professional development coordinator; in the Kingdom of Saudi Arabia, she coordinated a new information technology curriculum; at a teacher training college in the People's Republic of China, Linzi was a teacher trainer. She is a member of the British Academy of Management.

Website: Professional—http://www.aus.edu/info/200171/school_of_business_and_management/313/department_of_management/4#.UWVbmVEyHTp

Chapter 11
Intercultural (Mis-) Communication in Medical Settings: Cultural Difference or Cultural Incompetence?

Rana Raddawi

11.1 Introduction

The emergence of globalization in the latter half of the twentieth century contributed to the growth of the intercultural communication research (Jandt 2012). Intercultural communication occurs when people of different cultures send and receive messages (Jandt 2012; Asante and Gudykunst 1989; Brislin 1981; Condon and Yousef 1975; Samovar et al. 2011; Sarangi 2011).

Globalization has generated occasions for intercultural communication through immigration, global market activity, tourism, and other sectors. Intercultural communication in healthcare, which is the focus of this chapter, is highly affected by this mingling of cultures.

There are both linguistic and cultural challenges facing healthcare providers and patients in medical settings, most of which are taken for granted or neglected due often to the lack of cultural awareness of stakeholders. Literature on linguistic barriers between healthcare providers and patients is abundant (Baker et al. 1998; Bernstein et al. 2002; David and Rhee 1998; Hampers et al. 1999; Bischoff et al. 2003; Jacobs et al. 2003; Kirkman-Liff and Mondragon 1991; Halligan 2006). However, research on the relationship between language and culture, and the impact of intercultural communication mainly among non-Arabic-speaking healthcare providers and Arabic-speaking patients remains scarce. For instance, in their extensive study of literature on language barriers in medical settings in the USA, Elizabeth Jacobs et al. (2003), exclude Arabic even though it is a language spoken by more than three million individuals (US Census 2010) in the USA without counting the number of non-American citizens.

What happens when an English-speaking healthcare provider has to treat a patient with low-proficiency in English in the absence of professional translators?

R. Raddawi (✉)
American University of Sharjah, Sharjah, United Arab Emirates
e-mail: rraddawi@aus.edu

© Springer Science+Business Media Singapore 2015

R. Raddawi (ed.), *Intercultural Communication with Arabs*,
DOI 10.1007/978-981-287-254-8_11

What is the situation when the same patient has to fill out a form written in English and answer questions prepared by a healthcare provider who belongs to a different culture? What is the case when an Arab patient expects a Western doctor, who comes from a different cultural background, to share with him or her, the same values and beliefs that relate to healing methods and treatment decisions? How do patients react when doctors ask them culturally sensitive questions?

This chapter will attempt to answer these and other questions by shedding light on the main cultural issues that arise in medical encounters where multiculturalism is present.

11.2   Background

Both the USA and the United Arab Emirates (UAE) have a good number of individuals with low English proficiency rate whether citizens (UAE) or immigrants (USA), acting in many fields including the medical environment (Raddawi 2006). The use of human interpreters for the English–Arabic language pair is very common in large US hospitals despite its high costs (Garcia et al. 2004). English is the main medium of communication in healthcare, whether in the UAE or in the USA, whereas Arabic is the main language of communication between local citizens of the UAE and the third language spoken in the USA after English and Spanish (Raddawi 2006).

However, in parts of the USA, where an ethnically diverse population with limited English proficiency is present, a scarcity of professional interpreters is noted and communication barriers between healthcare providers and patients are often bridged by accompanying family members or staff (Suurmond and Seeleman 2006; Jacobs et al. 2003; American College of Physicians 2010; Hornberger et al. 1997).

According to these studies, 21 % of visits are with non-English-speaking patients. Trained medical interpreters or the AT&T Language Line are used, on average, in less than 6 % of these encounters, and 15 % are conducted without interpreters. In 27 % of the encounters with non-English-speaking patients, the doctor could speak the patient's language, in 20 % interpretation is carried out by a staff member who had no formal interpretation training, and in 36 % a family member or companion of the patient acted as interpreter. Physicians who have access to trained medical interpreters reported a significantly higher quality of patient–physician communication than physicians who used other methods.

Uncertainty remains about the best way to bridge language and cultural barriers. Trained interpreters and the AT&T Language Line are more costlier than using untrained staff or family members, but the quality of interpretation may suffer when untrained interpreters are used, placing the patient at risk for medical mishaps due to misunderstandings and the clinician at risk for medical malpractice suits, as will be demonstrated in the following pages of the study. Healthcare providers in the USA have documented that language barriers not only increase medical errors and the time needed to complete the encounter, they also reduce the ability of patients to understand the outcomes of treatment, potential side effects, and the personal actions necessary for optimal management of their illnesses.

This study reveals that in a large metropolitan area of the USA, different-language medical encounters are common and that in almost half of these encounters, no interpretation services are available or provided. The findings of this study are consistent with those of other studies showing that language and cultural barriers are a common concern in clinical practice. For instance, primary care physicians in the Greater Bay Area see a large number of non-English-speaking patients. Physicians reported, not sharing a common language with the patient in an estimated 15 % of patient encounters, yet trained medical interpreters are rarely available for these visits (Hornberger et al. 1997).

The emergence of the UAE as a center for trade, commerce, and tourism has fueled a rapid influx of multinational businesses and the people needed to support them. This growth rate has put considerable pressure on health care organizations, especially in the public sector, to provide high-quality, cost-effective care to individuals who are not fluent in the languages of their caregivers.

English is the current language spoken by the majority of healthcare providers in the UAE (the situation is not very different from that in the USA). According to a hospital manager in Dubai, when non-English patients from the local population, or a non-English speaking tourist from another country, present to an emergency care center, the language barrier often delays implementation of the appropriate therapy, or causes a misunderstanding by the healthcare provider of the patient's condition, or misunderstanding by the patient of the healthcare provider's explanations (Personal communication, October 2011). One way to facilitate asking a question with a high degree of accuracy in a foreign language is via an interpreter. Yet, the error rate in a medical situation by a live interpreter has consistently been published at over 50 %—an unacceptably high rate considering the importance of the task.

11.3 Methodology

The work that I have conducted over two years on a translation software project with a team of healthcare providers from both countries, the USA and the UAE, (see Raddawi 2006) prior to undertaking this study, enabled me to have access to some medical settings in both locations. Thus, I became acquainted with the work environment and the type of healthcare providers and patients frequently found in those settings, which I decided to include in the present study. Hence, the reason of selecting two multicultural and multilingual countries for the purpose of the study: the UAE, specifically Dubai and Sharjah and the Midwestern USA and the Great Lakes region (USA).

A mixed method approach was followed in the data collection phase of the research. Secondary sources, observations in different healthcare units, and semistructured interviews with patients and healthcare providers from two hospitals in both countries in addition to interviews conducted in two healthcare authorities in the UAE were the main methods of data collection. A stratified random sampling method was followed. The population was divided in subgroups (or strata) who all shared similar characteristics: first generation Arab immigrant adults in the USA (first strata) and Arab adults in the UAE (second strata). (Farmer et al. 1996).

The topics discussed included the patient's illness and treatment perspective, perceived barriers, and satisfaction with the encounter. Five interviews with physicians and ten interviews with patients in each of the medical settings were used in the present chapter. The tape-recorded interviews were transcribed verbatim. Some of the interviews were translated from Arabic by the researcher. A written consent was obtained from interviewees and an agreement to keep doctors' and patients' confidentiality and anonymity was signed by the researcher. Participants under scrutiny will be referred to anonymously or using pseudonyms upon their request.

11.4   Language Barrier

In the USA, more than 49 million people speak languages other than English and 22 million have low-proficiency in English (Samovar et al. 2011). "Almost a quarter of Americans speak a language at home other than English. Over 300 languages are spoken in the USA, with Spanish being the most common language spoken other than English" (Barrett et al. 2008, p. 54).

According to Youdelman (2008), communication is a critical component of the doctor–patient relationship. Linguistic barriers make it difficult for trust to be established between the two parties and physician recommendations to be followed. Patients with limited English proficiency (LEP) often receive poorer quality care and have worse access to care than fluent patients.

Children may be the only family members who speak English, but they should not be used as interpreters, as this may place them in situations beyond their maturity to handle. "Health care professionals should also use caution when using family members or friends of patients as interpreters" (Youdelman 2008, p. 125).

In one of Sharjah's private hospitals, the researcher observed the following situation. A female Arab patient was waiting outside the doctor's room in the general practitioner's (GP's) clinic with her teenage son. She was explaining her symptoms to him in Arabic so he could translate when she went to see the doctor. She was also telling him all the questions she wanted him to ask the doctor and the son looked overwhelmed and confused. When the woman's name was called, she and her son went into the doctor's room. After 10 min or so they emerged, and while she was walking with her son, she was asking him what the doctor said; however, the son seemed to have forgotten parts of the conversation and did not know how to translate it back into Arabic for his mother. He seemed to edit what the doctor said just to satisfy his mother with answers to her questions.

According to the American College of Physicians (ACP 2004, para 4) "only 12 states and the District of Columbia provide funding for interpreters for Medicaid and CHIP beneficiaries." Although ACP recognizes the important role of interpreters during medical encounters for ethnic and racial minorities, yet the cost of providing these services could be exorbitant, and keeping interpreters on duty would be impractical for most physician practices serving multiple ethnic and minority populations speaking many different languages (ACP 2004).

The lead principle of the ACP states that "effective communication between health care providers and patients is essential to facilitating access to care, reducing health disparities and medical errors, and assuring a patient's ability to adhere to treatment plans." (para. 4).

Although these principles of the ACP were endorsed by a number of other organizations, including the American Hospital Association, the National Council of La Raza, and the Joint Commission on the Accreditation of Health Care (ACP 2004), putting them into practice seems to be a far-fetched goal.

Language barriers affect multiple aspects of healthcare for the LEP patient, including access to care centers and use of health services. A six-page article informs about "Errors in medical interpretation and their potential clinical consequences in pediatrics encounters" (Flores et al. 2003). The article cites many examples of errors made by human interpreters in clinical encounters, which have potential clinical consequences. The rate of errors is 31 %per clinical encounter, with omissions as the most frequent type. Furthermore, language barriers negatively affect the ability of physicians to "elicit exact symptoms from patients, elicit treatment preferences" and even to "explain treatments" (p. 21).

In addition, there are inefficient ad hoc interpreters, and a shortage of interpreters available 24 h in hospitals in the USA (American College of Physicians 2004).

Amr (62-year-old) in a US hospital feels more comfortable with Arab American doctors as he can express himself easily:

> I wish all my doctors spoke Arabic … because it is my mother tongue and I express myself much easier than in my broken English … Most of the time, I do not understand what they are saying, they speak too fast. (Translated from Arabic)

Soha (70-year-old) in the same hospital stated that she could not understand what her healthcare giver usually says and she feels embarrassed to have one of her children translate from Arabic:

> Every time, I need to go to the hospital, one of my children has to accompany me and this is sometimes embarrassing to me and to my children because they have other business to take care of…. (Translated from Arabic)

Fatima (55-year-old) also feels embarrassed when accompanied by family members but for different reasons:

> I sometimes need privacy with my doctor and having someone from the family translate during the encounter makes it a bit embarrassing … to be honest sometimes I do not want anyone to hear what I have to tell my doctor

While a number of federal and state laws are in place to ensure that LEP patients have access to interpreters, such laws are insufficiently enforced and gaps in services persist (Youdelman 2008). For instance, one emergency department survey found that 87% of patients without an interpreter thought these services would have been valuable during the encounter (Baker et al. 1998). Additionally, 61 % of physicians surveyed stated that it was much more difficult to provide patient care to LEP patients when language services were not available (American College of Physicians 2010).

Similarly, in the UAE, there are 800,000 local Emiratis against five million expatriates, including Asians, Arabs, Americans, French, and Iranians (Rasheed 2009), who not only speak different languages but also come from different cultural backgrounds.

Moreover, globalization and technological advances have also brought healthcare providers from different parts of the world together. Global medical communication is taking place either through the establishment of Western medical schools in the region, such as Weill Cornell in Qatar (Gulf region) and The Royal College of Surgeons in Bahrain (Gulf region), or through medical exchange programs or even in international conferences.

The problem in UAE healthcare units is even greater than in the US due to the quasi-total absence of professional medical interpreters (The Emirates Center for Strategic Studies and Research 2008). Through a field trip to six healthcare units in different emirates of the country, the researcher could confirm the complete absence of skilled interpreters in healthcare. Specialists in the field and/or patients recur to staff, such as nurses, doctors, administrative employees, or even members of the patient's family to assist them in the communication process whenever a language barrier is present. According to the Emirates Center for Strategic Studies and Research, 30 % of the population is local while 70 % are divided between Arabic-speaking individuals (10 %) and other language speakers (90 %).

When interviewed by the researcher, senior healthcare providers and decision makers in one of the major hospitals in Dubai expressed the urgent need for professional medical interpreters The same was emphasized by officers at the Ministry of Health (MOH) and Development of Health and Medical Services (DOHMS) units. The latter stated that stakeholders in medical settings need to communicate, interchange ideas, beliefs, and principles, but are sometimes hit by linguistic barriers while communicating.

Sometimes, inaccurate nonverbal sign language is taken for granted in the process of coming to the correct diagnosis. The situation can be more serious in emergencies where time is an issue, and the delay of 1 s might endanger the life of the patient. Therefore, "poor communication is a barrier to good patient-centered care. Translation services are required in all facilities as part of Joint Commission accreditation" (DerGurahian 2008). In addition, the psychological status of the patient is part of the healing process, and the difficulty associated with finding medical translators will not ensure a good communication environment between the patient and the medical staff. "A number of studies show that misunderstandings that stem from cultural differences and language barriers have resulted in poor patient–provider relationships, incorrect diagnosis, lack of informed consent, lower patient satisfaction, and even malpractice suits" (Whitman and Davis, cited in Samovar et al. 2011, p. 23).

On a Friday morning (beginning of the weekend in the UAE), I had to drive to the nearest hospital in Sharjah for an acute stomachache. To my surprise, the receptionist, the doctor, and the nurse on duty, were non-Arabic-speaking staff. Curious, I inquired about a translator and the nurse, in very poor Arabic, informed me that she could do the translation! What would have been the situation if the patient in my place were non-English speaking? How would he/she have managed to communicate and convey his feelings to the doctor? How would the doctor have handled the encounter, the diagnostics, and treatment process?

80% of the interviewed patients in the UAE and 70% in the USA said they wished to have Arabic-speaking doctors and nurses in hospitals.

According to Ahmad a 56-year-old patient in Dubai:

One should not forget that it is one of individuals' basic rights to communicate and be communicated with in their mother tongue on their own soil.

And to Suad, a 39-year-old patient:

Also, native speakers express themselves and understand much easier and more effectively in their own language which is something indispensably needed for patients in a medical setting

To the researcher's surprise, when interviewed, the administrative manager of one of the major hospitals in Dubai, showed total unawareness of the language problems existing among patients and health caregivers knowing that at the time of the interview 75% of doctors and 100% of nurses were non-Arabs and around 60% of patients were locals This means that language barrier in these medical settings does not only exist due to the shortage of qualified interpreters but also due to the unawareness and probably denial of the existence of the issue by concerned decision makers.

11.5   Health and Cultural Awareness

Every time there is miscommunication among healthcare givers and patients, the blame is placed on "cultural differences" (Sarangi 2011, p. 262). This kind of analysis according to the same author may force an "analytic separation between language and culture." It may also presuppose a divide between "one homogenous cultural group" (healthcare provider in this case) and another (patients), thus, the risk of a unifying definition of culture and "thematization of cultural differences" (p. 261). For instance, although Dr. Maha (an Egyptian gynecologist working in her clinic in the USA for more than 20 years) and Sarah (a divorced Egyptian student living in the USA for more than 10 years) both are from Egypt and therefore according to many scholars in the field of intercultural studies belong to the same culture, the doctor does not mind asking her Arab patients who are single or married whether they are sexually active, this being part of the profession. For Sarah, however, this kind of question might be embarrassing especially given that she is separated and therefore expected not to have any sexual relations. What would be the situation if the gynecologist were from the USA? It would probably be no worse if the doctor were informed about the cultural background of her patient and most importantly if she or he had studied a bit about the Arab culture during their years of medical study.

This example illustrates and discredits the Sapir–Whorf hypothesis (1950) which states that language determines the way people think (Kay and Kempton 1984). How can language be separated from culture? Even if the healthcare provider and the patient share the same linguistic code, they may disagree on the way they think and translate their thoughts into words. Sherzer (2011) notes that discourse has to be considered as the concrete expression of the language–culture relationship because it is discourse that "creates, recreates, focuses, modifies, and transmits both culture and language and their interaction" (cited in Sarangi 2011, p. 265). In this context, culture is to be redefined as an open process of shared experiences (Raddawi 2007) rather than "a fixed inheritance of shared meanings," as stated by Thornton (1988, p. 26). Street (1993) also defines culture as "an active process of meaning making and contest over definition [...]." The very term "culture itself... changes its meanings and serves different often competing purposes at different times" (p. 25). Eisenstadt (1989) states that "[...] like scientific paradigm, elements of culture are used, modified, or discarded depending on their usefulness in organizing reality ... [...]. Sociologists now recognize that people continually choose among a wide range of definitions of situations or fabricate new ones to fit their needs" (p. 6).

The same author continues: "We need to subscribe to a dynamic view of 'culture' rather than attribute communicative breakdown to cultural differences" (Eisenstadt 1989, p. 11). A nonessentialist and action-oriented perspective on culture enables analysts interested in miscommunication to take on board the complexities related to the uses and functions of culture in contemporary societies (Hall 1981). There might also be a relationship of dominant/dominated or majority/minority cultures, or hosting/hosted, which determined the process of communication among healthcare providers and patients. Bourdieu (1976) points out that "[...] a speaker's linguistic strategies ... [...] are oriented not so much by the chances of being understood or misunderstood but rather by the chances of being listened to, believed, obeyed, even at the cost of misunderstanding" (p. 654). Sarangi (2011) sees that the unifying view of culture and attributing intercultural miscommunication to cultural differences may lead to a stereotyping of the field of intercultural research.

Another example of discursive analysis in cultural communication in the USA is the preprinted form, which a patient usually fills out for general admission or a particular medical encounter for general information. An excerpt reads:

How often do you drink?

Do you have AIDS?

Have you ever taken drugs?

Are you pregnant (for females)?

Compared to similar general information forms or encounters in the UAE, none of these questions are directly asked to the patients whether in written or face-to-face communications. If needed, patients are tested discretely for AIDS and for other culturally sensitive issues such as drugs or alcohol levels. And only married women are asked whether they are pregnant and never would a doctor or nurse ask an Arabic speaking patient how often they drink and even worse, whether they drink (Personal communication, with a senior officer in the Ministry of Health in Dubai, October 2012).

Is the Arabic-speaking patient in the USA supposed to have overcome these "cultural sensitivities?" Sarangi (2011) provides a cultural explanation to these situations when the interviewer (in our study the healthcare provider) is a "member of the majority culture, and has the situational power in the interview context" (p. 266) and therefore should be listened to and obeyed; whereas the interviewee (the patient) is "a member of the minority culture and therefore enjoys less situational power as far as the 'interview game' is concerned" (p. 267). Campbell and Levine (2009) add another possible component to intercultural communication which is "universal ethnocentrism" which has to do with "the universality of ethnic self-love and out-group hostility" (Rousseau and Garcia-Retamero 2007, p. 714). Out of 55 sample groups they examined, 35 turned out to be ethnocentric. "Westernization of the world brings with it new and powerful ethnocentrism, both through processes of diffusion and through reactions to a common out-group" (Rousseau and Garcia-Retamero 2007). In light of these explanations, one can wonder whether the medical world needs a democratization process. Could a sort of colonial and postcolonial power struggle exist?

However, Gumperz et al. (1979) account for miscommunication even in cases where the interviewee and interviewer have the same cultural background, claiming that perception about what is (not) acceptable in the interview context may differ just as in the example of the Egyptian gynecologist and her patient Sarah. In another example, Samia, a 21-year-old Pakistani college student in the UAE, blushed when her GP asked her about her menstruation cycle in front of her father:

> I did not know what to say nor where to direct my eyes and could not look my dad in the eyes for a certain period of time.

Although both Samia and her doctor were very good speakers of English, the cultural divide hindered the communication process. Suurmond and Seeleman (2006) describe four conceptual barriers in medical settings, one of which is when "physician and patient may not share similar values about health and illness" and based on the barriers they find that "the transfer of information, the formulation of the diagnosis and the discussion of treatment can be at stake and therefore the decision making process is impeded" (p. 258).

In the same context in the USA, "as the nation's population [the US] continues to grow and diversify, the health care system will have to change and adjust to meet the needs of an increasingly multicultural patient base" (American College of Physicians 2010, p. 1).

According to the same source: "All patients, regardless of race, ethnic origin, gender, nationality, primary language, socioeconomic status, sexual orientation, cultural background, age, disability, or religion, deserve high-quality health care (American College of Physicians 2010, p. 2) [...]As our society increasingly becomes racially and ethnically diverse, physicians and other health care professionals need to acknowledge the cultural, informational, and linguistic needs of their patients. Health literacy among racial and ethnic minorities must be strengthened in a culturally and linguistically sensitive manner" (American College of Physicians 2010, p. 4).

Culturally competent care providers are expected to ensure that all patients receive high-quality, effective healthcare irrespective of cultural background, language proficiency, socioeconomic status, and other factors that may be informed by a patient's race or ethnicity (Wu and Martinez 2006). Lack of cultural awareness can undermine the doctor–patient relationship. "While only half of all patients adhere to medical or prescription instructions offered by clinicians, rates of adherence are significantly lower for racial and ethnic minorities" (Chen 2009, p. 97). Cultural sensitivities must be understood and respected at all levels of a patient's care experience. The staff should receive preservice or on-the-job cultural competency training (CLAS 2009). Cultural competence is a key part of delivering effective patient-centered care: "both concepts stress respect for the patient, clear communication, shared decision making, and building of the doctor-patient relationship" (Beach et al. 2006, p. 67).

11.6   Cultural Differences and Treatment

According to Jandt (2012), culture is defined as a set of beliefs, traditions, and attitudes shared by a community. In other words, culture is a heritage of shared experiences.

In healthcare, these experiences can manifested as an attitude toward treatment, whether from the doctor's or the patient's side. For Western doctors (mostly low context cultures) including those in the USA, the common trend is to opt for the biomedicine, whereas Eastern healthcare providers or patients belonging to high context cultures, such as China, Japan, and Korea, may opt for alternative or holistic medicine (Samovar et al. 2011).

Other cultural differences in the medical field may arise from different religious and ethnic backgrounds between healthcare givers and patients. Being unaware of each other's cultures in this case may lead to culture shocks. Unintentionally mentioning a taboo or a sensitive issue, a healthcare provider is likely to hurt the feelings of a patient as confirmed by the interviewed patients. For example, when asking direct questions through a medical application form or through a medical encounter prior to prescribing medication, such as "are you pregnant?" or "are you virgin?" to a single Muslim teenager might be intimidating. Furthermore, asking a conservative Muslim patient, "how often do you drink?" or "are you sexually active?" may raise cultural conflicts.

The way a diagnosis or any negative message should be announced to the patient is another cultural difference healthcare providers should be aware of. For low context cultures, which include most Westerners, verbal communication is the principle means of communication among individuals and this, therefore, entails that the message content be direct, clear, and objective. Conversely, high context cultures like Japanese, Chinese, Korean, and Arabs focus more on physical context, i.e., nonverbal communication and other physical conditions that surround the communication. They also care about the harmony among the group, which requires a certain diplomacy and courtesy in the style, and subsequently, an indirect way of speaking (Samovar et al. 2011; Jandt 2012). Thus, a Western doctor informing the patient bluntly that they have cancer or any other lethal disease might have a distressful impact on the Arab patient. The latter, belonging to a collective culture, may not be used to receiving direct negative messages.

These cultural differences in the speech rules between high and low context cultures as referred to by Wolfson (1989) sometimes create a discrepancy in the way the truth should be conveyed to the patient and whether he or she has to right to know it (Samovar et al. 2011). Moreover, among the controversial issues that may arise in a diversified medical setting is the way the healthcare provider would like to treat the patient (for example, biomedical for low context cultures) or the mode of treatment that the patient wishes to receive (alternative medicine, holistic or supernatural for Confucian high context cultures), where the priority goes to the psychological status of the patient (Samovar et al. 2011).

Research in US medical settings has found that Hispanic, Asian, and African-American patients have diminished trust and feel less respect from their physicians than white patients (Blendon et al. 2008). Evidence reveals that the practice of medicine can have a "dehumanizing" effect on clinicians and that physicians may become so absorbed by the "culture of biomedicine" that it may become difficult to relate to those with differing views on the practice of medicine (Hutchinson and Dobkin 2009; Fox 2005). Evidence shows that cultural competency training can lead to improved patient outcomes and fewer liability claims, although more research is needed (Goode et al. 2006).

To understand and treat diverse ethnic communities better, whether in the USA or the UAE, physicians must engage in cultural competency training at all medical education levels. "An increasing number of medical schools offer pathways to cultural competence development, but more needs to be done" (Brotherton et al. 2004, p. 1036). Surveys report that nearly all residents believe that addressing cultural issues is moderately or very important.

Patients who were interviewed in this study, all felt that healthcare providers were not prepared to care for individuals whose beliefs were at odds with Western medicine, new immigrants, or those whose religious beliefs affect treatment (Weissman et al. 2005). Proper patient engagement takes time, and many of the interviewed physicians who provide care for racial and ethnic groups have expressed concern that time constraints and other pressures related to day-to-day medical practice do not facilitate crosscultural communication and understanding. Many residents also reported that they lacked professional mentorship in the area of crosscultural care and receive little evaluation of skills. Other evidence suggests that the existing cultural competency measures are insufficient to produce meaningful change among healthcare providers (Kumas-Tan et al. 2007).

To conclude, primary and secondary research in this study reveal the existence of language and culture barriers that are present in numerous medical settings in the USA and the UAE. These barriers can be summarized as follows:

1. Physician and patient may not share the same language.
2. Physician and patient may share the same linguistic but not cultural background.
3. Physician and patient may not share similar beliefs and values about health, illness and treatment.
4. Physicians do not have the required cultural competency to have unbiased and effective communication with patients.

11.7 Recommendations

As far as language barriers are concerned, there is an urgent need to hire qualified professional interpreters, whether ad hoc or permanent in most if not all multicultural and multilingual medical settings. A call center equipped with the most advanced technological means of communication for interpreting services is further recommended, especially when less common languages are present. Patient privacy and confidentiality needs should be respected and, therefore, language problems are not to be solved through the presence of nurses, family members, or acquaintances of the patient.

Funding should be continued and increased for programs and initiatives to train human medical interpreters as well as encourage the implementation of advanced machine aided translation and multilingual translation software in medical settings.

Cultural competency is the primary remedy to cultural issues in medical settings. Awareness of all parties involved in the process about each other's differences and diversity is indispensable for a successful interaction, better healthcare outcomes, and patient satisfaction. Traditional language learning and teaching have failed to acknowledge the importance of culture. "Learning to speak a language is not just about learning to produce grammatically correct sentences but about learning what to say in a culturally appropriate way" (Zhu 2011, p. 5). Second language acquisition needs to be rethought to include pragmatics and discourse abilities; also a nonessentialist redefinition of culture is required. No more cultural difference is confined to "memberships of different social groups nor are differences in beliefs and practices among groups a cause of mis- or nonunderstanding in intercultural communication" (Zhu 2011, p. 6). "Cultural differences are neither prescribed nor static and instead they are constructed through discursive practice" (Zhu 2011, p. 7)

Being culturally different "is a socially constructed phenomenon and needs to be studied through a fine-grained analysis of interaction on a case-by-case basis" (Zhu 2011, p. 29). Hence, there is a need to acknowledge the shifting nature of culture and the necessity of individual interaction between healthcare provider and patient prior to asking questions during the encounter and prior to distributing any form to be filled out by the patient. In these multilingual and multicultural settings, perhaps more than one language should be included in the forms, which the patients need to fill out. Sarangi and Nishizaka challenge the practice of using cultural categories such as "East," "West," "Indian," "European," etc. as independent variables and argue that whether a person is culturally different or not is something achieved in the actual course of the interaction (Zhu 2011, p. 26). Therefore "if the analysis of the intercultural event is made on a collective scale, the creation of a hypothetical individual is a means toward a generalization about cultures" (Zhu 2011). Furthermore, stereotyping and oversimplifying can stem out of this cultural unawareness; for instance statements such as "*Arabs like medication*" and "*Westerners are alcohol consumers*" are often heard in the Arab world.

The cultural competency of healthcare providers and patients should be fostered by the establishment of innovative training programs to support crosscultural care in both the UAE and the USA, such as the Navigator program developed in the Central Valley of California to help immigrant and nonnative English speakers deal with the complexities of the US healthcare system (Rideout 2007). This pilot program would help adult school students learn how to "navigate" the US healthcare system. The goal is to educate them about the healthcare system and make them culturally competent as potential healthcare givers and patients. Students can visit hospitals and clinics, and attend workshops and community presentations organized by healthcare professionals and medical students to spread healthcare awareness and cultural knowledge.

Mutual understanding of the different cultural perspectives of each party would enhance cultural competency to avoid stereotyping and the universalistic view that everyone is equal in behavior and perception. Cultural competency helps also reduce ethnocentrism when healthcare providers expect or impose certain styles of communication, treatment methods, or language on their patients just because these professionals believe that their own culture is superior to that of their patients.

The increase of diversity of healthcare professionals is another necessity to fight discrimination, biases, ethnic, and cultural conflicts between healthcare providers and patients. Diversity is a factor that can help enhance cultural sensitivity toward the patients' different ethnic, cultural, and linguistic backgrounds.

A diverse health care workforce that is more representative of those they serve is crucial to promote understanding among health providers and patients, facilitate quality care, and promote equity in the health care system. Therefore, medical schools need to put more efforts into recruiting and retaining minority and diverse faculty.

According to a senior faculty and healthcare consultant in a private hospital in the Midwestern USA, racial and ethnic minorities are severely underrepresented among American health care workers.

Having a multicultural workforce can have many benefits. The medical professor also emphasized that according to the IOM report "In the Nation's Compelling Interest, ":

> diversity in the health profession can lead to better access for minority patients, improved patient satisfaction, strengthened cultural competence and sensitivity among other health professionals, and overall improved academic performance for students of the health professions.

More research and data collection related to Arabic-speaking patients and non-Arabic speaking healthcare givers and vice versa in multicultural settings is needed to empower stakeholders to better understand and address any intercultural communication issues and guide potential solutions.

The shifting demographics and increased diversity in the communities of the USA and the UAE, highlighted by the most recent census in 2010, challenge health service providers to become more knowledgeable about and responsive to the diverse needs of their patients. Differences in perceptions of health, values, and practices, as well as diverse belief systems and worldviews, are realities that healthcare providers in service professions face when planning care and addressing their patients' needs. Lack of in-depth knowledge about these cultural differences, as well as an accompanying lack of sensitivity in addressing what is known, has been associated with health service disparities. Compelling evidence shows that minorities, and Arabs are no exception, in the US experience with higher incidence of disability, disease, and death compared with the mainstream population (Agency for Healthcare Research and Quality 2005; Betancourt et al. 2002; Flaskerud 2002; Smedley et al. 2003; cited in Munoz et al. 2009).

Conclusion

Linguistic and cultural diversity are a salient feature of today's globalized world and therefore, effective communication between stakeholders is indispensable. The medical setting is no exception. Medical caregivers and patients should engage in a cultural competency campaign for a successful healing process, better patient satisfaction, cost efficiency, and improved healthcare and research outcomes. This entails understanding and tolerance of the culture and language skills of each party.

Cultural differences are not always the reason for misunderstanding or miscommunication in intercultural interaction. Participants can create a common ground by seeking to know the other. In healthcare like in any other professional setting where humans are in constant interaction, the communication process should be based on the principle of altercentrism rather than egocentrism.

References

American College of Physicians. (2004). Racial and ethnic disparities in health care: A position paper of the American College of Physicians. *Annals of Internal Medicine, 141*(3), 226–232.
American College of Physicians. (2010). Racial and ethnic disparities in health care, Philadelphia: American College of Physicians; 2010: Policy Paper. (Available from American College of Physicians, 190 N. Independence Mall West, Philadelphia, PA 19106.)
Asante, M. K., & Gudykunst, W. B. (Eds.). (1989). *Handbook of international and intercultural communication.* London: SAGE

Baker, D. W., Hayes, R., & Fortier, J. P. (1998). Interpreter use and satisfaction with interpersonal aspects of care for Spanish-speaking patients. *Medical Care, 36*(10), 1461–1470. http://www.jstor.org/stable/3767075. Accessed 10 June 2012.

Barrett, S., Dyer, C., & Westpheling, K. (2008). *Language access: Understanding the barriers and challenges in primary care settings*. McLean: Association of Clinicians for the Underserved

Beach, M. C., Saha, S., & Cooper, L. A. (2006).The role and relationship of cultural competence and patient-centeredness in healthcare quality. The Common Wealth Fund, 36. http://www.commonwealthfund.org/~/media/Files/Publications/Fund%20Report/2006/. Accessed 19 June 2012.

Bernstein, J., Bernstein, E., Dave, A., Hardt, E., James, T., Linden, J., Mitchell, P., Oishi, T., Safi, C. (2002). Trained medical interpreters in the emergency department: Effects on services, subsequent charges, and follow-up. *Journal of Immigrant Health, 4*(4), 171–184. doi:10.1023/A:1020125425820

Bischoff, A., Bovier, P. A., Rrustemi, I., Gariazzo, F., Eytan, A., & Loutan, L. (2003). Language barriers between nurses and asylum seekers: Their impact on symptom reporting and referral. *Social Science and Medicine, 57*(3), 503–512. doi:10.1016/S0277-9536(02)00376-3

Blendon, R. J., Buhr, T., Cassidy, E. F., Pérez, D. J., Sussman, T., Benson, J. M., & Herrmann, M. J. (2008). Disparities in physician care: Experiences and perceptions of a multi-ethnic America. *Health Affairs, 27*(2), 507–517. doi:10.1377/hlthaff.27.2.507

Bourdieu, P. (1976). The economics of linguistic exchanges. *Social Science Information, 16*(6), 645–668. doi:10.1177/053901847701600601

Brislin, R. W. (1981). *Cross-cultural encounters: Face-to-face interaction*. New York: Pergamon.

Brotherton, S. E., Rockey, P. H., & Etzel, S. I. (2004). US graduate medical education: 2003–2004. *The Journal of the American Medical Association, 292*(9), 1032–1037. http://jama.jamanetwork.com/article.aspx?articleid=199359. Accessed 11 June 2012.

Chen, P. W. (16 July 2009). Doctor and patient: bridging the culture gap. The New York Times. http://www.nytimes.com/2009/07/16/health/16chen.html?_r=2&pagewanted=1&hpw. Accessed 25 Oct 2012.

Condon, J. C., & Yousef, F. (1975). *An introduction to intercultural communication*. Indianapolis: The Bobbs-Merrill Company.

David, R. A., & Rhee, M. (1998). The impact of language as a barrier to effective health care in an underserved urban Hispanic community. *Mount Sinai Journal of Medicine, 65*(5–6), 393–397. http://www.vdh.virginia.gov/ohpp/clasact/documents/CLASact/research3/13_David.pdf. Accessed 11 Nov 2011.

DerGurahian, J. (2008). Comparative satisfaction. *Modern Healthcare, 38*(13), 6–7. http://ez-proxy.aus.edu/login?url=http://search.proquest.com/docview/211942254?accountid=16946. Accessed 10 Jan 2013.

Eisenstadt, S. N. (1989). Introduction: Culture and social structure in recent sociological analysis. In H. Hafercamp (Ed.), *Social structure and culture* (pp. 5–11). Berlin: Walter de Gruyter.

Farmer, R., Miller, D., & Lawrenson, R., (1996). *Epidemiology and public health medicine* (4th ed.). Oxford: Blackwell Science.

Flores, G., Laws, B., Mayo, S., Zucherman, B., Abreu, M., Medina, L., & Handt, E. (2003). Errors in medical interpretation and their potential clinical consequences in pediatric encounters. *Pediatrics, 111*(1), 6–14

Fox, R. C. (2005). Cultural competence and the culture of medicine. *The New England Journal of Medicine, 353*(13), 1316–1319. http://ezproxy.aus.edu/login?url=http://search.proquest.com/docview/223926633?accountid=16946. Accessed 11 July 2012.

Garcia, E. A., Roy, L. C., Okada, P. J., Perkins, S. D., & Wiebe, R. A. (2004). A comparison of the influence of hospital-trained, ad hoc, and telephone interpreters on perceived satisfaction of limited English-proficient parents presenting to a pediatric emergency department. *Pediatric Emergency Care, 20*(6), 373–378.

Goode, T. W., Dunne, M. C., & Bronheim, S. M. (2006). The evidence base for cultural and linguistic competency in health care. The Commonwealth Fund, 37. http://commonwealthfund.org/usr_doc/Goode_evidencebasecultlinguisticcomp_962.pdf. Accessed 11 April 2013.

Gumperz, J. J., Jupp, T. C., & Roberts, C. (1979). Crosstalk: A study of cross-cultural communication. Souhthall: National Center for Industrial Language Training.

Hall, S. (1981). Cultural studies: Two paradigms. In T. Bennett, G. Martin, C. Mercer, & J. Woollacott (Eds.), Culture, ideology and social processes (pp. 19–38). London: Batsford (in association with the Open University Press).

Halligan, P. (2006). Caring for patients of islamic denomination: Critical care nurses' experiences in Saudi Arabia. Journal of Clinical Nursing, 15,1565–1573.

Hampers, L. C., Cha, S., Gutglass, D. J., Binns, H. J., & Krug, S. E. (1999). Language barriers and resource utilization in a pediatric emergency department. Pediatrics, 103(6), 1253–1256. doi:10.1542/peds.103.6.1253.

Hornberger, J., Itakura, H., & Wilson, S. R. (1997). Bridging language and cultural barriers between physicians and patients. Public Health Reports, 112(5), 410–417. http://www.ncbi.nlm.nih.gov/pmc/articles/PMC1381949/pdf/pubhealthrep00038-0056.pdf. Accessed 24 June 2013.

Hutchinson, T. A., & Dobkin, P. L. (2009). Mindful medicine practice: Just another fad? Canadian Family Physician, 55(8), 778–779. http://www.ncbi.nlm.nih.gov/pmc/articles/PMC2726084/pdf/0550778.pdf. Accessed 11 May 2013.

Jacobs, E. A., Agger-Gupta, N., Chen, A. H., Piotrowski, A., & Hardt, E. J. (2003). Language barriers in healthcare settings: An annotated bibliography of the research literature. Woodland Hills: The California Endowment.

Jandt, F. E. (2012). An introduction to intercultural communication: Identities in a global community (5th ed.). London: SAGE Publications.

Kay, P. & Kempton, W. (1984). What is the Sapir-Whorf hypothesis? American Anthropologist, 86(1), 65–79. http://www.jstor.org/stable/679389. Accessed 11 April 2012.

Kirkman-Liff, B., & Mondragon, D. (1991). Language of interview: Relevance for research of Southwest Hispanics. American Journal of Public Health, 81(11), 1399–1404. doi:10.2105/AJPH.81.11.1399.

Kumaş-Tan, Z., Beagan, B., & Loppie, C. (2007). Measures of cultural competence: Examining hidden assumptions. Academic Medicine, 86(6), 548–557. http://culturalmeded.stanford.edu/pdf%20docs/KurmasTan%20Examining%20Hidden%20Assumptions.pdf. Accessed 11 June 2011.

Munoz, C., Broka, C., & Mohamad, S. (2009). Development of a multidisciplinary course in cultural competence for nursing and human service professions. Journal of Nursing Education, 48(9), 495–503.

Office of Minority Health (2009). National Standards on Culturally and Linguistically appropriate Services (CLAS). http://www.omhrc.gov/templates/browse.aspx. Accessed 14 Sept 2011

Raddawi, R. (2006). Web based communication process to facilitate dialogue between English speaking healthcare providers and non-English speaking patients in United Arab Emirates and United States hospitals. TranslationWatch Quarterly, 2(2), 74–92. Sydney: TSI.

Raddawi, R. (2007). The role of translation in second language teaching: Customized software for vocabulary learning. In proceedings of the second international translation conference. experiences, expertise and technologies in translation. Amman. April 27–29th Arab Thought Foundation Press.

Rasheed, A. (2009). Expat numbers rise rapidly as UAE population touches 6m. Gulfnews. http://gulfnews.com/news/gulf/uae/general/expat-numbers-rise-rapidly-as-uae-population-touches-6m-1.505602. Accessed 5 June 2011

Rideout, V. (2007). Parents, children & media. A Kaiser family foundation survey. http://kaiserfamilyfoundation.files.wordpress.com/2013/01/7638.pdf. Accessed 11 May 2013

Rousseau, D. L., & Garcia-Retamero, R. (2007). Identity, power, and threat perception: A cross-national experimental study. The Journal of Conflict Resolution, 51(5), 711–744. doi:10.1177/0022002707304813.

Samovar, L. A., Porter, R. E., & McDaniel, E. R. (Eds.). (2011). *Intercultural communication: A reader* (13th ed.). Boston: Wadsworth Publishing.

Sarangi, S. (2011). Intercultural or not? In Zhu Hua (Ed.), *The language and intercultural communication reader* (pp. 261–276). London: Routledge.

Street, B. (1993). Culture is a verb. In D. Graddol, L. Thompson, & M. Byram (Eds.), *Language and culture* (pp. 23–43). Clevedon: BAAL and Multilingual Matters.

Suurmond, J., & Seeleman, C. (2006). Shared decision-making in an Intercultural context: Barriers in the interaction between physicians and immigrant patients. *PatientEducation and Counseling, 60*(2), 253–259. doi:10.1016/j.pec.2005.01.012.

The Emirates Center for Strategic Studies and Research periodical (June 2008). Abu Dhabi.

Thornton, R. (1988). Culture: A contemporary definition. In E. Boonzaier & J. Sharp (Eds.), *Keywords* (pp. 17–28). Cape Town: David Philip.

United States Census. (2010). Census, briefs and reports. Population distribution and change: 2000 to 2010. www.census gov/2010 census/. Accessed 11 Aug 2011.

Weissman, J. S., Betancourt, J., Campbell, E. G., Park, E. R., Kim, M., Clarridge, B., Blumenthal D., Lee K. C., Maina, A. W. (2005). Resident physicians' preparedness to provide cross-cultural care. *Journal of the American Medical Association, 294*(9), 1058–1067. doi:10.1001/jama.294.9.1058.

Wolfson, N. (1989). *Perspectives: Sociolinguistics and TESOL*. Rowley: Newbury House.

Wu, E., & Martinez, M. (2006). Taking cultural competency from theory to action. The Commonwealth Fund, 38. http://www.commonwealthfund.org. Accessed 15 July, 2013.

Youdelman M. K. (2008). The medical tongue: U.S. laws and policies on language access. *Health Affairs, 27*(2), 424–433. doi:10.1377/hlthaff.27.2.424.

Zhu, H. (Ed.). (2011). *The language and intercultural communication reader*. London: Routledge.

Rana Raddawi is Associate Professor in the English Department at the American University of Sharjah. She holds a Ph. D in Translation Studies from ESIT/Sorbonne. She teaches at the graduate and undergraduate levels. She has mastered five languages and has been teaching Intercultural Communication for more than seven years. She has lived and worked for many years in the West and the Middle East. She is a member of the editorial board of the International Journal of Bilingual and Multilingual Teachers of English (IJBMTE), member of the editorial board of the online Arab World English Journal (AWEJ), member of the Research Review committee of Qatar National Research Fund (QNRF). She is also a Peer Reviewer for American Education and Research Association (AERA) /Paulo Freire SIG, and member of the Review Committee of Global Conference on Education. She has various translations such as Natural Medicine for Flu and Cold.. (translated into Arabic, 250 pages)- and Happiness is a serious problem : a human nature repair manual (translated into Arabic, 200 pages) and publications in her areas of expertise. Her current research interests lie in Intercultural Communication, Critical Pedagogy, Emotional Intelligence in Healthcare and Education, and Gender Empowerment.

Chapter 12
The Political TV Interview, Tim Sebastian's Interview with an Arab: A Venue for Reconciliation or Discord?

Omar Fayez Atari

12.1   Introduction

The political television interview is an interesting venue for researchers to explore the dynamism of intercultural communication and its complexity; it is a highly structured speech event with norms of interaction and interpretation which are governed by sociolinguistic and discourse rules. An interview can be defined as question-and-answer exchanges between two or more participants, which sometimes are confrontational and challenging in nature. This interaction is produced for an audience that does not actively participate (Clyman and Heritage 2002; Jagtinani 2012). The formal interview is a speech event in which the interviewer and interviewee presumably cooperate and coordinate the activity of interaction to get across a message to viewers. Hence, an interview has its own structure, allowing interviewer and interviewee to construct knowledge and identity. The interviewer's conduct is influenced by the cooperativeness of the interviewee.

In order to achieve a highly structured, informative, and comprehensible speech event, participants are expected to cooperate in adhering to a set of unwritten interactional norms or rules and observe, among other things, Grice's (1975) cooperative principle and the maxims of quality, quantity, manner, and relation derived from it.

According to Riley (2007, p. 93), "The study of linguistic forms of coordination has shown that they are part of culture. Such culture-specific forms of language use are called communicative practices. They are the ways in which members of a given community exploit their linguistic resources." Culturally specific groups of various kinds select, pattern, and use those resources in different ways.

For instance, the speech act "requesting" can be realized in English in a number of different ways, for example:

The room is stuffy here.

You want to open the window as it is stuffy here?

O. F. Atari (✉)
UAE University, Al-Ain, United Arab Emirates
e-mail: atari_o@uaeu.ac.ae

© Springer Science+Business Media Singapore 2015
R. Raddawi (ed.), *Intercultural Communication with Arabs*,
DOI 10.1007/978-981-287-254-8_12

Can you open the window? It is getting stuffy here.

How can you stay in here? Is the AC on?

In political TV interviews, the interactional scenes become overshadowed by conflictual attitudes. These conflicts and adverse stances are bound up with the interviewer's and interviewee's conflicting norms of interactions, which in turn, are bound up with the two interactants' culturally specific strategies of communication. If the interviewer's communicative style is at any level not in harmony with the interviewee's style, these conflictual interactional scenes come to the surface.

This chapter attempts to describe the interviewer's/interviewee's communicative styles in terms of their indigenous social/cultural practices. Specifically, the interviewer's and interviewee's communicative styles will be attributed to what ethnolinguists and anthropological linguists call the "high-context" and "low-context" cultures and the high-dominant literate versus the high-dominant oral cultures: (cf. Hall 1982; Riley 2007; Biber 1988; Tannen 1980; Olson and Torrance 1991; among others). Hall views meaning and context as "inextricably bound up with each other" (1982, cited in Zaharna 1995, pp. 2–3). The difference between high- and low-context cultures depends on how much meaning is found in the context versus in the code. Low-context cultures tend to place more meaning in the language code and very little meaning in the context. For this reason, communication tends to be specific, explicit, and analytical. People raised in high-context systems expect more from others than do the participants in low-context systems. When talking about something that they have on their mind, a high-context individual will expect his interlocutor to understand what's bothering him so that he doesn't have to be specific. In high-context exchanges, much of the "burden of meaning" appears to fall on the listener. The result is that he will talk around and around the point, in effect putting all the pieces in place except the crucial one. In high-context culture, the meaning is in the context. In other words, high-context exchanges express the messages by heavy reliance on the context features rather than by language forms. Here is an example of contextualized language (borrowed from Hatch 1992, p. 237); "…take a tape recorder an…that you just punch…an y'work on the tape recorder…and y'talk the tape recorder."

A written low-context version would be as follows: "to solve writers' block use a tape recorder as a partner. Tell the tape recorder what you want to write. Then play back this message. As you listen. Type out…." In low-context cultures, the burden appears to fall on the speaker to accurately and thoroughly convey the meaning in his spoken or written message.

The analysis utilizes a range of concepts from speech act theory, conversational analysis, critical discourse analysis, and pragmatics, including implicatures and shared assumptions. Due to the "multilayerdness" nature of the political TV interview, the analysis will be conducted at the micro- and macro-levels. This involves analyzing each utterance produced by the interviewer and each interviewee's response to that including the implicatures, presuppositions, and shared assumptions which are associated with those utterances. The interview is perceived as a set of transactions, each of which consists of one exchange and each exchange of an interviewer's move followed by an interviewee's response.

12.2   Literature Review

The two pioneering approaches to the study of the political TV interviews have predominantly been the conversational analysis approach and critical discourse analysis (henceforth CA and CDA). The two approaches are both sociological approaches, analyzing social structure and activity.

According to Jagtiani (2012), contrastive analysts' approach is grounded in the observable orientations that interactants display when engaging in conversational interaction. In contrast, according to Jagtiani (2012, p. 1), CDA is mainly concerned with the way social power and dominance are practiced and challenged through written and spoken discourse within a social and political context.

Contrastive analysts consider communication a joint activity; they are interested in analyzing how such jointly organized interaction is produced (Sacks 1984). The focus is on naturally occurring talk, such as formal versus informal and institutional versus personal interaction.

Sequences and speaking turns within sequences are the primary units of analysis. In other words, CA is mainly concerned with explaining how coherence and sequential organization in discourse is constructed and understood in order to identify systematic properties in talk (Jagtiani 2012, p. 2).

Critical discourse analysts study "how social power abuse, dominance, and inequality are enacted, reproduced, and resisted by text and talk in the social and political context" (Van Dijk 2001 cited in Jagtiani 2012). In their analysis, they uncover how discourse discriminates against minority and powerless groups drawing from wider structural contexts (Jagtiani 2012, p. 3).

As for the analysis of political TV interviews involving an interviewer from the West and an interviewee from the Arab world, Al-aridi (1986) conducted a seminal piece of work on the analysis of political television interviews which included Israeli and Arab interviewees and the interviewer was an American. His analysis investigated the dynamics of political television interviews by describing and analyzing the operating forces in those speech events.

This speech event can have one or more transactions depending on the number of prepared topics for the interview. Transactions are made up of exchanges, and exchanges are made up of moves. An exchange has only two moves. The first one of these moves is an opening move and the second one is a responding move. The number of moves in an interview depends on the number of exchanges and number of transactions in that interview.

Al-aridi (1986) uses the term "move," as the smallest meaningful interactive unit with its various types, as the unit of analysis since moves combine to make up exchanges and exchanges make up transactions that make up the whole interview.

Types of moves:

a. Opening moves—they are structural and pragmatic elements of topic-carrying and transactional-initial opening moves.
b. Responding moves—they both determine discourse interconnectedness.

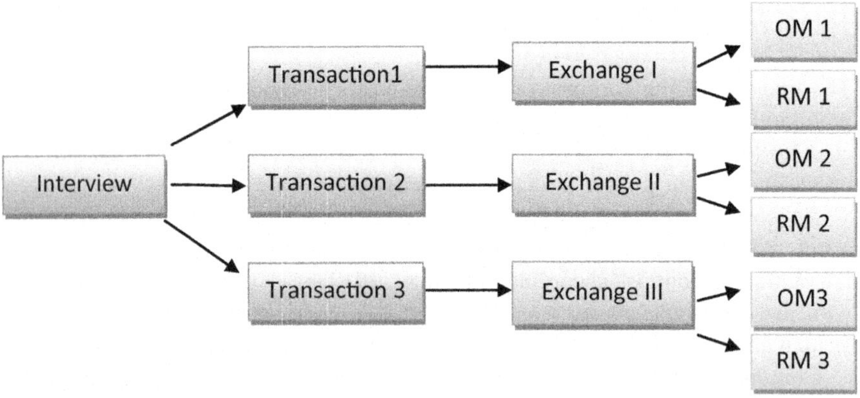

Fig. 12.1 Structure of an interview. (Al-aridi 1986, p. 44)

Al-aridi (1986, p. 44) studied interviewer's questioning strategies and interviewees' responding strategies.

Interviewer's questions are studied in terms of multilayerdness and content and the effect of interviewer's questions on interviewees' responses (Al-aridi 1986) is as illustrated in the following figure (Fig. 12.1):

It is worthwhile noting that the idea of measuring success in communication in political TV interviews on the basis of interviewees' supportive responses may not fully reveal the dynamism of the interactions. The sociolinguistic and pragmatic features of interviewees' styles of communication can be revealed on the basis of their literacy types and their cognitive consequence. The cultural and social practices which underpin the native English-speaking interviewer's communicative styles and those of the Arabic-speaking interviewee's have not adequately been incorporated in the previously conducted research studies. The ethnography of communication will be the basis of this study; specifically, how the native speaker of English interviewer employs certain communicative strategies and how the Arab interviewee responds is the major thrust of this chapter. The interviewer's and interviewee's communicative styles have not been explored cross-culturally in political TV interviews.

The analysis of each move-response as a single entity in its own right does not lead us to the entire genre interaction. Therefore, the norms of interaction and norms of interpretation between the two interlocutors in this complex dyad, should be examined in terms of the communicative styles/strategies employed by the two interlocutors of this genre, the interview. How the interviewer achieves his goals of making the interviewee respond by agreeing, disagreeing, challenge, etc., and how the interviewee can be expected to be supportive of the interviewer's move to make the interaction happen is another dimension.

In the following section, the interview will be presented (see appendix) followed by an analysis of a self-contained segment. The reason for the analysis of the first two pages is that this part is self-contained, it stands by itself and it ends as a normal conclusion of the interaction between the interviewer and interviewee. Specifically, the segment to be analyzed consists of 6 exchanges of 12 moves and responses. This in itself is one self-contained segment. The rest of the interview consists of other segments of similar structures.

The analysis is intended to pinpoint those moves in which the interviewer tries to manipulate language use to elicit the required responses from the interviewee. Then the interviewer's and the interviewee's communicative styles are interpreted in terms of cultural norms and practices of the two speech communities to which they belong.

12.3   Background

This interview was conducted on November 2, 2004, by Tim Sebastian for his show on BBC News 24 TV Program known as "HARDTALK." Sebastian interviewed Dr. Azzam Al-Tamimi from the Institute of Islamic Political Thought, London. The interview was conducted after the Oslo agreement for peace between Palestinians and Israelis. The Palestinians were split over the agreement into two opposing groups: those opposed to Oslo which is the Hamas group and those for Oslo, the Arafat group, Fatah.

12.4   Analysis

Here is a self-contained segment of the interview. It consists of 6 transactions with 12 exchanges comprising 24 moves and responses.
  Sebastian:

> As far as you're concerned with Yaser Arafat, good riddance—you don't want him back in the Palestinian territories and that goes for your friends in Hamas as well.

The interviewer starts off with a claim based on a presupposition that Al-Tamimi is a friend of Hamas and that both Al-Tamimi and Hamas do not want Arafat back in Palestinian territories.

The interviewer uses a British English cliché "good riddance" to make the claim more assertive. He uses an affirmative utterance to perform an assertive claim instead of a question. He uses the second person pronoun to confront the interviewee as a Hamas supporter. The interviewer is already practicing a controlling exercise technique.
  Al-Tamimi:

> Not really. The last few weeks he spent in Ramallah his relationship with Hamas was actually improving. They were doing very good business together.

Al-Tamimi performs a denial and tries to elaborate but ends up conceding to Sebastian's claim that Hamas and Arafat were not friends before. This comes in as support, unintentionally executed by Al-Tamimi to Sebastian's claim that Hamas does not want Arafat back in Palestinian territories.

Sebastian:

> But you say today his group no longer speaks for the Palestinians—these are your words

Sebastian is using a bound move to introduce a subtopic of the main claim that Hamas does not want Arafat and that Hamas and Arafat are not friends. Sebastian uses the quote: "these are your words" to maintain a neutrality stance while still challenging the interviewee.

Al-Tamimi:

> For some time they have not been speaking for the Palestinians. Since they accepted Oslo and went along the path of peace-making in accordance with the terms of Israel and its supporters in America they had stopped speaking for the Palestinians.

Al-Tamimi performs a confirmation that Arafat and his group have not been speaking for the Palestinians. He goes on to reiterate and substantiate his claim explaining that by signing the Oslo agreement, Arafat's group stopped being the representative of the Palestinians. He does this however by counting on the shared assumption that the peace path implies that the agreement is forged by the Americans in accordance with Israelis' terms. This is based on shared assumptions that are known by a certain segment of the viewers, such as some Palestinians, Arabs, etc. but not all viewers with all their different persuasions. In other words, the support for his claim is not expressed through language forms; it is all in the context. Here, he is perceived as flouting Grice's Maxim of Quantity and Relevance.

Al-Tamimi's resort to the strategy of shared assumptions appeals to just one minor segment of the viewers. Moreover, since Sebastian identified him as a Hamas supporter and friend at the outset, he is making him look bad to all those viewers who are against Hamas, namely the western viewers who think of Hamas as an illegitimate terrorist group.

This exchange shows how Sebastian sets up a trap for the interviewee by announcing in his first move in the first exchange that Al-Tamimi is a friend of Hamas.

Sebastian:

> But they may have stopped speaking for you and they may have stopped speaking for Hamas but there's plenty of popularity left among the Palestinians in the territories, isn't there?

Sebastian is using another bound move to introduce another subtopic which is the issue of representation/popularity of Arafat in Palestinian territories. This move links this subtopic to the preceding one:"speaking for Palestinians"; he presents a challenge to Al-Tamimi's claim that "Arafat stopped speaking for Palestinians since he signed the Oslo peace-treaty." Sebastian is challenging Al-Tamimi's claim by using this bound move. He uses repetition as a forceful strategy to concede momentarily to the claim in order to challenge Al-Tamimi by stating that "Arafat still has a lot of popularity in the Palestinian territories." His use of "they may have stopped speaking for you" followed by "they may have stopped speaking for Hamas" is an efficient strategy to serve as a concession that usually precedes the strong rebuttal:

the popularity for Arafat is still there. Sebastian is using the Aristotalian, Western, logical technique known as counter-argument (Behrens 2000). He accepts the opponent's claim (i.e., Al-Tamimi's claim that Arafat stopped speaking for Palestinians) and then starts to demolish it by the rebuttal; "there is still a lot of popularity for Arafat among the Palestinians."

Al-Tamimi:

> Well they speak for a certain segment of the Palestinians undoubtedly. This is like a tribe and Yasser Arafat was always the Chief of the tribe.

Al-Tamimi establishes another concession that Arafat and his group speak for a segment of the Palestinians. He then moves to use a nonsupportive response by way of contradicting the concession he has made by using his own personal opinion—"that the Arafat group behaves like a tribe acting according to their own interest irrespective of the law"; then he adds another personal comment that Arafat always acted as the chief of the tribe. Here, he is flouting the maxim of relevance.

Al-Tamimi is using the shared assumption strategy again. His presupposition is that Arafat and his group have always acted against the law and that they always controlled things the way they wanted with no respect to laws of the constitution, etc. All of these semantic relations are not explicitly expressed by language forms; they have to be inferred from the context, from the historical background of Arafat's presidency of the Palestinian authority. This response makes Al-Tamimi appeal to a very small minority of the viewers while not reaching out to the majority who may not be able to relate to Al-Tamimi's presupposition or assumptions. In this respect, Al-Tamimi's response is classified as a nonsupportive response and that classifies him as an unsuccessful communicator (see Al-aridi 1986 on supportive vs. nonsupportive responses). Al-Tamimi who is highly literate and almost a true bilingual is yet resorting to the oral culture strategy of counting on the viewers to add from the context information to his utterance. This orally based strategy associated with the Mediterranean oral culture values the interpersonal relationship between the communicator and the audience (Tannen 1980; Olson and Torrance 1991).

Sebastian:

> Exactly, so your slogan isn't exactly right is it? When you say today his group no longer speaks for the Palestinians; he speaks for quite a lot of the Palestinians doesn't he?

Sebastian uses another bound opening move to support his challenges of Al-Tamimi's preceding claim that "Arafat no longer speaks for Palestinians." He uses two question tags to confirm his move in this exchange: "is it …. " and "doesn't he?"

Sebastian links this substantiation of his challenges to the major claim that Al-Tamimi and Hamas are against Arafat. In this respect, Sebastian is seen as someone who manages to achieve discourse interconnectedness, cohesion, and coherence. He comes across to the viewers as a speaker who employs what Michaels calls "topic-centered" strategy (Michaels 1981, pp. 423–442); linking all the subtopics to the first major claim that Hamas does not want Arafat back in the Palestinian territories. He also comes across as a successful communicator because he uses the projected argument of a third party (Hyatt 1994, p. 221); he links one topic with the other; he doesn't use personal opinions nor does he resort to shared assumptions. Sebastian is employing the literate-based strategy associated with the literate Western culture which uses language forms as the message-carrying vehicle.

Al-Tamimi:

> Quite a lot or few that really depends. I mean we haven't had a (genuine) election and we cannot have general election because the current situation but...

Al-Tamimi uses a pre-answer topic-shift now using "quite a lot or a few"...which means his response is nonsupportive. He follows that up with an account which is based on the assumption that the viewers share with him the "fact" that they never had a genuine election and that "we" meaning the Palestinians or Hamas cannot have general elections because of the current situation. The current situation has to be understood by the viewers either as the Israeli occupation preventing elections or as the Arafat group manipulating the electoral process.

Al-Tamimi's response is nonsupportive and is based on a lot of background information that is shared by him and by a certain segment of Palestinians. Hence, he does not come across as a successful communicator by the other viewers. His use of the first person plural "we" is ambiguous as to whether it refers to Palestinians or to Hamas. Again, Al-Tamimi is flouting the maxims of relevance and quantity.

Sebastian:

> No, but you have opinion Polls don't you.

Sebastian is challenging Al-Tamimi's comment about elections and he asks Al-Tamimi to go back to the issue under consideration by referring back to the "Polls."

Al-Tamimi:

> ...there are indications and the indications tell us that today it is Hamas that really represents what the Palestinians want. The Palestinians want freedom.

Al-Tamimi uses a pre-answer topic-shift (Greatbatch 1986, p. 443) in order not to deal with the "Polls" issue, and then he introduces his own personal opinion as if it were a fact that "Hamas represents what the people want..."

Al-Tamimi is not being positively supportive and he resorts to his own personal views by ignoring the mention of "Polls." Interviewees do this in order to control the topic of their talk by ignoring the focus that has been established by the interviewer's previous question. They do not produce an answer but talk about something else (Greatbatch 1986 cited in Jagtiani 2012, p. 6).

Sebastian:

> Well you say that but that's not backed up by the opinion polls. The polls conducted by the Palestinians center for the policy and survey research between Sept. 23rd, and 26th gives Hamas 22% compared to, I think it's the 26% or more which is given to Fatah and the independence.

Sebastian confronts Al-Tamimi with facts, figures, percentages, and the polls which gave Hamas low percentages. Sebastian is maintaining a neutral stance while challenging Al-Tamimi.

Sebastian goes on to substantiate his counter-argument by elaborating and reiterating using examples. He adds:

> They were asked/people were asked: will you give your vote in the next local election to candidates from Fatah, Hamas, Islamic Jihad or Independence and only 22.2% said Hamas… isn't much of support is it?

Sebastian is using the "projected argument of a third party" to maintain a neutral stance while still effectively challenging Al-Tamimi's preceding claim. He even mentions the different Palestinian factions by name. At this moment the interviewer, Sebastian, is indirectly addressing the audience because he makes them aware of what political Palestinian factions other than Fatah and Hamas are talking about. Sebastian makes sure that the audience is being informed about the political scene and factions/groups in Palestine. He expresses the message through language forms. He doesn't count on shared assumptions that the audience may or may not share with the interviewer and interviewee in this interaction. His use of figures and percentages adds to the forcefulness of his second bound move used to substantiate his argument. His use of the question tag, his use of direct questions put to the audience appeals to the audience as he comes across as a successful communicator.

At this point, I would like to link the interviewer and interviewee's communicative styles to culture. At the outset, one has to establish that all forms of communication are to some degree cross-cultural. Cross-cultural differences in thought concern habits of thinking, not capacities for thought. All humans are capable of and do practice both *contextualized* and *decontextualized* thought (Denny 1991). By contextualized content, the speaker counts on the viewer/audience to add from the context information to the language forms. In decontextualized content, in contrast, the words convey the meaning. Furthermore, social scientists, anthropologists, ethnolinguists, and intercultural studies specialists associate contextualization with oral culture and decontextualization with literate culture. At this point in the interaction, Al-Tamimi's communicative style exhibits features of the oral culture while Sebastian's exhibits features of the literate culture. Western European cultures have been classified as literate-based cultures while the less industrialized Mediterranean culture as orally based culture (Denny 1991, p. 74–75). The fact that Al-Tamimi's responses do not fully and explicitly spell out the intended message by means of language forms is due to the oral culture emphasis on the interpersonal relationship between him as communicator and his audience. Thus, he uses words only as a convenient tool to signal shared social meaning. In contrast, the decontextualized literate culture strategies favor content whereby the words convey the message; that is the meaning is not in the context as in oral Mediterranean culture; rather, meaning is in the language forms. In this regard, Tannen (1980) has found that the strategies that have been associated with oral and literate cultures explain many of the differences in language use by members of varying ethnic, geographic, class, and cultural backgrounds (e.g., Greeks, New York Jews, and Turks employ oral culture strategies while Americans employ literate culture strategies).

Al-Tamimi:

> I question the credibility of this center and of the studies that it makes. What I would say is that give the Palestinians the freedom of choice for a change and see what they choose…

Al-Tamimi is performing an indirect nonsupportive response to Sebastian's counter-argument: "that the polls were taken and the percentages speak for themselves."

> If you give the Palestinians the freedom, they will do something else.

His hypothetical statement is based on the presupposition that the Palestinians were not given the freedom of choice because those opinion polls that Sebastian is referring to are not credible. Al-Tamimi does not explain how; he does not deal with Sebastian's preceding claim and its explicit substantiation. In this respect, Al-Tamimi's utterance is a nonsupportive response to Sebastian's statement. Al-Tamimi's response is an example of "topic associating" to use Michael's term (1981, pp. 423–442).

Sebastian:

> But you just don't like the results—that's the reason you reject this isn't it?

Sebastian is using a reopening new move as he decides that "Al-Tamimi's preceding response was nonsupportive." It is a new challenge, a new assertive claim that Al-Tamimi cannot accept the truth. Sebastian is linking this new challenge to his preceding moves of the polls, the substantiation of his original major challenge that Hamas and Al-Tamimi are against Araft's return to Palestinian territories, using "but you just don't like the results" which makes Sebastian's move antagonistic.

Al-Tamimi:

> No—there are many academics and many observers who have cast doubt on these centers which are funded by the United States of America and do research that serves the peace process and those who are involved in it.

Al-Tamimi's response is a substantiation, an elaboration of his previous statement that the polls are not valid because the centers that supervised the operation of voting are not credible. His topic shifting from dealing with results to casting doubt on the centers that conducted the polls is also based on the presupposition that the centers are controlled by the Americans and that they do what America wants. They are not credible according to Al-Tamimi, as they are funded by America for the purpose of serving the hidden agenda of the peace process which in Al-Tamimi's opinion is hurting the Palestinian cause. All of this topic-shifting response is based on a shared assumption, "that most Palestinians see in the peace process something against their common interest."

Al-Tamimi's response here is indirect and based on a hierarchical structure of presuppositions as I have just mentioned. To the viewers, Al-Tamimi's topic-shifting is vague and they cannot understand what went wrong with the peace process as Al-Tamimi is pointing out. Hence, his topic-shift response is nonsupportive, and Al-Tamimi here comes across as someone who assumes that all viewers share the same background with him.

Sebastian:

> Why does it serve the peace process? There hasn't been any peace process to serve, so it hasn't served anything has it…?

Sebastian's bound move here is to introduce a new concept about the peace process; he claims that the peace process which Al-Tamimi has referred to does not exist in the first place. Sebastian's move is Socratic (Hyatt 1994) in the sense that it leads to more and more questions and comments.

Al-Tamimi:

Well the Israelis killed the peace process.

Al-Tamimi's response is a direct challenge to Sebastian in the sense that there was a peace process but it was not allowed to survive because the Israelis did not want peace. Al-Tamimi's challenge opens the floor for more challenges and disputes. Yet, to the viewers, Al-Tamimi's challenge is not easily understood by the viewers who have different assumptions about the peace process. Some Western viewers see nothing wrong with the peace process. They cannot understand how the Israelis killed the peace process as Al-Tamimi has established.

Sebastian:

... apart from getting the opinion of Palestinians which you don't happen to like. The fact is, according to the polls, Hamas represents under a quarter of the population. That's maybe an unpalatable fact to you but that happens to be borne out by the figures.

Sebastian uses another reopening bound move to get Al-Tamimi back on track to deal with the issue of the polls, with the facts and percentages attesting to Hamas getting low percentages in comparison to what Fatah got. Sebastian's move is another challenge to Al-Tamimi's preceding comments about the polls and the centers that conducted the polls. He uses percentages to make his challenge substantiated and he draws viewers' attention to a distinction between Al-Tamimi's dislike of the results and the facts on the ground.

Sebastian's reopening bound move links his challenge with the major point of contention that he has used as a provocative challenge to Al-Tamimi from the very beginning: "you and Hamas are friends and you do not want Arafat back and Arafat does speak for the Palestinians; and it is not like what you claim that he doesn't speak for the Palestinians."

Al-Tamimi:

What Hamas represents today is actually what the Palestinians are hoping for. The Palestinians are hoping for freedom.

Al-Tamimi is using a pre-answer topic-shift that Hamas is the representative of the Palestinians. Then he follows that up with an elaboration or an account that Palestinians hope for freedom. This indirect nonsupportive response is based on the presupposition that the polls results which are in favor of Fatah are not what the Palestinians want. All of this is based on Al-Tamimi's personal opinion and for the viewers, it is difficult to make the implicit connection between the polls and Hamas as a representative of what the Palestinians want. Al-Tamimi's response does not achieve discourse interconnectedness; so some viewers are not being served by his indirect response which is based on several assumptions that the viewers are allegedly aware of.

Sebastian:

Some … some Palestinians are hoping (for) …

Interruption by Al-Tamimi … Interviewer is unable to continue.

Al-Tamimi:

The Palestinians, most of them want to go back home. The Oslo process, the peace process in which the PLO embroiled itself gave away the rights of the Palestinians ….

Al-Tamimi uses the pre-answer topic-shift to introduce a claim and that is "Palestinians want to go back home." This response is based on the presupposition that the Oslo agreement does not respect the Palestinians' right for return to Palestine. Again, Al-Tamimi's responses are nonsupportive as they do not address the issues put to the table.

Sebastian:

When the Palestinian human-rights group did a survey of the Palestinians and asked them whether they wanted to go home, the overwhelming majority said they didn't and their offices were trashed; the offices of the Palestinian Human-Rights Monitoring Group were trashed as a result of it. So you don't seem to like any results and Hamas and Islamic Jihad and people like that don't seem to like any results that go against their own orthodoxy, do they?

Sebastian uses a bound move to force Al-Tamimi to stick to the point and to challenge his personal value judgment of the issue at hand. Sebastian elaborates on his challenge to Al-Tamimi by referring to the facts on the ground—asking Palestinians about going back home and the results and how their offices were trashed by Hamas and Islamic Jihad. Sebastian is using a third party's utterance to maintain neutrality while challenging Al-Tamimi's rejection of the poll's results and the centers that conducted the polls.

Al-Tamimi:

You see that's nonsense. I am a Palestinian, I know many Palestinians around the world—I know my own family, I know my friends, we all want our homes back. Even if we live in villas, in palaces, we want our homes. Nobody has the right to bring people from outside and drop them on our land. Our land is our land.

Al-Tamimi's response is a direct challenge to Sebastian's claim about Palestinians not wanting to go home. Al-Tamimi elaborates on his challenge by repeating himself to assert his challenge. This can easily appeal to the majority of Palestinians and Arabs all over the world, but Al-Tamimi's antagonistic response (i.e., you see that's nonsense …) does not get across to some uninformed segments of western societies about the Palestinian/Israeli conflict. Hence, Al-Tamimi's challenge is quite good for some segments of the viewers but not necessarily to others.

Sebastian:

And for that, continuing violence-that's what Hamas and you your friends in Hamas speak for?

Sebastian uses a new opening move to introduce a new topic as a challenge to Al-Tamimi. This new opening move is exactly similar to his first original opening move which was meant to introduce a topic as a challenge for an explosive interactional scene to guarantee high ratings of his show.

Based on Al-aridi's (1986) model of the structure of an interview whereby an interview consists of a series of transactions, each comprising a series of exchanges with interviewer's moves and interviewee's response, I will present the interviewer's move structure as follows (Fig. 12.2):

12.5   Interviewer's Moves

The interviewer's communicative style exhibits feature of the decontextualized literate-based Western culture which dictates that meaning should reside in the language forms not in the context.

12.6   Analysis of Interviewee's Responses (Fig. 12.3)

The interviewer's communicative style exhibits features of the Mediterranean oral culture which favors heavy reliance on contextualization.

12.7   Interpreting Interlocutors' Moves and Responses

There are significant cultural differences imbedded in the communication styles of both the interviewer and interviewee. The interviewer's communicative style is based on a linear sequencing of the acts performed by his utterances and their subsequent subtopics. The subtopics are linked to the first main topic through the use of direct quotations, facts and figures, language forms that spell out the subtopic and its linkage with the first claim; in addition, the interviewer uses quotes of the interviewee's exact words, and use of a third-party statement to mitigate his own stance to maintain neutrality while still challenging the interviewee's claims. Further, he spells out everything to the viewers by making the language forms carry the message; he uses topic chaining.

Here is a sketch of the interviewer's moves and the acts performed and how they are linearly sequenced:

1. A provocative claim (i.e., you and Hamas don't want Arafat in Palestinian territories)
2. A substantiation of the claim (i.e., you and Hamas say that Arafat does not speak for the Palestinians).
3. A reiteration of the first main claim (i.e., Al-Tamimi's and Hamas's claim, the polls show that Arafat has a lot of popularity among Palestinians). The

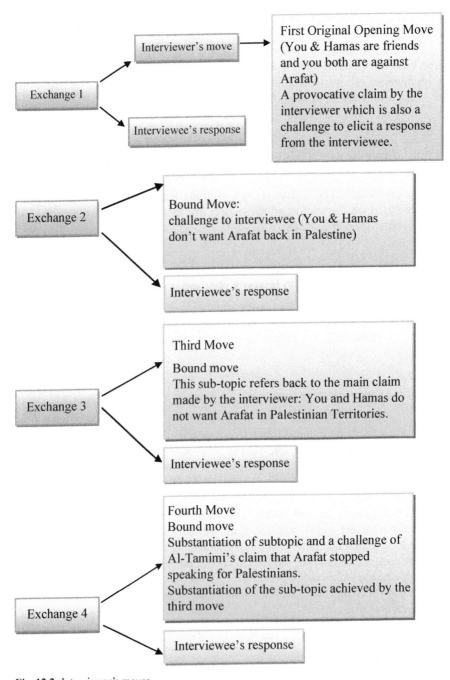

Fig. 12.2 Interviewer's moves

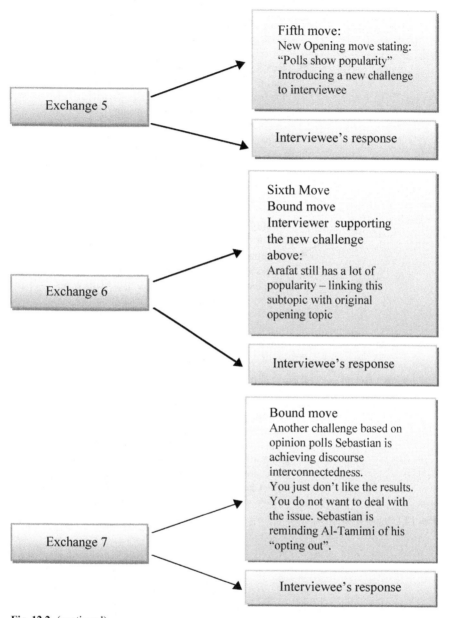

Fig. 12.2 (continued)

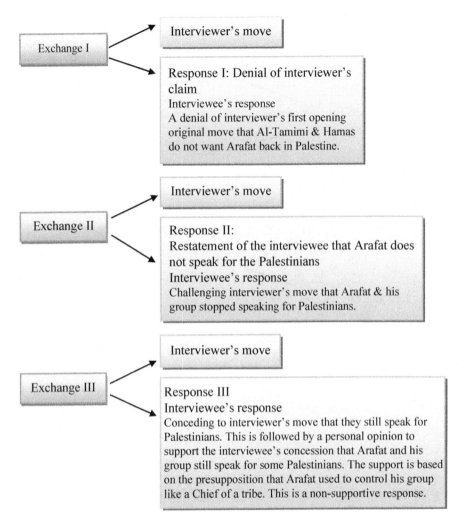

Fig. 12.3 Interviewee's responses

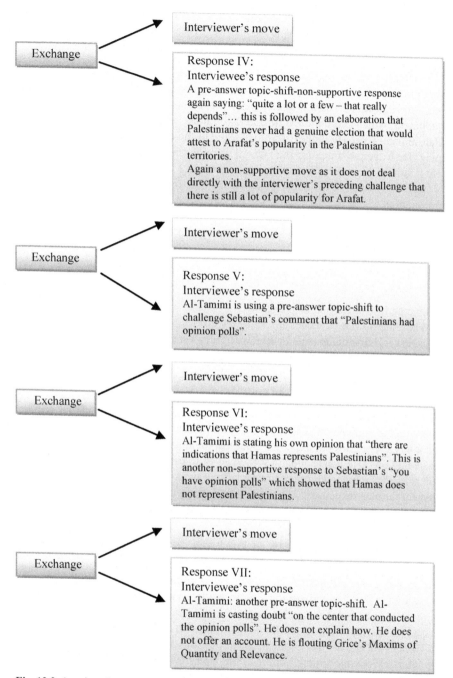

Fig. 12.3 (continued)

interviewer is referring to the polls result to support the claim that Arafat has popularity among Palestinians.
4. Another challenge to Al-Tamimi: (i.e., you don't like the results of the polls …)

The interviewee, in the meantime, gives responses which are based on shared assumptions and presuppositions that are known/shared by one segment of the viewers—the Palestinians supporting Hamas. The interviewee counts on personal value judgment, which can only be understood by those who are familiar with the Arab/Palestinian scene. He moves from one topic to the other. This is called topic hopping. He leaves so much for the viewers to understand what he intends to achieve. He flouts the Maxims of Quantity and Relevance.

Here is a sketch of the interviewee's responses to the interviewer's moves in one transaction.
Exchange I: Denial elaboration:
A denial of the interviewer's claim "that he and Hamas want Arafat out of Palestinian territories."

> Al-Tamimi: "not really". The last few weeks he spent in Ramallah his relationship with Hamas was actually improving. They were doing good business together.

Exchange II: Concession challenge:
The interviewee concedes to the interviewer's move in order to challenge the interviewer's first claim. The interviewee gives a supportive response but follows it up with a challenge of the interviewer's claim at the beginning:

> for some time they have not been speaking for the Palestinians. Since Oslo, … They stopped speaking for the Palestinians.

The second part of the interviewee's response is actually based on shared assumption with the audience who are familiar with politics in Palestinian territories. Here the interviewee does not explicitly establish the link between this response and the preceding one. He leaves much for the viewer to establish the connection between this act and the preceding one, the denial, but the language itself does not directly connect the two responses.
Exchange III: A pre-answer topic-shift by interviewee:

> Quite a lot or a few—that really depends.
> I mean *we* haven't had a [genuine] election and *we* cannot have general election because of the current situation, but …

Using "we" twice means that the interviewee is talking on behalf of all Palestinians.
Using his own pre-answer topic-shift, the interviewee is now seen as not being supportive as he is not responding to the interviewer's move. He is also counting on shared knowledge with those who are familiar with the situation in Palestine.

To the viewers, he may come across as not fully communicatively efficient. But the interviewer's moves put him, (i.e., the interviewee), on the defensive. He tried to be evasive, but to the majority of the viewers he is not looking good.
Exchange IV: Opting out:

Interviewee: …there are *indications* and the *indications* tell us that today it is Hamas that really represents what the Palestinians want. The Palestinians want freedom…

The interviewee's response is not considered a supportive one. He's not attending to the interviewer's move concerning the polls as a factual event.

The interviewee is using "fuzzy" elements namely, there are "indications," indications tell us…. To the viewers these expressions are empty clichés. He is not answering the question. He is using a reopening move himself that Hamas is the Palestinian representative with no explicit connectivity with the preceding responses. The connection is implicit as it is not expressed by language forms; the viewers have to find out on their own how the last response connects with the preceding one. This is an instance of the high-context culture style. Again, the nonsupportive response makes the interviewee look bad to some viewers. Perhaps it is not the interviewer's intention to make the interviewee look bad as much as creating an explosive interview which will command the attention of millions so that the ratings will be high.

Exchange V: A challenge but not directly related to preceding claims by the interviewer:

I question the credibility of this center and of the studies that it makes. What I would say is that give the Palestinians the freedom of choice for a change and see what they choose…

Exchange VI: Another challenge:

If your give the Palestinians the freedom, they will do something else.

Exchange VII: Opting out—Post-answer topic-shifting:

No—there are many academics and many observers who have cast doubt on these centers which are funded by the United States of America and do research that serves the peace process and those who are involved in it.

12.8   An Antagonistic Interview

This interview is antagonistic (Hyatt 1992). The interviewer uses his power to corner the interviewee by using the power exercising technique. From the outset, the interviewer identifies the interviewee as a Hamas spokesman. The interviewee has no other way but to decline, reject, and support his denials and rejections in his own way. This makes the interviewee look nonsupportive, flouting the maxims of quality, or manner. This is unavoidable due to the fact that the interviewer plays the devils' advocate and leads the interviewee to be at the opposite side of the argument. In other words, the interviewer is actually doing the following: forcing the interviewee to agree to his claims. If he agrees, he is saying something he does not believe in. If on the other hand, he does not agree to the interviewer's challenges, his responses will be perceived as being nonsupportive; this makes him look bad for some of the viewers. The interviewee's responses are based on shared knowledge with some viewers, personal opinion, and hedging of the interviewer's main provocative claim. The interviewee's responses are heavily dependent on the context of the interview. This makes his responses situation-dependent because his language use is not in itself the message-carrying vehicle. He does not achieve discourse interconnectedness as the second response is not linked by means of language forms to the preceding one. He assumes that the viewers will utilize their own background knowledge about Palestinian political factions and the Israeli conflict to understand the interviewee's implied relationship between one response and the other. He does not feel pressed to articulate the interconnections between one response and another by means of the proper language forms. This is typical of the oral Mediterranean culture which favors contextualization as language forms in this culture are perceived as ways to signal the shared social meaning between communicator and viewer. Hence, the interviewee will appeal to a certain segment of the viewers (i.e., Palestinians and Arabs supporting Hamas) while the interviewer will appeal to a different category of viewers.

In this respect, the interview adds to the divisiveness that already exists. It makes the interviewee appear to be not fully cooperative in this kind of interaction. Hence, he is made to look bad to the majority viewers.

12.9   Implications and Conclusion

Having analyzed the interviewer's and interviewee's utterances as speech acts, coupled with an analysis of the macro-structural components of the interview as establishing a challenge and following it up by a substantiation and reestablishing another challenge as a subtopic of the major challenge, I now interpret the interactants' communicative styles in terms of intercultural theoretical concepts. I will draw heavily on the work by some scholars in intercultural communication and others in ethnolinguistics and literacy studies (e.g., Hall 1982; Biber 1988; Gee 1989; Tannen 1980; Olson and Torrance 1991; among others).

According to Hall (1982), low-context cultures tend to place meaning in the language code and it tends to be specific, explicit, and analytical. The interviewer's communicative style is also associated with communication with these low-context culture strategies. These favor evidence, reasoning, and analysis. They place emphasis on accuracy and precision. This literate society culture represents a linear thought framework. It stresses beginnings and ends of events, unitary presenting of utterances starting off with a provocative claim substantiated by two or three subtopics which refer back to the main theme—the claim. The linkage was achieved by using explicit linkers, lexical items, quoting the interviewee (e.g., these are your words, you said that...) for staying neutral, detached and giving evidence to what he has established earlier. These are features of the Western European culture literate strategies.

In contrast, the interviewee's communicative style is associated with the strategies of the high-context culture whereby the meaning is embedded more in the context than in the code. Most of the information is either in the physical context or internalized in the person, while very little is in the code, the explicit, transmitted part of the message (Hall 1982). Thus, the listener (the viewer in this case) must understand the contextual cues in order to grasp the full meaning of the message. Hall (1982) states that people raised in high-context culture systems expect more from others than do the participants in low-context systems. While talking about something that they have on their minds, a high-context individual will expect his interlocutor to know what is bothering him so that he does not have to be specific. These are the strategies associated with the Mediterranean orally based culture.

The interviewee's responses are based on shared assumption between him and his viewers or some of them who share with him the background knowledge about Arafat; how he used to run the affairs of Palestinians in Ramallah, and how he acted like a chief of a tribe as Al-Tamimi put it. For westerners, they may not understand what Al-Tamimi is referring to, how and why Arafat was the chief of a tribe.... In fact at a later stage, the interviewer (i.e., Sebastian) in requesting a direct/relevant response from Al-Tamimi (i.e., the interviewee) on his stance about the killing of Israelis, says: "Answer my question, please." On another occasion, Sebastian uses the same prompt: "Answer my question."

The genre-based interaction (i.e., this interview) is essentially culture-bound and it is also an example of adversarial cross-cultural communication. The interviewer and interviewee have different rhetorical purposes. The interviewer is trying to make the interview an explosive news story that will provide interest or entertainment for the viewers in the hope that this will increase the viewing ratings of the interview. It is far from achieving an objective display of information to the viewers. In contrast, the interviewee finds himself in a difficult situation whereby he is on the defensive in the face of the adversarial moves by the interviewer. He tries to avoid an admission or an agreement which the interviewer is trying to elicit from him. This being the case, the viewers are addressed as consumers of a competition between interviewer and interviewee. Furthermore, the communicative styles of an interviewer who is employing the literate-based strategies and an interviewee employing orally based strategies make the cross-cultural communication more conflictual.

Appendix

BBC News 24 TV Program "HARDTALK"—Tuesday 2 November 2004 interview with Dr Azzam al-Tamimi. Institute of Islamic Political Thought
Tim Sebastian
As far as you're concerned with Yasser Arafat, good riddance—you don't want him back in the Palestinian territories and that goes for your friends in Hamas as well?
Dr Azzam Al-Tamimi
Not really. The last few weeks he spent in Ramallah his relationship with Hamas was actually improving They were doing very good business together.
Tim Sebastian

But you say today his group no longer speaks for the Palestinians—these are your words:

Dr Azzam Al-Tamimi

For some time they have not been speaking for the Palestinians Since they accepted Oslo and went along the path of peace-making in accordance with the terms of Israel and its supporters in America they had stopped speaking for the Palestinians.

Tim Sebastian

But they may have stopped speaking for you and they may have stopped speaking for Hamas but there's plenty of popularity left among the Palestinians in the territories isn't there?

Dr Azzam Al-Tamimi

Well they speak for a certain segment of the Palestinians undoubtedly. This is like a tnbe and Yasser Arafat was always the chief of the tribe

Tim Sebastian

Exactly. So your slogan isn't exactly right is it when you say today his group no longer speaks for the Palestinians; he speaks for quite a lot of the Palestinians doesn't he?

Dr Azzam Al-Tamimi

Quite a lot or a few—that really depends. I mean we haven't had a (genuine] election and we cannot have general election because of the current situation but.

Tim Sebastian

No, but you have opinion polls don't you?

Dr Azzam Al-Tamimi

... there are indications and the indications tell us that today it is Hamas that really represents what the Palestinians want. The Palestinians want freedom.

Tim Sebastian

Well you say that but that's not backed up by the opinion polls. The poll conducted by the Palestinian Centre for Policy & Survey Research between September 23rd and 26th gives Hamas 22% compared to, I think it's the 26% or more which is given to Fatah and the Independence.

They were asked/people were asked, *Will you give your vole in the next local election to candidates from Fatah, Hamas, Islamic Jihad or Independence and only 22.2% said Hamas....* isn't much of support is it?

Dr Azzam Al-Tamimi

I question the credibility of this Center and of the studies that it makes. What I would say is that, give the Palestinians the freedom of choice for a change and see what they choose....

Tim Sebastian

But you just don't like the results—that's the reason you reject this isn't it?

Dr Azzam Al-Tamimi

No—there are many academics and many observers who have cast doubt on these centers which are funded by the USA and do research that serves the peace process and those who are involved in it.

Tim Sebastian

Why does it serve the peace process? There hasn't been any peace process to serve, so it hasn't served anything has it…?

Dr Azzam Al-Tamimi

Well the Israelis killed the peace process:

Tim Sebastian

… apart from getting the opinions of Palestinians which you don't happen to like. The fact is, according to the polls, Hamas represents under a quarter of the population. That's maybe an unpalatable fact to you but that happens to be borne out by the figures.

Dr Azzam Al-Tamimi

What Hamas represents today is actually what the Palestinians are hoping for. The Palestinians are hoping for freedom.

Tim Sebastian

Some … some Palestinians are hoping [for]:

Dr Azzam Al-Tamimi

The Palestinians, most of them want to go back home. The Oslo process, the peace process in which the Palestinian Liberation Organization (PLO) embroiled itself gave away the rights of the Palestinians.

Tim Sebastian

When the Palestinian human-rights group did a survey of Palestinians and asked them whether they wanted to go home, the overwhelming majority said they didn't and their offices were trashed; the offices of the Palestinian Human-Rights Monitoring Group were trashed as a result of it. So you don't seem to like any results, and Hamas and Islamic Jihad and people like that don't seem to like any results that go against their own orthodoxy do they?

Dr Azzam Al-Tamimi

You see that's nonsense. I as a Palestinian, I know many Palestinians around the world—I know my own family, I know my friends—we all want our homes back. Even if we live in villas, in palaces, we want our homes. Nobody has the right to steal our homes from us. Nobody has the right to bring people from outside and dump them on our land. Our land is our land.

Tim Sebastian

And for that, continuing violence—that's what Hamas and your friends in Hamas speaks for?

Dr Azzam Al-Tamimi

We don't call it 'violence'. We call it 'legitimate struggle'; we call it 'jihad'…

Tim Sebastian

Well it doesn't matter what you call it. It's still murder isn' it?

References

Al-aridi, Y. (1986). *A discourse analysis of political television interviews: Variation in interactants' manipulation of language.* Unpublished Ph. D. Dissertation, pp. 6–50, Georgetown University, Washington, D.C.

Behrens, L. (2000). *Making the case: An argument reader*. London: Longman.

Biber, D. (1988). *Variation in speech and writing*. Cambridge: Cambridge University Press.

Clayman, S., & Heritage, J. (2002). *The news interview: Journalists and public figures on the air*. Cambridge: Cambridge University Press.

Denny, J. P. (1991). Rational thought in oral culture and literate decontextualization. In D. R. Olson & N. Torrance (Eds.), *Literacy and orality* (pp. 74–75). Cambridge: Cambridge University Press.

Gee, T. (1989). Orality and literacy: From the savage mind to ways with words. *Journal of Education, 17*(1), 8–25.

Greatbatch, D. (1986). Aspects of topical organization in news interviews: The use of agenda shifting procedure by interviewees. *Media, Culture and Society, 8,* 441–455.

Grice, H. P. (1975). Logic and conversation. In P. Cole & J. L. Morgan (Eds.), *Syntax and semantics 3: Speech acts* (pp. 41–58). New York: Academic Press.

Hall, E. T. (1982). Context and meaning. In L. Samovar & R. Porter (Eds.), *Intercultural communication: A reader*. Belmont: Wadsworth.

Hatch, E. (1992). *Discourse, Language and Education*. UK: Cambridge University Press.

Hyatt, D. (1994). *An analysis of text and tasks in the ESP area of English for politics*. Unpublished M. Ed. Dissertation. Bristol, UK.

Jagtiani, N. (2012). *Political news interviews: From a conversational analysis and critical discourse analytic perspective. Colorado Research in Linguistics 23*. Colorado: University of Colorado.

Michaels, S. (1981). Children's narrative styles and differential access to literacy. *Language in Society, 10*(3), 423–442.

Olson, D., & Torrance, N. (1991). *Literacy and orality*. Cambridge: Cambridge University Press.

Riley, P. (2007). *Reconfiguring identities. Language, culture and identity* (pp. 213–219). London: Continuum.

Sacks, H. (1984). Notes on methodology. In J. M. Atkinson & J. Heritage (Eds.), *Structure of social action*. Cambridge: Cambridge University Press.

Tannen, D. (1980). Implications of the oral/literate continuum. In J. Alatis (Ed.), *GURT: Issues in bilingual education* (pp. 334–335). Washington, D.C.: Georgetown University.

Van Dijk, T. A. (1999). Critical discourse analysis and conversation analysis. *Discourse and Society, 10*(4), 459–460.

Zaharna, R. S. (1995). Bridging cultural differences: American public relations and Arab communication patterns. *Public Relations Review, 21,* 241–255

Omar Fayez Atari PhD is a professor of sociolinguistics and translation studies. Prior to joining the UAE University, Al-Ain, he worked as full time faculty member at Sultan Qaboos University, Birzeit University, and Herriot-Watt University. His publications appeared in Meta, BABEL, IRAL, Journal of Literary Semantics, Turjuman and the Interpreter and Translator Trainer.

Chapter 13
The Role of "Cyber-Dissent" in Stimulating Democratization in the MENA Region and Empowering Youth Voices

Asiya Daud

13.1 Introduction

The call for democratization in the Middle East that led to the "Arab Spring" was stimulated by several factors: greater access to technology, the Internet, social media networking sites, and a unique youth demographic that distinguishes the region from the rest of the world. The Middle East region has the highest percentage of youth in the world: one out of five people of the Middle East are under the age of 24 (Assaad and Roudi-Fahimi 2007). The "Arab Spring" is largely a youth movement, and understanding the region's youth is crucial to understanding the social movement's dynamics. This research examines how the Internet and social networking sites are used for political dissent in order to circumvent severe press censorship and political restrictions imposed by the governments of the Middle East and North Africa region. The usage of the Internet and social media networking sites for political dissent is hereafter referred to as *cyber-dissent*. Cyber-dissent is defined in this research as: the usage of the Internet and social networking sites such as Facebook, YouTube, blogs, and Twitter to: (1) express political grievances and dissatisfaction; (2) criticize the government; (3) organize political dissent activities (i.e., protests and rallies); and (4) expose government behavior and articulate alternative political ideals.

Cyber-dissent exposes how a lack of freedom of speech and of the press, which is a direct result of authoritarianism, can stimulate a society to find other means to engage each other in deliberative discourse. The study of cyber-dissent and its relationship with press censorship provides an understanding of how legislation like "emergency laws" and "press laws" that claim to protect state security and promote national interest curtail freedom of expression. There is a strong relationship between the Internet and the enhancement of democratization, as cyber-social

A. Daud (✉)
University of California, Irvine, CA, USA
e-mail: doctor.asiya11@gmail.com

© Springer Science+Business Media Singapore 2015
R. Raddawi (ed.), *Intercultural Communication with Arabs*,
DOI 10.1007/978-981-287-254-8_13

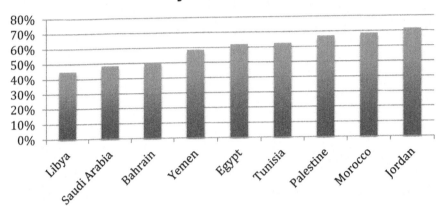

Fig. 13.1 Percentages of under-25 Facebook users in Middle East and North Africa (MENA) countries. (Adapted from Malin 2010)

networks are used to constructively exchange political, social, and religious ideals and increase political participation of civil society by reaching larger audiences. The data below in Figs. 13.1, 13.2, and 13.3 is suggestive data of the relationship between an increase in youth usage of social networking sites and democratization in the region. The Internet in the Middle East has been an effective tool for the people to voice their opinions freely, as press restrictions have inhibited freer expression. The Internet is also increasing political participation in the Middle East, by facilitating the inclusion of women, the youth and other marginalized groups in Middle East society (Etling et al. 2009). The inclusion of these marginalized groups is important to the success of democratization and development in the region.

Figure 13.1 shows MENA countries where more than 40% of Facebook users are under the age of 25. In fact, all of these countries have experienced either a regime change or significant unrest as a result of the Arab Spring. Cyber-dissent assesses the usage of social networking sites such as Facebook to express political dissent, thus, this figure indicates the direct causal relationship between the youth population and the level of cyber-dissent. In fact, the results in this research show that a country's youth population percentage of the ages 15–29 has a significant effect on cyber-dissent.[1] Furthermore, the results indicate that the higher a country's youth population, the higher the level of cyber-dissent. Egypt and Tunisia have the

---

[1] Refer to Table 13.4 results in "The Results" section. p value significance level was found to be 0.035 for youth population, which means that a higher percentage of a country's youth population between the ages of 15–29 increases the level of cyber-dissent, which ultimately leads to democratization.

Fig. 13.2 Tunisian Facebook demographics: age. (Adapted from Malin 2010)

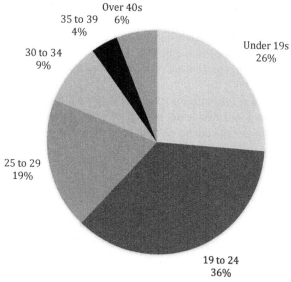

62% OF TUNISIAN FACEBOOK
USERS ARE UNDER 25 YEARS OLD

Over 40s
35 to 39   6%
4%

30 to 34
9%

Under 19s
26%

25 to 29
19%

19 to 24
36%

Fig. 13.3 Egyptian Facebook demographics: age. (Adapted from Malin 2010)

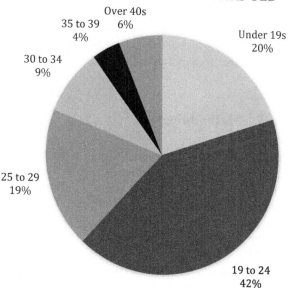

62% OF EGYPTIAN FACEBOOK
USERS ARE UNDER 25 YEARS OLD

Over 40s
35 to 39   6%
4%

30 to 34
9%

Under 19s
20%

25 to 29
19%

19 to 24
42%

highest levels of youth Facebook users in the MENA region under the age of 25. Tunisia, as indicated in Fig. 13.1, has a slightly higher level of Facebook users under 25, than Egypt; Tunisia was the birthplace of the Arab Spring. Indeed there are other factors that account for democratization movements, but the results show a compelling relationship. Nevertheless, both Tunisia and Egypt set a precedent for other countries in the region for their call for democratization. The figures below indicate the percentage of Facebook users in Tunisia and Egypt who are under the age of 25.

The results become even more compelling when the percentage of a country's youth population under the age of 29 is included, as this research further expands the impact of country's youth population from the age of 15 to 29 on cyber-dissent.

13.2   The Study

This research is significant because it is the first time this type of study has been attempted; therefore, it is unique and innovative. The data and research conducted in this study predate the Arab Spring; therefore, the data and results are a precursor to the factors that stimulated the democratization movements in the region. This research is unique, firstly, because assessing the level of cyber-dissent in the region has never been attempted. Secondly, it has never been attempted to define cyber-dissent by Internet usage in the MENA region. These two factors are also perceived limitations, as other studies of this nature have not been conducted. A major assumption in this study is that high levels of press censorship compel the people of the Middle East to engage in using the Internet for cyber-dissent, as high levels of censorship in the press prohibit the people from freedom of expression. It can be inferred that measuring for Internet usage as a means of cyber-dissent is a satisfactory measure, as the Internet provides a freer space for the people to express themselves, and to gather for political rallies and protests.

13.3   Methodology

This study employs a quantitative approach using panel data regression analysis of data between 2002 and 2007, to measure and test the effect of censorship on cyber-dissent. Cyber-dissent in this study is measured by Internet usage over a 5-year time period between 2002 and 2007, across 39 sample countries.[2] It is important to reiterate that censorship is the key independent variable to be tested, and cyber-dissent is defined in this study as the dependent variable.[3]

---

[2] Refer to Appendix II for a chart of Internet usage for MENA countries for 2007.

[3] Panel data are also referred to as a crosssectional time series data test. Panel data (or crosssectional time series) are used to examine a dataset in which the behaviors of entities are observed across time.

13.4 Research Questions

The key research question in this study is: What compels the people of the Middle East to engage in cyber-dissent? It is hypothesized that high levels of censorship in the press compel the people of the Middle East to engage in higher levels of cyber-dissent; thus, the higher the level of censorship in the press, the higher the level of cyber-dissent. There is a possibility of an unexpected sign result on press censorship, which may be due to the complex nature of press censorship policies in the Middle East. This is because some countries in the Middle East either do not have specific press laws, or they utilize other legislation to deter or punish those who engage in cyber-dissent.

The relationship between a country's level of cyber-dissent and its level of press censorship is a central aspect of this research. A highly censored press prohibits the people of the Middle East to constructively criticize the government and engage in political dissent; thus, the Internet in the Middle East has provided a free space for its citizens to constructively engage in criticism of the government. The nature of the press in the Middle East has been deemed "authoritarian" in that it seeks to promote a government agenda and curtail a challenge to government legitimacy through the usage of severe censorship. Tables 13.1 and 13.2 demonstrate the low level of press freedom and a high level of censorship in the press in the MENA region. It is important to make clear that in this study, press freedom and censorship levels are synonymous as what curtails freedom in the press is censorship.

The press in a legitimate democratic society serves as a tool of transparency that exposes and criticizes government behavior and decisions. Moreover, in a society where there is a free press, politicians are pressured by public opinion because the press openly criticizes their behavior, running the risk of reelection. In a society that does not have a free press, power is opaque and the press does not serve as a balancing tool to government power. The press serves as a voice for citizens, and restricting freedom in the press severely restricts healthy political participation. Aside from measuring the effect of press censorship on cyber-dissent, there are other research questions/hypotheses in this study. The following is a summary of other variables measuring their effect on cyber-dissent.

In this study, these entities are countries (encoded as "states"). The panel variable identified in this test is "states." "Countries" were encoded as "states" since "countries" was identified as a string variable, and could not be tested until encoded by STATA. "States" refers to the 39 countries tested in this model. The sample in this study includes MENA and non-MENA countries. Non-MENA countries were chosen by random selection. The time variable identified in this test was "year" and includes the time period of 2002–2007.

Table 13.1 Press freedom
in the Middle East and North
Africa (MENA) region.
(Adapted from Freedom
House 2007)

Rank 2007	Country	Rating	Status
1	Israel	29	Free
2	Kuwait	56	Partly free
3	Lebanon	59	Partly free
4	Jordan	61	Not free
5	Algeria	62	Not free
6	Egypt	62	Not free
7	Morocco	62	Not free
8	Qatar	63	Not free
9	United Arab Emirates	68	Not free
10	Iraq	70	Not free
11	Bahrain	71	Not free
12	Oman	71	Not free
13	Yemen	80	Not free
14	Saudi Arabia	82	Not free
15	Syria	83	Not free
16	Tunisia	83	Not free
17	Occupied territories/ Palestinian authority	84	
18	Iran	84	Not free
19	Libya	96	Not free

13.5 Other Expected Outcomes

Hypothesis 2: The higher the level of political repression, the higher the level of cyber-dissent

Hypothesis 3: The higher the level of democracy, the lower the level of cyber-dissent

Hypothesis 4: An increase in average level of education decreases cyber-dissent

Hypothesis 5: The higher GDP per capita income, the higher the level of cyber-dissent

Hypothesis 6: The higher the level of accountability, the lower the level of cyber-dissent

Hypothesis 7: The higher the population total, the higher the level of cyber-dissent

Hypothesis 8: The lower the control of corruption, the higher the level of cyber-dissent

Hypothesis 9: The higher the percentage of the youth population between the ages of 15–29, the higher the level of cyber-dissent

Hypothesis 10: An increase in the number of personal computers increases the level of cyber-dissent

Table 13.2 Percentage of
press freedom in the world.
(Adapted from Freedom
House 2007)

Status	Number of countries	Percentage of total
Free	1	5
Partly free	2	11
Not free	16	84
Total	19	100

13.6   Instruments/Data Measurement

The World Bank Database provides the number of Internet users in a country annually. The number of Internet users is the data measurement of cyber-dissent in this study. It will be proven in this research that places with higher Internet usage have a high level of cyber-dissent. The MENA region, as stated earlier, has the highest level of Internet usage growth in the world, even though the region has only 3.1 % of the world's population.[4] Internet usage growth in the MENA region between the years of 2000–2010 was 1825.3 %, as compared to the world total of 444.8 % (Internet World Stats 2010).

The key independent variable, censorship, is measured by the level of *press freedom*, and the data of this measurement is taken from a Freedom House variable called "freedom of the press." This variable measures the degree of a country's freedom of the press combining three categories. These categories are (1) the legal environment (0–30 points); (2) the political environment (0–40 points); and (3) the economic environment (0–30 points).[5]

This research also controlled for other factors such as: political repression, democracy, gross domestic product (GDP per capita), accountability, youth population (of the ages 15–29), total population, the number of a country's personal computers, average level of education, and corruption levels. Below one will find a brief description of each independent variable, and the way in which it is coded.

13.7   Data Collection

Other Independent Variables

1. **Political Repression:** Measures the level of political freedom and civil liberties.[5]
2. **Democracy:** (Polity IV Data) Measures the level of democracy and autocracy in a country.This score encompasses general qualities of political institutions and processes, including executive recruitment, constraints on executive action, and political competition. The ratings of these qualities are then combined into a single, scaled measure of regime governance: the *Polity* score.[6] Their *Polity*

---

[4] Refer to Appendix III for a chart on world Internet usage statistics.

[5] The data for this variable are taken from Freedom House's measurement of "Freedom in the World." Each country and territory is assigned a numerical rating—on a scale of 1–7—for political rights and an analogous rating for civil liberties; a rating of 1 indicates the highest degree of freedom, and 7 indicates the lowest level of freedom.

[6] The *Polity* scale ranges from − 10, fully institutionalized autocracy, to + 10, fully institutionalized. According to the polity IV data description, an anocracy is characterized by institutions and political elites that are far less capable of performing fundamental tasks and ensuring their own continuity. Anocratic regimes very often reflect an inherent quality of instability or ineffectiveness and are especially vulnerable to the onset of new political instability events, such as outbreaks of

scores range from -5 to $+5$. Collapsed or occupation regimes are assessed polity codes of -77 or -66 (Monty and Cole 2009).[7]

3. **GDP:** Refers to GDP per capita. The data are taken from the World Bank's development indicators.

4. **Accountability:** Refers to a countries level of government accountability. This variable refers to "voice and accountability," and the data are derived from the World Bank's "Governance Matters" project. It measures the extent to which a country's citizens are able to participate in selecting their government, as well as freedom of expression, freedom of association, and free media. The score is based on a percentile rating from 0 to 100, 0 being the lowest percentile rating and 100 being the best percentile.

5. **Corruption:** This variable measures a country's "control of corruption," and the data are taken from the World Bank's "Governance Matters" project.[8] Control of corruption measures the extent to which public power is exercised for private gain, including petty and grand forms of corruption, as well as "capture" of the state by elites and private interests (Governance Matters 2008). The score is based on a percentile rating from 0 to 100, 0 being the lowest percentile rating and 100 being the best percentile.

6. **Youth Population 15–29:**[9] Refers to a country's youth population between the ages of 15 and 29. This age group was chosen because the literature demonstrates that the youth in the Middle East are the ones engaging in cyber-dissent. Youth population is measured by the percentage of the combined male and female population between the ages of 15–29. Data are taken from the US Census Bureau, International Database (U.S. Census Bureau n.d.).

7. **Average Education:** Refers to a country's average literacy rate.[10]

8. **Personal Computers:** Refers to a country's number of personal computers; this data was taken from the World Development Indicators database.

9. **Population total:** Refers to a country's population total, and is taken from the World Development Indicators database.

---

armed conflict, unexpected changes in leadership, or adverse regime changes (e.g., a seizure of power by a personalistic or military leader).

[7] -88 refers to a transitional government; -77 refers to countries where central authority has collapsed or lost control over a majority of its territory; -66 refers to countries where foreign authorities backed by the presence of foreign forces provide a support structure for maintaining local authority. Countries in this sample that were assessed a score of -66, -77, or -88 were coded as 0.

[8] Control of corruption measures the extent to which public power is exercised for private gain, including petty and grand forms of corruption, as well as "capture" of the state by elites and private interests. The score is based on a percentile rating from 0 to 100, 0 being the lowest percentile rating and 100 being the best percentile.

[9] Coded as Youth pop 15–29.

[10] An average was taken because many countries did not list their literacy rates on a consistent basis, thus an average was taken for data management to remain consistent. The data on literacy rates were extracted from the World Bank Development Indicators database.

Table 13.3 Press the effect of press censorship on cyber-dissent

Random-effects GLS regression	Random effects u_i~Gaussian
R-sq: within=0.9164	Wald chi^2(10)=1730.94
Between=0.9707	Prob>chi^2=0.0000
Overall=0.9711	

As mentioned earlier, this study employs a panel data regression because the data includes a 5-year time span to test and observe the effect of censorship on cyber-dissent. There are two types of panel data regression models. These are a fixed-effects model and a random-effects model. This study uses a random-effects model, unlike a fixed-effects model, because it assumes variation across entities to be random and uncorrelated with the independent variables in a model. There is also an advantage in using a random-effects model; it allows for time invariant variables, such as gender. Figure 13.3 reports that the model is a random-effects model; it states Random effects u_i~Gaussian. This means that the differences across units are uncorrelated with the regressors.

Table 13.4 The impact of press censorship on cyber-dissent, regression results

Cyber-dissent	Coef.	Std. Err.	Z	$p>\{z\}$	[95% conf. interval]
Censorship	−124307.4	55403.45	2.24	0.025	−232,896.2 to 15,718.67
Political repression	−26711.99	690397.2	−0.04	0.969	−1,379,866 to 1,326,442
Democracy	366455	296750.2	1.23	0.217	−215,164.6 to 948,074.6
Accountability	−103373.7	82170	−1.26	0.208	−264,423.9 to 57,676.57
Personal computers	1.83379	0.0645457	28.41	0.000	1.707283 to 1.960297
Corruption	60908.21	37201.53	1.64	0.102	−12,005.45 to 133,821.9
GDP	104.8551	46.9988	2.23	0.026	12.73913 to 196.9711
Average education	−163605.3	55804.57	−2.93	0.003	−272,980.2 to −54,230.35
Population total	0.0037815	0.002832	1.34	0.182	−0.0017692 to 0.0093321
Youth pop.15–29	479450	227026.6	2.11	0.035	34,486.12 to 924,414
_cons	4621145	1.02e+07	0.45	0.651	1.54e+07 to 2.46e+07
Sigma_u 2477015.2					
Sigma_e 2405854.8					

13.8 The Results/Findings

Firstly, the results of our key hypothesis will be examined. As stated earlier, the key hypothesis in this study is that higher levels of censorship in the press lead to higher levels of cyber-dissent. We are seeking a significant effect of the level of censorship on the level of cyber-dissent. The results in Tables 13.3 and 13.4 show the effect of censorship on the level of cyber-dissent, using a panel data regression analysis of the years between 2002–2007, as mentioned in the methodology section above. Table 13.4 shows that cyber-dissent is the dependent variable (or Y variable), because it appears on the top of the far left column. Thus, all variables listed under cyber-dissent are the independent variables (X variables), and the results display each effect of X on Y. Table 13.3 demonstrates the overall "fit" of the model presented, which measures the effect of press censorship on cyber-dissent. Table 13.3

results show that the overall "fit" of the model is good, because the overall R-squared value is over 97%, which is close to the targeted goal of 100%.

The p value presented in Table 13.4 explains the relationship between censorship and cyber-dissent is 0.025. A p value that is equal to or less than 0.05 is considered to have a significant effect on the dependent variable, which in this study is cyber-dissent. Thus, a country's level of censorship in the press has a significant effect on its level of cyber-dissent. However, in the second column of Table 13.4, the Coefficient (abbreviated as Coef.) has a negative value, which means that the relationship is inverse. The key hypothesis was that higher levels of censorship lead to a higher level of cyber-dissent. However, the results state an unexpected story: the higher the level of a country's censorship, the lower a country's level of cyber-dissent.

In the section on expected outcomes, an individual hypothesis is stated for the desired relationship of X variables on Y. We find from the results that press censorship, education/literacy rates, GDP, the number of personal computers, and a country's youth population have a significant effect on cyber-dissent.[11] Average education presented in the data measures a country's average literacy rates. The desire to find an inverse effect of education on cyber-dissent supports the assumption in this study that higher education levels lead to greater satisfaction. Therefore, it was assumed that greater education decreases societal dissatisfaction and overall, the desire to engage in dissent is less. Higher levels of income (measured by GDP) allow greater access to the Internet. In fact, according to the literature on cyber-dissent in the Middle East, blogging and online political activism are an elitist trend. Mostly wealthy, young citizens of the Middle East have the personal disposal of a computer, and the leisure time to engage in online activities associated with cyber-dissent. In addition to this, in developing countries the wealthy can afford to pay a monthly subscription to have Internet access at home, and can afford a high-speed connection that makes cyber-activity more convenient (Brodock et al. 2009). In fact, a 2009 survey on digital activism concluded that "activism is an activity of the global elite" (Brodock et al. 2009).

The results also show that a country's percentage of youth population is more significant than its total population in regards to the effect on cyber-dissent. In this case, a higher youth population is more crucial than the total population. In this study, the youth population includes citizens between the ages of 15–29. The literature on cyber-dissent overwhelmingly states that the majority of those who engage in cyber-dissent are a part of the younger generation. One of the main goals of Egypt's blogger newspaper called *Wasla* is to bridge the generation gap of bloggers and online activists (Arabic Network for Human Rights Information n.d.). The majority of the Middle East's population is under the age of 30. However, there is a tremendous disconnect between them and the rulers in power who are of a much older generation. Those who have access to power in the Middle East are of an

[11] Table 13.4 results show that press censorship is significant with a p-value of 0.025, followed by the other significant results of average education, p-value of 0.003; personal computers, p-value 0.000; gdp, p-value 0.026; and youth population (ages 15–29), p-value 0.035.

older, well-connected society. Marina Ottoway (2003) in her discussion of Egypt as a semiauthoritarian society discusses this tremendous age gap in those who hold power. She states "…most Egyptian political parties are gerontocracies. In the opposition parties as in the government, leaders occupy their position for life" (p. 48).

However, a more tech-savvy youth generation of the Middle East has created greater opportunities of inclusion and participation in societies that marginalize them. As Mona Eltahawy (2008) states in her article entitled "The Middle East's generation Facebook, the Internet, blogs, and social networking sites now give voices to those most marginalized in the Middle East today—young people and women" (p. 75). Harvard University's study on the Arabic blogosphere concluded that Arabic bloggers are predominately male and young (Etling et al. 2009). A study completed on digital activism found that people between the ages of 26 and 30 were the most active—this age group made up 28 % of the total (Brodock et al. 2009). The second most active age group was between the ages of 30 and 36, representing 16 % of respondents who engage in activism via the Internet. Responses decreased after the age of 50.

The question is why is the age group more active? One theory argues that this age group is more politically active. A Pew Internet Research survey found that teenagers are more politically apathetic (Brodock et al. 2009). Going online for teenagers include social activities and "game playing." Harvard's Berkman's Center for Internet and Society found "the younger kids were very much politically disengaged—but very creative and active online—college age kids on the other hand and some high school [students] were much more civically aware and engaged, both online and offline" (Berkman Research Center Publication 2009, Blog). According to the digital activism survey report:

The 26–30-year group is out of school and into their first years of adulthood. They are in a sweet spot of technical expertise and political idealism, not as technologically immersed as the digital natives, but just slightly removed from that level of engagement. Yet, unlike the digital natives, who may be more concerned with gaming and pop music than human rights, the 26–30 cohort has been around long enough to mix the idealism of youth with the experience and education of adulthood (Brodock et al. 2009).

Activism indeed is associated with the younger generation. College students especially have led the way in many political and social revolutions around the world. However, the specific age of 20–29, measured in this study on cyber-dissent, have a different set of realistic concerns than college "idealists." They feel the effects of governmental policies and the economy more so; this age group is considered to be "young professionals." Unemployment, inflation, and the policy makers they choose affect their prosperity. As mentioned earlier, more than 40 % of the population is under the age of 30 in the MENA region. A 2007 MENA report called the Middle East a "demographic time bomb." The economies of the Middle East have failed to meet the job growth demands of a rapidly growing youth population. Thus, the biggest political and economic challenge of the Middle East regimes is to meet the demands of their youth.

The relationship between the number of personal computers and the level of cyber-dissent is also found to be significant. This result challenged the theory of the public option. Other research on Internet access found that increasing public access to computers is crucial to the increase of Internet usage. However, the 2009 Digital Activism Survey Report found that greater home access to computers increases digital activism—92% of respondents who stated they engage in digital activism have Internet access in their homes. In fact, respondents of this survey were most likely to use the Internet at home (90%) or at work (89%), while 40% accessed the Internet at a cyber-cafe and 46% found access at a school, library, or other free access point (Brodock et al. 2009).

In the Middle East some governments require cyber-cafe owners to have all computers face the front, and hold cyber-café owners accountable for Internet content, which makes privacy very difficult for customers. Cyber-cafes have also been targets of Islamist militants accusing patrons of chatting with the opposite sex and viewing pornography. Moreover, anonymity is a compelling characteristic of the Internet in societies that have severe ramifications for criticism from the government. Using the computer from the privacy of one's own home makes anonymity a lot easier.

13.9   Policy Implications and Conclusions

The test results in this study show that several variables have a significant effect on the level of cyber-dissent. These variables are a country's censorship level, percentage of youth population between the ages of 15 and 29, the number of personal computers, GDP, and educational level (measured by average literacy rate). The results of this study can be used to recommend policy in assessing the causal factors of cyber-dissent. The effect of press censorship on cyber-dissent is the key relationship that this study sought to measure. The results of the test show that press censorship has an inverse effect on cyber-dissent, meaning that higher levels of press censorship leads to a decrease in cyber-dissent. The question is, what may this result indicate? Firstly, the nature of press censorship in the Middle East may be a determining factor in this result, when it comes to cyber-dissent. Censorship of the press in this study literally refers to the extent to which a country's press is free; thus, the terms are interchangeable.

The measurement of censorship in this study was taken from a variable called "freedom of the press" by Freedom House. It was measured in three categories, and then an aggregate score was comprised from these categories. The first category was the legal environment. The legal environment examined laws and regulations that could influence media content and the government's inclination to use these laws and legal institutions to restrict the media's ability to operate. In the Middle East, press laws usually fulfill legal regulations of the media. Most countries in the Middle East do not have Internet-specific laws, and therefore, utilize their press laws to punish and intimidate those who engage in cyber-dissent. Thus, the results of this study might reveal a complex relationship between cyber-dissent and censorship because press legislation extends into cyberspace in the Middle East. Press laws in the Middle East are used to intimidate and detain bloggers. Egypt does not have a specific press law. However, as discussed earlier in this study, Egypt utilizes the "emergency law" to arbitrarily detain those deemed as a threat to the state, for an indefinite amount of time. Under the "emergency law" bloggers have been detained, arrested, and even tried in military courts. The test results show that an increase in censorship leads to a decrease in cyber-dissent. An explanation for this inverse relationship can be attributed to the utilization of press legislation to detain, arrest, and intimidate those who engage in cyber-dissent. Other aspects of a country's legal structure can also deter political dissent. Referring to the MENA region, aside from press laws, emergency laws, terrorism laws, and moral codes are also implemented and used to detain the opposition and consequently deter dissent. Thus, this creates a complex understanding of how the legal structure in the Middle East is used to suppress opposition. The legal structure in the MENA region has been used to detain protestors both before and during the "Arab Spring," and a demand for the abolishment of these laws has been a focal point of the protestors.

The second category that measures censorship in this study determines the political environment of the press. It examines the degree of political control over content of news media, the accessibility to information, official and self-censorship, and the ability of reporters to operate without intimidation. In regards to self censorship, the intimidating ramifications for criticizing the government both in the press media and in cyberspace are connected because press laws are used to punish both acts. Thus, the results of this study show that self-censorship might be affecting content used in cyberspace to criticize the government because of the fear of punitive actions by the governments of the Middle East, which is supported either by press laws or legislation that affect content in the press (e.g., the emergency law in Egypt). Fear of being detained or jailed might deter dissenters in cyberspace to thoroughly express grievances. Even though Arab bloggers blog under anonymity, the governments of the Middle East have been successful in uncovering and detaining bloggers (Etling et al. 2009). The question remains whether or not the results of this study reveal whether press censorship should still be lobbied against in the international community.

Indeed a free press is one of the attributes of a democracy. As Alex de Tocqueville states, the press is "the chief democratic instrument of freedom" (Whitten-Woodring 2009, p. 595). It would be a tremendous benefit to the societies of the Middle East to have a freer press where journalists do not have to fear the ramifications of criticizing the governments and their policies. As mentioned earlier, the press is used in the Middle East to promote government agenda. An "authoritarian press" in the Middle East has suppressed civil society from not only voicing opinions but from exposure to a diversity of opinions on issues. The grievances expressed by bloggers suggest that the people of the Middle East are seeking to challenge traditional ways of governing and the legitimacy of their governments. However, it is still crucial to continually promote freedom of the press in the Middle East, as government accountability and transparency are the results of a free press.

International organizations should continue to criticize and advocate against press laws that suppress press freedom and encroach on Internet freedom as well.

Secondly, cyberspace is still generally freer than the "authoritarian" press that exists in the Middle East. Internet content is harder to control. The Internet in the Middle East has proven to create greater inclusion in civil society, and is facilitating greater inclusion of civil society in the Middle East. The governments of the Middle East have been quite resilient to a freer press, and continually create a media environment that is tightly controlled. International organizations should continue to advocate greater transparency in the press, because the press has proven to be a tool of checks and balances on government power. In the meantime, the Internet in the Middle East is a phenomenon that has challenged the governments—their reactions to those who engage in cyber-dissent have proven this theory.

With regard to the importance of the youth generation of the Middle East, human rights and international organizations should reach out to the youth and listen to their grievances on the Internet, as lack of democratic freedom prevents civil society from openly criticizing their governments. The Internet has provided a space for the youth to express their opinions and political viewpoints. The youth generation of the Middle East is crucial, as one in five people of the Middle East are under the age of 24 (Assaad and Roudi-Fahimi 2007). A report from the Population Reference Bureau on the MENA countries stated in regards to a rapidly growing youth population, "the extent to which this large group of young people will become healthy and productive members of their societies depends on how well governments and civil societies invest in social, economic, and political institutions that meet the current needs of young people" (Assaad and Roudi-Fahimi 2007). So far, the governments in the Middle East have not been successful in creating jobs for this rapidly growing youth population; youth unemployment in the Middle East is the highest in the world at 26% (Assaad and Roudi-Fahimi 2007). In terms of political participation, change is yet to come in the Middle East, as the region rates the lowest in democracy and the highest in repression in the world (Freedom House 2009).[12] One of the focuses of this study is to also demonstrate how the Internet is creating greater political inclusion in the Middle East, and our discussion on the nature of cyber-dissent proves this. Thus, cyber-dissent for the youth population has a positive effect on democratic inclusion. This study showed that an increase in a country's youth population leads to a significant increase in cyber-dissent. This means the young generation is the most active participant in cyber-dissent. The international community should reach out to youth bloggers. The election protests in Iran in June 2009 not only showed the powerful effect of the Internet and technology on political participation in this society, it also was a means for the international community to communicate with civil society in a repressive society such as Iran. In addition, the Internet exposed human rights abuses that are prevalent in Iran.

The response to young bloggers in the Middle East has not been positive. An example of this is the case of the 24-year-old Egyptian blogger Kareem Amer, who was sentenced to 4 years in jail for his blog content that the government claimed

[12] The "Map of Freedom in the World" indicates the MENA region as being "not free."

"insulted Islam" and defamed the president (Free Kareem Campaign n.d.). Ahmed Mostafa, a 20-year-old Egyptian blogger was tried in a military court in March of 2010, and was found guilty and sentenced for his criticism of corruption in the Egyptian military (Human Rights Watch 2010). Ahmed Mostafa was a civilian, and not a member of the military. Human rights organizations have criticized the credibility and procedures of this trial, as his trial was referred to a military court for a more speedy decision (Human Rights Watch 2010). These are just a few examples of youth being detained arbitrarily, and without fair trial in the Middle East. Egypt under international human rights standards is obligated to allow its citizens to openly criticize corruption without ramifications—this should continually be enforced. Youth bloggers are increasingly coming under attack by their governments in the Middle East. Human rights organizations and the international community should continually pressure governments to stop these human rights abuses of arresting bloggers for expressing themselves freely.

Lastly, in regard to personal computers, this study demonstrated that an increase in a country's number of personal computers led to an increase in cyber-dissent. Greater personal access to computers increases participation in cyber-dissent. As discussed earlier, cyber-dissent is a positive activity in the Middle East, as it allows for greater inclusion and freer expression. Therefore, the international community should encourage accessibility to personal computers through the promotion of greater access to technology, and by ameliorating the inequality gap in technology. The United Nations has been active in trying to lessen the gap in access to technology. A United Nations report stated that "while the 'digital divide' between rich and poor countries may be shrinking overall, the gap is widening between the developed and developing worlds in the availability of broadband or high-speed Internet, a crucial tool for achieving economic and social goals" (United Nations News Centre 2009). The UN report also acknowledged that the Internet is a important connection tool between citizens and their governments, thereby endorsing the idea that the Internet can contribute to democratization.

References

Arabic Network for Human Rights Information. (n.d.). About us. http://www.anhri.net/en/?page_id=7. Accessed 11 May 2012

Assaad, R., & Roudi-Fahimi, F. (2007). Youth in the Middle East and North Africa: Demographic opportunity or challenge? http://www.prb.org/pdf07/YouthinMENA.pdf. Accessed 1 August 2012.

Brodock, K., Joyce, M., & Zaeck, T. (2009). Digital activism survey report. http://www.digiactive.org/wp-content/uploads/Research4_SurveyReport2009.pdf. Accessed 11 October 2013.

Eltahawy, M. (2008). The Middle East's generation Facebook. *World Policy Journal, 25*(3), 69–77.

Etling, B., Kelly, J., Faris, R., & Palfrey, J. (2009). *Mapping the Arabic blogosphere: Politics, culture, and dissent.* Berkman Research Center Publication 2009-06. http://cyber.law.harvard.edu/publications/2009/Mapping_the_Arabic_Blogosphere. Accessed 3 August 2013.

Free Kareem Campaign. (n.d.). Kareem FAQ. http://www.freekareem.org/kareem-faq/. Accessed 6 June 2013.

Freedom House. (2009). Freedom in the world 2009. http://www.freedomhouse.org/report/freedom-world/freedom-world2009. Accessed 23 January 2014.

Governance Matters. (2008). Worldwide governance indicators. http://info.worldbank.org/governance/wgi/faq.htm. Accessed 12 April 2013.

Human Rights Watch. (2010). Egypt: Free blogger in military court trial. http://www.hrw.org/en/news/2010/03/01/egypt-free-blogger-military-court-trial. Accessed 11 May 2013.

Internet World Stats: Usage, and Population Statistics. (2010). Internet usage statistics for Africa. http://www.internetworldstats.com/stats1.htm. Accessed 5 February 2013.

Malin, C. (2010). Spot on public relations. http://www.spotonpr.com/egypt-facebook-demographics/. Accessed 12 May 2013.

Marshall, M. G., & Cole, B. R. (2009). *Global report 2009: Conflict, governance, and state fragility.* Arlington: George Mason University Center for Global Policy.

Middle East and North Africa (2007). Freedom House. Retrieved from http://www.freedomhouse.org/regions/middle-east-and-north-africa#.VFfV-ed4Jo4

Ottoway, M. (2003). *Democracy challenged: The rise of semi-authoritarianism.* Washington, DC: Carnegie Endowment for International Peace.

United Nations News Centre. (2009). High-speed Internet gap between rich and poor widening, UN official warns. http://www.un.org/apps/news/story.asp?NewsID=32942&Cr=information+technology&Cr1=#. Accessed 2 April 2012.

U.S. Census Bureau. (n.d.). International data base (IDB). http://www.census.gov/ipc/www/ idb/ranks.php. Accessed 3 October 2013.

Whitten-Woodring, J. (2009). Watchdog or lapdog? Media freedom, regime type, and government respect for human rights. *International Studies Quarterly, 53*(3), 595–625.

Asiya Daud received her PhD in political science from Claremont Graduate University. She has lived and traveled to the Middle East, and was in Cairo, Egypt, during the climax of the Egyptian Revolution. She is a professor of international relations/Middle East politics at the American University (Washington, DC), and The University of California, Irvine. Dr. Asiya Daud frequently appears in the media providing Middle East analysis.

Chapter 14
The Political Discourse of the Arab Revolution: The Case of Egypt, Tunisia, Libya, and Syria

Radia Kesseiri

14.1 Introduction

Democracy, Arab Spring, and political rhetoric are topics that intersect in analyses of the recent Arab uprisings. Leaders, protestors, and users of social networks used language to mobilise, make arguments, and advance agendas. Language was used as the apparatus of mobilisation in order to express a common feeling of disarray and discontent amongst the protestors. Likewise, leaders deployed rhetoric to captivate their audiences and call upon them to unify against the chaos and those they consider rebels or worse as shown in this chapter. Language during the Arab Spring needed to be contextualised and adapted for audiences in order to be understood and accepted by the masses which would explain the use of dialectal Arabic as opposed to Modern Standard Arabic (MSA) in some instances. Ayalon (1987) theorises that patterns of dominance and subordination characterise the Arabic language. Based on my own observation, noticeably, since the start of the Arab revolutions, political discourse did not have to be substantially delivered in MSA; some Arab leaders showed linguistic flexibility in an attempt to contain people's disarray and displays of anger. This is particularly interesting when considering Holes' (2004) description of MSA as being the normal medium for formal discourse that is used for all news broadcasts, political speeches, official announcements, and education.

MSA remains the official intra-Arab tool of communication and in fact the official language of bureaucracy; colloquial/spoken Arabic is without doubt the language of the masses. Not all Arabs speak the same dialect however, a point Ferguson (1959) reiterates by saying, 'no variety of spoken Arabic is accepted as the norm or standard for the whole speech community, although of course important centres of prestige and communication may exert a considerable linguistic influence over a certain region' (p. 619). Arabs speak different dialects depending on the specific region which they hail from and an Arab from the Gulf region, for example, would

R. Kesseiri (✉)
University of Leeds, Leeds, UK
e-mail: r.kesseiri@leeds.ac.uk

© Springer Science+Business Media Singapore 2015
R. Raddawi (ed.), *Intercultural Communication with Arabs,*
DOI 10.1007/978-981-287-254-8_14

find it difficult to understand an Arab using the Algerian dialect, because of various influences on Algerian Arabic which make it difficult to understand, while it may be easier for an Arab from North Africa, to understand a Gulf Arabic dialect. Further, Badawi's (1973) five levels of Arabic distinguish among: Fus-ha t-turath (classical Arabic), Fus-ha l-asr (MSA), 'ammiyat al-muthaqqafin' ('high' educated spoken Arabic), Ammiyat al-mutanawwirin ('low' educated spoken Arabic), and Ammiyat al-'ummiyyin (illiterate spoken Arabic).

Generally speaking, politics and the media have always prioritised the use of Standard Arabic in writing and in speaking in the Arab world. Accordingly, it becomes crucial to understand that Arabic is a diglossic language with significant differences between the written and spoken form. Diglossia (1959) asserts that Arabic is a particularly interesting case as the written form of the language is significantly different from its spoken forms, which themselves vary from country to country, and even between different regions of the same country. This is certainly true with the major varieties of Arabic; MSA epitomises the lingua franca of the educated from Morocco in the West to Oman in the East. MSA is the pan-Arab language of communication in the Arab world, predominantly used in education, politics, and the media and regarded as the formal medium of communication. Furthermore, it remains the choice for political statements in the Arab world and the official language of over 250 million speakers. Chejne (1969) describes modern standard literary Arabic as binding of all Arabic-speaking countries and depicts standardized Arabic as the official language of literature and international communication in the Arab world. Abdelali (2004) insists that MSA has until now been the accepted form of the written language used in print media, literature, and formal correspondence.

Former Egyptian President Gamal Abdul Nasser was the first to include both Standard and colloquial Egyptian Arabic in his speeches. Mazraani (1997) comments that Nasser never completely delivered a speech in the everyday spoken language, always initiating his speech with the more formal standard Arabic. This was almost certainly an attempt at accessibility while maintaining the image of an eloquent, well-spoken leader. It is also safe to say that the use of MSA guarantees the maintenance of the fear factor that MSA always held which shall be discussed further later. Holes (1995) believes that Nasser was the first to 'go against the grain of the traditions of formal public speaking which has lasted until as late as the mid 1950s' (p. 283). Following his lines, both Qaddafi and Saddam Hussein equally used educated spoken Arabic to deliver their speeches. In the early 1950s, a poetic movement took colloquial poetry past the notion that the colloquial form is only appropriate for certain subjects (Radwan 2012). Poets such as Fu'ad Haddad, Bayram el-Tunsi, Salah Jaheen, Abdul Rahman al Abnudi, and Ahmed Fouad Negm have used colloquial Egyptian Arabic in their poems, while colloquial Arabic was also used in plays, novels, and short stories such as those of the Egyptian writers Tawfiq el-Hakim and Yusuf Idris. In literature, Muhammad Husayn Haykal (1888–1956) published Zaynab in 1914, the first Egyptian novel written in Egyptian Arabic.

Access to the Internet and social networks introduced new aspects of communication through web logs and forums which allowed new developments in the Arabic language to take place, such as the introduction of Latinised Arabic as a start to the

Table 14.1 Uses of the Arabic language

	*The birth of digital Arabic. This has allowed MSA to experience a breakthrough in its usages and initiate a digital phase after years of Latinised Arabic.*(Picture taken by author)
	*A snapshot of an Algerian advert promoting the French Bank Société Générale Algérie, which is aimed at an Algerian audience* Note the use of Colloquial Algerian Arabic aimed at reaching an Algerian audience only and epitomising a new phase in written Arabic
Société Générale Algérie (2011). Developpons Ensemble l'esprit d'equipe. El Moujahid Algerian Newspaper	

language revolution, the digitalisation of the Arabic language, and, most importantly, the use of colloquial Arabic as a written form in media and social forums. This meant that people no longer needed to be educated to the level of MSA in order to be able to communicate their thoughts (see Table 14.1).

In this respect, Younes (2006) stipulates that:

I believe that the main difference between Arabic and other languages resides in the unique status that the written version of the former enjoys for historical and religious reasons. It has not allowed, nor is it likely to allow at any time in the foreseeable future, the development of a writing system for any of the spoken dialects that closely reflects its structure. Any attempt at writing or codifying specific dialects is seen as a serious invasion of the territory of fuṣḥā, which is held in the utmost esteem by the overwhelming majority of Arabs. (p. 165)

Colloquial Arabic was never used on its own to express political opinions or used for official statements and in fact has not been recognised in its written form Recent events in the Arab world have to a certain extent liberated the language by allowing the use of dialects in official public statements and in their written forms as seen in certain revolutionary slogans. For instance, in a study of the slogans of the Tunisian and Egyptian revolution, Fawwaz Al-Abed Al-Haq and Abdullah Abdelhameed Hussein (2011) collected a sample of slogans from different places in Tunisia and Egypt using the Internet, TV channels, and newspapers. Some were in Egyptian Arabic, some in Tunisian Arabic, and others in MSA.

In Egyptian Arabic, 'yaa gamaal 'uul la'abuuk … ša'b miṣr biyikrahuuk' means 'O, Jamal tell your father that Egyptian people hate you'. Or 'Wallahi maa hanimši. wimalhaaš ḥali thaani inta hatimši w'ana baa'i bimakaani' means 'By God, we will not leave. No other solution, you will leave or I will stay here'.

In Tunisian Arabic, 'tuunis tuunis ḥurra ḥurra, bin 'ali 'aala barra' means 'Tunisia Tunisia free free, Ben Ali is out'.

14.2   Literature Review

In light of the recent political upheaval in some Arab countries, it has become a pressing need to understand the language used throughout these major historical events and shed light on how language was used to capture the attention of the masses, although in some cases to no avail. The Arab Spring represented a watershed in the way intra-Arab communication was conducted. The predominant use of MSA through political speeches was challenged with the attempt of leaders to reach their nations and hence use the language of their people, also known as *dialect*.

It is therefore helpful to examine the way Arabic evolved into this enthralling and enrapturing language, predominantly adopted by the educated middle class, politicians, and the powerful elite. Historically, Arabic was spoken by the Quraysh tribe. Chejne (1969) mentions that 'traditions handed down by Muslim writers give us good clues. They either attribute a divine origin to the language or trace it back through the Qur'an and pre-Islamic poetry to the Quraysh dialect' (p. 53; the Quraysh tribe is the tribe to which the prophet Mohammed belongs). It was the language of oral poetry prior to the rise of Islam and was of high importance in Arab society. It united Arabs into one people who communicated through language. Poetry described Arab life and the emotions of human frailty such as courage, love, war, and grieving. The correct and appropriate use of Arabic was also seen as a sign of wisdom, manhood, and eloquence. Ferguson (1959) asserts that:

> After the "Arabiyyah" became accepted throughout the world of Islam and was explicitly codified in the works of the grammarians, it remained essentially unchanged in phonology and morphology until the present time, when it is still accepted as the norm both for written and for formal spoken Arabic. During the centuries, however, spoken Arabic, even at the time of Muhammad quite different from the "Arabiyyah" in many parts of Arabia, diverged increasingly from this standard. (p. 617)

What was initially a tribal dialect evolved considerably into a venerated and adored language with Islam adding further significance and value. It was perceived as the language of fear and respect and was predominantly perceived as intruding upon the many well-established vernacular languages used by the tribes and peoples to which the language spread as part of the Islamic conquests.

From its early beginnings, Arabic evolved as a literary language in the Muslim empire and became the national language of Muslim states including Spain and Sicily. Chejne (1969) states that Arabic occupied an enviable position in a wide area of the Asiatic Middle East, throughout North Africa, and for a time in Spain and Sicily. By the eighth and ninth centuries, Arabic had acquired a universal character. Lyons (2010) asserts that 'Arabic replaced Greek as the Universal language of scientific inquiry' (p. 64) and in the twentieth century gained momentum and reinstated itself as the backbone of Arab nationalism. Another major fact that shaped the evolution of MSA is pan-Arabism with Gamal Abdul Nasser as the main driving force behind promoting the use of a single language that embodied unity for all Arabs. Unity was key to pan-Arabism and this was embodied through language. At this time, the political discourse of leaders configured language to further strengthen their ideology. Arabic had a symbolic importance, uniting Arabs and Muslims especially after the collapse of the Ottomans and the end of the First World War. It was pan-Arabism first in the 1920s, then Arab nationalism in the 1950s. These were the new ideologies of the time in the Middle East, mainly advocated by Arab leaders to unify the Arab world through a common language. Amin (2001) claims that Nasser's vision of a unified world focused on capitalising on the oral culture prevalent in the Arabic-speaking world at the time.

It is crucial to understand at this stage the close link between language and politics in order to understand the political discourse of pan-Arabism and consequently the language of the Arab Revolution. Safouan (2007) explains the closed nature of the intellectual world of classical Arabic and how Arab despotism was dependent on the use of writing as a means of power and exploitation. In fact, Suleiman (1999) states:

> The unequal distribution of power in society often leads to the emergence of patterns of dominance and subordination. These in turn are reflected in the unequal distribution of the linguistic capital in society, with the result that … speech accommodation starts to emerge and solidify in favor of the dominant group. (p. 26)

One rather pessimistic analysis leads us to stipulate that language had lost its liberty having been monopolised by the elite and the powerful and it became more difficult to articulate anger and frustration. Muslims in general and Arabs in particular continue to venerate and appreciate classical Arabic. One needs to understand that Arabic is seen not only as the language of religion but also as a means of cultural and national inspiration and stimulation. Arabic's hold on its listeners becomes more evident in public address when used to captivate the audience, an audience which if illiterate would be entranced by the Arabic if used correctly and properly. Hitti (1958) describes Arabic thus:

> No people in the world, perhaps, manifest such enthusiastic admiration for literary expression and are so moved by the word, spoken or written, as the Arabs. Hardly any language seems capable of exercising over the minds of its users such irresistible influence as Arabic. Modern audiences in Baghdad, Damascus and Cairo can be stirred to the highest degree by the recital of poems, only vaguely comprehended, and by the delivery of orations in the classical tongue, though it be only partially understood. The rhythm, the rhyme, the music produce on them the effect of what they call "lawful magic" (sihr halal). (p. 90)

14.3 Arabic Dialects and Social Media

With no threat to MSA, the advent of social media has encouraged the use of colloquial Arabic in a written form, which can be seen as mentioned by Khalil (2011) as a step towards the 'democratization' of the language as it became a means of mobilization and a source of enrichment to MSA. Colloquial spoken Arabic is the everyday language of both educated and illiterate people alike. Aboelezz (2009, p. 4) states that:

> Broadly speaking, there are two main classes of Arabic: Modern Standard
> Arabic (MSA), a descendant of Classical Arabic (which lives on in the Qur'an today), and
> regional Arabic vernaculars or Colloquial Arabic.

An increase in the use of Arabic in social network forums and tweets has been noted, which is seen as part of the language's evolution. Initially, software limitations as well as a foreign-language-educated elite led to the rise of 'Latinized' Arabic use on the Internet. 'With software support for Arabic script more readily available today than it was in 2003–2004, more recent developments which have potentially increased the applications of LA are offering a whole new perspective on its growing use' (Aboelezz 2009, p. 4). However, recent technological developments, along with modern software, have enabled more Arabic language use on the Internet. An important point is that the use of the spoken form of Arabic, rather than MSA, has allowed for greater liberty of speech and less censorship in comparison with the traditional state-owned media.

The *Facebook* page shown in Fig. 14.1 belongs to the 6th of April Youth Movement, which is an Egyptian activist group known to be 'the political Facebook group' in Egypt. In the Facebook page, the 6th of April Youth Movement addresses Mubarak's ministers. The group describes them as the corrupt people in the country and warns them of the group's imminent success and spread of their innovative and good ideas through big Egyptian Internet sites. The language used throughout

Fig. 14.1 6th of April Youth Movement (2011). Snapshot. (Facebook page. http://www.facebook. com/shabab6april/posts/181224031910132)

this page is spoken Egyptian and this is indicative of their wish to be understood by the populace which does not forcibly understand or can write MSA. The group target audience is the general public. This shows us the role social media had in revolutionising the use of Arabic and mobilizing thousands to take to the streets in protest in Tunisia and Egypt. It also illustrates the key role played by the Internet as it served to unite and mobilise and offer a different viewpoint to that of state-sanctioned media (Fig. 14.1).

Across the Arab world, young people are contributing their opinions to the new political map, through active participation in political life through social networks, blogs, tweets, and other forums which benefit from additional freedoms not afforded in more traditional means of communication. This leads us to infer that there is a clear shift in political trends in the Middle East and North Africa (MENA) region and it is obvious that social media constitute a breakthrough in the way politics is practiced from one side and a revolution in the way language is used on the other side.

14.4 Analysis

Egypt: The Language in Mubarak's Last Two Speeches It was against a backdrop of popular uprisings and demands for political, social, and economic reforms that Mubarak delivered his two principal speeches in 2011, a few days apart, addressing the demonstrators in Tahrir Square and other places in Egypt led by the youth movement. Unity, solidarity, and reform were the main themes in the president's first speech of 1 February 2011 whereby an attempt to calm the riots and unify the nation became increasingly urgent. This was a long-awaited speech intended to alleviate the severity of the riots and calm the tense situation. Mubarak initiated his infamous speech with an emphasis on the difficult time Egypt was experiencing and reasserting the legitimacy of his regime in an attempt to maintain his rule and authority. He was positioning himself as the figure standing for legitimacy and law beside other governing authorities and protesters with no legitimacy at the other end of the scale; they were the outlaws in his eyes. In fact, Mubarak distinguishes between two types of demonstrators, those who 'practise their rights to peaceful demonstrations and protests' and those who 'sought to spread chaos and violence and to violate the constitutional legitimacy and attack it' (Al Jazeera 2011). To emphasise the chaotic character of the demonstrations and to reinforce his legitimacy, he asked his people to choose between stability and chaos. Mubarak states:

> Those protests were transformed from a noble and civilised phenomenon of practising freedom of expression to unfortunate clashes, mobilised and controlled by political forces that wanted to escalate and worsen the situation. (Al Jazeera 2011)

Other themes present in his speeches include credibility and legitimacy which were mirrored by an emphasis of the systems in place to foster credibility and legitimacy by pointing at the brutality and lawlessness of the protestors who '…targeted the nation's security and stability through acts of provocation, theft and looting' (Al Jazeera 2011).

The protesters are represented as brutal outlaws which is probably intended to deter them from taking to the streets. In this respect, it is believed that:

> more repressive regimes are in principle better able to deter citizens from taking to the streets in the first place. Where citizens face significant risks of being jailed, tortured, or killed if they protest, the streets are likely to be deserted most of the time. Second, protest that takes place in a more repressive autocratic regime is more likely to cascade into a successful uprising. If citizens are willing to take to the streets to protest despite significant risks, their defiance will constitute a very powerful and informative signal about the strength of anti-government sentiment, and about the underlying weakness of the regime. (Kricheli et al. 2011, p. 9)

Mubarak's tenacity regarding his ability to hold onto power is justified through a resolute statement emphasising security:

> I am now absolutely determined to finish my work for the nation in a way that ensures handing over its safe-keeping and banner while Egypt is stable and safe and preserving its legitimacy and respecting the constitution. (PBSNewsHour 2011)

The second speech delivered on 10 February 2011 adopts a more specific and systematic approach predominantly using a more democratic language. One striking difference between Mubarak's speeches is the remarkable contrast between the views of the leader in each speech. In the second speech, Mubarak recognises people's right to demonstrate and promises to punish the police forces that attacked the protestors, even referring to the killed protestors as martyrs. In the first speech though, he attempts to show the potential risks and bleak future ahead should the protests continue. It is important to note that in the first speech, he does not give any legitimacy to the protestors and a week later he admits that the protests are legitimate and he even says that he is proud of the youth protesting in Egypt as he describes them as martyrs. Mubarak states: ' I am proud of you as the new genera-

Audience

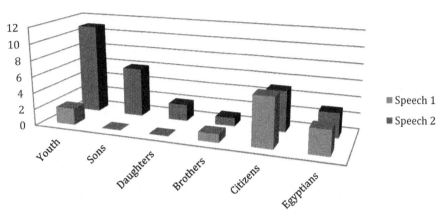

Fig. 14.2 The chart indicates the frequency of certain words in Speech 1 as opposed to Speech 2 and should help us establish the target audience in each case

tion calling for a change to the better, dreaming and making the future'. He goes further and asserts: ' The loss of the martyrs of the sons of Egypt in sad and tragic events has hurt our hearts and shaken the homeland's conscience' (BBC News 2011, para 23).

Mubarak opens both speeches with a religious sentence, which is the opening sentence of each and every Surah in the Quran: *In the name of Allah, the merciful, the compassionate*, a very common religious sentence for Muslims. Both speeches are tinted with a religious character through the use of expressions such as 'I ask God; what satisfies God; this is the pledge I have made before God'. The use of 'Bismillah' at the beginning of both speeches can be seen as an attempt to portray himself as a faithful Muslim. Mubarak addressed the nation as 'Dear brothers and citizens' in the first speech (PBSNewsHour 2011) but later portrayed the protestors, composed predominantly of young people with Islamic affiliations, as the main catalyst of the uprising. In fact, the young Egyptians are portrayed as a 'new generation' eager for a 'better change'. Protestors are not looters and vandals; instead, they are 'sons' whose 'demands are legitimate and right'. Furthermore, Mubarak expresses his desire to 'listen to the youth'. In a clear effort to draw sympathy from the youth, Mubarak tries to defend his achievements in a fatherly context saying, 'say again that I lived for the sake of this country, preserving its responsibility and trust. Egypt will remain above all and above everyone' (BBC News 2011, para 51). He also refers in his speech of February 10 to the days in his past in which he defended the nation saying: 'I lived days of occupation and frustration and days of liberation. Those were the best days. The best day of my life is when I raised the flag of Egypt over the Sinai' (BBC News 2011).

Below is an analysis of the main themes in his speeches and a comparison of their occurrences in both speeches (Fig. 14.2).

Audience for speech   Analysis shows that Speech 1 was directed at a more general audience, whereas Speech 2 was directed more at the youth of Egypt, whom he calls 'sons and daughters' (BBC News 2011).

Mubarak attempts to convince protestors to put an end to their rioting in Speech 1 but to no avail. Nine days later, demonstrations expanded throughout Egypt and the protestors across the nation were unified by one demand, *Asha'b yurid isqat anizama*, or 'people want to bring down the regime'. Mubarak's second speech was accordingly more personal, frequently using a paternalistic undertone to appeal to his people. His speech denoted the *Father Figure* talking to his children, trying to enlighten their ways and show them light at the end of the tunnel.

In the first speech, he is attempting to appeal to his own age group, rather than the younger generation with attempts to portray himself as the person who will advocate democratic reform and provide citizens with what they desire, namely jobs, social justice, and relief from poverty. He is very self-oriented which indicates that he is attempting to legitimise himself. He also tries to sensitise the older generation to control the youngest ones and keep them away from rioting.

Democratic Language Used (Fig. 14.3)   Speech 2 included terminology revolving around freedom, change, and transparency, whereas Speech 1 mentioned reform more than Speech 2, and also mentioned freedom and democracy. This indicates that Mubarak was referring to government reforms as part of a democratic process and was indeed considering the freedom of the people and independence of the nation.

Religious Words Used (Fig. 14.4)   Yet, in Speech 1, the top three words being part of the same phrase, one could say that religion was mentioned in both speeches three times. However, it is important to remember an actual Islamic phrase most probably carries more weight than mentioning God. The use of a religious phrase and religious words is informative about Mubarak's audience and the message being portrayed. It indicates that in some ways, the speaker is religious or wants to portray such an image to his audience. If Mubarak is using religious phrases and words to portray his religiosity to his audience, this indicates that his audience is religious or wants him to be religious. Mubarak started Speech 1 using an Islamic phrase which indicates that he is trying to give the audience of Speech 1 what they want to hear, hence indicating that Egyptian youth wants a religious leader. Seemingly, Speech 1 is attempting to appeal to his generation rather than the younger generation and Mubarak is attempting to gain their support and to emphasise that the demonstrations are wrong and are affecting Egypt negatively.

Apart from certain amendments in the constitution, Mubarak promises vague political and social changes to the protestors. He demonstrates his ability to deal with the crisis by showing that he has a plan for the crisis and a better future for Egypt and the Egyptians. At this stage, it is too early for him to be more precise and therefore he does not provide any particular examples. It is essential though to understand that he is already working on some changes. He discusses 'change' in the second speech as amendments were rejected by the people and demonstrations continued following previous speeches. Mubarak tried to address major demands

Democratic themes

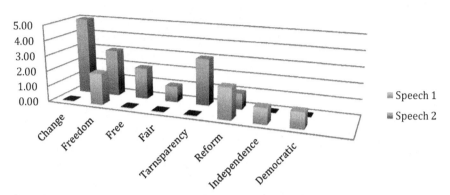

Fig. 14.3 The chart shows that more democratic language was used in Speech 2 than in Speech 1

Religious words

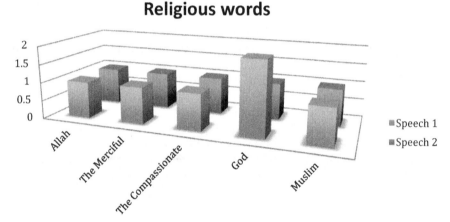

Fig.14.4 The chart illustrates that more words referring to Islam were used in Speech 1

that protestors had such as democracy and change in the government. In the later speech, he reinforces strongly the importance of democracy that many protestors claimed. In his speech, he mentions 'free and candid elections with guarantees of freedom and candor' (BBC News 2011, para 13). He also rectifies and defends his image by saying that: 'I trust that the overwhelming majority of the people know who Hosni Mubarak is. It pains me to see how some of my countrymen are treating me today' (BBC News 2011).

In the first speech, he talks only about amending constitutional articles and finishing his mandate after his last months in office. In neither of his speeches does he take responsibility for the problems that stalk the country. He does refer to some sort of responsibility in his second speech, saying, 'The mistakes can be made in any political system and in any state' (BBC News 2011). Of course, in both speeches,

Mubarak attempts to persuade people that a bright future for Egypt is ahead. He points out the need to stop the violence and in both speeches he argues that the protests are seriously detrimental to the future of Egypt. In the second speech, Mubarak attempts to portray himself as a compassionate and sympathising citizen. He indeed shares the same concerns and fully understands the protestors saying, 'I was as young as Egypt's youth today…' (BBC News 2011). This supports the belief that if the addressed audience thinks that the speaker is one of them, they are more willing to accept the message (Benoit and Benoit 2008). He also reiterates how much he has done for Egypt and talks about his endless love for the country. He legitimises his enduring tenure as constitutional imperative. Most importantly, Mubarak ends both speeches by evoking the mystery and power of Egypt's past saying, 'Egypt will remain eternal; …' (BBC News 2011; AL Jazeera 2011).The differences in tone and language between the two speeches is striking. For example, there is a dramatic increase in the pronoun I throughout the remaining part of Speech 2 with the word appearing a total of 51 times in the whole speech, 18 of which appear in the last few paragraphs. This is indicative of his eagerness to get his message across to the people and his will to be heard and acknowledged. Rather than using words such as *we, regime,* or *government,* he puts himself forwards as solely accountable and responsible to the people.

One major characteristic of both speeches is the use of MSA which affords Mubarak a level of notoriety as it conveys his attitude towards his people. In a country where only 72 % of the nation is literate, Mubarak's use of educated language highlights his disdain for the illiterate section of Egyptian society and perpetuates the image of a leader to be feared.

Language is a reflection of the culture. To a degree, the language of the speeches above reflects a culture of authority and power, tinted with an element of confidence. However, this was toned down through the use of certain terminologies throughout the speeches, meaning the leaders' culture often influences their language in context. The same applies to the audience and the way they perceive the speech, a fact that is also influenced by their culture.

Conversely, in the case of MSA, a strong resonance combined with the fear factor is conveyed through its use. While inspiring respect and admiration, MSA is the language of the educated, literate, and powerful as not everyone in the Arab world understands and speaks MSA. Historically, Arabs were united by this language that conveyed to them the word of God and instructed them in how to lead their lives. Audiences are often mesmerised by the structure and sound of MSA and its use in political speeches is intended to portray the speaker as someone from whom wisdom and the right to lead radiates. It is the eloquence, purity, and perfection of the language that is mirrored through its usage.

Tunisia Ben Ali of Tunisia delivered two major speeches during the revolution, the first on 27 December 2010 and the second on 13 January 2011. One striking contrast between both speeches is the use of a different register. While he uses MSA in the first, he switched to colloquial Tunisian in the second, even declaring 'I will talk to you in the language of all Tunisians' (Luc1f3rk0 2011). Prior to the second speech, most of Ben Ali's speeches to the nation are delivered in MSA but he switches in

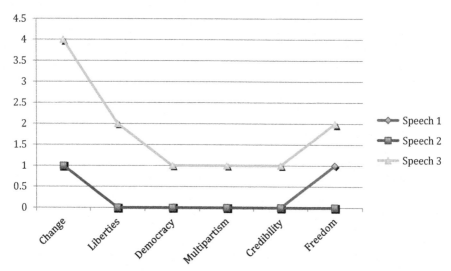

Fig. 14.5 The chart shows the frequency of use of democratic terms in the ousted president Ben Ali's speech of 13 January 2011 as opposed to his previous speeches on 27 December 2010 and 10 February 2011

an attempt to reach out to the nation, both educated and illiterate. This was probably dictated by the social upheavals and the cultural changes exemplified in the widespread unrest (Hudson 1980). The use of Tunisian dialect was a final attempt to be heard by the people and convey his pledge to the nation which is what Paradis (1978) identifies as the attitude towards an audience. He tries to convey sympathy to his people and his acknowledgement of the special circumstances. According to Scotten and Ury (1977), speakers may switch from one language to another for a variety of reasons, sometimes to redefine the interaction as appropriate to a different social arena. In the case of Ben Ali, the social arena includes uneducated and illiterate people who may not be familiar with MSA.

From a thematic aspect, Ben Ali's discourse revolves around themes of unity, patriotism, and, most importantly, change. His address to the Tunisian people was rich in promises of 'liberty', 'freedom of expression', and 'prosperity' (Luc1f3rk0 2011) in an attempt to respond to the demands of the demonstrators. Most importantly, Ben Ali is very defiant in his first speech and concentrates on past achievements and achievements he intends to perform in the future. In his first speeches of 27 December 2010 and 10 January 2011, he does not introduce themes of democracy and freedom directly, attempting instead to respond to the peoples' needs and maintain hegemony and power over the people by discussing unemployment, education, and development. He certainly adopts a more responsive and flexible discourse in his last speech of 13 January 2011. To begin with, he was reluctant to admit and recognise the failure of his rule but in his last speech he appeared more flexible in his approach, adopting democratic terms such as 'change', 'democracy', 'liberty', 'freedom', 'credibility', and 'multipartism' (Luc1f3rk0 2011; Fig. 14.5).

On 13 January 2011, Ben Ali introduced the intrinsic need for change, stating, 'I am addressing you because the situation dictates deep change, deep and comprehensive change'. He went further: 'I would like to affirm that many things didn't take place the way I would have wished, especially in the areas of democracy and freedoms. They misled me sometimes by hiding the facts, and they will be held accountable for that' (Luc1f3rk0 2011). It is interesting to note the use of the Arabic term *sayuhaassabun*: 'they will be held accountable and punished accordingly' which shed light on his approach towards the crisis by which he lays the blame for the lack of democracy and freedom on others.

In fact, 'sayuhaassabun' is a verb that occurs in verses of the Kor'an to inform who ought to be held accountable and punished. Fear and maybe even repentance is what Ben Ali wanted to instil in his audience, especially among the demonstrators. In this respect, he says, 'I would like to affirm that many things didn't take place the way I would have wished, especially in the areas of democracy and freedoms. They misled me sometimes by hiding the facts, and they will be held accountable for that' (Luc1f3rk0 2011). Clearly, Ben Ali refuses to take responsibility for the events in Tunisia and lays the blame on other members of his government. This can also be sensed in the use of the pronoun 'I' in his last speech which shows how he distinguishes himself from the rest of the political system and to affirm that he is blameless.

Repetition is also present in Ben Ali's speech as seen when he implores, 'I understand you, I do understand you' and 'I address you, I talk to you' (Luc1f3rk0 2011) which is intended to attract the attention of his audience and insist on his ability to interact with the people and be responsive to their requests. In this respect, Al-Khafaji (2005, p. 16) sheds light on the role of excessive repetition to appeal to the reader and attract attention.

Libya The case of Qaddafi's speeches in Libya was not different from that of Ben Ali's in Tunisia. Qaddafi shifted between colloquial and MSA throughout his speeches, though one would notice the predominance of MSA over Libyan Arabic. On 22 February 2011, Qaddafi addressed his nation and other Arab states. He also addressed the world and aimed to convey his message to whomever plots against him. For this reason, the use of MSA is necessary in order to be understood not only by Libyans but by the entire Arab-speaking community. Qaddafi's MSA is very eloquent and well spoken. He makes use of strong revolutionary terminologies in an attempt to remind the Libyan people of their rich history of fighting and nationalist stances, for instance 'masseera taarikhya Dhaafira' which means victorious historical path, 'al majd' meaning glory, 'al hadhidh' for rock bottom, and 'al intikaassa' for relapse (Aljamahiriya TV 2011). Most importantly, Qaddafi reiterates his intrinsic belonging to this glorious past and history, asserting: 'Muammar Qaddafi is history, resistance, freedom, victory, revolution' .(Valiente 2011)

Qaddafi not only makes use of words with strong resonance in Arabic but also makes use of Arabic prose and poetry as he makes an analogy between Libyan freedom and freedom in Bashir al-Saadawi's poetry. Qaddafi quotes Bashir al-Saadawi (a prominent freedom proponent) saying 'Freedom is a tree in whose shade no one can sit except the one who planted it with his hands and watered it with his blood' and compares it to Libyan freedom by stressing that 'Libya is a tree in whose shade we sit, for it is we who planted it with our hands and watered it with our blood' (Valiente 2011). Furthermore, Qaddafi also makes use of some Libyan literature heritage towards the end of his speech as he mentions a poem belonging to the Zentaan region. It is clear that Qaddafi wants to appeal to everyone in Libya. This highlights Qaddafi's strong knowledge of and ease with the Arabic language.

It is interesting to note in Qaddafi's speech the way he alternates between the use of MSA and the dialect. It is also important to note that Libyan Arabic is a variety of MSA that can be understood by most educated Arabs due to the resemblance between Libyan Arabic and MSA with some differences in pronunciation and some loan words. In fact, most vocabulary in Libyan Arabic is of classical Arabic origin with some Italian, Turkish, and Berber influences. Shagmani (2002) describes the influence of LA on MSA as syntactic while the influence of MSA on LA is lexical. He emphasises that 'Most of the vocabulary of MV [Misurata Vernacular] comes originally from MSA; however, hundreds of foreign words especially from Italian are present and are used in normal daily life situations. Also words from English, French and Turkish are used by the Misuratis' (p. 150).

The use of some Arabic Libyan words is present throughout the speech but a predominant presence of the dialect is clear as Qaddafi calls upon the people to take over the streets of Libya and recover control of their country through the 'People's Revolution', that is a revolution against those who want to destroy Libya. Qaddafi believes in a foreign conspiracy, and sees America as the number one culprit behind the destruction of Libya: 'We resisted the tyrannical might of America' (Valiente 2011, para 3) He also warns of following 'the agents of the foreign intelligence and those fundamentalists?' (Ironic Surrealism 2011). He asks, 'Do you want your country to be like Somalia and like Iraq as well? Same groups who caused the destruction of this country, are doing what they did, they want [it] to be like Fallujah' (Aljamahiriya TV 2011). Qaddafi aims his speech at an international audience and the presence of terminologies such as 'al-Qaeda', 'armed criminals', and 'foreign terrorists' gives the crisis an international dimension and rules out internal causes to the problem. In an interview with the BBC on 28 February 2011, after the crisis erupted in Libya, Qaddafi surprisingly responded in English despite not being fond of speaking in the language (mtribeproducer 2011).

Qaddafi's use of the language is very strategic and reflects his flexibility to the context of discourse. His speeches of February 22 and 28 mirror his determination to be heard by the international, Arab, and Libyan community. His use of MSA reflects an attempt to be communicative rather than powerful and authoritarian. This is supported with the fact that Qaddafi makes use of English in an attempt to communicate his response to the journalist. This is further stressed with an adult literacy rate in 2011 of 89.5 % in Libya according to the UNESCO records highlighting the fact that a high majority of adults is able to understand MSA with only 5 % of the nation speaking Berber. The use of eloquent language and poetry in the speech is certainly an emphasis of his belonging, culture, and heritage.

Syria Syria's uprising began on 26 January 2011, following the schoolchildren wall graffiti incident in Dar'a in the south of Syria. President Assad delivers various speeches using MSA with no language shift into Syrian Arabic. It is worth mentioning at this stage that the literacy rate amongst adults in Syria is 84.1% according to the UNESCO Institute for Statistics in 2011 meaning that a large section of the population understands and writes MSA. Add to that the fact that the Syrian dialect shares similarities with MSA in terms of vocabulary and it is actually one of the closest dialects to MSA in comparison with other existing dialects in the region. A Syrian or someone who understands Syrian should have no difficulties understanding MSA. In a reading booklet series, *Teaching Eastern Arabic III*, it is asserted that differences between spoken Syrian and MSA exist at phonological levels and constitute differences in pronunciation. (Rettig and Heinle Eds. 2009, p. 8)

Security and stability are overwhelming themes in Assad's speech of 20 June 2011. Having said that, though he is addressing the Syrian people, he does want his message to be heard by Arabs and by the international community, which would certainly justify the use of a register that is understood by all Arab speakers. When he addresses the Syrian people, he recognises the death toll and attributes the status of martyrdom to those who died, saying, 'Peace be upon the souls of our martyrs' (Al-Bab 2011b, para 1). In his speech of 10 January 2012, the word 'reform' is more prevalent. Even though there is a lack of terms referring to the demonstrators, the president does not deny the loss of life. It could be argued that with this avoidance of mentioning demonstrators, he has failed in his task to reach out to the people. Nevertheless, he is confident *conspiracy* is behind the crisis. With this in mind, Assad has successfully conveyed his message and tackled the presence of conspiracies and sabotage with initiatives to strengthen immunity.

In fact, what is striking in the speech of 06 January 2013 is the lack of terms such as *democracy, freedom, demonstrations,* and *down with the regime.* These are terms that echoed through the streets during the Arab Spring and are therefore more or less expected to be dealt with in a speech. President Bashar al Assad uses terms such as *homeland, plot, sabotage, achievement, dialogue, reform,* and a shift between the pronouns *I* and *we.* The issue in using such a range of terminology lies in the existing contradiction between a term such as *plot* and a term such as *reform. Reform* entails a discontent within the people and the need to instil changes in order to bring improvement. This is rather incompatible with a state that suffers external plotting and is the victim of a conspiracy. This also shows that for Assad, the conspiracy is the fuel of the revolution and not the people. In other words, a conspiracy does not require reform but rather *defence.* While the term *defence* does not occur directly, Assad speaks about immunity and ways to boost it.

Assad does not remove references to demonstrators completely from his speech. Although there are no mentions of them at the beginning of the speech, the president does recognise the existence of demonstrators as he introduces the substance of his speech, being a dialogue with all sections of the society, namely demonstrators and non-demonstrators. He mentions: 'We will have dialogue with all those who don't agree with us in politics and who have stances contrary to ours providing that those stances are not based on affecting the national principles and basics' (Global Research (Jan 7, 2013). The notion of democracy is without a doubt present in Assad's speech as he introduces the concept of national dialogue between the sections of society, which is characteristic of democracy. Johnson and Johnson (2000, p. 9) assert that:

> In a democratic society, psychology (and the other social sciences) has the responsibility of increasing the understanding of how to enhance the health of the democratic process and socialize new citizens into the attitudes and competencies they need to participate actively in political discourse.

In fact, this can also be seen as another contradiction in the speech as the president relates the crisis to a conspiracy yet admits he has conversed with demonstrators and non-demonstrators. Equally, the term dialogue, which is very predominant in the president's speech (31 occurrences), firstly introduces the idea that there are many parties to the crisis who ought to work together to solve it. Amnesty is also present in the speech and it expresses the wish of the state to forgive the people who are causing destruction and this, in a certain way, is an admittance that people have taken to the streets and that the problem is not a conspiracy only. An alternative view is that the protestors are actually part of a bigger picture, manipulated by a conspiracy.

Moving to the shift in the use of the personal pronoun *I* and *we,* it is apparent that the president considers himself one of the people and shares with them the same feelings towards current events. This is apparent in the multiple uses of *we:* 'We have been through difficult time, we have paid a heavy price' (Al-Bab 2011). However, the shift to using the pronoun '*I*' entails a disparity in the level of addressee. By using *I,* President Assad emphasises an existing delineation between himself and the others: 'I said this before in my speech before the People's Assembly and at the Cabinet' (Al-Bab 2011). We cannot, however, be categorical in saying that the president was placing himself at a higher level.

There are thus two potential cases to be analysed. First, considering that the demonstrators and the government are the main actors in the Syrian crisis, the contradiction between the terminologies of the streets and the terms used in the speech indicates a gross misunderstanding between them as each side discusses different themes and does not recognise the other's right to exist. Of course, we need to give credit to the original speech given in Arabic and the strength of the words used for its purpose. It is important to mention that listening to the original speech in Arabic, the listener is left with a thorough account of the situation in Syria and how the president sees the crisis and tries to understand and offer solutions to it. It is because the president had to explain and relate initiatives he had taken that he needed to make the shift in order to emphasise his active role and concern about the situation.

The second case places the conspiracy as a major actor in the crisis to which the layout of the speech responds appropriately. In Syria, at this specific time, the objectives behind a political speech would be to put an end to protests and return to a state of alchemy.

Of course, there are two analyses we can make: if we were to base our decision on the reactions in the streets, one ought to decide that President Assad's speech has

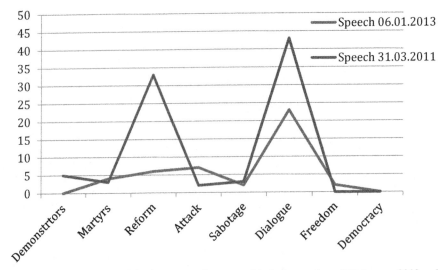

Fig. 14.6 A comparison of the frequency of terms used in both speeches of 06 January 2013 and 31 March 2011. This should help show a change in 'attitude towards' the revolution

failed to complete the intended purpose, as the message has not been conveyed or received by the audience. In other words, the crisis has gotten worse. From a linguistic perspective, some could argue that the speech is contradictory as it includes terms that are better not used together. For example, the occurrence of the term 'conspiracy', either as one word or understood from context, contradicts the occurrence of reform. Lack of credibility can be argued in such discourse, as terms do not support each other. In an attempt to contain the crisis, Assad has touched on various paradigms, even though they do not fit together in some instances. The speech is instructive and educational providing an account of major facts and narratives in the history of Syria and the many issues that evolved throughout the nation that are being dealt with or are in the process of being dealt with. It also explains the process of reform and constitutional amendment (Fig. 14.6).

Conclusion

MSA written Arabic is inaccessible to the illiterate although most of the educated class can read it and feel they can produce it competently. Yet, colloquial/spoken Arabic remains the everyday language of both educated and illiterate people alike. Writing in colloquial Arabic is a step towards 'the democratization of the language' in the case of Arabic. It is the democratization of written Arabic which enjoys a revered status for historical and religious reasons that cannot be altered. The Arab uprisings facilitated a convergence between written and spoken Arabic, representing a shift in political discourse manifested in the speeches of political leaders in 'Arab

Spring' nations. The new discourse is characterised by a change of register and the introduction of democratic ideas. It also ended an era of language subordination by authoritarian rulers.

Further, the online and social media aspect of the uprisings created a new forum for written Arabic. In fact, one can stipulate the start of a new era in the use of Arabic, namely one of democratization in which Arabic is no longer solely reserved for literary and media writers. One needs to bear in mind that colloquial Arabic has neither threatened nor replaced MSA throughout the last wave of revolutions. On the contrary, the Arab uprisings facilitated a convergence between written and spoken Arabic through social networks and blogs. Furthermore, new terminology came to the surface which was created to serve the purposes of the Arab Revolution, for instance: 'jum'a al ghaDab' for 'Friday of wrath', 'jumu'at al raheel' for 'Friday of departure', 'ahad al shuhadaa' ' for 'Sunday of martyrs', 'al balTaguiyya' for 'thugs', and 'mawqi'at al jamel' for 'battle of the camels'. In fact, the 'Revolution Terminology' Facebook group which is a closed group created in Egypt introduced the 'Revolution Terminology' in an attempt to facilitate the understanding of the terminology used. One can safely infer that the Arab Spring has marked a new turn in the development of the Arabic language by defining new words to be used in the context of the Arab Spring in order to express new themes. This primarily features the democratization of the language, whereby writing is not only limited to the use of MSA but rather extends to spoken Arabic, seen essentially in Internet forums, social media, and the slogans of the demonstrators. The Arab Spring emancipated the language of political statements, with essentially the democratization of the Arabic language, thus marking a watershed in the development of the Arabic language.

Revolution terminology and democratization of the language are certainly a major feature that characterised the development of MSA throughout the Arab Spring. Equally, the culture of fear and veneration towards Arab leaders was revolutionised with the Arab Spring, as people went on to the streets to put an end to years of dictatorial ruling. Likewise, the use of MSA was no longer required for official statements and for written forums. People wrote in the dialect they spoke. In other words, spoken Arabic was to be used in its written form. This reflects a culture of democracy reflected in the language. In other words, language is influenced by culture, and the culture of democracy, freedom, and justice created by the people in MENA has affected the structure and the terminology (language) of the leaders' speeches directly or indirectly. The Arabic language has witnessed a breakthrough that allowed for spoken Arabic to be written and used for written communication.

References

Abdelali, A. (2004). Localization in modern standard Arabic. *Journal of the American Society for Information Science and Technology, 55*(1), 23–28.

Aboelezz, M. (2009). Latinised Arabic and connections to bilingual ability. *Papers from the Lancaster University Postgraduate Conference in Linguistics and Language Teaching (LAEL PG) 3* (December), pp 1–23. http://www.ling.lancs.ac.uk/pgconference/v03.htm. Accessed 2 April 2013.

Al-Bab. (10 Jan 2011a). *Tunisia: speech by President Ben Ali*. http://www.al-bab.com/arab/docs/tunisia/ben_ali_speech_10012011.htm. Accessed 15 Sep 2013.

Al-Bab. (20 June 2011b). *Syria: speech by Bashar al-Assad*. http://www.albab.com/arab/docs/syria/bashar_assad_speech_110620.htm. Accessed 16 Jan 2014.

Al Haq, F, & Hussein, A. (2011) The slogans of the Tunisian and Egyptian revolutions: A sociolinguistic study. http://media.leidenuniv.nl/legacy/fawwaz.pdf. Accessed 18 Sep 2013.

Aljamahiriya TV. (24 Dec 2011). Al Gaddafi's full speech February 2011, Tripoli. http://www.youtube.com/watch?v=1n_G0vIeGqw. Accessed 20 Sep 2013.

Al Jazeera. (2011). *Full text of Mubarak's speech*. http://www.aljazeera.com/news/middleeast/2011/02/20112221313603381.html. Accessed 21 Sep 2013.

Al-Khafaji, R. (2005). Variation and recurrence in the lexical chains of Arabic and English texts. *Poznan Studies in Contemporary Linguistics, 40*(2005), 5–25.

Amin, H. (2001). Mass media in the Arab states between diversification and stagnation: An overview. In H. Kai (Ed.), *Mass media, politics, and society in the Middle East* (pp. 23–44). Cresskill: Hampton.

Arabic enabled keyboard (n.d.). http://www.istockphoto.com/stock-photo-239353-arabic-enabled-keyboard.php?st=d51e3c9. Accessed 15 Sep 2014.

Ayalon, A. (1987) *Language and change in the Arab Middle East: The evolution of modern political discourse*. New York: Oxford University Press.

Badawi, El-Said. (1973). *Mustawayat al-arabiyya l-mu'assira fi misr*. Cairo: dar al-ma'arif.

BBC News. (2011). *Egypt unrest: Full text of Hosni Mubarak's speech*. http://www.bbc.co.uk/news/world-middle-east-12427091. Accessed 22 Sep 2013.

Benoit, L., & Benoit, J. P. (2008). *Persuasive messages: The process of influence*. Oxford: Blackwell Publishing.

Chejne, A. (1969). *The Arabic language: Its role in history*. Minneapolis: University of Minnesota Press.

Diglossia. (1959). *In word* (Vol. 15, pp. 325–340). New York: Linguistic Circle of New York.

Facebook page. (2011). 6th of April Movement. [Screenshot]. http://www.facebook.com/shabab6april/posts/181224031910132. Accessed 16 Sep 2013.

Ferguson, C. (1959). The Arabic Koine. *Language, 35*(4: October–December), 616–630. http://www.jstor.org/stable/410601. Accessed 15 Dec 2013.

Global Research. (10 Jan 2012). *President Bashar Al Assad's 2012 Damascus University speech*. http://www.globalresearch.ca/president-bashar-al-assad-s-2012-damascus-university-speech/31250. Accessed 17 Sep 2013.

Global Research. (7 Jan 2013). *The West has brought terrorists to Syria: President Bashar Al Assad's historic speech. Full transcript*. http://www.globalresearch.ca/the-west-has-brought-terrorists-to-syria-president-bashar-al-assads-historic-speech-full-transcript/5317977. Accessed 17 Sep 2013.

Hitti, P. K. (1958). *History of the Arabs*. New York: Palgrave Macmillan.

Holes, C. (1995). *Modern Arabic: Structures and functions*. London: Longman.

Holes, C. (2004). *Modern Arabic: Structures and functions. Revised edition*. Washington, D. C: Georgetown University Press.

Hudson, R., A. (1980). *Sociolinguistics*. New York: Cambridge University Press.

Ironic Surrealism. (2011). *Gaddafi speech Feb 2011—Full translated video*. http://www.ironic-surrealism.com/2011/02/24/gaddafi-speech-february-2011-full-translated-video/. Accessed 27 Sep 2013.

Johnson, W. D., & Johnson, T. R. (2000) Civil political discourse in a democracy: The contribution of psychology. *Peace & Conflict: Journal of Peace Psychology, 6*(4), 291–317. http://www.co-operation.org/wp-content/uploads/2011/01/Controversy-Political-Discourse.pdf. Accessed 15 Dec 2013.

Khalil, A. (2011). A wounded father figure. *Foreign Policy*. 76–77. http://www.foreignpolicy.com/articles/2011/02/01/a_wounded_father_figure. Accessed 22 Sep 2013.

Kricheli, R., Livne, Y., & Magaloni, B. (2011).Taking to the streets: Theory and evidence on protests under authoritarianism. http://www.stanford.edu/~magaloni/dox/2011takingtothestreets.pdf. Accessed 17 Sep 2013.

Luc1f3rk0. (17 Jan 2011). *Tv7 Tunisia–Zine al-Abidine Ben Ali's last speech [13 Jan 2011]*. http://www.youtube.com/watch?v=RdCwCVHzMh0. Accessed 19 Sep 2013.

Lyons, J. (2010). *The house of wisdom: How the Arabs transformed western civilization*. London: Bloomsburry.

Mazraani, N. 1997. Aspects of Language Variation in Arabic Political Speech Making. Richmond, Surrey: Curzon Press.

mtribeproducer. (28 February 2011). Muammar Gaddafi interview with BBC. http://www.youtube.com/watch?v=T65wx9ByFq0. Accessed 9 Sep 2013.

Paradis, M. (1978). *Aspects of bilingualism*. Columbia: Hornbeam Press.

PBSNewsHour. (1 Feb 2011). *Egyptian president Mubarak says he will not seek re-election [Arabic]*. http://www.youtube.com/watch?v=EgrQ6qghzvU. Accessed 15 Oct 2013.

Radwan, N. (2012). Egyptian Colloquial Poetry in the Modern Arabic Canon. NY: Palgrave MacMillan.

Rettig, U., & Heinle, B. (Eds.). (2009). Eastern Arabic III: Reading booklet. Concord: Simon & Schuster. http://www.neiu.edu/~fldept/Pimsleur_Arabic_(Eastern)_III.pdf. Accessed 15 Sep 2014.

Safouan, M. (2007). *Why are the Arabs not free: The politics of writing*. Oxford: Blackwell.

Scotten, C.M., & Ury, W. (1977). Bilingual strategies: The social functions of codeswitching. *International Journal of the Sociology of Language, 1977*(13), 5–20.

Shagmani, A. (2002). The structure of Libyan Arabic discourse as depicted in two Arabic interviews recorded by the Libyan jihad studies centre in tripoli. Unpublished PhD thesis.

Société Générale Algérie. (2011) Developpons Ensemble l'esprit d' equipe. [photograh] Retrieved from *Le Matin* newspaper. 26 Dec 2011.

Suleiman, Yasir. (1999). Language and political conflict in the Middle East. In Y. Suleiman (Ed.), *Language and society in the Middle East and North Africa* (pp. 10–37). Cornwall: Curzon Press.

UNESCO Institute for Statistics. (2010). National adult literacy rates (15+), youth literacy rates (15–24) and elderly literacy rates (65+). http://stats.uis.unesco.org/unesco/TableViewer/tableView.aspx?ReportId=210. Accessed 5 Sep 2014.

Valiente, A. (8 July 2011). Muammar Gaddafi speech made in the early days of the crisis. http://libyadiary.wordpress.com/2011/07/08/muammar-gaddafis-speech-made-in-the-early-days-of-the-crisis/. Accessed 12 Sep 2013.

Younes, M. (2006). Integrating the Colloquial with *Fuune* in the Arabic-as-a-foreign language classroom. In M. Kassem, Z. Wahba, A. Taha, & L. England (Eds.), *Handbook for Arabic language teaching professionals in the 21st century* (pp. 157–166). Mahwah: Lawrence Erlbaum.

Dr. Radia Kesseiri graduated from the University of Algiers in 1998 with a BA in interpreting and translation (Arabic–French–English). In 2000, she obtained an MA in interpreting and translation (Arabic–English–Arabic) from Leeds University. Dr. Kesseiri is a language expert, specialised in Arabic. She has been teaching Arabic since 2001 and translating and interpreting at higher education institutions since 2006. She is currently teaching at Leeds University.

Part III
Societal Contexts

Chapter 15
Impact of Parental Communication Patterns on Arab Women's Choice of Careers

Case Study: Lebanon

Hayfaa A. Tlaiss

15.1 Introduction

Lebanon is an Arab country that is bordered by Syria to the north and east and the Palestinian territories to the south. After being under the influence of the Ottoman and French powers for hundreds of years, Lebanon today is an independent country that is economically highly dependent on tourism and banking sectors. Demographically, unlike the majority of the other Arab countries that are predominantly Muslim, Lebanon is characterized by its religious diversity as it has substantial Muslim and Christian populations. This religious diversity, as Feghali (1997) argues, along with its geography and location at the crossroads of the East Mediterranean and the Arab region, has contributed to Lebanon's cosmopolitan and plural nature.

One of the most prominent aspects of the country's nature is the status that women enjoy in Lebanese society. Unlike some of their Arab counterparts who are still struggling for the right to vote or to travel freely without a male guardian, Lebanese women have been enjoying voting rights and equality in all political arenas since the early 1950s. There have not been any restrictions on their mobility for more than six decades (Tlaiss and Kauser 2011a). Additionally, Lebanese women have always been able to work in any domain they choose, pursue education and graduate studies, and participate in all forms of public life (Barakat 1977). Moreover, Muslim women in Lebanon can choose to wear the veil or not and are not restricted in their relations and interactions with men (Neal et al. 2005). These somewhat relaxed codes regarding women's participation in economic and political activities (Sidani 2005) have been historically explained in terms of the country's tolerance of the Western way of life (Barakat 1977).

H. A. Tlaiss (✉)
University of New Brunswick, New Brunswick, Canada
e-mail: htlaiss@unb.ca

© Springer Science+Business Media Singapore 2015
R. Raddawi (ed.), *Intercultural Communication with Arabs,*
DOI 10.1007/978-981-287-254-8_15

261

Based on these freedoms, one would expect the cultural values of Lebanon to be relaxed, reinforcing the relaxed societal codes. However, reality begs to differ. Using Hofstede's (2001) famous taxonomy of cultural values, the societies of the Arab states, including Lebanon, demonstrate high masculine and collectivist values. On the one hand, the masculine cultural values of the Arab world draw sharp distinctions between gender roles (Hofstede 2001). For example, while females in these societies are socialized to be communal, to focus on their domestic responsibilities, and to meet their socially ascribed primary role as mothers and wives (AlAjmi 2001), males are socialized to pursue education and career and to be financially successful (Omar and Davidson 2001). On the other hand, the collective cultural values of the Arab world emphasize the importance of the family and the group, and encourage family needs to take precedence over personal goals (Pringle and Mallon 2003). These masculine and collective values are further empowered by the patriarchal nature of the Arab societies. While emphasizing the importance of the family as the backbone of the society (Barakat 1977), patriarchy in the Arab world also allocates the responsibilities and the duties of males and females in the family by virtue of gender. Hence, women are expected to attend to the family's needs within the domestic arena, leaving the decision making and financial authority to the male figures (Barakat 1993). As such, Arab women are not expected to consider employment, even on a part-time basis, unless there is a financial need for it (Goby and Erogul 2011).

Interestingly, although research is readily available regarding the general social life in Arab societies (Feghali 1997), studies that explore how gender stereotypes are socialized, endorsed, and communicated by Arab parents within the context of Arab families are rare. This lack of information generated an important knowledge gap, given that childhood socialization is not only integral to every culture but also instrumental to the creation of gender stereotypes. According to the gender socialization perspective, societies produce and reinforce gender differences in values and interest throughout the course of individuals' lives (Ku 2011). Societies and the resulting cultures also reflect the cognitive beliefs about the differences between masculinity and femininity (Best 2004), and support traditional gender roles (Omair 2010). The sociocultural values result in socially different expectations of how men and women should behave. In turn, these differing expectations are firmly woven into the framework of social life (Loscocco and Bird 2012) and lead to gender stereotypes that are aligned with the cultural values and further reinforce these values. Hence, the communication that takes place during the socialization phase is critical given that females and males are taught gender-based attitudes and behaviors during this phase (Powell and Graves 2003). This study is therefore particularly interested in exploring the extent to which the parents of Lebanese women managers communicated and emphasized the traditional gender stereotypes regarding education, employment, and marital status.

15.2   Parental Communication, Childhood Socialization, and Gender

Gender socialization in the Arab countries is closely linked to the strongly held values of patriarchy and masculinity. Since childhood, many females in Arab families are socialized by their parents to assume domestic responsibilities and to focus on meeting the societal expectations of being good wives and mothers (AlAjmi 2001). For example, females are expected to learn how to perform the domestic chores of cooking and cleaning to realize their objectives in life as homemakers and caregivers. Notwithstanding the modernization that several Arab states have been undergoing during the past decade, in a more recent study, Tlaiss and Kauser (2011a) confirm the salience of these beliefs in Lebanon as well as the rest of the Arab world.

Interestingly, this male supremacy that has been reinforced by the patriarchal social structures (Sharabi 1998) and is visible in the various social and economic domains of life (Abou Chedid 2007) extends to the education curriculum in Lebanon. To further explain, in a study examining textbooks in Lebanese schools, Kallab (1983) found that a large number of lessons emphasized gender-based employment roles such as limiting mothers' function to cleaning, cooking, and sewing and fathers' activities to reading or assuming leadership in the public domain (Abou Chedid 2007). More than a decade later, another study in Egypt found that the traditional gender roles in employment were also accentuated in the civics curriculum (Wassef 1996). Therefore, when and if Arab females are encouraged to further their education, they are encouraged to pursue educational majors that are socially accepted as feminine (El-Ghannam 2002; Wassef 1996). Unfortunately, the same applies for employment.

The social role theory argues that women who choose to have a career outside their homes seek employment in line with the socially ascribed roles (Eagly and Carli 2007; Ku 2011); hence, the concentration of women in the Arab world is in a handful of traditionally female sectors (Omar and Davidson 2001) such as health, education, and social work (Metcalfe 2008; Salloum 2003; Tlaiss and Kauser 2010, 2011a). Moreover, while women in Western countries can choose to remain single, this choice is rarely granted to females in the Middle East given that marriage, especially for females, is perceived as a social necessity (Kausar 1995; Khattab 1996). Marriage and having children is of such importance in Arab societies that a significant number of families in this region encourage their daughters to pursue a university degree because higher education would increase their chances of marriage, not for reasons related to having a career or for self-development (El-Ghannam 2002).

Although the review of the literature describes these stereotypes, few studies empirically try to explore the realities experienced by Arab women. In an attempt to attend to this gap, this study explores the socialization experiences of Lebanese women managers and the extent to which the traditional gender roles have been communicated and emphasized to them by their parents during their pursuits of education and career. It also looks at the extent to which marriage and family creation were stressed as a priority versus having an education and/or a career. In other words, this study is interested in exploring the impact of cultural values in defining the importance of women's education and work and the expectations regarding the responsibility of women to their families.

15.3   Research Methodology

This study is particularly interested in exploring the parental communication of traditional gender stereotypes during childhood socialization as experienced by employed Lebanese women. In the absence of previous studies that empirically try to solicit the experiences of women on this subject matter, this research is exploratory in nature. To meet its exploratory objective, and given the high-context nature of the Arab region where most of the meaning is implicit and defined by the context itself (Feghali 1997; Zaharna 1995), the utilization of a mixed method research design that uses qualitative and quantitative data collection and assimilation and analysis techniques was deemed most suitable.

Of the various mixed methodologies, sequential exploratory strategy was used given its compatibility with the exploratory nature and purpose of the current study (Creswell 2007). The sequential exploratory strategy is composed of a sequential triangulation of two phases: first, qualitative data collection and analysis; and second, quantitative data collection and analysis (Creswell 2007).

To probe beyond the common elements and to be immersed into the uniqueness of the cultural tradition of the Lebanese context, semi-structured face-to-face in-depth interviews were used in phase one of the study. This qualitative research method was used to explore the communication of traditional stereotypes in its broad forms. Phase two of the study included the preparation, administration, and analysis of a survey questionnaire. This quantitative methodology was prepared in line with the findings of the interviews and the most prominent themes in the literature. The survey was very useful as it helped the researcher to identify new themes and interconnections between new and old themes and to confirm the qualitative results.

Data collection in the Arab region has always been one of the main obstacles for researchers for several reasons including the absence of reliable postal systems and the reluctance of organizations to grant access to their employees. Because of these difficulties, obtaining a representative sample through conventional sampling was difficult. Hence, a convenience sample (Atkinson and Flint 2000) was used during data collection throughout the various phases of this study. In particular, a quasi-theoretical strategy based on snowballing, word of mouth, and chain referral sampling was used to overcome data collection difficulties and to increase sample size in the qualitative and quantitative phases of this study (Berg 2004; Bernard 2000).

15.4   Phases and Instruments

Phase One: In-depth, Face-to-Face, Semi-structured Interviews

As previously mentioned, the first phase of data collection and analysis in this study entailed the use of a qualitative methodology. In particular, in-depth, face-to-face, semi-structured interviews were conducted with 32 women managers across different levels of managerial hierarchy from a wide range of industries. The interviews took place in several locations, including the offices and homes of the interviewees, and ranged in length from 45 to nearly 90 min. The interviews were guided by the research questions and were tape-recorded. At the beginning of every interview, the researcher emphasized the confidentiality of the study as well as its objectives in an attempt to create a certain level of rapport, comfort, and trust with the interviewees. The interviews were conducted mostly in English. For the few interviews conducted in Arabic or French, the interviews were translated and back-translated to confirm the validity of the findings.

While analyzing the interviews, the researcher adopted a constructivist ontological and an interpretivist epistemological approach. By adopting a constructivist ontological approach, the researcher was accepting the notion that there are multiple subjective realities as seen by the participants in the study contexts (Guba and Lincoln 1989). By adopting an interpretivist epistemological approach, the researcher was able to get closer to the participants to understand their perspective on the phenomena under study (Creswell 2007) and to give their experiences a voice (Leitch et al. 2010).

Methodologically, the in-depth interviews were initially analyzed using thematic analysis. During this phase, the transcribed interviews were systematically coded and recoded based on the theses that were most prominent in the literature, guided by the research questions. In line with the suggestions of King (1994), the analysis guide or the list of codes was frequently adjusted based on the new themes that emerged during this analysis phase. To verify the persistency of certain recurring themes and to give the occurrence of these themes a quantitative perspective, content analysis was conducted based on the frequency of occurrence of a particular theme.

Profile of the interviewees. More than half of the interviewees in this study were married (18/32) with children (16/18). Most of the women were between the ages of 30 and 50 years and had tertiary education (14/32 had an undergraduate degree and 16/32 had a postgraduate degree). Most of the women worked for large organizations (more than 100 employees), in the service sector (26/32). Typical employers include banks, insurance companies, and educational and training and development institutions. As for their positions in the managerial hierarchy, the majority of the women in this study were clustered at the lower levels of management (17/32). This is illustrated in Table 15.1.

Table 15.1 Demographic information of the interviewees

Demographic information		Percentage (n)
Marital status	Single	43.75 (14)
	Married with children	50 (16)
	Married without children	6.25 (2)
	Total	100 (32)
Educational attainment	High school or equivalent	6.25 (2)
	Undergraduate degree	43.75 (14)
	Postgraduate degree	50 (16)
	Professional qualifications	18.75 (6)
Age	Range	25–59 years old
	Mean	41.9 years old
Management level	Junior	53.125 (17)
	Middle	28.125 (9)
	Senior	18.75 (6)
Economic sectors		
Services sector	Education	25.00 (8)
	Banking and insurance	28.125 (9)
	Marketing and advertising/ arts and media	12.50 (4)
	Travel and transport/health services/hospitality	15.625 (5)
	Total	81.25 (26)
Manufacturing	Fashion/food and beverage/ printing/others	18.75 (6)
	Total	100 (32)

Results of Interviews The results of the qualitative methodology highlighted the particularity of the context settings and the resulting cultural values on the experiences of Lebanese women managers. Put another way, when asked about their parents' influence over the interviewees' educational choices, the majority of the interviewees stated that they were not given as much freedom as their male siblings when choosing their fields of study. (See Table 15.2). Notwithstanding the fact that some interviewees said they had the support of both their parents in choosing their field of studies, the majority stated that their choice of educational field was restricted by their parents and the pressure to conform to what is socially acceptable for females. One junior manager in the banking sector said:

Table 15.2 Parental influence on the choice of educational field and career

Parental influence	Percentages (n)
Received encouragement/given freedom of choice	46.875 (15)
Not given the freedom of choice unlike their male siblings	28.125 (9)
Restricted their choice to what is socially acceptable for a female	25 (8)

My father was a very strict man [.]… I wanted to study law but he did not allow me [to] because he thought that law is a man's education field and job and that a girl cannot work with men all the time [.]…so I studied business because[,] for him[,] a job at the bank or a teacher is the best for a woman.

Interestingly, following the same logic of adhering to societal expectations, the parents who emphasized gender stereotypes in guiding the interviewees' choice of education also stressed these stereotypes in guiding their choice of careers. For example, a middle manager in the education sector stated:

My parents encouraged me to study education at the university to be able to get a job as a teacher …. [T]hey always stated that if I am to work, I have to work in a job that is suitable for a woman and teaching is considered…a good job for a woman in Lebanon.

At the same time, the parents of the majority of the interviewees reportedly stressed the importance of marriage and having children. Sometimes, the parents placed the interviewees' being married and having children above the interviewees' career aspirations. Therefore, by communicating the necessity to have "socially suitable careers" and marriage, the parents, according to the interviewees, thought that they were helping their daughters both to have a career that is socially acceptable and to meet their primary role as women in terms of being wives and mothers. As one senior manager in the hospitality industry said:

My father wanted me to have a job from 8:00 to 2:00 so that I can have enough time to prepare food for my husband and children before they come from work or school.

She further explained:

My parents were very conservative, and they made me and my sisters get married early to have children [because] this is the cultural thing in this country.

Phase Two: Surveys

In an attempt to further explore the results of the interviews and to provide stronger support, the second phase of this study involved the development of a survey questionnaire derived from the interview findings and the literature review. The survey consisted of three parts. The first part asked the respondents to provide personal (age, marital status, education level) and organizational demographics (i.e., the organizations they worked in and their classification in the managerial hierarchy). The second part of the questionnaire included three categorical questions that asked the women to indicate the party that influenced their choice of education, career, and career progress (refer to Table 15.3). The third part requested that the respondents indicate their level of agreement or disagreement on six statements using a Likert five-point scale (1 = strongly disagree; 5 = strongly agree).

Procedures Surveys were originally crafted in the English language. However, an English-only questionnaire would have significantly reduced the response rate and sample population given that Arabic and French are frequently used by the Lebanese population. Therefore, the English version was translated to French and Arabic

Table 15.3 Items in the survey questionnaire

Construct	Childhood socialization
Items	1. Your choice of educational field was mainly influenced by
3 Categorical	2. Your choice of career was mainly influenced by
	3. Your career progress was mainly influenced by:
	□ Father □ Mother □ Parents
	□ Husband □ Yourself □ Other (please specify:)
6 Metric	4. My parents encouraged me to get a good education
	5. My parents encouraged me to pursue a career
	6. My parents stressed the stereotypical female–male role divisions in the choice of education
	7. My parents stressed the stereotypical female–male role divisions in the choice of careers
	8. My parents put/are putting pressure on me to get married/and have children
	9. My parents put/are putting greater weight on my personal/family life than on my career
Sources	1. Analysis of the interviews
	2. Review of literature

by professional translators, and then the translated versions were back-translated to English to ensure the validity of the translated versions (Tlaiss and Kauser 2011a). A comparison between the initial versions and the back-translated versions was carried out by three language professors at the Lebanese University and minor changes were made. The linguistic aspects of the final Arabic version were examined by a Lebanese journalist and an Arabic language scholar, and those of the French version were examined by a French language professor.

Using the three versions of the surveys in the English, French, and Arabic languages, a total of 650 questionnaires were distributed. With a response rate of 69.2%, 450 were answered and 411 of these were complete and in usable condition. The completed surveys were analyzed using the Statistical Package for the Social Sciences (SPSS) statistical software package. Descriptive statistics were used to understand the experiences of the women. In addition, factorial analysis of variance (one-way analysis of variance (ANOVA)) was conducted for mean comparisons based on some of the organizational (position in management) and personal (marital status/age/education) demographics of the respondents. Levine's equality of variance was used as a guide in selecting the appropriate test values and all the statistical inferences were made at the 95% confidence level.

Profile of the Survey's Respondents The descriptive analysis of the survey respondents revealed that the majority of the 411 respondents were between 31 and 40 years of age and approximately 52.3% of them held a bachelor's degree. More than half the total sample were married (69.3%) and almost 55% of the married respondents had more than one child.

Table 15.4 Demographic information of the survey participants

Demographic information	Percentages (n)
Marital status	
Single	30.70 (126)
Married	69.3 (285)
Total	100 (411)
Educational attainment	
High school or equivalent	7.30 (30)
Undergraduate degree	52.3 (215)
Post graduate degree	40.40 (166)
Age	
<25 years old	1.90 (8)
25–30 years old	16.30 (67)
31–40 years old	38.70 (159)
41–50 years old	30.70 (126)
>50 years old	12.40 (51)
Management level	
Junior	196 (47.7)
Middle	114 (27.7)
Senior	101 (24.6)
Economic sectors	Percentages (n)
Services sector	84.18 (346)
Finance	(105)
Education/research/training	(91)
Health care/health services	(48)
Travel and transport	(25)
Marketing and sales	(24)
Others	(53)
Manufacturing	15.82 (65)

The organizational demographics revealed that the respondents worked in a wide range of organizations including financial institutions like banks and insurance companies (27.4%); educational, training, and development institutions (22.1%); health-care and medical firms (11.7%); and other industries like hospitality and catering (6.1%). They mostly held junior managerial positions (47.7%; refer to Table 15.4)

Results of the Survey Questionnaires The descriptive analysis of the categorical items (1, 2, 3 as outlined in Table 15.3) revealed that the educational pursuits of the respondents were mostly impacted by their parents individually and/or collectively (i.e., influenced by: father, 57/411, 13.9%; mother 56/411, 13.6%; parents 144/411,

Table 15.5 Descriptive results

(Percentages)

Research items	Father	Mother	Parents	Husband	Yourself	Others
1.Your choice of educational field was mainly influenced by	13.9	13.6	35.0	0.5	34.5	2.4
2.Your choice of career was mainly influenced by	10.5	4.4	14.8	3.7	62.0	4.6
3.Your career progress was mainly influenced by	3.4	2.7	9.0	3.6	77.1	2.2

35%; total 357/411, 62.5%; 37.7% were not influenced by either parents). Interestingly, the majority of the participants in the survey reported that their choice of career (255/411, 62%) and career progress (317/411, 77.1%) was individually crafted (refer to Table 15.5).

In their responses to items 4 and 5 of the survey as outlined in Table 15.3, the majority of the respondents did not report receiving any parental encouragement to pursue an education (52.6% strongly disagreed and 24.6% disagreed to the statement stating that they received parental encouragement) or a career (40.1% strongly disagreed and 31.4% disagreed to the statement stating that they received parental encouragement). Interestingly, the ANOVA test with position in management as the independent variable revealed significant results ($p < 0.05$). Middle and senior managers compared to their junior counterparts were more likely to disagree about getting parental encouragement for pursuing an education or a career.

In response to items 6 and 7, the majority of the survey's participants stated that their parents stressed the stereotypical female–male role divisions in the choice of education (20.2% strongly agreed and 46.5% agreed) and career (14.6% strongly agreed and 45.7% agreed). The ANOVA test revealed statistical results between age and educational attainment levels as independent variables and item 7 ($p < 0.05$). The group of managers who were more than 50 years old were significantly more likely to emphasize how their parents stressed the stereotypical female–male role divisions in the choice of career (mean = 3.71 vs. 2.63, respectively). Moreover, the less educated managers (high school diploma or equivalent; mean = 3.63) were significantly more likely to highlight the focus of their parents on the stereotypical female–male role divisions in the choice of career in comparison to their more educated counterparts (e.g., undergraduate degree; mean = 3.29).

As for the last two items, 8 and 9, the majority of the respondents reported experiencing parental pressure to get married and to prioritize personal life over career life. To further explain, 62.3% of the respondents stated that their parents put/are putting pressure on them to get married/have children (37.7% agreed and 24.6% strongly agreed). The ANOVA test using marital status revealed significant results ($p < 0.05$) with the single women more likely to agree than the married with no children and with children (mean = 3.64, 3.41, 3.25, respectively).

Similarly, the respondents also reported that their parents put/are putting greater weight on their personal/family life than on their career (46.2% agreed and 8.5% strongly agreed). The ANOVA test with the position in management as the independent variable revealed that the middle and junior managers were more likely to feel this pressure when compared to their senior counterparts (mean = 3.43, 3.07, and 2.96, respectively).

15.5 Discussion of the Results (Interviews and Surveys)

The demographic profile of the women in the samples from the two phases of the study strongly supports the findings of previous studies regarding the age of Lebanese women managers. As suggested by previous studies (see for example Jamali et al. 2006), Lebanese women managers are more likely to be in their middle age.

As for their marital status, more than half of the total sample of participants in the interviews and questionnaires were married and had children. Hence, the Lebanese women managers in this study are unlike their Western counterparts in the USA or UK who are less likely to be married or have children (Granleese 2004; Greenhaus and Parasuraman 1999; Parasuraman and Greenhaus 1994). These results can be explained in terms of the collective aspect of Arab society that focuses on the importance of marriage and having children to foster its family-orientated nature. The findings also resonates with Kausar (1995) who argues that marriage in the Middle Eastern countries has always been perceived as a social necessity, where women were pressured to get married (Jandt 2012; Khattab 1996).

As for the educational attainment levels, the results of this study highlight the high educational levels of Lebanese women as more than 92% of the total sample had undergraduate and postgraduate degrees. This finding was not surprising as it lends credence to previous studies that highlight the high human capital investment of the Lebanese and Arab women.

Yet despite these high levels of education, the majority of women managers in this study cluster at lower management. Supporting previous studies in the Middle East (Tlaiss and Kauser 2010, 2011a, b), this chapter argues that the high educational attainment levels of the women, while perhaps increasing their chances of finding employment, do not foster their advancement into and within the managerial hierarchy. Unlike their counterparts in the Western world who have made impressive managerial advancement in terms of moving up in the ranks of middle and senior management (Eagly and Carli 2007; Omar and Davidson 2001), the Lebanese women managers, similar to their counterparts in other Asian and Arab countries (Al-Lamki 1999; Benson and Yukongdi 2006; Omar and Davidson 2001) continue to cluster at the junior levels (48% of total sample) and are unable to access senior and middle management.

As for the type of industries they work in, the majority of the women in this study work in services-based industries and thus are similar to their Asian (Yukongdi 2006) and other Arab (Abdallah 1996) counterparts. The women in this study cluster in the feminine industries and hold traditionally female jobs (Omar and Davidson 2001) in the financial and education sectors.

The results of this research highlight the role of childhood communication and socialization in guiding the choices and the priorities of Lebanese women managers. In terms of the role that parents have in their daughters' choices of educational fields, the findings of the interviews were supported by those of the survey. Generally speaking, the survey respondents did not report parental encouragement for their pursuit of education or career.

This finding supports previous studies (see, for example, El-Ghannam 2002) and suggests that many Lebanese families resist education for their daughters on the grounds of the cultural values that promote masculinity. Accordingly, the researcher suggests that the Lebanese women managers were not encouraged to pursue an education due to the salient cultural value that women do not need an education because they do not need to have careers outside the domestic sphere. Using El-Ghannam's (2002) argument, it could also be that the families of the women in this study did not encourage the women to pursue an education because education for females is a bad investment. In other words, if women are indeed to have a career outside the home, their education is less capable of generating a financial return when compared to males.

When the pursuit of higher education did occur, the interviewees and survey respondents both underscored the role of their parents in guiding their choice. Moreover, the interviewees and the survey respondents stressed the emphasis that their parents put on traditional gender stereotypes in selecting their choices of educational fields. The interviewees also reported some discrimination within the households between the siblings—their brothers were free to choose their educational majors while they females were steered towards traditionally feminine majors. These findings demonstrate how the collective values that focus on the family can influence women and cause them to adjust their aspirations to meet family expectations (Pringle and Mallon 2003). They also demonstrate how the Lebanese women managers allowed their families' needs to take priority over their personal preferences and guide their choices.

As for the impact of parental communication on the choice of careers, the majority of the survey respondents stated that their parents did not encourage them to pursue a career. This finding supports previous studies (El-Ghannam 2002; Omar and Davidson 2001) and follows the same theory previously stated concerning education. In other words, the women in the study were not encouraged by their parents to pursue a career because of the parents' perception that a woman's career path should lead to the home, not professional employment.

And while the majority of survey respondents stated that their choice of careers was made independently, they nonetheless stressed the emphasis that their parents put on choosing a career that is traditionally acceptable for women, thus supporting the findings of previous studies (Metcalfe 2008; Salloum 2003; Tlaiss and Kauser 2010, 2011a) regarding the emphasis that the Arab communities place on women in terms of having careers that are socially acceptable for women. While acknowledging the possibility that the Lebanese women managers may indeed be choosing occupations that allow them to more easily manage their family and work responsibilities (Greenman 2011), this study brings to light the minimal freedom of choice and the high parental pressure to embrace a feminine career.

Although the interviewees were less likely to state that their choice of career was a personal choice, they highlighted the emphasis that their parents put on choosing a career that is socially and culturally acceptable for women. The interviewees also stated that their brothers were given more freedom in choosing their education and careers. This finding is explained by the tendency of the majority of families in the Arab world to expect males rather than females to have careers, be financially independent, and be successful so that they can support their families. Moreover, by virtue of patriarchy, males in the Arab families are typically given the decision-making authority because females are often perceived as needing the males in the families to take care of them (Omar and Davidson 2001).

Interestingly, the majority of the survey respondents stated that their career progress was mostly encouraged by "themselves," with only a minority referring to external encouragement from parents. This finding was not a surprise given the lack of parental encouragement to pursue education or career that the Lebanese women managers in this study experienced. It not only emphasizes the fact that women have been pushed to enter feminine careers but also sheds light on the complexity of the careers of women in the Lebanon and the Arab world in general and the multiple factors that interfere in the process of having an education and a career. Amidst all the cultural values that restrain their attempts to develop and progress by focusing on their primary roles as caretakers, Lebanese women, and Arab women by extension, strive for education, employment, and career advancement. This strive highlights the agency of these women and their determination to pursue higher education and careers as they navigate through the traditional values of their societies and construct their futures.

Another aspect of the Arab cultural values that was expressed by the Lebanese women managers' parents was the emphasis put on marriage and children and the expectation that the Lebanese women managers put their family above their career aspirations. Not only does this finding support previous studies documenting the significance of marriage and motherhood in the Arab world (Jandt 2012; Jawad 1998; Omar and Davidson 2001) it also underscores the masculine, collective, and patriarchal values of the society. In other words, by pushing their daughters toward marriage and motherhood, the parents of the Lebanese women managers were perpetuating the masculine values by emphasizing the stereotypical gender roles of women. As for collectivism, it is emphasized not only by emphasizing the significance of marriage and having children but also by expecting women to adjust their aspirations to meet the needs of the family, in terms of prioritizing their family's needs and expectations over having a career of their own choice.

Collectively, these cultural values bolster the patriarchy of the Arab societies and the superiority of men. In addition, they diminish the significance of women's education and careers. Further, they hinder women's career advancement and progression not only by limiting women's choices but also by restricting their ability to construct and negotiate their own identity and future.

15.6   Implications and Conclusion

To the author's best knowledge, this is the first study to explore the extent to which the division of gender roles between the sexes has been communicated by the parents of Arab women as perceived, experienced, and recollected by the career women themselves. It also investigates the role this division of labor and gender roles plays in controlling their choice of educational disciplines, career choices, and encouragement to advance in their careers. Through empirical data, this study clearly portrays the socially constructed patriarchal ideology that continues to confine women's primary roles to that of being mothers and wives. This patriarchal ideology encouraged the parents of the Lebanese women in this study to grant their sons the freedom to choose their education and career, and confine their daughter's education and careers to what is socially acceptable and feminine. This confinement and attachment to the traditional, conventional gender-roles stereotypes also granted the males in the Arab families the support to advance their careers and the females the sermons on how to focus on their primary roles as mothers and wives. Therefore, despite the Lebanese women's increased educational attainment levels and participation in the workforce, there has been little change to the content of the messages and stereotypes communicated during childhood. The communication and endorsement of the traditional masculine cultural values by the Arab parents to their children, particularly the females, during childhood education and throughout adolescent years outline the futures of these children. In other words, these traditional cultural values do not only endorse the traditional gender-role stereotypes during childhood socialization but also limit women's choices of educational disciplines and types of careers, and prioritize marriage and having children over all other endeavors. Hence, the majority of the Arab women continue to join the traditionally feminine disciplines and hold jobs in feminine sectors such as the services sector. Moreover, women who attempt to complain about this hegemony and focus on their careers are usually described as wearisome and socially aberrant. These findings imply that although Lebanon's cosmopolitan nature has granted women some freedoms that their Arab counterparts are still denied, these freedoms are surpassed by gender-role stereotypes.

Therefore, if Lebanon and other countries in the Arab world are to become truly equal societies or societies that enforce gender equality, the need to "cut loose" from the rugged traditional values that hinder the modernization of these societies and the liberation of their people must be clearly communicated and firmly endorsed. By no means is this though to be misunderstood or interpreted as a call for abandoning the traditions of the Arab world. In other words, this study is neither calling for the abandonment of the Arab culture and traditions nor the family-oriented values in which the Arabs take extreme pride in. On the contrary, this chapter is calling for a greater focus on communicating the rather forgotten true Arab values that promote fairness and equality among all the members of the society as emphasized by Islam and the teachings and practices of the Prophet. It is calling for preparing women to play an active role in the development of their turbulent countries rather than confining their abilities and competencies within the walls of their domestic heavens. It is also calling for the need to capitalize on the large number of women graduate and the talents they bring to their local economies and society through encouraging and facilitating the departure of the society away from the single-lens visual image of women solely as "mothers and wives."

To effectively transform the Lebanese society and the societies of the majority of the Arab world, the change needs to start from home and with the parents. Parents must realize the importance of childhood socialization and communication and the role it plays in determining the lives of their children. This message could be transferred to the parents by various oral and written communication channels including audio and visible media that help create and motivate change and explain to the parents their role in removing barriers to gender equality. Parents need to understand that childhood socialization should focus on motivating children to realize their potential and improve their human capital, rather than on emphasizing gender stereotypes and the sharp distinction of gender roles. Furthermore, parents need to be educated to communicate freedom of choice rather than the need to adhere to gender stereotypes. Children, males and females alike, should be given the freedom of choice in education, careers, and personal lives by their parents. One way to achieve this is by changing the educational curricula that emphasize the cultural representation of these gender stereotypes. To further elaborate, school textbooks can show females as lawyers, judges, managers, doctors, university professors, and presidents as opposed to constraining their representation at the workplace as secretaries, assistants, or nurses. These messages, if properly communicated to children at young ages, can create a new generation of educated future parents empowered with the spirit of gender equality.

15.7 Limitations and Suggestions for Future Studies

This chapter drew conclusions without exploring how the parents' employment status, education, socioeconomic status, class, and religious affiliation might have impacted their communication with their children. Therefore, it will be extremely interesting to see future studies exploring these aspects.

References

Abdallah, I. A. (1996). Attitudes towards women in the Arabian Gulf Region. *Women in Management Review, 11*(1), 29–39.

Abou Chedid, K. E. (2007). Correlates of religious affiliation, religiosity and gender role attitudes among Lebanese Christian and Muslim college students. *Equal Opportunities International, 25*(3), 193–208.

AlAjmi, A. (2001). The effect of personal characteristics on job satisfaction: A study among male managers in the Kuwait oil industry. *International Journal of Commerce and Management, 13*(3/4), 91–110.

Al-Lamki, S. (1999). Paradigm shift: A perspective on Omani women in management in the Sultanate of Oman. *Advancing Women in Leadership, 5,* vol. 2, no. 2, Spring 1999. www. advancingwomen.com/awl/spring99/Al-Lamki/allamk.html. Accessed 19 Sep 2012.

Atkinson, R., & Flint, J. (2000). Accessing hidden and hard-to-reach populations: Snowball research strategies. *Social Research Update, 33,* 1–4.

Barakat, H. (1977). *Lebanon in strife.* Austin: University of Texas Press.

Barakat, H. (1993). *The Arab world: Society, culture, and state.* Berkeley: University of California Press.

Benson, J., & Yukongdi, V. (2006). Asian women managers: Participation, barriers, and future perspectives. In V. Yukongdi & J. Benson (Eds.), *Women in Asian management* (pp. 141–151). New York: Routledge, Taylor and Francis.

Berg, B. (2004). *Qualitative research methods* (5th ed.). USA: Pearson Education, Inc.

Bernard, H. (2000). *Social research methods: Qualitative and quantitative approaches.* London: Sage.

Best, D. L. (2004). Gender stereotypes. In C. R. Ember & M. Ember (Eds.), *Encyclopedia of sex and gender: Men and women in the world's cultures, vol. I: Topics and cultures A-K.* Dordrecht: Kluwer/Plenum.

Creswell, J. W. (2007). *Research design: Qualitative, quantitative, and mixed methods approaches.* London: Sage.

Eagly, A. H., & Carli, A. L. (2007). Women and the labyrinth of leadership. *Harvard Business Review, 85*(9), 62–71.

El-Ghannam, A. (2002). Analytical study of women's participation in economic activities in Arab societies. *Equal Opportunities International, 21*(1), 1–18.

Feghali, E. (1997). Arab cultural communication patterns. *International Journal of Intercultural Relations, 21*(3), 345–378.

Goby, V. P., & Erogul, M. S. (2011). Female entrepreneurship in the United Arab Emirates: Legislative encouragements and cultural constraints. *Women's Studies International Forum, 34,* 329–334.

Granleese, J. (2004). Occupational pressure in banking: Gender differences. *Women in Management Review, 19*(4), 219–225.

Greenhaus, J. H., & Parasuraman, S. (1999). Research on work, family, and gender: Current status and future directions. In G. N. Powell (Ed.), *Handbook of gender and work* (pp. 391–412). Thousand Oaks: Sage.

Greenman, E. (2011). Asian American–White differences in the effect of motherhood on career outcomes. *Work and Occupations, 38*(1), 37–67.

Guba, E. G., & Lincoln, Y. S. (1989). *Fourth generation evaluation.* Newbury Park: Sage.

Hofstede, G. (2001). *Culture's consequences: Comparing values, behaviors, institutions and organizations across nations.* Thousand Oaks: Sage.

Jamali, D., Safieddine, A., & Daouk, M. (2006). The glass ceiling: Some positive trends from the Lebanese banking sector. *Women in Management Review, 21*(8), 625–642.

Jandt, F. E. (2012). *An introduction to intercultural communication: Identities in a global community.* London: Sage.

Jawad, H. A. (1998). *The rights of women in Islam: An authentic approach.* New York: St. Martin's Press.

Kallab, E. (1983). *She cooks he reads: The image of women in Lebanese textbooks.* Beirut: Center of Feminist Studies in the Arab World.

Kausar, Z. (1995). Women in feminism and politics: New directions towards Islamization. In Omar, A. & Davidson, M. J. (2001). Women in management: A comparative cross-cultural overview. *Cross Cultural Management, 8,* 35–67.

Khattab, H. (1996). *The Muslim woman's handbook*. London: TA-HA Publishers.

King, N. (1994). The qualitative research interview. In C. Cassell & G. Symon (Eds.), *Qualitative methods in organizational research: A practical guide* (pp. 14–36). London: Sage.

Ku, M. C. (2011). When does gender matter? Gender differences in specialty choice among physicians. *Work and Occupations, 38*(2), 221–261.

Leitch, C. M., Hill, F. M., & Harrison, R. T. (2010). The philosophy and practice of interpretivist research in entrepreneurship: Quality, validation, and trust. *Organizational Research Method, 13*(1), 67–84.

Loscocco, K., & Bird, S. R. (2012). Gendered paths: Why women lag behind in small business success. *Work and Occupation, 39*(2), 182–219.

Metcalfe, B. D. (2008). Women, management and globalization in the Middle East. *Journal of Business Ethics, 83*(1), 85–100.

Neal, M., Finlay, J., & Tansey, R. (2005). My father knows the minister: A comparative study of Arab women's attitudes towards leadership authority. *Women in Management Review, 20*(7), 478–497.

Omair, K. (2010). Typology of career development for Arab women managers in the United Arab Emirates. *Career Development International, 15*(2), 121–143.

Omar, A., & Davidson, M. J. (2001). Women in management: A comparative cross-cultural overview. *Cross Cultural Management, 8*(3/4), 35–67.

Parasuraman, S., & Greenhaus, J. H. (1994). Personal portrait: The life-style of the woman manager. In E. A. Fagenson (Ed.), *Women in management: Trends, issues, and challenges in managerial diversity*. London: Sage.

Powell, G. N., & Graves, L. M. (2003). *Women and men in management* (3rd ed.). London: Sage.

Pringle, J. K., & Mallon, M. (2003). Challenges for the boundaryless career odyssey. *International Journal of Human Resource Management, 14*(5), 839–853.

Salloum, H. (2003). Women in the United Arab Emirates. *Contemporary Review, 283*(1651), 101–104.

Sharabi, H. (1998). *Neopatriarchy: A theory of distorted change in Arab society*. New York: Oxford University Press.

Sidani, Y. (2005). Women, work, and Islam in Arab societies. *Women in Management Review, 20*(7), 498–512..

Tlaiss, H., & Kauser, S. (2010). Perceived organizational barriers to women's career advancement in Lebanon. *Gender in Management: An International Journal, 25*(6), 462–496.

Tlaiss, H., & Kauser, S. (2011a). The impact of gender and family on career advancement: Evidence from Lebanese women. *Gender in Management: An International Journal, 26*(1), 8–36.

Tlaiss, H., & Kauser, S. (2011b). Career success of Arab women managers: An empirical study in Lebanon. *Education, Business and Society: Contemporary Middle Eastern Issues, 4*(1), 43–61.

Wassef, H. (1996). Constructions of gender in middle and secondary school curriculum in Egypt. Paper presented and published at the proceedings of the Arab Regional Conference, International union for the scientific study of population, Cairo, Egypt, 324–351.

Yukongdi, V. (2006). Women in management in Thailand: Advancements and prospects. In V. Yukongdi & J. Benson (Eds.), *Women in Asian management* (pp. 126–141). New York: Routledge, Taylor.

Zaharna, R. S. (1995). Understanding cultural preferences of Arab communication patterns. *Public Relations Review, 21*(3), 241–255.

Hayfaa A. Tlaiss is an associate professor with the Faculty of Business at the University of New Brunswick, Saint John, Canada. In addition to a PhD from Manchester Business School, Dr. Tlaiss has a Diploma in University Teaching (DUT), a Master's of Business Administration (MBA), passed the Financial Risk Management (FRM) and level II of the Chartered Financial Analyst (CFA) designations tests. She teaches a variety of graduate and undergraduate courses including leadership, corporate strategy, and organizational behavior. Her research interests are diverse including intersectionality of gender, class, and ethnicity, the interplay between gender and culture in entrepreneurial and employment careers, and business ethics. Dr. Tlaiss has published her research as chapters in several books and as articles in a variety of journals such as International Journal of Human Resources Management (IJHRM), International Small Business Journal (ISBJ), International Journal of Cross Cultural Management (IJCCM), Employee Relations, and Gender in Management: An International Journal. She has presented her work at national and international meetings including the Academy of Management (AOM) and the Academy of International Business (AIB). Dr. Hayfaa Tlaiss serves on the board of directors of several organizations and as a reviewer and/or on editorial boards for several journals and conferences.

Chapter 16
Different Cultures, One Love: Exploring Romantic Love in the Arab World

Michael J. Oghia

> *Life without love is like a tree without blossoms or fruit.*
> —Khalil Gibran

16.1 Introduction

During my first semester of graduate school at the American University of Beirut (AUB), a topic of discussion seemed to constantly recur among AUB students: the opposite sex. In fact, it is difficult to walk through AUB's campus without passing two lovers cuddled on a bench, or a huddled group of students talking in between classes about dating, love, and relationships outside of Jafet Library or on the steps of West Hall. Moreover, looking around Lebanon, you see couples holding hands in Byblos, lovers professing their affection and devotion through heart-shaped graffiti in Beirut, books dedicated to love and romance on display in shop windows in Hamra and along Bliss Street, and overbooked restaurants on Valentine's Day. I became increasingly curious about how young Arabs perceive dating, romantic relationships, and love, and how they compared and contrasted to my own perceptions as an Arab–American. For instance, I was interested in discovering if globalization affects the narratives to which they subscribe, and how their family influenced their romantic decisions or antagonized their personal desires. However, I found it concerning that, while love seemed to saturate Lebanese society, it was largely unaccounted for in social scientific academic literature.

A wealth of academic research does exist addressing romantic love in the Arab world within history, literary studies, and Arab, Middle Eastern, and Islamic studies (Abu-Lughod 1998b; Allen et al. 1995; Heath 1987; Murani 1972; Giffen 1971), and in regard to sexuality (Massad 2007; Khalaf and Gagnon 2006; Joseph 2005). Yet large gaps exist within the social scientific literature on the subject of romantic relationships

M. J. Oghia (✉)
American University of Beirut, Beirut, Lebanon
e-mail: Mike.oghia@gmail.com

Daily Sabah (1st floor), ATV – Sabah Binası, Barbaros Bulvarı, No: 153, Balmumcu, Beşiktaş, Istanbul 34349, Turkey3

© Springer Science+Business Media Singapore 2015
R. Raddawi (ed.), *Intercultural Communication with Arabs,*
DOI 10.1007/978-981-287-254-8_16

in the Arab world. On closer inspection, this is not surprising. Taking the larger Arab world into account, emotions and the role of emotions in the region have generally been ignored (Abdallah 2009), and love is such an understudied topic, that Armbrust (2009) declared, "As a topic in its own right, love between men and women scarcely articulates with conventional preoccupation in the study of the Middle East" (p. 256). Exacerbating this issue, love is something that has also been almost entirely excluded from crosscultural studies and the sociology of emotions, specifically framed within an Arab context. This is not just disappointing, but frustrating because love in the Arab world is, in fact, incredibly contentious. While gathering research and data for my graduate thesis, I discovered that love permeates the very core and essence of Lebanese society.

The relevance of love arises from the many cultural constrictions placed on romantic relationships and love within the Arab world. For instance, this includes emphasizing compatible religious and social backgrounds, and even geographic and political backgrounds over personal desires and feelings or individual choice. Moreover, as Abu-Lughod (1998a), Armbrust (2009), Oghia (2012), and others demonstrate, love is seemingly intertwined with such social institutions and concepts as family, power, gender dynamics, globalization, resistance, modernity, social change, religious sectarianism, intergenerational relationships, individualization, and patriarchy. In fact, love is often associated with politics in the Middle East (Armbrust 2009); "[love] has no intrinsic connection to nationalism, war, modernity, resistance to domination, discourses about "East and West," or "modernity and tradition," yet it can easily be attached to any of these" (Armbrust 2009, p. 256). For instance, Armbrust (2009) acknowledges that love is a central thematic narrative of many Arab cultural outlets such as Egyptian cinema. When love is the central theme, however, such narratives are often constructed as a tension between an individual choice of a marriage partner or an arranged marriage that is "patriarchally controlled" (Armbrust 2009). As this alludes to, the tensions between the two forms of marriage often manifest as foreign versus local discourses, such as Western ideas of romantic love being in direct contrast to more traditional practices of courtship, relationship formation, and marriage—specifically within an Islamic tradition (Oghia 2012; Armbrust 2009; Abu-Lughod 1998a).

Bearing in mind love's connection to almost every aspect of Arab culture, in this chapter, I explore this contention in detail, discuss how Arab conceptualizations of love adhere to and deviate from dominate Western romantic discourses, and illustrate contemporary perceptions of love. Moreover, this chapter aims not to address crosscultural romantic relationships with Arabs, but the cultural characteristics and intercultural tensions related to romance and love in the Arab world, specifically due to competing discourses, narratives, and social norms and expectations.

16.2   The Relationship Between Culture and Love

Romantic love is a concept that is foreign to few cultures (Jankowiak and Fischer 1992; Buss 1989). When taking a social constructionist perspective of romantic love, most scholars uphold it as a cultural universal (Berscheid 2010; Jankowiak

1995; Buss et al. 1990); however, the definition of love is culturally determined (Beall and Sternberg 1995). There are key components of the Arab romantic narrative that differ from other cultural discourses. These include the contentious nature of love, the cultural context of defining love, and the role of sexuality, marriage, the family, and individual choice.

Love is also a difficult concept to operationalize. Beall and Sternberg (1995) even argued, "It is difficult, if not impossible, to answer [this] question…because any answer must reflect its time period and place, and in particular, the functions that romantic love serves there" (p. 417). When conducting crosscultural research specifically, instead of one restrictive, all-inclusive definition of love (Jankowiak and Fischer 1992), it is advantageous to take an inductive approach and allow cultural narratives to frame romantic conceptualizations as "there is…no way of exploring love except through the ways in which it is talked and written about" (Jackson 1993, p. 207). Additionally, and particularly within an intercultural context in the Arab world, one must take into account the intersection between local and foreign discourses as an increasing volume of new, globalized, external discourses and narratives saturates the region. These provide alternatives to the socially prescribed and sanctioned avenues of romantic love and relationships that can potentially challenge the preexisting romantic discourses (Padilla et al. 2007; Giddens 1992), encourage increased individualization, and undermine traditional power structures (Beck and Beck-Gernsheim 1995; Giddens 1991). For instance, the family is one of the most powerful influences on courtship, romantic relationships, and ultimately, marriage among Arab individuals (Barakat 1993), yet love is becoming increasingly important to Arab youth (Barakat 1993), and marriages based on romantic love are increasing (El-Haddad 2003).

Thus, it is problematic to actively juxtapose culture as it often influences subjective perceptions of love, dictates which individuals constitute acceptable romantic partners, and sanctions what is acceptable and unacceptable romantic behavior (Coates 1999; Beall and Sternberg 1995). How is then the Arab cultural narrative of love portrayed? For one, Arab society is often contrasted between the concepts of collectivism and individualism. While some scholars consider this polarized dichotomy problematic (Earley and Gibson 1998), certain features do reflect Arab culture in general, particularly related to the importance placed on marriage and the family within cultures labeled as collective (Dwairy 2002). For instance, love is often more important for marriage in societies where individualism is the dominant cultural value (Dion and Dion 1993). A significant difference also exists between cultures that emphasize individualism versus ones that emphasize collectivity through the importance individuals in each place on romantic love. Whereas romantic love is highly emphasized in cultures referred to as individualistic where personal choice and loose kinship networks are normative, strong kinship networks and extended family ties exist in cultures often referred to as collectivist; thus, romantic relationships are often viewed as negative, and are actively discouraged in cultures that value strong familial networks because they may disrupt the tradition of family-approved marriage choices, or kinship ties (Abu-Lughod 2009; Al-Thakeb 1985; Gupta 1976).

16.3   Romantic Love and Arab culture

According to Armbrust (2009), a popular—albeit, incorrect—assumption is that romantic love was introduced to Arab society by European colonialism, and, thus, became desired and connected to marriage. While some scholars emphasize that love is a predominately modern concept within Western societies (Giddens 1992; Luhmann 1986), love in fact has an extensive history in the Arab world (Armbrust 2009; Inhorn 2007; Sharma 2006).

Identifying the pertinence of romantic love to the contemporary Arab world can be explained by providing a contextualization to the region's history. It is evident how love is rich in Arab literature, language, music, and history. Additionally, love follows "culturally prescribed patterns" (Jackson 1993, p. 213), which is relevant because traditional cultural artifacts supply individuals with a repertoire of scripts and narrative forms (Barthes 1978). These forms often become familiarized in childhood, and act as a reference point for defining and understanding love (Shumway 2003; Jackson 1993; Barthes 1978). For instance, the concept of love is active and deeply rooted in Arab literature. It often invokes strong emotional forces and intense themes of passion, romance, and sexuality. Specifically, romantic poetry (*ghazal*) often becomes a cathartic outlet for romantic expression in the Arab world (Abu-Lughod 1985, 1999); this occurs even when deep and personal emotions are not sanctioned by the overarching Arab social environment (Abu-Lughod 1999).

However, written expressions of love and romance are consistent themes within Arab literature and history. Some of the first documented and well-known stories of love, romance, passion, desire, and sexuality are love stories such as *Majnun Layla*, *'Antar wa 'Abla*, *The Thousand and One Nights*, and *Hadith Bayāḍ wa Riyāḍ*. These stories are instrumental in creating vivid Arab illustrations of romance and love, as they not only historicize love within the region, but they also challenge the notion that love is a foreign concept in the Arab world. Furthermore, these romantic themes are also apparent in mainstream literature written by Arab authors, such as in the writings of the influential twentieth-century artist and mystic poet Khalil Gibran (1923, 1997) as well as being infused into Arab music, which acts as a salient and cathartic avenue for emotional and romantic expression (Racy 2003).

As the aforementioned literature illustrates, contextualizing how romantic love manifests in various cultural outlets establishes a historical and cultural foundation that roots romantic love within Arab societies, and illustrates its active role in the Arab social imagination. Outside of Arab cultural artifacts though, crosscultural scholarship regarding romantic love and dating in the region is limited. A significant crosscultural study that actively juxtaposed Arab perceptions of love with other cultural conceptualizations was that of Buss et al. (1990). The authors found that almost all men and women in 37 societies from around the world ranked love as being an important and desirable quality for a mate, and the sample included 43 Palestinian Arabs. Although it was a small sample, it is relevant because the males in the sample ranked love the most important quality of a mate, and the females ranked love as the second most important—consistent with their other global findings.

Later, Khallad (2005) replicated Buss et al.'s (1990) study, and examined mate preferences for long-term relationships using an expanded Arab sample of 288 Jordanian university students. Related to mate selection, he found that the male students showed greater interest in potential mates' good looks and youth whereas female students displayed greater preference for mates exhibiting economic ability and commitment. Nevertheless, he also found that students "value the same attributes that have been universally considered important to have in a mate, namely love, kindness, and a pleasing disposition" (p. 155).

Overall, studies point to an evolving relationship between love and marriage, and a recurring theme of much of this literature is the reflection of external romantic narratives by Arab youth (Kaya 2009; Volk 2001; Al-Thakeb 1985). For instance, Volk's (2001) observation of Lebanese adolescent dating habits found that, "Dating in the American sense does not exist, as young people rarely go out with 'a date,' but are more likely to spend an evening with a group of friends" (p. 232). The author acknowledged that because dating was often accompanied by the fear of being seen and talked about, "most 'Lebanese dating' happens on the phone, or in the company of friends" (p. 232).

Together, the scholarship available points to an increasing value being placed on love within certain Arab societies—even as established cultural customs and practices remain normative. Love often works as a binding force that assists individuals to both form and maintain their romantic relationships, and challenge the dominant discourses related to relationships and marriage. These studies also allude to the contentiousness that saturates Arab love and romance.

16.4   The Contentious Nature of Arab Love

Love—and more generally, dating—are especially contentious topics in the Arab world because traditionally, courtship and marriage have "been a family and community or social affair instead of a personal, individual one" (Barakat 1993, p. 107). Romantic relationships in Arab society are inextricably connected to marriage, which is relegated to the family and kinship networks. This includes a large proportion of arranged marriages or "family-facilitated" romantic matches that are common in Arab society (Barakat 1993; Al-Haj 1988; Al-Thakeb 1985), and familial endorsement of romantic partners (Barakat 1993). However, the contentious nature of love in the Arab world permeates not just the family institution, but also the very notion of power itself.

In the late 1950s, Goode (1959) identified common events that occur among Arab families. He noted the importance of familial investment in mate selection, as kinship ties are invariably linked to perpetuating social status and stratification as well as creating a link with another kinship line. For Arab families, kinship networks are invaluable because it is generally through kinship that individuals and families may access social capital (Barber 2001). Social capital includes all of the potential or actual resources available that are linked by a network shared by individuals (Bourdieu 1986), and is paramount to understanding the way Arab families operate. Romantic relationships often act as ties to other kinship networks, reinforce family ties and interests, and preserve "private property through inheritance, socialization, and the achievement of other goals that transcend the happiness of the individual to guarantee communal interests" (Barakat 1993, p. 107).

Due to the familial interests embedded within romantic relationships and the emphasis on collective family goals versus individual ones (Farhood 2009; Dwairy 2002), the success or failure of an individual member resonates throughout the family as a whole (Barakat 1993). The importance of being successful and the pressure of failure are inextricably linked to the discourse of patriarchy that governs the socialization of Arab children and the preservation of social capital. Within this discourse, agency and individual choice are limited, dominated, and deemphasized for the benefit of the family (Olmsted 2005; Abu-Lughod 1999; Joseph 1993), and love is constructed within the family as inherently connected to patriarchy (Armbrust 2009).

Strict social norms and rules are situated within the family to further regulate behavior, and deviation from these rules may lead to dire consequences for both the individual as well as the family. Thus, romantic love might directly challenge the dominant discourse of patriarchy by facilitating an individual's rebellion against community norms and values. This occurs through choosing a romantic partner that could potentially undermine kinship solidarity, disrupt social capital, and erode social network connections (Abu-Lughod 2009; Joseph 1996).

One instrument of power that is infused within the discourse of patriarchy is the overutilized and somewhat problematic dichotomy of honor and shame (Abu-Lughod 1999, 1989; Wikan 1984; Dodd 1973). This system is directly linked to control through family socialization, and, related to love, individuals are socialized into knowing what does and does not constitute an acceptable romantic partner. Moreover, Watts (1991) reinforced the importance of and connection between the family and power. His definition of power encompasses the ability of an individual to achieve his/her desired goals, "...[and] if this involves conflict with the interests of others, power will entail the ability to impose one's will. The amount of power one possesses is thus relative to the status one has in the social group with respect to others" (p. 145). Hofstede (1997, 2001) later further validated Watts' (1991) assertion with the power distance dimension of culture identified by Hofstede. In the case of the Arab world, it ranked 7 out of 53 countries and societies in the power distance dimension, meaning that less powerful members of society (such as children) accept that power is distributed unequally, and obedience to more powerful figures within institutions (such as parents and teachers) is expected absolutely (Hofstede 1997, 2001).

When considering Hofstede's framework as well as the amount of power that is socially prescribed to the patriarch (and males in general) in Arab society, it is clear how they have the ability to control the individual interests of family members. This seems especially pertinent if an individual's actions—such as being in love with someone who does not merit familial or social approval—are perceived to endanger the family's ability to access social capital, or do not reinforce the solidarity that is necessary for social, economic, and political survival (Joseph 1993, 1999). Moreover, this is particularly applicable to Lebanon, which is plagued with a weak, corrupt, and inefficient state (Khalaf 2002; Joseph 1993, 1994). Thus, the responsibilities and provisions of the weak Lebanese state often shift to families, which supply individuals not only with (social) capital and resources, but also safety, security, and personal identity (Joseph 1993, 2004; Khalaf 1971, 2002).

In addition to having power over whom one can and cannot love, Al-Thakeb (1985) noted, "Love and dating in Western styles are considered likely to lead to premarital sexual relationships, [which could damage the family's honor and reputation]...there is a large segment that believes that love is to come only after marriage" (p. 578). This further underscores the importance of upholding family honor because if shame is brought to an individual, it is not just hurting the future of the individual, but endangering the family's access to social capital, the amount of social capital that is available, or the social perception of the entire family (Abu-Lughod 2009; Joseph 1994; Dodd 1973).

Logically then, Sabbah (2010) suggested romantic relationships compose a powerful weakening agent that challenges and destabilizes patriarchy, particularly if an Arab woman is unable to find a husband—further meriting the importance of controlling romantic relationships. Additionally, the Arab family is facing potentially dramatic changes, as a fluid entity that continues to adapt to social changes, modernity, and demographic transformations (Rashad et al. 2005). Two of the most relevant changes facing the Arab family include the declining influence of the extended family (Farhood 2009; Volk 2001; Faour 1998; Al-Thakeb 1985) and the generational gaps between grandparents, parents, and children (Nasser 2010; Schvaneveldt et al. 2005; Al-Tawila et al. 2002; Davis and Davis 1995).

Reflecting on these changes, Barakat (1993) stated, "Increasingly, marriage is seen as an individual choice that does not depend on parental approval. Love, which could serve as a reason for opposing a marriage in traditional communities, is increasingly becoming a prerequisite in the minds of young Arabs" (p. 107). Thus, clashes often occur between the discourses that govern love, romance, sexuality, social expectations, and personal choice. This has a direct influence on individuals who are increasingly caught between social norms and obligations that require respecting and following certain familial expectations and cultural traditions, and their own ideas and personal desires (El-Osta 2010; Volk 2001).

In sum, Arab families regulate and govern behavior to ensure that social capital held within kinship networks is protected, and do so by managing relationship formation and conditioning mate selection. However, relationships based on romantic love have the ability to challenge the dominating discourses linked to patriarchy, honor, and shame. Moreover, unlike the typical frame of Western contexts, traditionally, romantic relationships did not relate to happiness in the Arab world; they are related to pragmatism: uniting families to secure and safeguard social capital and resources.

16.5 Love in the Contemporary Arab World: An Exploratory Study of American University of Beirut Students

As demonstrated earlier, there is much insight into the Arab conceptualization of love. While much is known about North American university students and their relationship habits (Goodwin 2005), one key aspect of this conceptualization that has generally been overlooked is the basic question of what *is* love, and how is it defined and perceived by a sample of the Arab population?

Methodology and Instruments

To explore this in detail, a mixed-methods qualitative/quantitative study was designed. The primary method employed was a nonprobability exploratory qualitative component. It consisted of 22 in-depth, semistructured, personal interviews with students at the AUB completed in spring 2011. The open-ended interview instrument used included 16 primary questions in total with subquestions available for probing. It also included supplemental information collected from 193 students who completed questionnaires related to their relationship and dating habits and perceptions of love. This information was used to corroborate the qualitative findings across the larger AUB student population. However, this chapter only addresses results gleaned from the qualitative findings.

Participants

The participants include undergraduate and graduate students from AUB who were mainly from Lebanon, Syria, and the United Arab Emirates (UAE), and whose ages ranged from 18 to 26. They hailed from various religious and sectarian backgrounds. While a sample of the AUB student population was largely unique to Lebanon and had its limitations, it was advantageous for multiple reasons including the students' fluency in English, the availability of literature documenting their changing values vis-à-vis the post-Civil War society (Farhood 2009; Faour 1998), and their easy access to both globalized discourses and cultural capital. Additionally, the sample recruitment method employed was a convenient, purposeful sample for the quantitative and qualitative participants. Both types of the participants were recruited voluntarily by three primary ways: classroom visits, direct solicitation, and flyers.

Procedure and Data Analysis

Data collection lasted 3 weeks, beginning 28 February 2011, and concluding 18 March 2011. After obtaining approval from the AUB Institutional Review Board

(IRB), I pretested the instrument, and began conducting interviews. The interviews lasted 90 min, on average. They were conducted both on campus and off campus in Beirut at various cafés around AUB in a private setting. All of the qualitative data gathered were kept private and confidential, and all interviews were conducted in English. Before the interview began, I ensured that the interviewees were comfortable, introduced myself to them, informed them of why I was doing this research, and instructed them to read over the informed consent form. After consent was received both verbally and in writing per IRB protocol, I began asking the interview questions, and took extensive notes detailing the interviewee's responses.

The analysis of the qualitative data included the following steps as outlined in Marshall and Rossman (1999): I transcribed field notes into organized, electronic files; I observed and identified salient themes and patterns drawing from the theoretical framework and the literature review; I coded data consistent with these themes that assisted in generating understanding about their responses and answers to the research questions; I then tested consistent themes and patterns by scrutinizing their frequency and importance, and evaluated these themes drawing on the theoretical framework and literature reviewed. After the qualitative data were analyzed, the results of both the questionnaire and the interviews were drafted and compared. In the reporting of the results the interviewees were referred to using pseudonyms.

Results and Discussion

When asked how they define love, the interviewees revealed definitions that were inextricably linked to their experiences with romantic relationships, and saturated with subjective perceptions, attitudes, and interpretations. These perceptions included conceptualizing love through attachment and inclusion, accepting or rejecting popular culture narratives, intense attraction and passion, or through sacrifice.

One of the most common thematic narratives that surfaced was defining love based on attachment, inclusion in their lives, and companionship. Descriptions such as not being able to live without someone; wanting to spend quality time together and be around each other often; being supportive; being comfortable with each other; sharing an emotional bond; working together to overcome obstacles and hard times; and being connected were consistently mentioned. One interviewee, Sarah, a 25-year old senior, described her definition of love, "Whenever I am with this person, I feel like I'm at home…[you] become part of each other." For May, a 19 year-old sophomore,—love is when "you're with your best friend that you're passionate about," while Tanya, a 19-year-old junior, expressed that love is "being with someone who makes everything better. Anything we do together is fun, and you give everything the other person needs."

Another salient theme emerged defining romantic love by comparing it to popular culture narratives communicated through the mass media. These are often evoked linguistic archetypes such as "soul mate," "Prince Charming," "the one," and "happily ever after." For instance, Shireen, a 20-year-old junior, stated, "I don't know what love is. I've never been in love, at least the Princess/Prince Charming movie [kind of] love." Others expressed sentiments related to mass media or popular culture; however, these narratives were often viewed paradoxically as both ideal and unrealistic. Joanne, a 19-year- old sophomore, imagines "the overdramatized, the *Layla and Majnun* kind of love [and] romanticized images of romantic love. Romantic love does contain some of this fantasy, [but] some of these feelings and outcomes are usually a lie, like in Hollywood movies."

The third major theme pertained to attraction and passion. The interviewees often expressed the sentiment that attraction was both a requirement and a necessity for love, and it was common for them to relate love to strong emotional feelings. For instance, Mazen, a 19-year-old sophomore, stated that love occurs when "a person is intensely attracted to another person." Rana, 21-year-old senior, expressed a related conception, but with a more optimistic tone:

> There's no definition for romantic love. It's very intangible; not concrete. [It's] feelings, emotions, gut feelings, instances—an aura. Something that at the end of the day, after certain thoughts, words, and gestures, my heart squeezes for this one person. It's a connection; you know it when you feel it.

The fourth major theme that arose from the interviews was related to sacrifice. For some individuals—almost all of them females—making sacrifices defines love, even if that means at the expense of their own wants, needs, and goals or taking risks in order to be together with someone. "I know it's wrong," explains Yara, a 19-year-old junior. "But it's putting him before myself. [It's] sacrificing for him." Overall, by incorporating different aspects of these themes into their definition, many of the interviewees recognized the subjective and personal nature of romantic love. For instance, Joanne believed love is defined by the "sacrifice of one's own wellbeing for the other person and a real understanding of each other" in addition to the overdramatization/overromanticization of love mentioned previously. For May and Munira, a 19-year-old sophomore, love is a much more fluid concept. Munira stated that love can "be whatever you want it to be." "It's not roses, or candles, or gifts," explains May, "romance can be found in a lot of things, like little gestures."

Still, many others were vocal about their reservations with defining love. Raja, a 22-year-old graduate student, underscored how "each person has a definition." Najwa, a 21-year-old senior, echoed this, insisting, "Your relationship with a person determines your definition of love." Michel, a 19-year-old junior, expressed a similar feeling, yet also emphasized the ephemeral nature of love:

> I don't understand it one bit. I can't define it because I don't know. Love is not just defined. It's defined differently by everyone, and through people's experience. It's subjective. I don't believe in love that lasts forever. People change, but love doesn't always change too.

In addition to various definitions and perceptions of romantic love, the interviewees made meaning of love—that is, signifying how they perceive love exists within their lives vis-à-vis society—by associating it with marriage, economics, social class, luxury, and Western culture, yet also recognized the inherent contradictions society communicates.

One of the most pervasive ways the participants made meaning of love was by relating it to marriage. Most of the interviewees either directly or indirectly alluded to marriage as being the final outcome of a romantic relationship. In fact, all of the 22 interviewees mentioned marriage or connected love with marriage even without being prompted to do so. Illustrating the link between love and marriage, Joanne emphasized how love is "a prerequisite for marriage. You need love for marriage. Men and women stress love. We're taught to fantasize about it. You see it in the weddings, the engagements. Effort is put to show they're in love. Does marriage equal love? Here it does." Yet some were critical of this link, indicating both weddings and marriage display love through a lavish, though empty, façade. According to Najwa, "Getting married doesn't mean you're in love, especially in Lebanon." Munira reinforced this as well. "Love is advertised in society, but society doesn't want you to marry for love; it's supposed to come later."

As the interviewees revealed, a closely related aspect of love and relationships to marriage is the connection between marriage, economics, and the utilization of romantic relationships for the social exchange of resources. As Sarah, a 25-year-old senior, noted, for instance, "Relationships here are like a business. They ask, "How are we going to benefit from this?" "How do we match [with sect, land, etc.]?" "What can I get out of this?"" However, Mohammad, a 19-year-old sophomore, pointed out that as individuals have become more financially secure, love has been able to flourish:

> People are marrying more for love now, not just [for] family status. In the past, people weren't financially secure or stable, so that is something they wanted to give to their children. But now, more people are financially stable, so love is becoming more important. It's a system. The grandparents didn't have money, so they want their kids to have what they didn't have. They worked hard to give them money. So, the kids had money, but not happiness. Thus, they want their kids to be happy and loved.

Also tied to economics was the perception that love is often a luxury available to few, and is inherently connected to social stratification and class. For instance, according to Michel, "Arab culture is based on hardship. Love is a luxury. And this luxury in the past wasn't affordable."

Some interviewees made meaning of love by identifying how foreign, Western cultural constructions of love are imported into and commercialized within Lebanon, and are becoming typical and normative. Some highlighted how the increase in globalization is creating an environment that is emphasizing more individualism. However, there are also many contradictions that are constrained by society. For example, although lasting romantic relationships are considered desirable and are encouraged, Zayna, a 20-year-old senior, feels, "Love is choked, suffocated, distorted by social pressures and rules. There's always going to be something wrong: different class, different sect. People—parents, peers, family—always have a say in your romantic life." Related to Zayna's sentiments, Noura, also a 20-year-old senior, not only discussed contradictions that exist, but also described how society sends particularly confusing and hypocritical messages about what is appropriate and sanctioned regarding love:

There are so many constraints on love; we've even transformed love into something sectarian. You only talk about love after you get married. If you don't get married, you don't talk about it. Because they feed you the idea that love and marriage are related, you think you have to find love to get married. This is not just in Arab societies. Even in Disney, Cinderella marries the Prince.

Similarly, Sarah described how these contradictions are particularly frustrating as a woman:

We adopt Western and foreign standards but in our Lebanese way, and we're sent contradictory messages. We are sent mixed signals from our parents who raise us as girls and boys with strict gender roles. For instance, it's ok for men to have sex, but women can't. They tell women to have fun, socialize. But also ask, "when are you going to find a husband?"

Overall, the meaning of love is often connected to such concepts as marriage, economics, social class, luxury, and Western culture, but is saturated with contradictions that originate from social institutions and varying culture constructions. This raises the question, what further steps can be taken to rectify these contradictions?

16.6   Implications and Conclusion

Embedded within the interviewees' responses was a strong sense of subjectivity related to their definitions of romantic love, and a reflection of the personal nature of these definitions. They also indicated that objectifying the concepts of both romance and love was problematic. Furthermore, the interviewees often communicated definitions that incorporated elements of attachment, companionship, attraction, and/or sacrifice. Although it was difficult for some to define romantic love, the majority professed a familiarity with love; they have spent substantial time thinking about what love means, and critically assessing their perspective of and their opinions regarding love. The interviewees also frequently connected love to Western cultural conceptions, such as individualism, that they indicated clash with or challenge other cultural conceptions such as honor, shame, familial collectivity, and traditionalism. It was also indicated that love is a luxury, linked to social class, and inherently connected to marriage, but also saturated with contradictions by society and the family. The participants affirmed that love is important, and they ascribed a high value to love. Furthermore, many indicated it is essential to human existence. The majority also considers being in love with someone a requirement for a successful relationship, and rank being in love as an important factor in choosing a romantic partner. Paradoxically, they see romantic love as something hidden in romantic relationships, or as contradictorily emphasized and portrayed but not expected or practiced in reality.

Although the findings presented here are but a snapshot of the larger results, they illustrate how the research participants were not passive actors vis-à-vis the social forces that affect them; they recognized the forces at hand, acknowledged them, and these forces are apparent throughout their narratives. Moreover, the interviewees reflected globalized discourses, often stating that they incorporate local Lebanese attitudes or behaviors with more "Western" attitudes or behaviors communicated through outlets such as the mass media. Crossculturally speaking, this may hint at converging romantic conceptions, and it will be very interesting to observe how young Lebanese individuals will increasingly want to incorporate romantic love into their lives while also reflecting elements of Lebanese culture and society. There is not enough information available to know if there has been a fundamental shift of the focus of romantic relationships from pragmatism to individual happiness, but there are clues available signifying that it is developing—at least at AUB.

This research constituted an exploratory study; thus, further research is needed such as with representative samples of Arab youth. Nevertheless, the perceptions of what is desired and acceptable in relation to romantic relationship formation and love seem to be changing, at least among this small sample of Arab youth. Quite simply, they desire romantic love. Understanding more about Arab love is pertinent to a number of entities, such as researchers, demographers, economists, governments, and counselors, especially because love is not merely a "romantic" topic; it is an active proxy battleground for the forces of modernity, individualization, and globalization. Thus, more research is needed to understand how demographic shifts and exposure to transnational media, rapid modernization, and globalization will affect the future of the basic building block of the Arab world—the family—and the individual atoms that they consist of—romantic relationships and married couples. Although one of the goals of this research was to partially fill some of the gaps within the social scientific literature concerning romantic love in the Arab world, there is still an abundance of potential research opportunities related to this topic. However, one of the most explicit ways that could expand information available on this topic is simply better inclusion in crosscultural studies.

Regardless, in the future, when scholars are considering the factors that contribute to the happiness of Arab youth or what contributes to a successful romantic relationship in the Arab world, perhaps they should focus more on love, for it seems love is pointing to the answer.

References

Abdallah, S. L. (2009). Fragile intimacies: Marriage and love in the Palestinian camps of Jordan (1948–2001). *Journal of Palestine Studies, 38*(4), 47–62.

Abu-Lughod, L. (1985). Honor and the sentiments of loss in a Bedouin society. *American Ethnologist, 12*(2), 245–261.

Abu-Lughod, L. (1989). Zones of theory in the anthropology of the Arab world. *Annual Review of Anthropology, 18,* 267–306.

Abu-Lughod, L. (1998a). The marriage of feminism and Islamism in Egypt: Selective repudiation as a dynamic of postcolonial cultural politics. In L. Abu-Lughod (Ed.), *Remaking women: Feminism and modernity in the Middle East* (pp. 243–269). Princeton: Princeton University Press.

Abu-Lughod, L. (Ed.). (1998b). *Remaking women: Feminism and modernity in the Middle East.* Princeton: Princeton University Press.

Abu-Lughod, L. (1999). *Veiled sentiments: Honor and poetry in a Bedouin society* (2nd ed.). Berkeley: University of California Press.

Abu-Lughod, L. (2009). Shifting politics in Bedouin love poetry. In M. Damon & I. Livingston (Eds.), *Poetry and cultural studies: A reader* (pp. 116–132). Urbana–Champaign: University of Illinois Press.

Al-Haj, M. (1988). The changing Arab kinship structure: The effect of modernization in an urban community. *Economic Development and Cultural Change, 36*(2), 237–258.

Al-Tawila, S., Ibrahim B., & Wassef, H. (2002). Social change and parent—Adolescent dynamics in Egypt. In N. S. Hopkins (Ed.), *The new Arab family, Cairo papers in social science series, 24*(1/2) (pp. 214–246). Cairo: The American University of Cairo Press.

Al-Thakeb, F. (1985). The Arab family and modernity: Evidence from Kuwait. *Current Anthropology, 26*(5), 575–580.

Allen, R., Kilpatrick, H., & de Moor, E. (Eds.). (1995). *Love and sexuality in modern Arabic literature*. London: Saqi.

Armbrust, W. (2009). Love live patriarchy: Love in the time of 'Abd al–Wahhab. *History Compass, 7*(1), 251–281.

Barakat, H. (1993). *The Arab world: Society, culture, and state*. Berkeley: University of California Press.

Barber, B. K. (2001). Political violence, social integration, and youth functioning: Palestinian youth from the Intifada. *Journal of Community Psychology, 29*(3), 259–280.

Barthes, R. (1978). *A lover's discourse: Fragments*. New York: Hill and Wang.

Beall, A. E., & Sternberg, R. J. (1995). The social construction of love. *Journal of Social and Personal Relationships, 12*(3), 417–438.

Beck, U., & Beck-Gernsheim, E. (1995). *The normal chaos of love*. Cambridge: Polity.

Berscheid, E. (2010). Love in the fourth dimension. *Annual Review of Psychology, 61*, 1–25.

Bourdieu, P. (1986). The forms of capital. In J. G. Richardson (Ed.), *The handbook of theory and research for the sociology of education* (pp. 241–258). New York: Greenwood.

Buss, D. M. (1989). Sex differences in human mate preferences: Evolutionary hypotheses tested in 37 cultures. *Behavioral and Brain Sciences, 12*, 1–49.

Buss, D. M., et al. (1990). International preferences in selecting mates: A study of 37 cultures. *Journal of Cross-Cultural Psychology, 21*, 5–47.

Coates, D. L. (1999). The cultured and culturing aspects of romantic experience in adolescence. In W. Furman, B. B. Brown, & C. Feiring (Eds.), *The development of romantic relationships in adolescence* (pp. 330–363). New York: Cambridge University Press.

Davis, S. S., & Davis, D. A. (1995). Love conquers all? Changing images of gender and relationships in Morocco. In E. W. Fernea (Ed.), *Children in the Muslim Middle East* (pp. 93–108). Austin: University of Texas Press.

Dion, K. K., & Dion, K. L. (1993). Individualistic and collectivistic perspectives on gender and the cultural context of love and intimacy. *Journal of Social Issues, 49*, 53–69.

Dodd, P. C. (1973). Family honor and the forces of change in Arab society. *International Journal of Middle East Studies, 4*(1), 40–54.

Dwairy, M. (2002). Foundations of psychosocial dynamic personality theory of collective people. *Clinical Psychology Review, 22*(3), 343–360.

Earley, P. C., & Gibson, C. B. (1998). Taking stock in our progress on individualism-collectivism: 100 years of solidarity and community. *Journal of Management, 24*(3), 265–304.

El-Haddad, Y. (2003). Major trends affecting families in the Gulf Countries. United Nations Programme on the Family Division of Social Policy and Development, United Nations Department of Economic and Social Affairs (UNDESA). http://www.un.org/esa/socdev/family/Publications/mtelhaddad.pdf. Accessed 15 May 2011.

El-Osta, S. H. (2010). *Sexual graffiti and changing sexual morality: Bathrooms as uncensored settings*. (Unpublished master's thesis). American University of Beirut: Beirut, Lebanon.

Faour, M. (1998). *The silent revolution in Lebanon: Changing values of the youth*. Beirut: American University of Beirut.

Farhood, D. N. (2009). *Family, culture, and decisions: A look into the experiences of university students in Lebanon*. (Unpublished master's thesis). American University of Beirut: Beirut, Lebanon.

Gibran, K. (1923). *The prophet*. New York: Alfred A. Knopf.

Gibran, K. (1997). *The beloved: Reflections on the path of the heart* (Trans: J. Walbridge). New York: Penguin Group.

Giddens, A. (1991). *Modernity and self-identity: Self and society in the late modern age*. Cambridge: Polity.

Giddens, A. (1992). *The transformation of intimacy: Sexuality, love, and eroticism in modern societies*. Cambridge: Polity.

Giffen, L. A. (1971). *Theory of profane love among the Arabs: The development of the genre*. New York: New York University Press.

Goode, W. J. (1959). The theoretical importance of love. *American Sociological Review, 24*(1), 38–47.

Goodwin, R. (2005). Why I study relationships and culture. *The Psychologist, 18*(10), 614–615.

Gupta, G. R. (1976). Love, arranged marriage, and the Indian social structure. *Journal of Comparative Family Studies, 7*(1), 75–85.

Heath, P. (1987). Romance as genre in "*The Thousand and One Nights*," Part I. *Journal of Arabic Literature, 18*, 1–21.

Hofstede, G. (1997). *Cultures and organizations: Software of the mind* (Rev. ed.). New York: McGraw-Hill.

Hofstede, G. (2001). *Culture's consequences: Comparing values, behaviors, institutions, and organizations across nations* (2nd ed.). Thousand Oaks: Sage.

Inhorn, M. C. (2007). Loving your infertile Muslim spouse: Notes on the globalization of IVF and its romantic commitments in Sunni Egypt and Shi'a Lebanon. In M. Padilla, J. S. Hirsch, M. Muñoz-Laboy, R. E. Sember, & R. G. Parker (Eds.), *Love and globalization: Transformations of intimacy in the contemporary world* (pp. 139–160). Nashville: Vanderbilt University Press.

Jackson, S. (1993). Even sociologists fall in love: An exploration in the sociology of emotions. *Sociology, 27*, 201–220.

Jankowiak, W. (1995). *Romantic passion: A universal experience?* New York: Columbia University Press.

Jankowiak, W. R., & Fischer, E. F. (1992). A cross-cultural perspective on romantic love. *Ethnology, 31*(2), 149–155.

Joseph, S. (1993). Connectivity and patriarchy among urban working-class Arab families in Lebanon. *Ethos, 21*(4), 452–484.

Joseph, S. (1994). Brother/sister relationships: Connectivity, love, and power in the reproduction of patriarchy in Lebanon. *American Ethnologist, 21*(1), 50–73.

Joseph, S. (1996). Patriarchy and development in the Arab World. *Gender and Development, 4*(2), 14–19.

Joseph, S. (Ed.). (1999). *Intimate selving in Arab families: Gender, self, and identity*. Syracuse: Syracuse University Press.

Joseph, S. (2004). Conceiving family relationships in post-war Lebanon. *Journal of Comparative Family Studies, 35*(2), 271–293.

Joseph, S. (2005). Learning desire: Relational pedagogies and the desiring female subject in Lebanon. *Journal of Middle East Women's Studies, 1*(1), 79–109.

Kaya, L. P. (2009). Dating in a sexually segregated society: Embodied practices of online romance in Irbid, Jordan. *Anthropological Quarterly, 82*(1), 251–278.

Khalaf, S. (1971). Family association in Lebanon. *Journal of Comparative Family Studies, 2*(2), 235–250.

Khalaf, S. (2002). *Civil and uncivil violence in Lebanon: A history of the internationalization of communal conflict*. New York: Columbia University Press.

Khalaf, S., & Gangon, J. H. (Eds.). (2006). *Sexuality in the Arab world*. London: Saqi.

Khallad, Y. (2005). Mate selection in Jordan: Effects of sex, socio–economic status, and culture. *Journal of Social and Personal Relationships, 22*, 155–167.

Luhmann, N. (1986). *Love as passion: The codification of intimacy* (Trans: J. Gains & D. L. Jones). Cambridge: Polity.

Marshall, C., & Rossman, G. B. (1999). *Designing qualitative research* (3rd ed.). Thousand Oaks: Sage.

Massad, J. A. (2007). *Desiring Arabs*. Chicago: University of Chicago Press.

Murani, N. G. (1972). *Parallels between medieval Arabic literature and patterns and themes of courtly love*. (Unpublished master's thesis). American University of Beirut: Beirut, Lebanon.

Nasser, K. (2010). *"Do it for me my dear:" Structuration and relational dialectics among mother-daughter dyads in Lebanese arranged marriages*. (Doctorial dissertation). Louisiana State University: Baton Rouge, Louisiana.

Oghia, M. J. (2012). *What's love got to do with it? An exploratory study of relationship formation and romantic love among American University of Beirut students*. (Published master's thesis). American University of Beirut: Beirut, Lebanon.

Olmsted, J. C. (2005). Gender, aging, and the evolving Arab patriarchal contract. *Feminist Economics, 11*(2), 53–78.

Padilla, M., Hirsch, J. S., Muñoz-Laboy, M., Sember, R. E., &. Parker, R. G. (Eds.). (2007). *Love and globalization: Transformations of intimacy in the contemporary world*. Nashville: Vanderbilt University Press.

Racy, A. J. (2003). *Making music in the Arab world: The culture and artistry of tarab*. Cambridge: Cambridge University Press.

Rashad, H., Osman, M., & Roudi-Fahimi, F. (2005). *Marriage in the Arab world*. Washington, DC: Population Reference Bureau Policy Brief. http://www.iiav.nl/epublications/2005/MarriageInArabWorld.pdf. Accessed 25 Jan 2011.

Sabbah, D. M. (2010). *Social inclusion or exclusion? Never-married singles in West Amman*. (Unpublished master's thesis). American University in Cairo: Cairo, Egypt.

Schvaneveldt, P. L., Kerpelman, J. L., & Schvaneveldt, J. D. (2005). Generational and cultural changes in family life in the United Arab Emirates: A comparison of mothers and daughters. *Journal of Comparative Family Studies, 36*(1), 77–92.

Sharma, S. (2006). Love: Premodern discourses, Persian, Arabic, Ottoman, Andalusian, and South Asian. In S. Joseph, et al. (Eds.), *The encyclopedia of women and Islamic cultures, volume 3: Family, body, sexuality, and health* (pp. 236–241). Leiden: Brill.

Shumway, D. R. (2003). *Modern love: Romance, intimacy, and the marriage crisis*. New York: New York University Press.

Volk, L. (2001). *Missing the nation: Lebanon's post-war generation in the midst of reconstruction*. (Doctorial dissertation). Harvard University: Cambridge, Massachusetts.

Watts, R. J. (1991). *Power in family discourse*. Berlin: Mouton de Gruyter.

Wikan, U. (1984). Shame and honour: A contestable pair. *Man, 19*(4), 635–652.

Mike Oghia graduated with a Masters of Arts in sociology from the Department of Sociology, Anthropology, and Media Studies at the American University of Beirut in 2012. While at AUB, his course work included a variety of topics from Arab mass media and Arab Internet to social movements, but his main focus areas in sociology were family, romantic relationship formation, and the effects of globalization among Arab youth. Michael is the author of #LOVEanon, a blog about love, relationships, and dating, with a Lebanese/Arab emphasis. He has worked as consultant with a conflict resolution and dialogue center in Bangalore, India and is currently working in Istanbul, Turkey as Copy Editor for Daily Sabah.

Chapter 17
In the Zone: Female Athletes and Intercultural Contact in Iraq

Geoff Harkness

17.1 Introduction

In May 2011, a rumor circulated on the campus of the American University of Iraq Sulaimani (AUIS) that the administration intended to remove "Sulaimani" from the school's name and shorten it to the American University of Iraq. This led to an outcry from AUIS students, who mobilized via Facebook, and organized a lunchtime demonstration. The protest was large and loud, bringing out droves of angry students who decried what they viewed as a loss of Kurdish identity. Chanting, "We love Sulaimani," wearing Kurdish-themed clothes, and waving the Kurdish flag, the students took part in the largest protest in the university's history (Fatah 2011). During the demonstration, a petition was circulated and signed by 200 students, some reportedly penning their names in blood.

A 20-year-old Kurdish business administration major named Nagham Haidar assailed the proposed name change to a reporter from the student newspaper: "I am against the idea of removing the 'S' from the name of our university," he said. "All the students who are Kurds are against this idea because they want to have a separate country, so their country will not be viewed by world as a colony of Iraq" (Hussein 2011, p. 1).

Other students supported the proposed name change. Safa, an Arab student from Baghdad, was ambivalent about the protest and did not participate. "People were upset," she recalled. "Kurdish students, they localized the thing. [They say,] 'This can't happen. We want the S there in the name. This represents our identity.' From 1991, they have been separated from us. So anything that happens, they think that we're attacking their territory, their culture, their traditions, [and] their name. They think that this is what made them Kurd. They have this feeling to protect their nation, to protect their identity."

G. Harkness (✉)
Grinnell College, Iowa, USA
e-mail: harkness@grinnell.edu

1501 Morninside Drive, Sioux City, IA 51106, USA

© Springer Science+Business Media Singapore 2015
R. Raddawi (ed.), *Intercultural Communication with Arabs,*
DOI 10.1007/978-981-287-254-8_17

Provost Athanasios Moulakis issued a statement decrying the conflict between Arab and Kurd students, and called upon the "entire academic community to set aside ethnic and sectarian passions and to move together in a spirit of toleration and mutual understanding as befits a community devoted to the dignity of human individuals regardless of class, race, gender, religion, or ethnicity" (Hussein 2011, p. 4).

The proposed name change was dropped, with the university administration denying that it had intended to remove the "S" in the first place. The reversal, however, did not do away with ethnic animosities on the AUIS campus altogether. "In regards to tensions between Arabs and Kurds, of course, yes there is," former AUIS director of Student Affairs Dashnye Daloye explained. "You can't wipe out 30 years of violence, aggression, and war" (cited in Lewis and Fine 2011, p. 45)

Kurdistan is not a country but a symbolic geographic territory that intersects four Middle Eastern nations: Iraq, Iran, Syria, and Turkey. The Kurds are an ethnolinguistic group of Aryan origin that has inhabited, among others, this region for centuries. Currently estimated to number between 20 and 36 million, the Kurds represent the fourth largest ethnic group in the Middle East (Shoup 2011). The Kurds have long called for the establishment of an independent Kurdish nation, a goal that remains unrealized. In Iraq, the central government in Baghdad has resisted Kurdish secessionist efforts, in part, because the province is located on a land rich in natural resources, including a large portion of the nation's water supply and approximately two-third of its oil production and reserves (Gunter 2004).

While the two regions of Iraq constitute a single country, they sometimes function as separate entities. This can lead to social and political obfuscations. For example, both Kurdish and Arabic are the official languages of Iraqi Kurdistan, but each region has its own flag and national anthem. A visa is required to travel across the Kurd–Iraq border. Crucially, while the Iraqi Kurds view themselves as distinct, they remain under the rule of Iraqi Arabs.

Kurds make up approximately 15–20% of Iraq's total population, and there is an extended history of political, territorial, economic, and social tension between Iraqi Kurds and Arabs (Bengio 2012). The Kurds were targeted by former Iraqi president Saddam Hussein, who terrorized Iraqi Kurdistan with a genocidal strategy that included economic sanctions, the destruction of villages, mass slaughters, and lethal chemical weapons attacks that by some estimates killed upwards of 100,000 Kurds (Katzman 2010; Genocide in Iraq 1993). The central government's tendency to disregard these atrocities remains a point of contention between Kurds and Arabs (Bengio 2012).

Adding to this complexity, movements of populations within Iraq have resulted in a Kurdish region characterized by ethnic and cultural heterogeneity (van Bruinessen 2000). In the 1970s, thousands of Iraqi Arabs were relocated to oil-rich Kirkuk as part of Saddam Hussein's strategy of "Arabization." In 1991, more than 100,000 non-Arabs were forced to leave the city under Hussein's policy (Aziz 2011). The displacement of more than 1 million Iraqi Arabs from the southern region of Iraq following the 2003 US military intervention created northern cities populated by Kurds, Arabs, Turkmens, and other ethnic groups that were "deeply divided by chasms of race, religion, history, region, ethnicity, and the asymmetries of political power and control over economic resources" (Mutua 2006, p. 932).

The geopolitical, economic, and cultural differences between Iraqi Kurdistan and the remainder of the country have resulted in social tensions between Kurds and Arabs that exist to this day. In contested oil-rich border cities such as Kirkuk, where there are large numbers of Kurds, Arabs, and Turkmens, ethnic infighting and violence are prevalent.

Tensions between Arabs and Kurds are found in many facets of life in Iraq, including at university campuses. Aziz (2011), conducted a survey of 450 college students in Iraqi Kurdistan, and found that 90 % believed that Kurdistan should become independent from Iraq. More than 86 % of respondents felt "very proud" upon seeing a Kurdish flag, while 40 % felt "very hostile" upon seeing an Iraqi flag. When asked how proud they were to be Kurdistani, nearly 89 % replied "very proud." When asked how proud they were to be Iraqi, 76 % responded that they were "not Iraqi." Almost 97 % of Aziz's subjects self-identified as Kurdish. Therefore, while this survey data are useful for understanding the attitudes of Kurdish college students, it reveals little about Arabs and other ethnic groups, and the communicative processes that exist between these factions on university campuses in the Kurdish region.

This chapter fills that gap by employing ethnographic and interview-based research methods in an ethnically heterogeneous setting. Specifically, I examine sports as an intercultural contact zone, and the role of athletics in alleviating existing conflicts between ethnic groups within the Arab world. I analyze discursive practices used by Kurd and Arab female athletes to invoke categories of difference and similarity. Ultimately, I demonstrate how the basketball court and soccer pitch functioned as intercultural contact zones that led to a degree of accord between different ethnic groups. The social processes described here illustrate how ethnic tensions were moderated through a combination of communicative practices, intercultural contact zones, and athletics.

17.2 Literature Review

Intercultural communication (IC) has traditionally been defined as "a transactional, symbolic process involving the attribution of meaning between people of different cultures" (Gudykunst and Kim 2002, p. 14). This definition can be problematic because (a) the notion of "culture" is elusive and complex; (b) it assumes that people have a defined sense of culture, and see themselves (or can be seen) as culturally akin or divergent from others; and (c) scholars regularly conflate culture with concepts such as ethnicity and nationality. Indeed, "the essentialist assumption that people belong to a culture or have a culture, which is typically taken as a given in intercultural communication studies, has given the field a somewhat old-fashioned, dowdy, not-quite-with-it, even reactionary image" (Piller 2012, p. 3).

In recent years, scholars of IC have increasingly considered how large-scale social forces, such as globalization and transnationalism, shape interactions and social exchanges between people from disparate cultural backgrounds in a global context (Patel et al. 2011; Asante et al. 2008; Baraldi 2006; Jandt 2003). Despite these advances, however, IC within "transnational space remains underresearched, in particular within transnational communities, transnational issue networks and small groups" (MacDonald and O'Regan 2012, p. 559).

There is also a growing interest in IC involving Arab populations. Studies of Arabs and IC have focused largely on communicative practices between Arabs and Westerners in realms that include education (Love and Powers 2004), public relations (Zaharna 1995), health care (Halligan 2006), collective identity (Witteborn 2007), the Internet (Warschauer et al. 2002), communication styles (Nelson et al 2002), and discursive strategies (Umale 2011). Few studies have examined IC between Arab populations, and even fewer examine these processes within Arab nations. In part, this is due to the difficulties in conducting research in the Middle East: "Travel restrictions, inadequate language skills, government censorship, and potentially threatening sociopolitical environments have made conducting research within the Arab world extraordinarily difficult and continue to hide the culture behind the 'Muslim veil'" (Love and Powers 2002, p. 218). While the Middle East is often viewed as a monoculture, a burgeoning generation of scholars is challenging this notion by pointing to the "tapestry of culture" within the Arab world (Zaharna 2009). The present study adds to this body of literature by exploring IC between Arabs and Kurds in Iraq.

Rather than imposing essentialist definitions of culture upon Kurds and Arabs, I instead examine discursive practices used by Arab and Kurd participants to invoke categories of difference and similarity. Halualani and Nakayama (2010) note that "culture as a site of struggle imbues 'communication' not as some equalizing, neutral channel of expression.... Communication involves the creation, constitution, and intertwining of situated meanings, social practices, structures, discourses, and the nondiscursive" (p. 7). In other words, communication is a means by which groups with divergent levels of power and status create, maintain, and upend social boundaries.

Canagarajah (2012) reminds us that "diverse strands of a culture are not equal and neutral. Certain strands serve to define those who enjoy more status, while other strands struggle for greater acceptance or representation" (p. 113). Moreover, Kim (2012) notes that environmental factors help shape contextual variation vis-à-vis IC. Among these factors is ethnic group strength, defined as the "relative status or standing of a particular ethnic group in the context of the surrounding host society" (p. 237). While ethnic group strength can be beneficial to members of that ethnic group, it can also discourage social engagement for nonmembers. Ting-Toomey (2012) proffered four types of identity threat that increased prejudice, ethnocentrism, and conflict between disparate groups: intergroup anxiety, stereotypes, tangible threats, and symbolic threats. Such phenomena "can color our biased expectations and intensify our perceived identity threat levels in dealing with culturally and linguistically dissimilar strangers or what we consider as our 'enemies'" (p. 284). Finally, Watson et al. (2012) point out that, "Two interactants from cultural groups in conflict (e.g., a militant Israeli and a Palestinian) may not desire a mutually effective interaction" (p. 512). The Arab-Kurd tensions examined in the present study are situated within a context where the Kurds form the majority and the Arabs a minority, coloring the communicative exchanges between the two.

Conversely, scholars of IC point to transformations of identity that can occur through intercultural exchanges. "As an individual's cultural identity evolves toward intercultural identity, that person's definition of self and others becomes simultaneously less restricted by rigid cultural and social categories and more broadened and enriched by an increased ability to, at once, particularize and humanize his or her perception of each communicative event" (Kim 2012, p. 238). These changes in perspective may be more available in certain settings, including the realm of sports, which involves voluntary intercultural contact. Studies (Kramsch and Uryu 2012) demonstrate that those interested in other cultures sometimes seek voluntary intercultural contact.

Numerous studies have examined sports' role in identity transformation, particularly for women (Bell 2004; Brace-Govan 2002; Gilroy 1989; Palmer 2009; Kelly et al. 2008; McDermott 1996). The use of sports as a mechanism for personal transformation and the creation of new understandings between divergent groups has been described by scholars such as Soubhi (1977), who noted that in the aftermath of the 1958 Iraqi revolution, "The development of physical culture exerted [a] positive influence on changes in inter-human relations" (p. 109).

The relationship between athletics and IC is understudied, yet organized sports serve as a site of intercultural contact, which occurs when culturally diverse groups have physical interaction in spaces known as contact zones: "social spaces where disparate cultures meet, clash, and grapple with each other, often in highly asymmetrical relations of domination and subordination" (Pratt 1992, p. 12). This study examines sports as an intercultural contact zone, and the role of athletics in alleviating existing conflicts between groups within the Arab world.

17.3 Setting and Methodology

The AUIS, an American-style postsecondary institution that opened its doors in fall 2007, features men's and women's soccer and basketball teams. The women's teams were formed at the behest of female students interested in developing extracurricular activities. In part, this desire was fueled by local customs, which dissuade females from pursuits that take place outside the home. Because of their connection to the university, athletics enjoy a slight reprieve from these attitudes, offering institutional legitimacy that reduces cultural anxiety about female sports participation (Sfeir 1985).

This study is based on ethnographic observation and interview-based research methods. Thirty-two open-ended, in-person interviews were conducted with 19 female basketball players, nine female soccer players, and four members of the coaching staff. Interviewees were prebriefed as to the nature of my research and gave verbal consent at the beginning of each interview. With their permission, I use their real first names throughout this chapter; for some quotations I opted to omit names altogether. All interview quotations are transcribed verbatim. I also observed the basketball team during practice. Reflecting their status as college students, all of the team members were in their late teens or early twenties. All players were Iraqi. Most were Kurds, but the basketball team had four Arab and two Turkmen players, and the soccer team had two Arab players. The Kurds and Turkmens had lower levels of religiosity compared to the Arab players, some of whom wore the *hijab* at all times, including while playing sports. The majority of the team members hailed from Sulaimani and the surrounding area. A few came from nearby Kurdish cites such as Kirkuk and Dohuk, and about 35 % of the players—mostly Arabs but also some Kurds—grew up in Baghdad and moved to Sulaimani to escape the war.

Initially, my interest in these women was vis-à-vis their status as female athletes within a country steeped in patriarchy and traditional gender roles. During our interviews, many participants spoke of tensions between various ethnic groups, particularly Arabs and Kurds. Because this topic was invoked repeatedly and early on, I began asking all participants about Arab-Kurd tensions. Doing so revealed the primacy of ethnic identity for participants. The women also spoke of the transformative experience of playing sports, how joining a team and interacting with different ethnic groups had led to marked changes in personal perspective. Thus, the creation, maintenance, and upending of social boundaries can be found in the discursive practices of these groups.

17.4   Data

Ethnic Conflict At the AUIS, ethnic discord was found in many arenas of the campus. Kurd and Arab participants described how long-standing conflicts reduced interactions between the two groups. An Arab participant who moved to Sulaimani from Baghdad told me that, "Some of the Kurds here just hate Arabs. They ignore me most of the time. I don't have that many Kurdish friends. They look at us like we are from outer space or something because we are from Baghdad and don't speak Kurdish."

When describing the engines of ethnic conflict at the AUIS, nearly all Kurdish participants mentioned Iraq's tenuous political situation, the history of war, and Hussein's *Arabization* policies and terrorism of the Kurdish territory. A Kurdish participant named Nina insisted that the grievances between Kurds and Arabs were largely political, but that political problems led to personal issues.

Some believed that political fissures between Kurds and Arabs were related to territorial claims and the movement of ethnic populations across borders within Iraq, particularly in contested cities located near the Kurdistan–Iraq dividing line. Kurdish participants asserted that Iraqi Arabs wanted to forcibly wrest control of these territories. "I don't really understand Arabs," one Kurdish participant told me. "I don't understand the reason they consider themselves the owners of Kirkuk. Because it's obvious and it's written in history books that Saddam used to transfer the Kurds from Kirkuk to Sulaimani or Erbil and bring in Arabs." In this participant's estimation, only the Kurds had the right to populate or claim ownership of ethnically heterogeneous territories in Iraqi Kurdistan.

For other Kurdish participants, the problems were described as stemming from the Iraqi Arabs' refusal to recognize the Kurdish region as an independent country. Again, it was emphasized that these matters were political rather than personal, but became personal because government maneuverings sparked animosity between ethnic groups. This was described as working in both directions: Arabs were wary of Kurds for the same reasons Kurds were wary of Arabs. For example, one Kurdish participant stated:

> We're not satisfied with having our own region; we want our own state; and we think that Arabs are the people who do not give us the right to have that state. So psychologically we have that feeling against Arabs. I have a lot of [Arab] friends that are from Baghdad. On a personal basis, I don't hate them. But when it's about Kurds and Arabs, I hate them. I don't know the reason; it's just a feeling. I think with them as well. It's probably because of two different ethnic groups have one country. And [the Arabs] think they have a right to govern the country, and we [Kurds] are a minority. I don't want to be a part of Iraq. I never say I'm an Iraqi. I say I'm a Kurd and that's it.

This participant's conceptualization of herself as Kurd, rather than Iraqi, illustrates the role of large-scale social forces in shaping IC. The political and economic strategies of the Kurdistan Regional Government, abetted by the US military, helped forge the belief that there were two distinct nations within a single country. These actions cemented this participant's resolve to define herself as Kurd, rather than an Iraqi.

Identity, Language, and Culture? The relationship between national identity, a sense of belonging to and affiliation with one's nation, and ethnic identity, a sense of representation and affinity with one's ethno-racial culture, has been explained through theories such as ethnic pluralism and social dominance. The ethnic pluralism model is grounded in the belief that "individuals can simultaneously maintain a positive identity with their nation while remaining identified with their heritage culture" (Rodriguez et al. 2010, p. 326). Conversely, social dominance theory asserts that ethnic and national identities are wrought with conflict in locations where "the individual's ethnic group was subjugated through conquest or domination by the majority culture" (Rodriguez et al. 2010, p. 327). Both theories lend explanatory weight to my findings in Iraq.

For some participants, the lack of a cohesive, inclusive Iraqi national identity was problematic. From this perspective, Kurds felt singled out and marginalized by Iraqi Arabs because of their ethnicity. It was believed that Arab recognition of Kurds as a distinct ethnic category, and refusal to acknowledge Kurds as part of a collective Iraqi identity, led to the conflict between the groups. For example, Nina told me that, "Not everyone thinks that we are Iraqi. We always have arguments with our friends. I say we are Iraqi, we have Iraqi passports, and they say, 'No, you are Kurds.' And it's not that [Kurds] hate Arabs, but you want to be recognized as what you are."

Others attributed the conflict between Arabs and Kurds to cultural and religious differences. Although many Kurdish participants were Muslim, they perceived themselves to be far more liberal and tolerant than the supposedly conservative and fundamentalist Iraqi Arabs. These ideological distinctions were thought to create behavioral differences. For example, one participant opined that,

> The problem with Kurds and Arabs, we do really have really different cultures. Arabs are more judgmental. It's probably their religion that allows them to be hateful. Even the Kurds who do practice religion, they're still more liberal because our culture allows it. Kurds are willing to help things get better more than Arabs are. I think Arabs want things to go their way. It's either their way or no way, and that's not possible.

While some critics of IC contend that culture is sometimes used as a proxy for ethnicity and/or nationality (Piller 2012), the above response illustrates how these concepts are used interchangeably in communicative practices. The participant viewed the distinction between these two ethnic groups as largely stemming from differences in culture, including the level of religiosity. Thus, while it may be possible to separate these concepts analytically, it is important to remember that they are often conflated at the ground level.

Along the same lines, linguistic differences were another reason proffered for the tensions between Arabs and Kurds. Dawisha (2009) noted that young Kurds in post-Hussein Kurdistan "no longer cared to speak, or make an effort to learn, Arabic. Indeed, young Kurds who were inclined to take Arabic as a second language were looked at with bemusement at best and suspicion at worst" (p. 264). Aziz(2011, p. 141) found that 89.1 % of college students in Iraqi Kurdistan believed that speaking Kurdish was "very important." One Arab participant at the AUIS opined that conflicts arose because Kurds refused to speak Arabic. "The Kurds don't even know how to speak Arabic. They don't want to learn; they hate the language."

The bringing together of Kurd and Arab students at the AUIS required some degree of interaction between two ethnic groups with long-standing political, social, and cultural divisions. Therefore, the AUIS functioned as a site of contestation, resistance, and negotiation for conflicts that were in place well before the construction of the campus. Faculty members hoped that these social exchanges between students would foster greater understanding. Student participants stated that these exchanges resulted in a subtle lack of solidarity between the Arabs and the Kurds on campus. According to one Arab participant:

> In terms of the university, it exists, even if it's not [defined as] a problem where there's Kurds and Arabs and this is why this is happening. But the underlying tension is because of that. Just in terms of the groups: When we study or when we eat lunch or when we go out, you see this is the Kurd group, this is the Arab group. It's so obvious.

In addition to self-segregation along ethnic lines, sometimes heated debates between Arabs and Kurds took place inside and outside of classrooms. Students argued, called each other ethnic slurs, and used social networking sites to wage interethnic battles. The crowded campus dormitories—where Arab and Kurd students had little choice but to intermingle in close proximity—were another site of ethnic antagonism. "We had a student who lived in the dorm, and she used to say bad words about Kurds," one Kurdish participant recalled. "For example, once she saw a donkey and she said, 'Oh that's a Kurd, a Kurdish donkey.'"

For some, interethnic tensions did not stop them from pursuing friendships outside of their ethnic group, but affected the content and character of these relationships. In these instances, Arabs and Kurds could be friends to a point, but politics prevented them from becoming closer. For example, one Arab participant opined that:

> I've got friends who are Kurd. I get along with them, but when it comes to the talking about the issues, it doesn't seem like we are friends anymore. No matter how much you think that okay she's a Kurd and she's my friend, when it comes to politics there are problems between us.

When Safa arrived at the AUIS campus 4 years ago as a 17-year-old freshman, her first thought was to turn around and go back home to Baghdad. For the first time in her life, Safa was an ethnic minority, an Iraqi Arab in a city where Kurds were the overwhelming majority. She spoke English and Arabic, but not Kurdish, which made communication with Kurds more difficult. In addition to adjusting to adult responsibilities such as time management and fiscal budgeting, Safa found it challenging to make friends. Living in the campus dorms, she felt isolated and alone. Her fellow students tried to be helpful, offering advice and inviting Safa to dine or watch movies together, but Safa kept to herself. She recalled this time as alienating and confusing:

> It was a difficult transition. When I first moved here, I was like, "This is not where I belong." You're still in Iraq, you're still in your country, but you feel very strange. Everybody here is Kurd. They don't speak my language, they don't have the same traditions and cultures, and I don't know how to interact with them. I felt strange for the first year and a half. I was always thinking about going back home.

Safa eventually befriended Meriem, an Arab member of the basketball team who encouraged Safa to join. Safa was wary, in part because she came from a conservative family that frowned upon physical activity for women. As one of the few players who wore a *hijab,* Safa was concerned that playing basketball would convey the wrong message. Rather than joining as a player, Safa came aboard as a team manager, assisting from the sidelines but not participating in practices or games. Being a manager required that Safa interact with Kurdish players, which she initially resisted.

> For the first year and a half, I was only with my group, the Arab group. I didn't want to interact with these people or get to know them more, and I didn't care. "I don't know you, I don't care about you, even if we are a team." I put this wall between me and them…. So there wasn't that bond. I caused some of the problems. I was the issue because I didn't want to get to know these people more. I really regret doing stuff like that, but I think that was part of the process: to learn more about them and to know how to handle these problems.

In 4 years at the AUIS, Safa has not limited her extracurricular activities to the basketball team. She has written for the student newspaper, deliberated issues in the debate club, and tutored children as part of a university outreach program. It was basketball, however, that inspired Safa to reconsider her views on members of different ethnic groups:

> There's more interaction when you play basketball and you're on a team. You spend more time together, you interact with these people and you get to know them more. You're in

class for an hour, or in the other clubs, we meet for one hour a week. But for basketball we meet for four hours per week, and all the extra activities we do together: The games, we travel together, we go get something to eat after practice, or watch a movie together. So we spend more time together. And also because of the nature of basketball: we interact more because it's a team and to play well you depend on the player next to you and how you interact with each other. You cannot play as an individual on a team.

Safa spoke from firsthand experience. Once a team manager whose involvement was limited to the sidelines, she has now joined the basketball team as a player, suiting up twice a week for practice. Safa's transformation, however, did not eliminate tensions on the basketball team. As with any group, conflicts arose, but sharing mutual goals and a collective team identity mandated that problems be resolved quickly. Students committed to the basketball team, Safa said, were those willing to set aside differences and work together:

Of course there is tension and there are problems. But we have a main goal, which is to keep this basketball team together. And we deal with the problems that come along in order to achieve that goal. If we have a problem, let's solve it together, try to work it out. And it's the duty of both parties to get involved in that. Because if only Kurdish try or only Arab try, it won't get solved. Once you live with them and have problems and you solve them, this is where you really start to see people. So basketball changed me inside as a person.

17.5   Transformations of Identity Within Intercultural Contact Zones

As Safa's story illustrates, sports at the AUIS offered a space for IC between Arabs and Kurds that led to personal transformations. The basketball court and the soccer pitch served as contact zones where improved relations between divergent groups occurred via IC. While cultural discord was sometimes amplified in campus classrooms and dormitories, many described the basketball court and the soccer pitch as spaces where these tensions were muted. "You feel it during class, but you don't really feel that diversity when we are playing," Bery explained. "We sort of put aside our differences." From this perspective, interactions between Arabs and Kurds on the AUIS campus could be seen as involuntary intercultural contact, while interaction on the sports teams was voluntary and thus sought out by those interested in greater understanding between culturally divergent groups.

Maryam asserted that during basketball practice, ethnic and religious distinctions were minimized, and the team's shared gender identity became more salient: "We forget everything when we play basketball. We never say, 'She is Christian, she is Kurd, she is Arab, she is Muslim.' We are girls; we are a bunch of sisters."

In part, these findings may be a function of team sport. As Safa noted, playing basketball forced culturally divergent groups to work together as a unit and view themselves collectively. During practices, if a player was late or made a mistake, the entire team might be punished collectively by having to run laps or perform additional drills, reinforcing the team's collective identity. Scholars of IC have noted the role of teamwork in conflict resolution: "If team members feel that there exists a good relationship between them, their efforts towards resolving existing or emerging conflicts are greater than if no such relationship has been established" (Glaser 2010, p. 186). Being on the team fostered communication and dependency between culturally dissimilar groups. This sometimes led to new understandings and brought the members closer together. For example, Hanar noted that, "The best part about it is communicating with other people. Before I joined the team, I wasn't so close to them, but when you become a team, you depend on each other."

Rather than exacerbating existing tensions, working together as a team, communicating, and setting aside differences led to players helping each other during practices. The better players coached those struggling to learn the techniques of the game. During scrimmages, players encouraged each other and cheered one another on. Participants noted that collaborations on the sports teams sometimes led to players helping each other outside of athletics. For example, team members would tutor players who were having academic difficulties. Meriem, an Arab, recalled that, "I was one of the girls who was in trouble [academically] and lots of them came to say, 'Do you need help? We can help;' and I didn't expect such a thing to happen. I was surprised to see this kind of strong union that we have among the team members. It is not only in front of the audience or in front of the coaches, we are kind of a family who care for one another and help one another."

Through the IC of sports, players learned to care for one another. Many players used terms such as "family" and "sisters" to describe the relationship between team members. "We are like a family," an Arab player named Ola avowed. "Maybe for some people it's strange because we are all from different backgrounds, but that means nothing for us. We are like one person."

17.6   Implications

These findings do not suggest that IC in the realm of sports is a panacea for reducing cultural conflict. Not every player claimed to be "sisters" with other members of their team. Some participants described a lack of kinship with teammates, and some—though not all—attributed this distance to cultural or ethnic differences. For example, one Kurdish player told me that, "I'm not close friends with Arabs and Turkmens [on the team]. I know all of them, I'm friends with them, but we are not so close. We don't go out together. It's just sports that we have in common." Overall, however, the majority of the participants described their teams as highly unified, a claim that rang true in my observations and interactions with them.

Education is sometimes touted as an idyllic means by which to reduce differences between disparate groups of people, but education seemed to underscore and even exacerbate the tensions between ethnic groups in Iraqi Kurdistan. The differences in ethnic tensions between the sports teams and the other arenas of the AUIS might be attributed to the diversity of the teams, which was greater than found on the campus as a whole. While Kurds still outnumbered other groups, about 25% of the basketball and soccer players were ethnic minorities. Likewise, both teams were home to Muslims, Christians, and even atheists. There may have been a process of self-selection, where this relatively diverse setting was appealing to those who joined. The teams may have attracted players with higher levels of tolerance than the student body as a whole. Arab, Kurd, and Turkmen students who were not interested in interacting outside of their ethnic group could seek less diverse extracurricular activities. Furthermore, participants may have been predisposed towards IC because this highly physical sensation takes place in a country where women are often discouraged from this type of activity. Morgan and Arasaratnam (2003) found that "high sensation seekers find intercultural interactions to be more enjoyable and satisfying than low sensation seekers do" (p. 183).

Worth considering are the broader implications of IC in the realm of sports, and what impact these types of exchanges may have on ethnic relations in Iraq over time. For Dashne, the unity found on the AUIS basketball team gave her hope for the nation's future. "In our team you can see Turks, Kurds, and Arabs," she said. "There are many ethnic groups but we are just one team. If Iraq is that way one day, it will be the great Iraq."

Recent events in the Middle East make it clear that the region's future is in the hands of its young people. While these youth have inherited the baggage of previous generations, they have new understandings of age-old concepts such as race and gender. Whether the youth can navigate this terrain remains to be seen, but sports seem like a potential avenue for social progress. Governments, educators, and policymakers should take seriously the potential of sports to foster such changes.

Conclusion

For decades, scholars have documented the tensions between the various ethnic groups in Iraq. These tensions, which have persisted for centuries, were exacerbated by the 2003 US military invasion of Iraq and the subsequent displacement of Iraqi Arabs. This chapter is an attempt to explore how ethnic tensions, even those deeply engrained within populations, may be alleviated through communicative exchanges that take place in intercultural contact zones. At the AUIS, a location rife with ethnic tension, sports served as a site for such exchanges. Although playing sports together did not eliminate all ethnic discord between every member of the team, the personal transformations described by many of the players render athletics worthy of consideration in future attempts to reduce existing ethnic tensions.

References

Asante, M., Miike, Y., & Yin, J. (2008). *The global intercultural communication reader*. New York: Routledge.

Aziz, M. (2011). *The Kurds of Iraq: Ethnonationalism and national identity in Iraqi Kurdistan.* New York: I.B. Tauris.

Baraldi, C. (2006). New forms of intercultural communication in a globalized world. *The International Communication Gazette, 68,* 53–69.

Bell, M. (2004). "Knowing what my body can do:" Physical moments in the social production of physicality. *Waikato Journal of Education, 10,* 155–67.

Bengio, O. (2012). *The Kurds of Iraq: Building a state within a state.* Boulder: Lynne Rienner.

Brace-Govan, J. (2002). Looking at body work: Women and three physical activities. *Journal of Sport and Social Issues, 26*(4), 403–20.

Canagarajah, S. (2012). Postmodernism and intercultural discourse: World Englishes. In C. Paulston, S. Kiesling, & E. Rangel (Eds) *The handbook of intercultural discourse and communication* (pp. 110–132). West Sussex: Wiley-Blackwell.

Dawisha, A. (2009). *Iraq: A political history from independence to occupation.* Princeton: Princeton University Press.

Fatah, S. (2011). Is 's' worth protesting? *AUI-S Voice, 3*(4): 2.

Genocide in Iraq: The Anfal campaign against the Kurds. (July, 1993). *A Middle East watch report.* New York: Human Rights Watch. http://www.hrw.org/reports/1993/iraqanfal/. Accessed 12 Sept 2011.

Gilroy, S. (1989). The emBody-ment of power: Gender and physical activity. *Leisure Studies, 8*(2), 163–71.

Glaser, E. (2010). Working in multicultural teams. In M. Guilherme, E. Glaser, & M. Mendez-Garcia (Eds.), *The intercultural dynamics of multicultural working.* Bristol: Multilingual Matters.

Gudykunst, W., & Kim, Y. Y. (2002). *Communicating with strangers: An approach to intercultural communication.* New York: McGraw Hill.

Gunter, M. (2004). The Kurdish question in perspective. *World Affairs, 166*(4), 197–205.

Halligan, P. (2006). Caring for patients of islamic denomination: Critical care nurses' experiences in Saudi Arabia. *Journal of Clinical Nursing, 15,* 1565–1573.

Halualani, R., & Nakayama, T. (2010). Critical intercultural communication studies at a crossroads. In R. Halualani, & T. Nakayama (Eds.), *The handbook of critical intercultural communication* (pp. 1–16). West Sussex: Wiley-Blackwell.

Hussein, H. (2011). Students protest to save Sulaimani 's.' *AUI-S Voice, 3*(4), 1, 4.

Jandt, F. (Ed.). (2003). *Intercultural communication: A global reader.* Thousand Oaks: Sage.

Katzman, K. (2010). *The Kurds in Post-Saddam Iraq.* Washington: U.S. Congressional Research Service.

Kelly, D. M., Pomerantz, S., & Currie, D. H. (2008). You can break so many more rules: The identity work and play of becoming skater girls. In M. Giardina & M. Donnelly (Eds.), *Youth culture and sport* (pp. 113–125). London: Routledge.

Kim, Y. Y. (2012). Beyond cultural categories: Communication, adaptation and transformation. In J. Jackson (Ed.), *The routledge handbook of language and intercultural communication* (pp. 113–125). London: Routledge.

Kramsch, C., & Uryu, M. (2012). Intercultural contact, hybridity, and third space. In J. Jackson (Ed) *The Routledge handbook of language and intercultural communication* (pp. 211–226). London: Routledge.

Lewis, B. (Producer), & Fine, D. (Director). (2011). *Salaam Dunk,* DVD. San Francisco: Seedwell Films.

Love, D. E., & Powers, W. G. (2002). Communicating under uncertainty: Interaction between Arab students and western instructors. *Journal of Intercultural Communication Research, 31*(4), 217–231.

Love, D. E., & Powers, W. G.(2004). Differences in the persuasion strategies of Arab female students toward western instructors. *Journal of Intercultural Communication Research, 33*(1), 1–13.

MacDonald, M., & O'Regan, J. (2012). A global agenda for intercultural communication research and practice. In Jackson, J. (Ed.), *The Routledge handbook of language and intercultural communication* (pp. 553–567). London: Routledge.

McDermott, L. (1996). Towards a feminist understanding of physicality within the context of women's physically active and sporting lives. *Sociology of Sport Journal, 13*(1), 12–30.

Morgan, S. E., & Arasaratnam, L. A. (2003). Intercultural friendships as social excitation: Sensation seeking as predictor of intercultural friendship seeking behavior. *Journal of Intercultural Communication Research, 3*(31), 175–186.

Mutua, M. (2006). The Iraq paradox: Minority and group rights in a viable constitution. *Buffalo Law Review, 54,* 927–955.

Nelson, G., Batal, M., & Bakary, W. (2002). Directness vs. indirectness: Egyptian Arabic and US English communication style. *International Journal of Intercultural Relations, 26,* 39–57.

Palmer, C. (2009). Soccer and the politics of identity for young muslim refugee women in South Australia. *Soccer and Society, 10*(1), 27–38.

Patel, F., Li, M., & Sooknanan, P. (2011). *Intercultural communication: Building a global community.* Thousand Oaks: Sage.

Piller, I. (2012). Intercultural communication: An overview. In C. Paulston, S. Kiesling, & E. Rangel (Eds.), *The handbook of intercultural discourse and communication* (pp. 3–18). West Sussex: Wiley-Backwell.

Pratt, M. L. (1992). *Imperial eyes: Travel writing and transculturation.* London: Routledge.

Rodriguez, L., Schwartz, S. J., & Whitbourne, S. K. (2010). American identity revisited: The relation between national, ethnic, and personal identity in a multiethnic sample of emerging adults. *Journal of Adolescent Research, 25*(2), 324–349.

Sfeir, L. (1985). The status of muslim women in sport: Conflict between cultural tradition and modernization. *International Review of Sport, 20*(4), 283–306.

Shoup, J. (2011). *Ethnic groups of Africa and the Middle East: An encyclopedia.* Santa Barbara: ABC–CLIO.

Soubhi, A. (1977). Physical education and sport in the life of Iraqi Women. *International Review for the Sociology of Sport, 12*(2), 107–109.

Ting-Toomey, S. (2012). Understanding intercultural conflict competence: Multiple theoretical insights. In J. Jackson (Ed.), *The Routledge handbook of language and intercultural communication* (pp. 279–295). London: Routledge.

Umale, J. (2011). Pragmatic failure in refusal strategies: British versus Omani Interlocutors. *Arab World English Journal, 2,* 18–46.

van Bruinessen, M. (2000). Transnational aspects of the Kurdish question. (Working paper) *Robert Schuman Centre for Advanced Studies.* European University Institute: Florence.

Warschauer, M., El Said, G., & Zohry, A. (2002). Language choice online: Globalization and identity in Egypt. *Journal of Computer Mediated Communication, 7,* 4.

Watson, B., Gallois, C., Hewett, D., & Jones, L. (2012). Culture and health care: Intergroup communication and its consequences. In J. Jackson (Ed.), *The Routledge handbook of language and intercultural communication* (pp. 510–522). London: Routledge.

Witteborn, S. (2007). The situated expression of Arab collective identities in the United States. *Journal of Communication, 57,* 556–575.

Zaharna, R. S. (1995). Understanding cultural preferences of Arab communication patterns. *Public Relations Review, 21*(3), 241–255.

Zaharna, R. S. (2009). An associative approach to intercultural communication competence in the Arab world. In D. Deardorff (Ed.), *The Sage handbook of intercultural competence.* Thousand Oaks: Sage.

Geoff Harkness, PhD is assistant professor of sociology at Morningside College. He has a PhD in sociology from Northwestern University, where he was awarded the Helen O. Piros Dissertation and Research Fellowship and the Karpf Prize. His scholarship focuses on the interactive practices of youth cultures, and the role of stratification in shaping the content and character of culture and identity. His scholarly research has been published in *Cultural Sociology, Poetics, American Behavioral Scientist, Soccer & Society, the International Journal of the History of Sport, Journal of Workplace Rights,* and *Contexts.* The University of Minnesota Press will publish his first book in 2014.

Chapter 18
"Why Am I Black?" Gendering Hip-Hop, and Translocal Solidarities in Dubai

Zenzele Isoke

18.1 Introduction

Contrary to the racist and misogynist antics of entertainers like Nicki Minaj, Eminem, and Lil' Wayne, hip-hop provides young women with an important cultural venue to express discontent with gender relations, articulate new readings and interpretations of Islam, as well as examine the increasing impossibilities of national belonging in the context of migration, gendered racialization, and cultural exchange. In this chapter, I pose the following questions: What happens when two or more distinctive ways of being, understanding, and living blackness operate side-by-side in the same space and time? What new truths and narratives emerge when distinctive histories of migration and identity converge by way of extended dialogues between women involved in global hip-hop culture and politics? To answer these questions, I first develop a black feminist ethnographic methodology grounded in a transversal understanding of both black feminism and hip-hop politics. I then use my ethnographic fieldwork in Dubai, UAE to map a translocal geography of black female political agency using the voices of Afro-Arab female hip-hop generation artists. Lastly, I argue for the importance of locating translocal solidarities to frame analyses of global black women's political expression. I draw on the theoretical and methodological innovations of scholars who write within and across the fields of contemporary hip-hop politics and culture, contemporary black feminism, and translocal geographies. I show how hip-hop remains a central mode of cultural and political insurgency for young women by enabling multiple articulations of the dis/continuities of race-gender-culture that persist within urban neoliberalization in late modernity. Hip-hop also provides an important space for alternative mappings of geopolitical relationships between women of diverse ethnic and cultural backgrounds, while providing the context to interrogate the continuing appeal of "blackness" as a marker of identity and solidarity for women of color globally. It

Z. Isoke (✉)
University of Minnesota, Minneapolis, USA
e-mail: isoke001@umn.edu

is an important point of encounter to negotiate local-to-local connections in ways that undermine the national boundaries erected by states and reinforced through the racist cultural logics of capitalist heteropatriarchy. Hip-hop offers a unique glimpse into the lives of Afro-Arab "third culture" women who live in or around the margins of the Khaleeji culture (Gulf culture) in the Arabian Gulf. The term "third culture kids" refers to children who spend a significant portion of their developmental year living in a culture that is outside of their parent's passport culture, or, more specifically country of origin (Al-Otaibi 2012).

In this chapter I am most interested in amplifying the voices of Arab black female hip-hop artists who reside in and move through global cities in the Islamic world. Using this vantage point, I direct attention to how hip-hop can operate as a galvanizing cultural force that provides opportunities for the forging of political intimacies between diverse black women.

18.2   Background and Literature Review

An older generation of hip-hop scholars defined its form by four defining elements: emceeing/rapping, deejaying, break dancing, and graffiti. Scholars who interpreted hip-hop through its earliest geographic "origins" consolidated this understanding of hip-hop: its rightful *birthplace* is the South Bronx borough of New York (Watkins 2005; Ogden 2007). This perspective has been routinely critiqued, as it builds primarily upon the nation-oriented, male-centric histories that relied exclusively on US regional biases to evaluate and authenticate what "real" hip-hop was (Brown 2008; Sharpley-Whiting 2007; Durham 2007; Perry 2004). Today, hip-hop exceeds its four elements as the art form has metastasized to different parts of the globe. What we now call "hip-hop" is understood to be characterized by a synergy of factors that includes but is not limited to its eclectic musical qualities (Chang 2006). Terkourafi (2010), locates the transformative quality of hip-hop in the genre's stubborn inclination toward cultural hybridization and the incitement of border-bouncing oppositional youth politics (p. 12). For Terkourafi, hip-hop is neither confined, nor necessarily defined by its original four elements. Instead, hip-hop's genius is realized through the iconoclastic ways that artists and activists transform the original elements by infusing them with the shifting cultural and aesthetic character of specific geopolitical locales. Hip-hop draws attention to what Osumare (2007) has described as "connective marginalities" between youth from diverse geographic and cultural settings (p. 172). She explains, "connective marginalities in each global site become bridges across late capitalist manipulations of hip-hop culture, and also help link issues of collective social continuity and individual experience of local realities" (p. 173). Within this framework, hip-hop functions as both an object of commodification and an embodied philosophy of cultural resistance that have morphed and shifted with the heightened realities of travel and cultural osmosis produced expansion of digital technology and globalization in the neoliberal era.

Globally, women of color have embraced hip-hop as means to articulate political critique and discontent. It is a dialogic mode of expression for personal and spiritual exploration and agency within and against a broader male dominated society (Lane 2011; Fernandes 2011; Malone and Martinez 2010). Gender, ethnicity, and culture operate as powerful organizing concepts and discourses in hip-hop. Together they are foundational to its inherent expression (Jeffries 2007) For example, rappers Abeer Al Zinati and Safa Hathoot locate women's subordination in the interstices of intra-Arab sexism and racist Israeli militarism, actively linking Palestinian national liberation to women's liberation from patriarchy (Eqeiq 2010). Hip-hop is an important point of encounter between the marginalized youth in the global North, providing opportunities to (bear) witness (to) the contradictions of hyper-invisibility of urban youth culture and the increasingly dismal economic opportunities for young people coming of age in the second decade of the new millennium. Popular British recording artist, M.I.A., of Tamil (South Indian) descent exemplifies this trend. Not only do her beats blend American hip-hop, soul, rhythm and blues (R&B), reggae, and electronica, but also her lyrics take on themes such as immigration and the violence of "citizenship." She makes connections between Muslim women's right to drive in Saudi Arabia and the futility of using militarism to solve deeply entrenched social cleavages. Several of her songs invoke the term "third world democracy" in order to underscore the political and economic interdependence between first world and third world. Without falling into the artistic dead-end of proselytization, she advocates for the achievement of global youth solidarity by calling attention to the widespread problem of racialized poverty while highlighting the social and political disenfranchisement of the children of migrant workers. M.I.A.'s music also provides insights into the creative ways that racialized migrants both subvert and manipulate global capital at first world borders.

Political hip-hop played a central role in the ignition of youth led revolt during the Arab Spring. In November 2010, a Tunisian rap artist from Sfax called "El General" produced a four-minute music video called "Head of State" that showcased the problems of hunger, poverty, unemployment, and discontent among Tunisian youth. After the self-immolation of Mohammed Bouazizi in Sidi Bouzid, El General's music video spread exploded on Facebook, helping to set off the Jasmine revolution in Tunisia. Muslim women also use hip-hop as a tool for social change. Soultana, a Moroccan rapper, debunks the stereotypes of Muslims as religious extremists and terrorists in her music. Rapping uncovered, Soultana declared, "Our Islam is peace, love and respect. We are a generation calling for peace." In spite of persistent threats and dismissals by Muslim men in her audiences, she was reported to have countered, "I read the Koran" (Robin 2007). Her own personal readings and understanding of the text trump the opinions of men who relied upon masculinist and patriarchal attitudes to interpret the holy book. By rapping, dancing, and singing in public *while* embracing Islam, Soultana refused to capitulate to the ideology of Islam as articulated, practiced, and regulated by the heteromasculinist state and its enforcers.

18.3 Methodology

This essay relies upon ethnographic fieldwork conducted in the summer of 2011 in Dubai, UAE. Dubai is a fertile site to examine the negotiation of new modes of translocal cultural expression and political storytelling that center the lives of black-identified Arab women. Known for its shopping malls, mega engineering projects, and ultra-luxurious hotels, the city takes the form of a desert paradise in the larger public imagination. However, beneath the veneer of a gilded city, Dubai is a globalized city that relies heavily on the labor of people of color from all over the world, including African and other women racialized as "black."

Within a period of 4 weeks, I interviewed eight women of diverse racial and ethnic backgrounds involved in some aspect of hip-hop culture and politics. Three were Palestinian (one half African American and half Palestinian), two were Lebanese, two were Sudanese, and one was Emirati (UAE citizen). All of the women were identified as "black." As an African-American feminist doing ethnographic work in Dubai, hip-hop served what Anaya McMurray (2008) has called an "improvisation zone:" a dynamic space in which questions of culture, identity, and artist/political expression between the hip-hop generation women of diverse racial, ethnic, cultural and ethnic backgrounds were worked through. McMurray explains, "Improvisation occurs within a space structured by the experiences and histories of the people involved (p. 75)." Ethnography was an improvisation zone in which I, my collaborator John Thabiti Willis, a scholar of African history, and the artists we interviewed collectively theorized how our own personal, musical, cultural, and political histories informed our relationships to hip-hop culture. We met in restaurants, hookah lounges, nightclubs, and/or in the women's homes. Our conversations lasted from one and a half to three hours long. I met with each of the women, except Rafiyah and Zenaib (who will be profiled later) on two or more occasions. We always shared meals and nonalcoholic beverages including tea and coffee. We all agreed that hip-hop was "very political" and spoke openly about how hip-hop had shaped our identities as young black people living in different parts of the world. Most of the women were brown-skinned, and about two had a light olive complexion and straight hair that Americans might typically describe as "Middle Eastern." We all spoke American English fluently, often times falling into what Imani Perry (2004) calls African American Vernacular English (AAVE). Throughout our conversations there were slippages into Arabic between our informants to clarify points made that were easily misunderstood because of the way Thabiti and I framed comments and questions. All participants shared equally about themselves, our personal and familial histories and our various relationships with hip-hop culture. Over the course of spending about 3 or 4 h together almost everyday, we became very familiar with one another.[1] In this chapter, to do justice to the complexity of the conversations that we

---

[1] Our conversations were unscripted, spontaneous, and had a collaborative quality. We learned from each other. All of us were between 25 and 35 years old, with the exception of Rafiyah's mother (aged 65) whom she insisted that we interview with her. All of the artists were college educated and either employed or seeking employment in their chosen field. We were a part of what

had, as well as to honor the intimacy shared between us, I will analyze and present the findings of three of the eight interviews.

18.4 The Study

It became clear that Dubai was an important locale in which to examine how hip-hop is used as a mode of discursive intervention to the larger structures of power, identity, and location in the Middle East. Some of the major themes that emerged in our conversations included the continued relevance of blackness as a category of identity in the Arab world, the sexual politics of black womanhood, spiritualized Islamic feminism that both praised and critiqued Arab doctrinal practices and traditions, and what can only be described as the struggle for freedom. This included the freedom to make personal decisions about marriage without being overly beholden to male family members; the freedom to live without military occupation and violence; and the freedom to practice Islam in expressive, nonconventional ways and still be respected as a Muslim woman. There was a mutual sharing of stories that resulted in the development of both emotional and political bonds between us all. These bonds have persisted over the last 2 years, maturing into strong and meaningful friendships that are sustained digitally through the internet and return visits. During our conversations in Dubai, considerable time was spent both debunking and confirming stereotypes of black women (especially African-American women) as "strong," and Muslim women as "religious" and "devout." Consistent effort was made between all of us to expose and critique racializing discourses that are rooted in anti-black/anti-Arab/anti-Islamic attitudes, policies, and state practices. Especially important was the need to distinguish between Arab culture and Islam. Our conversations were consciousness-raising sessions for us all.

18.5 Theoretical Framework

I employ a transversal theoretical framework to explore blackness and black femininity in Dubai. Transversality, as I am using it here, refers to a particular identity that coalesces with two or more other similar, yet distinct, identities within the same place or geographic locale over extended periods of time. Transversality is different from intersectionality. Intersectionality is based upon the intersection of two or more coherent identity categories or structures of domination that come together to

---

Bakari Kitwana has called the "hip hop generation," young people who came of age during the maturation of neoliberalism. Born between 1965 and 1985, the hip hop generation has had to deal with the roll-back of the welfare state under Margaret Thatcher and Ronald Reagan and the widening gaps between haves and have-nots, the decades long vilification of young black and Arab men as "criminals" and "terrorists" respectively.

forge a specific location based upon race, gender, class, nation, and other relevant axes of social differentiation (See for instance, Crenshaw and Peller 1995; Berger and Guidroz 2009; Isoke 2013).

Alternatively, transversality refers to the relational context that occurs when two or more similar structures of identification produced by differential racialization converge in the same locale. I argue that blackness should be understood as a transversal political identity, rather than one that is static or homogeneous. Collins (2000) explains, "transversal politics requires rethinking of cognitive frameworks used to understand the world and to change it. Transversal politics require rejecting the binary thinking that has been so central to oppression of race, class, gender, sexuality and nation" (p. 245).

Following Collins, I theorize blackness as a relational identity that is reproduced by the use of hip-hop as a resistive cultural and political practice. In other words, I argue that blackness gets made and remade through what Gilroy (2005) describes as "proliferating encounters with otherness" that form the everyday context of globalization. Hip-hop—for at least two generations of young people coming of age in late modernity—often serves as the context through which young people are exposed to the black or "blackened" other. As such, it makes sense to think about blackness as shifting mode of identification that is produced by the travel of bodies and narratives about blackness. Within a transversal framework, we can better trace how understandings and practices of blackness morph within and around hip-hop as a discursive site. Throughout my fieldwork, I learned to recognize diverse iterations and manifestations of both hip-hop and blackness, while learning to "shift and to pivot as an ongoing aspect of methodological practice" (Pryse 2000, p. 112). For example, while I brought my particular "rootedness" in black culture and politics and investments in black feminism, I had to learn to be strong and agile enough to work while "suspended across cultural gaps" in order to facilitate the development and exchange of knowledge across cultural, geopolitical, intellectual boundaries (Yuval-Davis 1999).[2]

Taking this shifting methodological stance, my portrayal and analysis of black womanhood is constituted through my personal, political, and intellectual interests in hip-hop and politics and time spent building relationships with black-identified women in Dubai. Subsequently, any knowledge about "blackness" women was produced dialogically—through exchange and multidirectional communication. Blackness within a transversal knowledge-making process indicated more than just skin color and phenotype; it also acted as a rhetorical strategy used to make sense of being a minoritarian subject (some times of African-descent and other times not).

---

[2] I write as a feminist, transdisciplinary scholar. I seek to transcend the false demarcations produced by disciplinary territorialism. Instead, taking the lead from M. Jacqui Alexander (2005), I am more concerned with the "imperative of making the world in which we live intelligible to ourselves—in other words teaching ourselves" (6) rather than teaching white dominated, and historically racist and racializing academic disciplines about black women's culture and politics. Toward this aim, I both center and contribute to the intellectual-activist itineraries of feminists who have advocated for the decolonization of the academy, the de-territorialization of disciplines, and the inclusion of voices from the global margins.

In other words, blackness was short hand for expressing feelings of otherness, discontent with and tacit opposition to the political status quo, and the prolonged experience of alienation and secondhand citizenship in relation to the dominant class in the city. This spontaneous appeal to blackness during our conversations enabled the negotiation of multiple social boundaries and identities including but not limited to blackness, femaleness, "Middle-Eastern," "American," and "hip-hop" (Rose 1994). In Dubai, transversality occurred when I, an African-American woman, came face-to-face with other black-identified women who experience blackness in distinctive ways as a result of ongoing and somewhat paralleling histories of racialization—mine in the USA and theirs, in the Arabian Gulf. The enactment of transversal politics required a shared and collaborative storytelling, as a well as a sustained commitment to insistently interrogate structures of power and marginality that frame knowledge-producing dialogues (Yuval-Davis 1999). Within the context of hip-hop, transversal politics emphasizes both the resonances and limitations and opportunities for knowledge-making that emerge through neoliberalizing social, political, and economic configurations in different parts of the world (Spence 2011; Osumare 2007). It also provides a more honest self-reflexivity about how one can go about creating knowledge, meanings, and enactments of black feminism across geographic locales in ways that are grounded, interpretative, and deeply contextual.

Speaking about blackness in the Middle East is not without its risks. First, the historic relationship between Africans and Arabs is shaped by centuries of enslavement which, not surprisingly, coincided with the dissemination of Islam in Africa (Mirzai et al. 2009). By the seventeenth century, blackness of skin/Africanness became virtually synonymous with slaves or *abid* (Hunwick and Powell 2002; Segal 2001). Historically, acceptance into Islamic communities via conversion to Islam was essential for inclusion, status, and social recognition in the conquered regions of north and west Africa (Ghazal 2009). The violent history of the importation of African bodies to the Arabian Gulf, and the conquering of territories across northern Africa by Arabs is more easily forgotten than remembered in a region of the world that publically prioritized obeisance to *sharia* and the Islamic *hadiths* over skin color, yet privately discriminated against people of African descent in business transactions, marital and inheritance practices, and other areas of everyday life (Mirzai et al. 2009; Hunwick and Powell 2002; Segal 2001). With this said, the liberatory *potential* of Islam (both historically and in contemporary times) to transgress the limitations of human identitarianism—including race, phenotype, and highly restrictive modalities and practices of nationalism and citizenship—must be fully appreciated in order to understand how the comingling of hip-hop and Islam fuel cultural resistance among women of color in the Arab world. Today hip-hop provides room for a critical remembrance of this (living) history of racial subordination, enabling young women to openly speak about how "blackness" itself still shapes the experience of living as a Muslim woman in a region that is ethnically heterogeneous, yet operates within a consolidated field of theocratic state practices that claim not to "see" race.

Dubai is a highly diverse metropolitan area that attracts immigrants from all over the world. Dubai is part of an Arab coastal kingdom nestled between Saudi Arabia,

Qatar and Oman, and the Arabian Gulf. According to the Dubai government, in 2011 the total population of Dubai was 1,675,906. Emirati citizens make up just over 7% of the population in the city. The rest of the population (1,552,111) is compromised of non-citizen migrant workers from all over the world. In 2005, 51% of the city's resident migrant workers were from India, 16% from Pakistan, 11% from Bangladesh and Sri Lanka, and 11% from Arab countries, 7% from Africa, and less than 2% from the USA and Europe (Elsheshtawi 2010). White Europeans and Americans are granted visas to work in highly skilled white-collar jobs in corporate satellite offices and universities. However, migrant workers from India, Pakistan, Philippines, and Africa are typically granted visa to work as taxi drivers, construction workers, and even lower paying jobs like cooks and servers in restaurants and hotels, and as domestic laborers (i.e., nannies, housekeeping, and janitors).

18.6 Findings

I begin my analysis with my dialogue with Rafiyah and her mother Zenaib. When I interviewed Rafiyah Karimi a.k.a. "Miss Lyrical Nuisance," she was a 29-year-old Sudanese spoken word artist raised by her mother who was widowed in her late thirties. Thabiti and I interviewed Rafiyah and her mother, Zenaib, jointly at Rafiyah's request, in their apartment in Dubai. In 1975, at age 19, Rafiyah's mother, Zenaib, moved to UAE from Sudan. She and her husband moved to Dubai in search of "freedom from the pressure of family." I found this somewhat strange because Zenaib initially described her family as "very liberal, very intellectual. My mother was a teacher before she became a housewife, and my father was a chief accountant. They spoke good English." She also described her father as "liberal" because she and her husband were able to marry without too much interference from male relatives. Zenaib recalled, "I went to my father and said, 'Dad, I love him!' and he said okay and let us marry."

Zenaib and her husband chose the UAE for not only the opportunity to get a pay job but because, "Dubai was a good place for entertainment. You know, we were thinking at that time that Sudan was not the right place for us. We liked music, we liked clubs!" Zenaib was married for nearly 5 years before giving birth to her first child. During those years she and her husband worked in Dubai and lived a very "contemporary lifestyle." She proudly proclaimed that she was "one of the first Sudanese women in Dubai to drive a car." During the interview Zenaib showed us photos of herself during her twenties. At the end of our interview, Zenaib shared old pictures of herself. At first she was very reluctant to do so, as she is now covered, and did not find it appropriate to revel in photos of herself uncovered. However, after so many laughs and tears, several cups of tea, dates, and fresh fruits, she decided it was okay. In the pictures she showed us she sported a bouffant hairstyle styled to look like blown-out Afro. In one she wore colorful button-up shirts with elegant butterfly collars. She flashed long, thickly mascaraed eyelashes with dramatically arched eyebrows and brilliant eye shadow to match. This came as no surprise as

Zenaib donned a burgundy and black, fringed head scarf with her abaya for our interview.[3]

Zenaib fondly remembered attending several R&B concerts in Dubai, including Diana Ross and the Supremes and Boney M. She hummed and re-sang tunes by Al Green, Isaac Hayes, and the Temptations to help her remember the artists she followed closely during that time. Blues music especially resonated with her. When I asked her why, she explained, "You feel like you are listening to Sudanese music, it was…part of my identity. The hits and the rhythms…it affects you. It feels like you are listening to Sudanese music; and also, because it was black music. I liked it because they are black. I am black! I like it!" In our time spent together, we found out that Zenaib was a poet. She composed what her daughter described as "classical Arabic poetry" throughout her life. They were simple, rhythmic poems, interlaced with lyrical embellishments that showcased the beauty and tenderness of the Arabic language or what Thabiti and I interpreted as "soul."

Zenaib's daughter, Rafiyah, clearly shared her mother's love of "blackness" and poetry, although she attributed much different meanings and practices to these concepts. Mother and daughter signified differently, both imbuing different cultural and temporal locations and imperatives to their appreciation of black music. While Zenaib admired black American culture, she did not tell the story of her life through its signifying practices. Instead, her affinity for black American musicality was more closely tied to her yearning to be understood as a *Sudanese Arab*. Alternatively, Rafiyah has spent most of her entire life living in a small apartment in Dubai. With this said she is not, nor will she likely ever be, a citizen of the UAE. She is a citizen of Sudan. The only way that a female can become citizen of Dubai is through legal marriage to an Emirati male. Since Rafiyah married a Sudanese man, she will always be beholden to her work visa and guaranteed through the sponsorship of her husband's employer. Although Rafiyah lives and works in Dubai, her work visa must be renewed every 3 years in order to remain in UAE legally.

Rafiyah's first experience with understanding that she is "black" occurred when she was 9 or 10 years old. She recalled, "I attended school in Dubai. Sometimes kids would tease me. I remember one day a young boy came up and asked, "Why are you black?" Rafiyah was shocked because before then she only understood herself to be "Sudanese" and "Muslim." This experience came as some surprise. Rafiyah was raised not to think about or acknowledge the significance of skin color, let alone "race." While her mother had a deep affinity for black music, Rafiyah believed that Zenaib was in denial about how antiblack racism from lighter skinned Arabs impacted her experiences while growing up. Zenaib, whose father and ancestors were Egyptian and Saudi and migrated to Sudan, considered herself "Arab." However, in the minds of others blackness indicated difference, if not blatant inferiority, because her "Arabness" was placed into question.

In contrast, Zenaib made a point of letting us know that she was often mistaken as an "Egyptian," which was code that she could pass as "Arab" which confirmed a

---

[3] An abaya is a long black robe that is commonly worn by some women in Muslim countries mainly in the Arabian Gulf.

sense of belonging and, perhaps even, entitlement. Her looking "Egyptian" was reference to her fair skin and loosely curled hair texture. Zenaib's perspective became a point of contention between the mother and daughter during our conversations. Rafiyah, who would likely be described as "brown skinned" by black women in the USA, had a heightened awareness of her darkness, although she was essentially taught by her parents that her blackness was not real. Rafiyah did not understand how to consciously articulate her "blackness" until she immersed herself in hip-hop music. Incidences of what black Americans would plainly call "racism" were explained by both Rafiyah's mother and her father (before he died) as the "moral lapses in wrong-headed individuals." In other words, racist comments and taunts were explained as examples of individuals not being "good Muslims." Rafiyah recalled an incident, when she was 10 years old, of her father going up to the school and confronting the boy about the shaming of his daughter. As she related the story, Rafiyah's father explained to her that in the Qur'an, and throughout history, Islam was a religion that did not distinguish between "the races," but only between the devotion of Muslims and the commitment to practice the Five Pillars of Islam.[4] However, as a school girl, Rafiyah faced taunts and questions from her classmates about why she was a different color than her mother, and why her "neck was black." As a result, Rafiyah's relationship to "blackness," vis-à-vis her relationship to African-American music, was different from her mother's. Rafiyah explained, "The difference between my mom's generation and my generation is that we relate more to African American music because of the racism we felt here. But with my mom's generation there was no racism. Black people and their music, for them, was about pure enjoyment and beauty. But for us it was more of like a salvation, freedom thing. We were the ones who actually went through the racism in this country. We've undergone a lot of racism from Arabs of different nationalities."

Throughout the interview there was clear generational tension about significance of relationship between Zenaib's generation and Rafiyah's generation and the role that "blackness" played in their cultural/social identities. For Zenaib, racism was not particularly salient. She felt respected and honored as an Arab Sudanese woman in the UAE. Somehow, R&B affirmed her "Sudanese" identity. Alternatively, Rafiyah felt that she was frequently harassed because of her dark skin along with her family's fragile class status. When her parents left Sudan, they also left the honor and status that came from being part of a wealthy "Arab" Sudanese family. In Dubai, Rafiyah's family was basically working class. The fact that Rafiyah attended private school and college was culturally and socially irrelevant, except to the extent that it improved her ability to marry into a "good" (read Arab) family. While one was free to consume, consumption did not necessarily transfer into social clout. In Dubai, if you are not Emirati then you are just a "visitor." Even if a person is born or a permanent, lifelong resident they are still guaranteed few, if any, political or civil rights.

---

[4] The Five Pillars of Islam are (1) Shahada: To know and believe that there is one God, and that Muhammud (Peace Be Upon Him) is God's messenger, (2) Salat: To pray five times a day facing Mecca in Saudi Arabia, (3) Sawm: To fast and pray diligently during the Holy Month of Ramadan from sun up to sun down, (4) Zakat: To provide a portion of one's income to charity, (5)Hajj: To make a pilgrimage to the holy city of Mecca.

For Rafiyah, hip-hop music and culture offered a dynamic cultural space to speak out against the antiblack colorism in Dubai that was often subtly and not so subtly practiced by wealthy and lighter skinned Emiratis, and those who could afford to assimilate into the wealth driven culture of the city. In the UAE, Emiratis are both the bearers and cultural and economic beneficiaries of Khaleeji culture, others were simply guests—temporary, permanent or, like Rafiyah, somewhere in between. Rafiyah's poetry focuses on the hyper-materialism of Arab culture in Dubai. In "Let it Be Told—Collecting Sense to Make Change" Rafiyah contrasts worship of wealth and consumption in Arab Khaleeji as practiced in Dubai to the deep spiritualism of Islam.

> Why has materialism substituted spiritualism as a religion?
> And why can't we petition against politicians
> Who have turned us into slaves
> in a decaying political system?
> "Divinity" and soul prostitution,
> Blinded in mental destitution
> Why has the media become a parenting institution?
> This is neither philosophy nor rhetoric.
> This rhyme is not meant to be a mnemonic.
> Open your mind and embrace the logic.
> Permit the goodness within to shine
> Compassion, faith, and integrity are a wise man's shrine.

In "Let it Be Told," Rafiyah works through the alterity of black cosmopolitan subjects who live in hyperdeveloped urban landscapes without formal political voice. For her, hip-hop becomes a way to forge and enact forms of cultural citizenship that are built upon critique of urban neoliberalization in unexpected places. As a Sudanese poet, her agency hinges upon the sharing of new and evolving histories of displacement, while quietly yet insistently pushing for achievement of quotidian literacies that enable young people to articulate civic, cultural, political, and spiritual intellectualisms that open up the possibilities for translocal solidarities (Gilroy 2005). For Rafiyah, hip-hop is not simply about mimesis and repetition that so often structure popular rap music, rather, it is a way to question the logics of late capitalism in ways that articulate local desires for voice and belonging. In her music, she publically asks questions that Sudanese migrant workers and their children are not allowed to ask. She uses hip-hop to speak against Dubai's alienating and hostile social and spiritual landscapes that are created by the intersection of antiblack sentiments and neoliberalism. As an expectant mother, Rafiyah wants to impart her love of hip-hop onto her children. Ironically, while Rafiyah was deeply skeptical of what she called "patriarchal Arab culture" she, like her mother, has a deep affinity for the Arabic language. For her, Arabic language is a way to instill reverence for her and her husband's imaginings of Sudan as their true "home" and "culture."

I saw a publicity image of Lynn "Malikah" Fatouh before I met her. On her CD cover image she was wearing shorts, sitting spread eagled, and looking defiantly at the camera. I was shocked that most of our conversations were focused on Islam, her staunch and unapologetic commitment to end the Israeli occupation in Palestine, and her insistence that she "is the Queen of Arab Hip Hop"! In person, Lynn was short, slender, and had the demeanor of a college activist. However, once we began smoking shisha and chatting, our conversation turned into a lively political discussion that touched on issues of imperialism, militarism, and misogyny in Arab culture. We first met in the terrace lounge of a luxurious hotel in downtown Dubai. The hotel atrium was elaborately decorated with creamed colored roses, tiger orchids, and gentle pools of cool water. The air smelled of candles, fresh cut flowers, and burning oils of blended patchouli and lavender. The terrace was lit only by candlelight and our lounge sofa was less than 50 ft from the Arabian Gulf, and Malikah's story was center stage.

Malikah, is half-Lebanese and half-Algerian. She grew up in a town near the Lebanon-Israeli border. She is fair skinned, and could easily pass as white. That is, until she starts talking. She spoke with a strong Lebanese Arabic accent that was often interlaced with slang with origins in AAVE. From her perspective, the western world has basically "declared war" on both Islam and the Palestinian people. Her music talks explicitly about the lives taken by Israeli bulldozers, the Israeli rockets that often flew into parts of Lebanon that inevitably kill and maim civilians, and the world community's active complicity in sanctioning human rights abuses against Palestinians. To her, the US occupations in Iraq and Afghanistan were wholly unjustified because the perpetrators of the 9/11 attack "were terrorist [...] extremists. The Iraqi people had nothing to do with that. Muslims are peaceful people. We don't go and start wars with other countries...Why do Americans hate us? Muslims used to look up to Americans and respect Americans." This, however, was clearly no longer the case. Our conversations touched on questions of Americans complicity in the ongoing "war" against Muslims, and the myths and stereotypes of Muslim women and African-American women.

Malikah was proud to have produced two records and to have received regional and international notoriety and respect for her lyrical skills. She performs uncovered often wearing jeans, a bandana, and or a cap with big hoop earrings. While Malikah wears makeup, it is usually sweated off because she is such an energetic and aggressive vocalist. In previous years, Malikah sang hooks for other male rappers, but was determined to claim and celebrate her own prowess on the microphone. She understands her role as a woman in hip-hop and showing young women and girls—and men—that women can be "strong" and "powerful" and "in control." Malikah takes pride in dominating male rappers in freestyle competitions and in her own ability to work with and employ other women to now sing hooks for her. Malikah also has a deep and passionate commitment to Islam and the Arab language. She often weaves her own gender progressive interpretation of passages of the Qur'an into her lyrics. For Malikah, hip-hop is about "Resistance. It is all about resistance, to patriarchy, to war, to suffering. Hip hop is about trying to start a revolution to stop the oppression of people."

Malikah's music takes a strong stance against the abuse and subjugation of women both in Arab culture and in mainstream hip-hop culture. In her words, her music "seeks to empower women and girls to be strong and to be all of who they are." Part of her project includes preserving young people's knowledge, use and reverence of the Arabic language. The Emirates, like other countries in the region, conduct formal schooling either in Arabic (in public schools) or in English (in most private schools). As a result, young peoples' knowledge about and proficiency of the Arabic language is quickly waning. Malikah now only raps in Arabic, which forced her to study and master the intricacies of the language—its registers, its cadences and its localized stylist conventions as she performs throughout the Middle East. While Malikah deeply respects American artists, she feels that it is important to instill pride in being Arab. She declared, "I'll start rapping in English when English rappers start rapping in Arabic! Although we love American hip hop, we have our own stories to tell and our own histories to learn. Young people, especially girls, have to learn how to love and respect themselves." Her cultural resistance involved encouraging girls and young women to critique Arab sexist and patriarchal practices in the name of Islam—in its language and culture.

We went on to discuss stereotypes about black women. From Malikah's perspective, African-American women like Beyoncé and Rihanna represented "the most beautiful people on earth." However, when I pointed out that we are also the least likely group of women to be married, the tenor of the conversation shifted. Thabiti and I were raised by single mothers. Unlike Thabiti and me, Malikah (and Sara whom I will discuss later) had the privilege of growing up in relatively stable upbringings unmarked by extreme poverty. This was evidenced in their ability to trace their family histories over many generations, and tie their culture to a particular place. Thabiti and I talked a lot about the alienation from family and community which was a result of our mothers moving around the country to find a good job and safe community to live in. While Arab women were often surveilled by male family members, many African-American women spent time disconnected from their families, often only seeing them a few times per year. This is especially true for first generation college students from working poor families. In fact, as Thabiti and I explained, what was often interpreted as "black women's strength" is more often a sign of us having to cope with so much social and economic vulnerability on a daily basis, rather the rather romanticized celebration of strength that is promoted in the media. Especially, embarrassing and awkward was our need to debunk the broadly circulated stereotypes of black women as "bitches," "hos," and "gold-diggers" who wielded our sexuality for the sake of our own economic advancement. What became clear throughout the evening was that our understanding of each other's culture and positionality is sharply mediated by racial stereotypes that circulate in global media.

As we became more absorbed into Malikah's deep and passionate articulation for justice in Palestine, it became clear that it was more than fiery rhetoric and nationalist extremism—rather her story unfolded within the context of a longstanding family history and culture that is tied to the land of Palestine. At face value, the deployment of "blackness" as a political identity was used to showcase the problems of the powerless that is undergirded by a ferocious critique that "liberal democracy" fails to acknowledge and respect long histories of violence and land dispossession. However, her claiming of blackness goes deeper than this, signaling a deep sense of solidarity between Africans Americans who had, in her mind, managed to successfully stand up and challenge racial oppression in the USA. In our conversations, hip-hop was the language that was used to articulate, debate, and affirms diverse modes of "black" politics, perspectives, and positionalities.

Of all the women I spent time with in Dubai, I developed the closest relationship with Sara Nasar. At the time, Sara was 25 years old, she was 5 months pregnant, and was only married for 7 months. Sara is half-Palestinian and half-African American. She has golden brown skin, wavy black hair with auburn highlights, and deeply set black eyes. Her father is a wealthy Palestinian businessman and her mother a working-class black woman who lives in Kansas. Sara speaks AAVE and Arabic fluently. She was taken from her mother when she was 1 year old and raised as a Palestinian Muslim by her father and his second wife. Sara has lived in Lebanon, Kuwait, Saudi Arabia, the USA, Russia, and Dubai. She now lives in Kuwait. She is a US citizen; however she married a Russian to appease her father. Sara is a songstress who provides the seductive, throaty vocals of urban lounge music and Arabic hip-hop. Her voice is a deep and sultry contralto. Her style can be described as blues melodies on top of house beats. She writes many of her own songs; however, she collaborates with Malikah and other producers by singing hooks (the choruses to hip-hop songs) to keep a steady flow of income while she struggles to get a record deal of her own.

Sara and I became very close during my time spent in Dubai. I learned that Sara is a survivor of a severely abusive relationship and had recently entered into a marriage of convenience. With this said, she is very proud of the extravagant wedding she planned with her father. She showed us pictures of her stunningly wearing a snug fitting white wedding gown, standing with her beautiful younger sisters and her debonair father. While she took extreme pleasure in the visuals of her wedding ceremony and reception, she was scared to death of marriage, particularly the prospect of having to move permanently to Russia with her husband.

Sara quit her job as a marketing analyst shortly after getting married and finding out that she was pregnant. In her mind, her marriage secured her dowry, and ensured that she would continue to enjoy the patronage of her father. During her pregnancy she continued to write and record music, collaborating with Malikah. However, she stayed with her father in a large compound in the wealthier section of Dubai. While living with her father, she enjoyed the assistance of housekeeper, a luxurious home, and access to the family Hummer. While on her own, with or without her husband, she lost any and all privileges associated with her father's wealth and good name. She was tethered to her father, and her father used her husband to keep her firmly under his control. Sara wanted desperately to live in Dubai, to escape her husband's increasingly violent outbursts and what she described as his "shady business practices." However, her father would not permit her to stay in Dubai without her husband. Without her father's permission and without a work visa, Sara had to either go back to the USA or go back to Russia to her husband. In 2012, she left her husband and moved to Kuwait with her aunt. She is now recording her second album. After leaving Dubai, Sara and I spoke regularly about our relationships, especially the way our economic standing compromised our ability to be happy and secure. When we first met, Sara was pregnant and vulnerable, while at the same time defiant and brave. She spoke eloquently and passionately about her situation, and was determined to live the best of both worlds at all costs. Sara's fragile economic standing was tied to her consistently defying her father's wishes—trying but failing to place her own needs over his demands.

Sara wrote songs about getting hit by her lover and wanting to stay through heartbreak, and infidelity. She envied my ability to be "independent," to be a "single mom and a professor," but was simultaneously afraid of that independence. She understood that if she left her husband—she would also leave behind her father's blessings and most likely end up as a black single mother in Arkansas, or a severely isolated black, Muslim woman in Russia. While she was raised as "Arab," her affinity for her black "American roots," including hip-hop, marked her as an oppositional "bad girl" to be reigned in and put in her place. Sara, who was close to her mother via Skype and cell phone calls, was often challenged to break away from her bad relationships and to take the necessary risks to establish her independence. However this move would require that she forsake all privileges that were associated with her father's wealth and status—in fact such a move would further jeopardize the fragile contingency of her "Arabness."

Today, as a recording artist and mother of an 18-month-old boy, Sara is slowly but surely coming fully into her own self-defined womanhood. She and I continue to walk this path together. Sara and I bonded not only because we found each other culturally familiar and comforting, but because, for a time, both sacrificed our African American mothers' taste for independence and autonomy for survival in an expensive, hyper-materialist, consumer-driven culture. I did it in my first relationship with my children's father, and Sara was going through it with her new husband. We were both pregnant within a year of meeting our partners. As result, we had to reconcile our personal ambitions for success with our grudging economic dependence on men. We found that our experiences as young black women of the hip-hop generation struggling with motherhood, were quite similar although we lived over 10,000 miles away from each other. We both risked our independence to engage in ambitious and risky career endeavors—mine in women's studies studying hip-hop, and hers as an aspiring R&B vocalist in the Middle East. Predictably our conversations were personal and intimate. In September of 2012, Sara released her first single while I was editing the proofs of my first book. Hip-hop feminism was the cultural space through which this new relationship was built. Our politics consisted of building strong and resistive relationships across rigid geopolitical and cultural boundaries. We contested the alienating tendencies of neoliberalization through the building of trust, rapport, and cross-racial and cross-ethnic solidarity—something that was only achieved through the cultural rubric of hip-hop.

Conclusion

Hip-hop provides the field of engagement for personal sharing, and truth-telling about the intricacies and intimacies of blackness in a globalized world. It is a space in which we can engage and flow across our differences with passion, respect, and admiration. Hip-hop was the cipher in which a transversal politics was enacted: it was the common discourse in which we gave voice to histories and realities on our own terms without fear of condemnation or judgment—with attention paid to questions of justice, representation, recognition, and solidarity. Hip-hop, as Paul Gilroy (2005) writes, provided the "spirit of connection…that can be recycled and employed to transform our understanding of how translocal solidarity can work so that we are more informed, more sensitive, less intimidated, and more likely to act (p. 79)."

In Dubai, hip-hop is used as a space to wrestle the spiritual fruit of Islam from the dogmas of state patriarchy, and to contend with the contemporary challenges of motherhood in the hyper-material, fast-paced, and high-stress digital age. Artists like Malikah, Rafiyah, and Sara, and many others, have created a political and cultural space within hip-hop where the voices, perspectives, interests, and experiences of contemporary Middle-Eastern women can redefine the parameters of cultural resistance in places that deny the very existence of race. All women we spent time with participated in the creation of cultural spaces in their communities to transform the meanings and practice of art, politics, and activism, while redefining the contours of antiracist, antisexist, class conscious revolutionary struggle.

Hip-hop feminist ethnography created opportunities for women, especially to engage with questions of social location and identity from a translocal vantage point. The concept of transversality enabled us to situate our conversations about hip-hop within a larger context of traveling bodies and discourses about blackness and black womanhood. Furthermore, a transversal epistemological standpoint enabled us to productively interrogate how place, migration, and the search for personal, intellectual, political fulfillment could be actualized through conversations about hip-hop (broadly construed) and our life's work as resistant hip-hop cultural practitioners. We opened some very important new questions for further research in the Middle East, and particularly Dubai. These questions include: Will hip-hop generation women be content with the lack of formal political representation in Arab states? Will "blackness" as a social and political identity remain a useful marker to call attention to patterns of racialized poverty, urban containment, and political disenfranchisement among new generations of people of color in the Arab world? Finally, how will blackened hip-hop generation Arab women incorporate their love and appreciation of hip-hop music and culture into their approaches to motherhood? While answers to these questions remain outside the purview of this chapter, they are well within the project of transversal feminist ethnography. These are the kinds of questions that will provide insight into the lives and perspectives of emerging generations of multinational, multiethnic black-identified women all over the world. This work will provide new ways of understanding the emergence and consolidation of cultural identities vis-à-vis cultural citizenship, as well as demonstrate how art itself can be a springboard into telling new stories about place, politics, and cultural resistance among diverse women in the Global North and South, including especially women in the Arab world.

Finally, this provides a glimpse into the cultural and social minefields that are produced by largely unacknowledged racial and cultural hierarchies that persist as a by-product of antiblack prejudice, US cultural imperialism, and race-based social inequities. Hip-hop continues to be a rich cultural space in which to articulate the paradoxical state of societies that claim to be colorblind, yet in both formal and informal ways, restrict the building of deep and abiding social relationships across racial and ethnic difference. As consumers and practices of global hip-hop in the academy, in studios and clubs, and in popular culture, new generations of young women are able to articulate deeply personal social grievances that arise in transnational family and society. Hip-hop provides a cultural space in which profoundly different women can in small, yet meaningful ways, make place and community in territories that deny us the rights of citizens and, as a result, full participation in the cultural landscapes of the places that we live our lives, but that we are never fully allowed to embrace as home.

References

Al-Otaibi, Gh. (2012, March). Third culture kids. *Khaleejesque Magazine.*
Brown, R. N. (2008). *Black girlhood celebration: Toward a hip hop feminist pedagogy.* New York: Peter Lang.
Berger, M. T., & Guidroz, K. (2009). *The intersectional approach: Transforming the academy through race, class, and gender.* Chapel Hill: University of North Carolina Press.
Chang, J. (Ed.). (2006). *Total chaos: The art and aesthetics of hip hop.* New York: Basic Civitas Books.
Collins, P. H. (2000). *Black feminist thought: Knowledge consciousness and the politics of empowerment* (2nd ed.). New York: Routledge.
Crenshaw, K. & Peller, G. (1995). *Critical race theory: the key writings that formed the movement.* US: The New Press. p. xxiv.
Durham, A. (2007). Home girls make some noise: hip-hop feminism anthology. In Pough et al. (Eds.) (1st ed.), *Mira Loma.* Calif.: Parker Pub. pp. 304–310.
ElSheshtawi, y. (2010). *High-Rise Dubai urban entrepreneurialism and the technology of symbolic power Cities, 27*(4), 272–284.
Eqeiq, A. (2010). Louder than the blue ID: Palestinian hip hop in Israel. In R. A. Kanaaneh & I. Nusair (Eds.), *Displaced at home: Ethnicity and gender among Palestinians in Israel.* Albany: State University of New York Press.
Fernandes, S. (2011). *Close to the edge: In search of the global hip hop generation.* London: Versa Press.
Ghazal, A. (2009). Debating slavery and abolition in the Arab Middle East. In B. Mirzai, I. M. Montana, & P. Lovejoy (Eds.), *Slavery, Islam and diaspora.* Trenton: Africa World Press.
Gilroy, Paul. (2005). *Postcolonial melancholia.* New York: Columbia University Press.
Hunwick, J., & Powel, E. (2002). *The African diaspora in the Mediterranean lands of Islam.* Princeton: Markus Wiener.
Isoke, Z. (2013). *Urban black women and the politics of resistance.* New York: Palgrave-MacMillan.
Jeffries, M. (2007). The name and game of hip hop feminism. In G. Pough, E. Richardson, A. Durham, & R. Raimist (eds.), *Home Girls, Make Some Noise!: A Hip-Hop Feminist Anthology.* Mira Loma: CA: Parker Publishing, 208–227.
Lane, Nikki. (2011). Black women queering the mic: Missy Elliot disturbing the boundaries of racialized sexuality and gender. *Journal of Homosexuality, 58,* 775–792.
Malone, C., & Martinez, P. (2010). The organic globalizer: The political development of hip-hop and the prospects for global transformation. *New Political Science, 32*(4), 441–445.
McMurray, A. (2008). Hotep and hip hop: Can black Muslim women be down with hip hop? *Meridians: Feminism, Race, Transnationalism, 8*(1), 74–92.

Mirzai, I, Montana I. M., & Lovejoy, P. (2009). Introduction: Slavery, Islam and diaspora. In B. A. Mirzai, et al. (Eds.), *Slavery, Islam and diaspora*. Trenton: Africa World Press.

Ogden, J. (2007). *Hip hop revolution: The culture and politics of rap*. Lawrence: University of Kansas Press.

Olumare, H. (2007). *The Africanist aesthetic in global hip hop: Power moves*. New York: Palgrave MacMillan.

Perry, Imani. (2004). *Prophets of the hood: Politics and poetics in hip hop*. Durham: Duke University Press.

Pryse, M. (2000). Trans/feminist methodology: Bridges to interdisciplinarity thinking. *National Women's Association Journal, 12*(2), 105–108.

Rose, T. (1994). *Black noise: Rap music and black culture in contemporary America*. Hanover: Wesleyan University Press.

Robin, w. (2007). The Koran. Penguin Classics.

Segal, R. (2001). *Islam's black slaves: The other black diaspora*. New York: Farrar, Straus and Giroux Press.

Sharpley-Whiting, D. (2007). *Pimps up, ho's down: hip hop's hold on young Black women*. New York: New York University Press.

Spence, L. (2011). *Stare in the darkness: The limits of hip hop and black politics*. Minneapolis: University of Minnesota Press.

Terkourafi, M. (Ed.). (2010). *Languages of global hip hop*. New York: Continuum International Publishing Group.

Watkins, C. (2005). *Hip hop matters: Politics, pop culture, and the struggle for the soul of a movement*. New York: Beacon Press.

Yuval-Davis, N. (1999). What is transversal politics? *Soundings*. Issue 12.

Zenzele Isoke is assistant professor of gender, women, and sexuality studies at the University of Minnesota. She is the author of "Urban Black Women and the Politics of Resistance" (Palgrave-MacMillan, 2013). Her new book project titled "Unheard Voices at the Bottom of Empire" uses a translocal approach to understanding black women's cultural activism and resistances across multiple urban sites. Her work has appeared in "Gender, Place, and Culture: A Journal of Feminist Geography," "Souls: Journal of Black Politics Culture and Society," and "Transforming Anthropology: The Journal of the Association of Black Anthropologists.

Chapter 19
Integrating People with Disabilities into Society in the UAE

Sarah Abdul-Hadi, LoriAnn Alnaizy, Bashaer Aref and Asma AlShamsi

19.1 Introduction

Persons with disabilities have often lived on the margins, with little hope of education, employment, and autonomy over their own lives. Beginning several decades ago, many Western societies began implementing laws and programs to protect those living with disabilities to ensure them the best possible lives for their situations. Currently, approximately 20 % of the world's population lives with some kind of disability (UN 2013). Unfortunately, for the disabled minority of the Gulf region, this area has consistently lagged behind in progressive reforms for disabled persons (Lawati 2011). Only recently, the United Arab Emirates (UAE) has taken important steps toward protecting the rights of disabled people with laws and public awareness programs; however, there is still much room for improvement, especially in encouraging a change in societal mentality concerning those living with disabled family members and associated stigmas. The UAE is ranked as the most desirable place to live in the Middle East (Duncan 2011). The UAE must maintain its appetite for excellence by broadening its agenda to include the needs of the disabled population. The UAE has recently taken important steps to protect the rights of disabled people through passing laws and making future commitments; therefore, their next agenda must be to correct culturally negative feelings and stigmas associated with disabled people and/or family members and to enforce current laws by holding schools and employers accountable for not following procedures concerning disabled people. The UAE needs to encourage integration and acceptance of people living with disabilities to gain a respectable stature as a progressive nation that upholds the dignity of all its citizens.

S. Abdul-Hadi (✉) · L. Alnaizy · B. Aref · A. AlShamsi
American University of Sharjah, Sharjah, United Arab Emirates
e-mail: sarah.abdulhadii@gmail.com

© Springer Science+Business Media Singapore 2015   327
R. Raddawi (ed.), *Intercultural Communication with Arabs*,
DOI 10.1007/978-981-287-254-8_19

In 1976, the World Health Organization (WHO) internationally defined the term disabilities as "any restriction or lack (resulting from any impairment) of ability to perform an activity in the manner or within the range considered normal for a human being." However, because language constitutes our world and meaning is attributed to an idea in the human mind, the definition given to disabled people back then seemed to degrade the status of a person with a disability as someone less human simply because they were less able. Nowadays, a disability simply refers to limitations and possible restrictions to an individual's activity and participation levels, and it also includes impairments, which are difficulties in body structure or function (WHO 2013). Terms once appropriate, like handicapped, retarded, or crippled, are now viewed by many societies and advocates for disabled persons as having derogative connotations and should be avoided.

Western societies have made significant progress to relieve disabled individuals from feeling like burdens on society. Hence, the WHO developed a new strategy in 2002 that included two models, the medical model and the social model, to explain the differences in specific societies concerning their outlook on disabilities. The WHO defines the two models as:

> The *medical model* views disability as a feature of the person, directly caused by disease, trauma or other health condition, which requires medical care provided in the form of individual treatment by professionals. Disability, on this model, calls for medical or other treatment or intervention, to "correct" the problem with the individual. The *social model* of disability, on the other hand, sees disability as a socially created problem and not at all an attribute of an individual. On the social model, disability demands a political response, since the problem is created by an unaccommodating physical environment, brought about by attitudes and other features of the social environment (pp. 9–10).

The WHO immediately acknowledges that neither model is sufficient on its own, and both are only partially correct because a disability is such a dynamic and complex situation. Therefore, the organization encourages bringing both models together in a "biopsychosocial model" which, in essence, combines the most prudent ideas from both plus the psychological impact on the individual as a result of the biosocial factors. The most striking aspect of this model is its focus on changing society's problems and issues in dealing with disabled people instead of the other way around. Emphasis is placed on changing the environment and cultural attitudes of a society, and furthermore, *society* needs to adapt to living with the disabled, not the disabled making all the adjustments and feeling alienated in the process; a patient becomes a citizen, and the *us-against-them* attitude of exclusion is replaced with an inclusive society of tolerance (WHO 2002).

Upon finding out that a family member or child has a disability, most people go through certain steps before ultimately accepting and acknowledging the disability, explain Hanoch Livneh and Richard F. Antonak (2005). The steps are shock, isolation, adaptation, and integration. The first step, shock, can include feelings of grief, denial, and agonizing over their self-image and associated stigmas they worry are associated with a disability. After the shock, begins the isolation phase, which can include depression, anger, and continuing anxiety over physical appearances and/or body image issues. The depression is normal when the individual must come to a realization that their disability is permanent and the magnitude of being permanently disabled settles within them. The disabled individual may fear the unknown and often lash out in anger at those responsible or even those trying to help (Livneh and Antonak 2005). Adaptation comes at varying times to people and has a lot to do with the resilience and personality of the individual. The person begins to have a restored sense of self-worth, values, and goals. Finally, the integration and adjustment phase involves refinding their place in society but now with new challenges, and sometimes a new direction in life can develop from the disability, taking the individual down a path they may never have chosen otherwise (Livneh and Antonak 2005). Whatever the way a disability is acquired, through birth, injury, or otherwise, the society in which that individual lives must acknowledge them as one that has contributions to offer instead of hiding them shamelessly out of public sight or stigmatizing them as pitiful members of society, as is often the case in the Gulf region. In response to this accusation, the government of the UAE finally became proactive and took a great step in the form of enacting laws to protect their disabled citizens.

19.2 Background

The UAE ratified the United Nations (UN) convention on the Rights of People with Disabilities; Maryam Mohammed Al Roumi signed the convention in the UN headquarters. The convention stressed that any country that ratifies it should abide by the UN laws and regulations in giving disabled individuals equal rights, opportunities, and services (Al Roumi 2008). This entails that the government will provide disabled individuals with public positions, facilities in all public administrations, and provide them with special education. In Abu Dhabi schools such as Al Noor Speech, Hearing, and Development Centre and the Future Centre have been built to accommodate disabled students. Dubai is the emirate with the largest support for disabled individuals as it has nine different schools that are the best equipped and staffed. The most prominent is Dubai Autism Center and Dubai Center for Special Needs. Although other centers exist in the remaining emirates, there is only one per emirate, or none at all ("Special Education" 2011). According to Maryam Mohammed Khalfan Al Roumi, these centers and the rising awareness "is a great achievement for this segment of society which has suffered so much in isolation, neglect and maltreatment and abuses," and the ultimate aim is to change social perception of disabled individuals from individuals in need to individuals who deserve equal rights, opportunities, and could handle the same responsibilities as a well-functioning person (Al Roumi 2008, p. 2). The UAE government realizes that the essential change is social; the need to overcome the barrier of distinguishing a disabled individual as an outsider to an insider who can participate and engage in society on an equal basis with others.

However, Arab governments recognize that this transformation is not going to be easy or fast, as Sheikha Hessa, the first Arab woman to be appointed as the UN Special Rapporteur on Disability in 2003, described: "disabled people are more marginalized and more isolated than other people. Yet, specifically in the Arab region, they are invisible, because of negative social attitudes and lack of a human rights culture" (Reinl 2008, p. 1). As noted by James Reinl (2008), a journalist of *The National,* the largest hindrance to disabled people in the Arab world is not the lack of government support for facilities but societal perception of disabilities. The obstacle remains the social attitude toward disabled people as individuals who are lacking, individuals who need help and are a burden to their families, and society as a whole. Sheikha Hessa is aware of the culture and states that change would not happen in regard to disability unless people begin to give them rights out of equality rather than pity. As long as disabled individuals are looked at as a charity case, society will continue to exclude them out of socioeconomic or political roles as they are regarded as less capable in fulfilling these roles (Reinl 2008).

19.3   Methodology

There is great need for additional information concerning societal perceptions and the extent of integration concerning the disabled in the UAE. It is equally intriguing to discover how a fairly new and progressive nation, such as the UAE, positions itself on the models of disabilities as presented by the WHO so that areas of concern can be highlighted and addressed. Primary and secondary sources are used to obtain credible information on the subject for this chapter. However, there is a lack of secondary sources available; only database articles, websites, and newspaper articles were located. Hence, our group decided to conduct two interviews and a survey in an attempt to capture local inclinations toward people with disabilities. The survey was e-based and mass distributed to university student participants. The two interviews were conducted at (1) Al-Thiqah Handicapped Club in Sharjah and consisted of interviews with a disabled member, a trainer, and the supervisor of the women's department, and (2) An Emirati mother whose son has been diagnosed with autism.

19.4   Survey Results and Discussion

In order to analyze social perception of disabilities, our group distributed surveys as primary research to examine the extent of discrimination disabled individuals encounter. We distributed our survey online and received 52 responses; the respondents were American University of Sharjah (AUS) students as well as students of Zayed University and other universities in the Emirates. The results of the surveys were not surprising; in one of the questions we asked what feelings do individuals have toward disabled people and the majority felt either empathy or gratefulness. This reveals how social stigma is still dominant and the lack of facilities and acceptance from society make many feel grateful they are not in the disabled person's shoes, as the future for disability holds no positive light. A qualitative study led by Sara Ashencaen Crabtree with the backing of the Sharjah City for Humanitarian

Fig. 19.1 Survey question 1

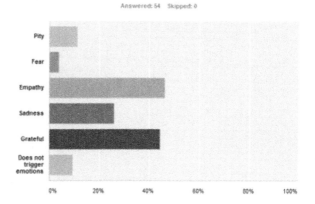

Upon coming across a physically disabled
student, what are your feelings towards
them?

Answered: 54   Skipped: 0

Services in 2007 revealed that families in the UAE who struggle with a disabled member sustain social stigma arising from the misinterpretation of religion, culture, and an overall lack of knowledge about the requirements and necessities of disabled children. A disabled child continues to be considered a disability for the whole family; families complain that having a disabled child disrupts their outings and social image (Crabtree 2007). Also, disabled individuals are constantly, directly or indirectly, devalued because of their physical appearance. The study conducted revealed a disturbing assumption made by many families with a disabled child, that a disability to some families is a curse or a test from God for their patience. This belief makes the disabled individual less of a human but more like a burden. Consequently, this mentality has damaging results in both the treatment and upbringing of a disabled child who is considered a shame to the family (Crabtree 2007). Accordingly, when a disabled child is perceived as a divine punishment it hinders a positive outlook for the child's future and the parents' role. Another problem that is common across Arab states is the gendered fault that a woman bears if she delivers a disabled child. The mother becomes responsible for raising the child, and there is a high possibility that her husband will distance himself from her in fear of her bringing another disabled child into the family (Crabtree 2007, Figs. 19.1, 19.2 and 19.3).

Survey results complemented the secondary research conducted on social perception of disabilities. Nearly 60 % of participants believed that society would have a different opinion of their family if they had a disabled family member. However, many did agree that the government is trying to provide for people with disabilities; -58 % agreed that the government has provided enough while 42 believed it is not enough. This result is not surprising, as the government continues to make substantial strides by building centers and schools; however, in terms of public facilities, the disabled are still restricted to malls and well-known hotels and universities. Therefore, life is easier for disabled people in Dubai, but not in Ras al-Khaimah where there is only a single center with minimum facilities ("Special Education" 2011). Question six on the survey reveals how much society perceives disabled

Fig. 19.2 Survey question 2

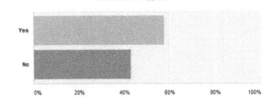

If you had a disabled family member, be it
physically or mentally, do you think society
would look differently at your family? If you
ticked 'yes' please provide reasons.

Answer Choices	Responses	
Yes	57.41%	31
No	42.59%	23
Total Respondents: 54		

Fig. 19.3 Survey question 3

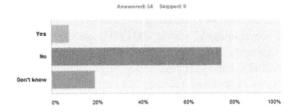

If you needed help in carrying equipment,
would you feel comfortable asking a
physically disabled student for help?

Answer Choices	Responses	
Yes	7.41%	4
No	74.07%	40
Don't know	18.52%	10
Total		54

individuals as incompetent and needing help rather than providing it. The participants were asked whether they would feel comfortable asking a disabled student if
they wanted help carrying equipment and the results showed that 75% would not
and only 6% did, while 20% said they did not know. Another revealing question
was how often the participants encounter physically or mentally disabled individuals in public places. The majority (57%) answered, rarely. This answer reflects how,
still, disabled people are not welcome in society as normal, capable human beings
who are able to contribute and make a change. This represents the ultimate challenge the government confronts, which is the removal of social stigma and discrimination that ultimately excludes a substantial portion of society from leading a
productive life (Figs. 19.4 and 19.5).

Fig. 19.4 Survey question 4

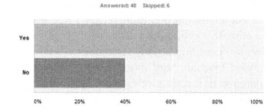

Do you think the government is doing enough to help sustain people with disabilities in the UAE If yes, provide 2 examples. If no, provide 2 suggestions as to what should be done.

Answered: 48   Skipped: 6

Answer Choices	Responses	
Yes	62.50%	30
No	39.58%	19
Total Respondents: 48		

Fig. 19.5 Survey question 5

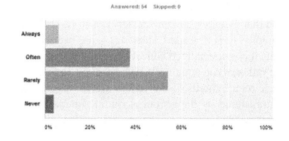

How often do you encounter physically or mentally disabled people? (Whether in university, mall, street)

Answered: 54   Skipped: 9

Answer Choices	Responses	
Always	5.56%	3
Often	37.04%	20
Rarely	53.70%	29
Never	3.70%	2
Total		54

Inclusion of Dyslexic Children in Mainstream Education in the UAE

The population of the UAE is diverse and multicultural with a large number of expatriates hailing from developed nations. The UAE prides itself as having an atmosphere that appreciates changing attitudes, especially those that seek to highlight traditionally ignored concerns, such as children with learning disabilities, autism, and physical disabilities. The UAE has taken the rights and inclusion of the disabled seriously; hence currently, the country does have an integration educational program in the official law books that mandates a right for children with special needs to achieve an education. It is, however, inadequate and mostly unenforced. Public and private schools alike do not provide a "safety net" within their curricula to detect at-risk children from an early age and reroute them to a more specialized education that will greatly increase their chances of success in school and further integrate them into society later in life. Workshops and training programs run by qualified teaching staff must be put into place by the UAE government to spot children with learning weaknesses and/or disabilities; and, just as importantly, the current law needs to be executed to the fullest extent to make inclusion a reality, as most schools do not uphold any stipulated requirements of the law, reports Carolina D'Souza in her March, 2013, *Gulf News* article.

To better illustrate the shortcomings of the Gulf region, it is relevant to compare the progress of Western nations concerning implemented integration programs. For example, in the USA, there are usually two kinds of education in an educational school system curriculum: general education and special education, explains the National Center for Learning Disabilities (NCLD) which is a long-established advocate and resource group for the disabled in the USA (2013). The American public school systems have an inclusion program through the Individuals with Disabilities Education Act (IDEA) titled, "Free Appropriate Public Education" (FAPE). FAPE ensures that every child, regardless of their abilities, is guaranteed a general education that includes specialized services to be provided for them free of charge by the school system if needed. However, it has been defined further through the court systems that a specialized education need not exceed the limits of a general education, but rather, to be equal to it. The special-needs children in return must complete the basic requirements of the school system to graduate and pass state-approved tests administered by the school at routine intervals. Hence, it is apparent that the law is intended to protect those special-needs children with an ability to learn (NCLD 2013).

FAPE began in 1975 when the "Education for All Handicapped Children Act" was implemented by law. The original act allowed for special-needs education within a short distance of the disabled child's home so that the child could remain at home and still receive an education. The result of that act still meant two different paths had to be taken to receive an education, and in two different facilities—either a normal education system or a specialized one. In 1990, the law was changed, and, thereafter, specialized education was merged into the general education system and under one roof as well. The public school system is now required to provide assistance and specialized education to the best of their abilities and to integrate children with specialized needs as much as possible into the general education program. By doing so, the child has the best possible atmosphere to grow into a self-sufficient, dignified adult. In addition to many other benefits, the normally functioning children within the school are exposed from an early age to accepting and tolerating children with special needs through integration. This method helps rid a society of many social stigmas and intolerance toward people with special needs (NCLD 2013).

Since the learning disability (LD), dyslexia, is one of the most diagnosed LDs throughout the world, it will be used as an example to underscore the difficulties that diagnosed children and their parents face in the UAE with regard to being accepted into mainstream education, and actually locating schools that are sensitive to their children's needs and accessible to all nationalities. Dyslexia is a neurological language-processing disorder that greatly affects the ability of the person to read, write, spell, and speech sometimes as well. It is a lifelong disability that affects up to 15 % of any given population in varying degrees (NCLD 2013). As previously mentioned, in 2006, the UAE government explains on its website that they have signed an optional protocol of the UN Convention on the Rights of Persons with Disabilities that guaranteed disabled people within the UAE the same rights to work and equal opportunity in the workplace and equal access to public and private schools throughout the nation as stated in the UAE government website for cultural division ("Special Education" 2011). However, the actual implementation of the law is obscure and, in most cases, ignored (D'Souza 2013). D'Souza and other professionals, like Dr. Sabah Al Lawati in her 2011 *Middle East Health Magazine* article, contend that the UAE continues to lag behind progressive nations with respect to integrating the disabled into mainstream society and taking significant steps toward removing the social stigma of being disabled. Moreover, the law does not specifically state the definition of a person with special needs, and, therefore, provides schools with an excuse to claim they do not have specialized facilities or staff to assist children with disabilities such as autism or dyslexia. They also argue that schools rarely are prepared and properly staffed to accommodate any child who fails to keep up with the other children in the classroom. Private schools have obstacles like general placement tests instead of tests specific to a child's condition that could ensure their enrollment; hence, though the law may exist, in most cases, it is not implemented. Dr. Al Lawati insists that refusing to integrate children with learning and physical disabilities leads some families, without the financial means to afford specialized centers, to keep their children at home, uneducated, and disconnected from society (Lawati 2011).

It will be extremely difficult to integrate children with learning disabilities like dyslexia until attitudes concerning the disabled change not only within society but, more specifically, also among educators who will have the task of actually integrating the children into the mainstream school system, explain Emad Alghazo and Eman Nagger-Gaad (2004). Alghazo and Nagger-Gaad conducted surveys in an attempt to explore the teachers' willingness and openness to having children with dyslexia in their classrooms alongside normally functioning children. The results of the surveys concluded that, in general, educators in the UAE had a negative attitude toward the inclusion of children with learning disabilities, preferring children with all types of other disabilities, including physical or visual, above mental/learning disabilities such as dyslexia (Alghazo and Nagger-Gaad 2004). Male and female educators were near equal in their negative attitudes toward inclusion. The general conclusion from the researchers regarding the negative feedback stems from "the idea that teachers may find it demanding to work with students with such disabilities. Specifically, working with such students requires more time and preparation for planning and the provision of teaching aids" (2004, p. 97). Interestingly, the survey revealed the most willing teachers favoring inclusion in the classroom came from two groups of teachers: Those with between 1 and 5 years experience, and those with more than 12 years of teaching experience. The researchers assume that a general acceptance of new ideas and challenges for new educators may explain their willingness to include children with disabilities. Thereafter, the more experienced group having more than 12 years experience may feel more comfortable because they are already familiar with having slower-paced children in their classrooms, and, therefore, are accustomed to dealing with different levels of learning among their pupils. Alghazo and Nagger-Gaad conclude by stressing the importance of proper training through workshops and governmental programs designed at promoting the positive factors of integration. These steps are crucial to the success of inclusion in the classroom and an overall change in attitudes toward children with special needs (Alghazo and Nagger-Gaad 2004).

The Lexicon Reading Center in Dubai (2013) echoes the recommendations of the many advocates for inclusion. They suggest simple strategies that can make a big difference to dyslexic children. They suggest teachers help the student look at words as a whole unit; phonetic learning, which is very successful for other students, does not work well for dyslexic children. Using tangible items to explain mathematical concepts works much better for them than single-digit numbers on a page or board; such traditional methods are quickly forgotten which leads to failure to learn and low self-esteem. Schools need to introduce such techniques that are geared toward helping children with dyslexia learn better and faster.

Afshan Ahmed reported for *The National* in March, 2013, that dyslexic children learn more and at a faster pace when their learning accompanies images and different colors; the addition of music helps also if the situation is appropriate. Dyslexic children find the normal task of traditional note-taking and copying very frustrating because the words seem jumbled and out of place in their minds. Using colorful images associated with new words or stories is a tremendous help to dyslexic children. Ahmed reported that simple allowances for mild-to-moderate dyslexic children, such as using different colored pens for writing, made a huge difference in their ability and in their attitude. Especially in primary schools, teachers need to be trained to know the small steps and benefits of small changes and special allowances for these children that can make the child more eager to listen and learn. Purely mechanical writing is very stressful for dyslexic children, often making the child dislike learning altogether; hence, it is vital to discover and hone skills and techniques by teachers in mainstream education that can make inclusion and integration very successful. The special-needs children and society both reap the benefits of inclusion (Ahmed 2013).

It must be acknowledged, however, that not all parents with special-needs children are advocates of the inclusion program, as was revealed in the interview with an Emirati mother of an autistic child. Their reasons are many; from fear of the child's ability to cope, to their needs not being met in the mainstream education, and many more reasons in between, they feel adamant that a special-needs child should be in a special-needs facility. This has a lot to do with the previously mentioned social model of accepting disabled people and embracing them into mainstream society. It will take time and much focused effort from the UAE government to make such parents comfortable with the decision of integration in education and to evolve the UAE society into a culture that embraces the social disabilities model of inclusion. The parents must first be assured that the teachers are qualified and the education is comprehensive. Additionally, parents must be confident that special-needs children are safe from ridicule and harassment. This will only come with a change in cultural attitudes toward the disabled.

Autism in the UAE

According to the American Medical Association (n.d), autism is defined as a mental disorder, characterized by great difficulty in communicating and forming relationships with other people and in using verbal and nonverbal language. In the UAE, there is a growing awareness regarding autism, with an increasing number of children being diagnosed with the condition every year. However, there are no official figures released. Across the world, the causes for autism remain unknown.

The Dubai Autism Center has gained recognition as one of the first and most prominent centers for autism in the UAE. In 2012, the Gulf News reported that the Dubai Autism Center had enrolled 46 students, with a waiting list of 200 children hoping to enter the school (Chaudhary 2012). In Abu Dhabi, the Emirates Autism Center faces more or less the same dilemma. Such figures are staggering in light of the fact that these centers have been the most acclaimed in the region. The centers are often to both local and expat children. However, they are still unequipped to accommodate more than half of the children in need. Sarah Ahmed Baker, head of the community service unit in the Dubai Autism Center, claimed that "autism is definitely on the rise. There is more awareness of the condition and improved diagnosis and assessment techniques so more cases are coming to light. However, the more worrying factor is that there could be an as yet unidentified reason for this rise, something psychiatrists and doctors have yet to ascertain" (Chaudhary 2012).

Parents of autistic children might find themselves facing expenses that they cannot afford. The financial burdens can add to the emotional distress and, of course, this factor can hinder a child's ability to develop. Without the necessary therapeutic treatments for children, their conditions may worsen. Thus, the lack of help may constitute further isolation from social communities at large. In addition, both of the prominent autism centers within the region are facing financial struggles, which hinders their provision of sufficient resources. The Dubai Autism Center charges each parent 30,000 DHS for the child, when the actual fee is 140,000 DHS on average per year (Chaudhary 2012). The Emirates Autism Center in Abu Dhabi charges parents 42,000 DHS, although the cost per student reaches 70,000 DHS (Chaudhary 2012). Both centers rely on donations, fund-raisers, and even government funds to cover the costs. However, they acknowledge that their budgets are never enough. The financial challenges are bound to represent significant sacrifices and shortages in the availability of essential therapy (Chaudhary 2012).

A young Emirati mother, Shaikha, sheds light on her experience as a parent with a child with autism. At the age of 25, Shaikha already had two boys. Her first-born son, Majed, was diagnosed with autism at age 3.

> People knew something was wrong because Majed always seemed detached from the other kids. I have a very supportive family," she says. "So that, for me, has helped. I haven't enrolled my child in any of these centers. (Personal Communication, April 2nd, 2013)

Shaikha was asked whether she was familiar with autism before the birth of her son.

> You know, because I have a nephew who was autistic himself, so autism is not something new for me. I've learned about autism as a teenager in school and I had gone to visit the Dubai Autism Centre. I know the symptoms. Of course, you don't want to believe it as a parent. That's not your immediate response.

When asked about the actions she took after her son had been diagnosed, she stresses her commitment to helping him.

> My husband and I took him to the United States as soon as we could. We decided to enroll him in the schools there; we spent quite a significant period of time and we definitely saw changes in Majed that we were happy with. I don't believe that the schools here are sufficient enough. I try to keep myself informed all the time; I read about the new case studies and I don't lose hope. I've experimented with my son a lot, to be honest. I've tried all the diets that have been recommended and I've tried different therapies as well.

Shaikha does imply that her attitude may not represent the majority in her society.

> I've seen too many parents in my society who just kind of gave up on their kids and never made an effort. I find it to be so irresponsible. Thankfully money isn't an issue with us, so we can afford that. My son's condition has improved so much because we never stop trying to help him grow and to give him opportunities to develop as healthily as he can. Majed has responded really well. Every little bit of effort has helped him in one way or another.

Although Shaikha believes to have seen a positive difference in her son, she acknowledges the personal challenges that she faces with him.

> It's difficult, of course. I have another son, a younger son who's not autistic, and [there are] differences in bringing them up. If your child, God forbid, has some disability, then it can consume you. My son will always need more time, more attention, more care. Communication is one of the biggest challenges.

Upon inquiry, Shaikha rejects the idea of sending her son to a school with a more inclusive educational system. She is adamant about never enrolling her child in a school that is not primarily focused on autism, as she does not believe that this would benefit her child. Her main concerns revolve around improving his autism.

> I don't want him to be in a classroom with kids who won't understand and a teacher who doesn't know how to handle it. I don't believe a school that's not focused on helping kids with special needs could benefit my son. I believe this requires proper training. He has to be in an environment that gives him the attention that he needs to grow.

Nonetheless, Shaikha finds ways to encourage her son to interact with other children in order to help him develop social skills.

> He plays with other kids who have no disabilities, because we have a large family and we are all close to our relatives, who are quite supportive. There has never been judgment. I

take him to birthday parties and I have birthday parties for my son. So I don't keep my son isolated. I try to involve him in normal activities and I take him out of the house often. Thankfully, I've never faced anything drastic. I think that largely has to do with the fact that my son has been getting excellent help early on. The earlier you start, the better.

Shaikha's relatively positive experiences reflect the way in which social and environmental factors may significantly influence parental behavioral attitudes toward their children (Mandell and Novak 2005). Her testimony affirms that the improvement of conditions as autism is contingent upon effective parenting, supportive environments, and collective concern (ibid.). Her determination to involve her son in wider familial and social spaces can be attributed to the fact that she receives regular help and support from her family (ibid.).

Physical Disabilities in the UAE

The idea of integrating the physically and mentally challenged into society is a topic of heated discussion across the world. However, particularly in developing countries, those with disabilities do not enjoy the same rights and treatment as their able-bodied counterparts. However, in the rapidly developing Gulf States, more attention has been given to this issue, and several facilities have been created to accommodate the needs of those with disabilities, to better assimilate them into society. In a study conducted by Lamya Abedin from Tanmia, the National HR Development and Employment Authority, a 2002 census showed more people in the UAE suffer from physical disabilities (63 %) than from mental ones (19 %), with sight, speech, and hearing impairments making up 45 % of the results. Physical disabilities, unlike mental ones, are most often acquired during a person's lifetime than at birth. A recent survey by the Dubai Health Authority has linked disabilities with chronic diseases and age, where 40 % of the 5000 surveyed disabled were over 60 years of age (Al Hassani 2012). These results mean that it is imperative that the UAE nation be well prepared to cater to the physically challenged, as they comprise a significant amount of the overall population.

Until recently, in the UAE, and the Middle East in general, the disabled were considered a hindrance and shunned away from society; however, significant efforts have been made to turn this around. Several facilities have been set up in different emirates to provide their disabled residents with much-needed services. An example of such a facility is Nadi Al-Thiqah for Handicapped, located in Sharjah. The club offers persons with disabilities, from all nationalities, free access to intellectual and sports services. Established by Her Highness Jameela Al-Qasimi, the club offers lessons in Quran recitation and storytelling, as well as several physical activities such as strength sports, throwing and running, swimming, and Boccia (Personal Communication, April 9, 2013). Most of the members at the club were physically disabled, with sight and hearing impairment being the most common forms of disability (Personal Communication, April 9, 2013); these facts correspond to the results of the census.

A common misconception concerning the disabled is that they do not pursue an education/career, nor do they marry; yet, the staff at the club denies this myth and emphasizes the importance of early intervention in determining the life of a disabled person. They explained that one of their physically challenged female members recently got married to an able-bodied partner and that several of their members are employed (Personal Communication, April 9, 2013). Samira Azmi, an instructor at the club, explained that it is important to provide moral support to the disabled person, so as they are psychologically able to handle their situation and are therefore motivated to achieve. Public figures such as Jessica Cox and Nick Vujicic, who appeared on the BBC News and TedXTalks video series, further testify to this theory; both explain that the psychological well-being of a physically disabled person is in direct correlation to their accomplishments. Cox was the first licensed armless pilot, and can drive a car, play piano, as well as Taekwondo (Brown 2013). She has a degree in Psychology and is married to her former instructor, which further dismisses the misconceptions that disabled people do not marry or receive an education. On the other hand, Vujicic (2012) states he was the first physically challenged student to be integrated into the mainstream educational system in Australia and is a university graduate with a double major. He contends that unconditional love and support from family members, especially parents, is vital to increasing the self-confidence of disabled persons (Vujicic 2012).

When asked about inclusive education, Salmana Abdel-Baqi, the manager of the women's section of Nadi Al-Thiqah Club, explained that this was a great method to implement in UAE schools, as long as the teachers were patient and trained to understand the needs of disabled students (Personal Communication, April 9, 2013). She mentioned that early intervention is the key to helping those with disabilities, in order to build their confidence and teach them independence from an early age. This corresponds to the results of the survey conducted by the Dubai Health Authority, which linked functional disabilities to education (Al Hassani 2012). Among the behavioral problems of students with special needs are violence and excessive shyness, which need to be handled by experts (Personal communication, April 9, 2013). Abdel-Baqi also states that inclusive education is more likely for the physically disabled than the mentally disabled (Personal Communication, April 9, 2013).

The physically disabled comprise a small percentage of the UAE labor force, where most are concentrated at the bottom of the hierarchical pyramid. In a 2002 survey conducted by Lamya Abedin from Tanmia, the National HR Development and Employment Authority, a total of 30 employees with varying disabilities were interviewed about their roles at their companies. Of these employees, 40% worked in clerical positions, 33% in auxiliary positions, as opposed to only 3% as managers, and 7% as senior officers (Abedin 2002). Clerical positions include basic tasks in the office, such as typing, reporting, and scheduling. Auxiliary workers are considered additional help, and carry out tasks such as stamping documents, record keeping, and delivering messages. These jobs do not demand any particularly advanced skills and do not pose a challenge to those with disabilities. A similar trend was observed with members at Nadi Al-Thiqah, where most were employed in the fields of pottery, farming, carpentry, cooking, and sewing (Personal Communication, April

9, 2013). This is likely because most companies are not equipped to hire disabled persons, due to the lack of facilities incorporated at their buildings (Abedin 2002). These include wide corridors and lifts, as well as toilets and parking spaces specifically designed for the disabled. The deaf–mutes are particularly affected in the employment sector, as most companies believe hiring them will lead to communication problems (ibid.).

At the schools in the UAE, significant efforts must be made to ensure that the needs of disabled students are met. In order for inclusive education to be implemented, schools must provide all the necessary building facilities for easy transportation, as well as invest in high-tech equipment, such as electrical wheelchairs and walkers (Abedin 2002). In the UAE, most physically disabled prefer to study abroad, especially in places with more accessible public transportation (ibid.).

A largely ignored, yet important, aspect to consider is the use of language in the description of persons with physical disabilities. Words such as retarded, crippled, and handicapped have become recently unacceptable in the West due to their negative associations. In their book *Understanding Disability: Inclusion, Access, Diversity, and Civil Rights*, associate professor of literacy education Cynthia Bowman and manager for research development Paul Jaeger (2005) wrote that handicapped is derived from "cap in hand," which is an old English term for begging. Yet in the East, where English is often not the first language, this word continues to be used in formal translations to refer to matters of the disabled; this is true of Nadi Al Thiqah for Handicapped, and others. This also brings to mind the issue of colloquial Arabic using the word *mo'awaq* (literally "hindered" as an insult, and how Gulf culture casually refers to persons with Down syndrome as "Mongolian" (Personal Communication, April 9, 2013). Moreover, services for the disabled are usually categorized under charities, which is problematic. For example, Barbara Ibrahim and Dina Sherif (2008), directors of John D. Gerhart Center, mention that Beit Al-Khair in the UAE, and Charity Foundation in Qatar, offer aid for the disabled. While this is a positive gesture, it continues to encourage the long-held stereotype of associating pity and charity with those who are disabled, which was discussed by Dr. Tenbroek and Dr. Matson in their article The Disabled and the Law of Welfare (1966). In order to fully integrate the disabled into society, it is important that society is made aware of the impact of linguistics.

19.5 Limitations

The main difficulty we encountered during our research was the general lack of information on the topic of disabilities in the region, which forced us to depend more on primary sources than secondary ones. We noticed a severe lack in anthropological and sociological data, as well as quantitative data and statistics; official information available to the public was either outdated or vague. Furthermore, the topic is traditionally considered a social taboo, and this was reflected in our interviewees "requests for anonymity."

19.6   Recommendations

The following section suggests methods that the UAE government and society at large could implement within its country, to better accommodate the needs of individuals with disabilities and ease their integration into society.

Raising Awareness In an article from Gulf News, journalist Huda Tabrez (2009) states that many individuals in UAE society do not feel confident interacting with persons with disabilities. In order to fully assimilate the disabled into society, individuals should be made aware of the more empathetic ways to communicate with and behave around a person with disabilities. Schools and media can play a major role in educating members of society on this topic, and the UAE should take full advantage of these methods.

Grant System and Funding In her research paper, Abedin (2002), from the Tanmia National HR development and Employment Authority, explains that businesses and schools will be more encouraged to provide facilities for the disabled, if the government assists in the costs. In order to fully provide for the needs of disabled students and employees, schools and companies in the Gulf must invest in expensive equipment and consider the needs of the disabled in the physical infrastructure of their buildings. High-tech equipment such as electrical wheel chairs or walkers, disabled toilets and parking, as well as ramps, all must be incorporated into the environment (Abedin 2002)

Quotas Abedin (2002) gives the example of the Japanese employment quota system for the disabled, which obliges businesses to hire a certain percentage of persons with disabilities, and how this helps further integrate them into the labor force. Such quota systems could be very beneficial if applied in the UAE and other Gulf States, as they help improve society's perception of people with disabilities. These can be enforced on schools as well, to ensure a certain percentage of students with disabilities are enrolled in educational institutes. Although the UAE bill of rights for persons with disabilities, which was issued in 2006, is a good move toward an inclusive society, significant progress will not be visible unless it is made mandatory for private institutes to incorporate those with disabilities into their environments. Furthermore, it is important to integrate these laws into the education system, so that all members of society are aware of their existence.

Standardized Infrastructure It is beneficial if a standardized infrastructure was enforced on all schools and businesses, in order to accommodate the needs of those with disabilities (Abedin 2002). This includes wide corridors and elevators, toilets and parking spaces specifically designed for the disabled, as well as ramps and automatic doors.

Change Society's Viewpoint on Disabilities Throughout history, several models of disability have emerged to help steer the attitudes and policies a government and society implements with regard to its disabled. The UN encourages the social model of disability, which considers disability a social problem; thus, an individual's lifestyle is not hindered due to a physical or mental disability, but because society does not sufficiently accommodate the needs of this individual (www.un.org). This is compared with the medical model of disability, which sees persons with disabilities as being deficient and in need of charity, pity, and care (www.un.org). The social model of disability emphasizes the government's role in providing the disabled with the same quality of life that is ensured for the able-bodied population. This includes equal opportunities in the employment sector, and in education as well as enabling those with disabilities to live independent lives. The current model of disability embraced by the Gulf States is the medical model of disability, and this can be seen from the various charitable organizations that provide care for the disabled. For example, Barbara Ibrahim (2008) and Dina Sherif (2008), who are directors at the John D. Gerhert Center for Philanthropy, give the example of Beit Al-Khair in the UAE, and Charity Foundation in Qatar, which cater to the needs of the disabled in their societies. The Gulf States should adopt the social model of disability if they are to fully assimilate those with disabilities into society.

More Universities to Offer Degrees in Special-Needs Education More universities within the UAE need to offer 2-year master's degree programs in special-needs education to acquire the sufficient number of specialized teachers needed so that their current inclusion laws can be properly implemented and sustained. They must be able to produce their own qualified specialists to make their dream a reality. Currently, there are only two universities in the UAE, Zayed University and Abu Dhabi University, which offer master's degrees in special education (Swan 2011). This number must increase so they can begin to be less dependent on foreign specialists who may not speak Arabic and begin to cater more to the percentage of the population that only speaks Arabic; in addition, there will be an increase in national pride from having demands met by its own citizens.

Conclusion

This chapter attempts to highlight a prevailing tendency of cultural stigmas and aversion toward integration of the disabled in the UAE society. As demonstrated, there are key obstacles that must be overcome before inclusion and integration can be achieved and prevail. The role of disabled people within society has largely been predestined for them starting from diagnosis of any problem. Unfortunately, for this portion of society in the Gulf region, they can hope for little more than to meagerly exist on the edge of society, discriminated against, stereotyped, and largely ignored. If such cultural norms are to ever change, serious efforts need to be made, including government public awareness programs and integration programs, to change the mentality toward such people. The trend is reversible; the UAE is a relatively young country compared to most progressive nations. As the UAE continues to develop, it can align its infrastructure to include the many necessary elements that will create a tolerant atmosphere for disabled people. Most importantly, a cultural change is on the horizon due to a general drift toward global awareness of the challenges confronting the disabled; these minorities deserve lives enriched with dignity, education, and hope for a bright future as any normally functioning majority of the population strives to have.

References

Abedin, L. (2002). *Enabling the disabled in the UAE labour market*. Dubai: Tanmia, Centre for Labour Market Research & Information.

Ahmed, A. (17. May 2013). Dyslexic children benefit from visual lessons, mind guru tells Dubai teachers. *The National*. http://www.thenational.ae/news/uae-news/education/dyslexic-children-benefit-from-visual-lessons-mind-guru-tells-dubai-teachers. Accessed 15 Aug 2013.

Al Hassani, Z. (5. Sept 2012). Dubai health survey to help cater for disabled. *The National*. http://www.thenational.ae/news/uae-news/health/dubai-health-survey-to-help-cater-for-disabled. Accessed 15 May 2013.

Alghazo, E. M., & Naggar Gaad, E. l. (2004). General education teachers in the United Arab Emirates and their acceptance of the inclusion of students with disabilities. *British Journal of Special Education, 31*(2), 94–99. doi:10.1111/j.0952–3383.2004.00335.x

Al Roumi, M. (2008). UAE ratifies UN convention on rights of people with disabilities. *Gulf News*. http://gulfnews.com/news/gulf/uae/general/uae-ratifies-un-convention-on-rights-of-people-with-disabilities-1.83978. Accessed 19 Aug 2013.

American Medical Association. (n.d.). Genetics of autism. American Medical Association Website http://www.amaassn.org/ama1/pub/upload/mm/464/geneticsofautism.pdf. Accessed 3 May 2013.

Brown, K. (18. Feb 2013). Jessica Cox: Pilot born without arms on flying with her feet. *BBC News*. http://www.bbc.co.uk/news/magazine-21377627. Accessed 3 Oct 2013.

Chaudhary, S. B. (11. May 2012). The rise of autism in the UAE. *Gulf News*. >http://gulfnews.com/life-style/health/the-rise-of-autism-in-the-uae-1.1020114. Accessed 5 Oct 2013.

Crabtree, S. (2007). Family responses to the social inclusion of children with developmental disabilities in the United Arab Emirates. *Disability and Society, 22*(1), 49–62.

D'Souza, C. (2013). Disability law needs enforcement, says advocates. *Gulf news*.http://gulfnews.com/news/gulf/uae/society/disability-law-needs-enforcement-say-advocates-1.1164600. Accessed 3 Jan 2014.

Duncan, G. (30. Nov 2011). Abu Dhabi and Dubai are best places to live in the Middle East, survey says. *The National*. http://www.thenational.ae/business/economy/abu-dhabi-and-dubai-are-best-places-to-live-in-the-middle-east-survey-says. Accessed 4 Oct 2013.

Embassy of the United Arab Emirates, Cultural Division (2011). *Special Education*. Embassy of the United Arab Emirates Website http://www.uaecd.org/special-education. Accessed 9 Oct 2013.

Ibrahim, B. L., & Sherif, D. H. (2008). *From charity to social change: Trends in Arab philanthropy*. Cairo: The American University in Cairo Press.

Jaeger, P. T., & Bowman, C. A. (2005). *Understanding disability: Inclusion, access, diversity and civil rights*. London: Praeger.

Lawati, S. (15. Aug 2011). Mentally disabled children in the Middle East and their integration into society. Middle East Health Magazine. Middle East Health Magazine.http://www.middleeasthealthmag.com/cgi-bin/index.cgi http://www.middleeasthealthmag.com/jul2011/feature5.htm. Accessed 10 Oct 2013.

Livneh, H., & Antonak, R. (2005). Psychosocial adaptation to chronic illness and disability: A primer for counselors. *Journal of Counseling and Development: JCD, 83*(1), 12–20.

Mandell, D. S., & Novak, M. (2005). The role of culture in families' treatment decisions for children with autism spectrum disorders. *Mental Retardation and Developmental Disabilities Research Reviews, 11*(2), 110–115. Accessed 3 May 2014.

National Center for Learning Disabilities. (2013). *What is FAPE?* National Center for Learning Disabilities Website http://www.ncld.org/parents-child-disabilities/ld-rights/what-is-fape-what-can-it-mean-my-child. Accessed 3 May 2014.

Reinl, J. (03. Sept 2008). Arab region 'lacks' disability awareness. *The National.* http://www.thenational.ae/news/world/middle-east/arab-region-lacks-disability-awareness. Accessed 23 Sep 2013.

Swan, M. (2011). New college courses to end special needs crisis. The National. http://www.thenational.ae/news/uae-news/education/new-college-courses-to-end-special-needs-crisis. Accessed 21 Oct 2013.

Tabrez, H. (1. Dec 2009). Media, employers can do more to help disabled. *Gulf News.* http://gulfnews.com/news/gulf/uae/general/media-employers-can-do-more-to-help-disabled-1.542411. Accessed 27 Nov 2013.

Tenbroek, J., & Matson, F. W. (1966). The disabled and the law of welfare. *California Law Review, 54,* 809–840.

United Nations Human Rights. (2013). Combating discrimination against persons with disabilities. United Nations Human Rights Website http://www.ohchr.org/EN/ABOUTUS/Pages/DiscriminationAgainstPersonsWithDisabilities.aspx. Accessed 12 Oct 2013.

Vujicic, N. (17. Oct 2012). Overcoming hopelessness: Nick Vujicic at TEDxNoviSad [Video File]. http://tedxtalks.ted.com/video/Overcoming-hopelessness-Nick-Vu. Accessed 4 Oct 2013.

World Health Organization. (2002). Towards a common language for functioning, disability and health. http://www.who.int/classifications/icf/training/icfbeginnersguide.pdf. Accessed 18 Oct 2013.

World Health Organization. (2013). Health topics: Disabilities. World Health Organization Website http://www.who.int/topics/disabilities/en/. Accessed 24 Jan 2014.

Sarah Abdul-Hadi Bachelor of Science in Multimedia Design Alumna.Cum Laude.

LoriAnn Alnaizy Bachelor of Arts in English Language and Literature Alumna.Cum Laude. She made the Dean's List For Fall 2012 and Spring 2013 semesters

Bashaer Aref Bachelor of Arts in English Language and Literature Alumna.Cum Laude. Her interests include creative writing, poetry, film, history and anthropology

Asma AlShamsi Bachelor of Arts in International Studies Alumna.Cum Laude.

Index

CPSIA information can be obtained at www.ICGtesting.com
Printed in the USA
LVOW04*1017160315

430735LV00001B/113/P